D0722159

THE TRIAL
OF DOCTOR
SACHEVERELL

THE TRIAL
OF DOCTOR
SACHEVERELL
by Geoffrey Holmes

EYRE METHUEN
LONDON

First published 1973
© *1973 Geoffrey Holmes*
Printed in Great Britain for
Eyre Methuen Ltd
11 New Fetter Lane, London EC4P 4EE
by Richard Clay (The Chaucer Press) Ltd
Bungay, Suffolk

SBN 413 27750 X

TO MY MOTHER

CONTENTS

viii *Contents*

ILLUSTRATIONS

PLATES

between pages 16 and 17

1a Henry Sacheverell, 1710, by A. Russell, mezzotint engraved by J. Smith (*Ashmolean Museum, Oxford*)

b Magdalen College, Oxford, 1675, engraved by David Loggan (*The President and Fellows of Magdalen College, Oxford*)

2a The parish church of St Saviour's, Southwark, from a drawing of 1737, published 1739 (*The Trustees of the British Museum*)

b The parish church of St Andrew's, Holborn, 1754 (*Guildhall Library, London*)

between pages 32 and 33

3a Henry Compton, Bishop of London, by Sir Godfrey Kneller (*National Portrait Gallery*)

b Gilbert Burnet, Bishop of Salisbury, *c.* 1690, copy after John Riley (*National Portrait Gallery*)

c 'The Church in Danger', 1709: Ben Hoadly, Latitudinarian rector of St Peter-le-Poor. Dutch engraving (*The President and Fellows of Magdalen College, Oxford*)

4a 'The Church in Danger', 1706: impression of an inn sign put up at Stoke by Naland, Suffolk (*The President and Fellows of Magdalen College, Oxford*)

ACKNOWLEDGMENTS

The suggestion that I should write an account of the Sacheverell trial was first made to me by Professor John Kenyon in 1966. Now that it has at last borne fruit, in a book for which the trial provides the centrepiece, I should like to thank him for planting the idea.

Surprisingly there were only three pioneers before me: Falconer Madan, who printed a hundred copies of his *Bibliography of Dr Henry Sacheverell* in 1884; his son, F. F. Madan, whose vastly more ambitious bibliography was well advanced at the time of his death in 1961; and Dr Abbie Scudi, who published a short study of *The Sacheverell Affair*, including an excellent bibliography, in America in 1939. My debt to all three is considerable; that to the Madans being profoundly increased by the readiness of F. F. Madan's executors, particularly Mr C. W. Brocklebank, to sanction the loan to me for the past year of the unique Madan collection of Sacheverelliana, including F. F. Madan's manuscript notes.

Bill Speck brought this collection to my notice, and the fact that he was producing his edition of the younger Madan's Bibliography while I was working on this book was a boon to me in all manner of ways. As if this were not enough, it was Dr Speck who unearthed at Yale and xeroxed for me the anonymous diary of the trial which proved perhaps the most exciting find of my research. I am grateful to the Curators of the James Marshall and Marie-Louise Osborn Collection at Yale University Library for permission to quote from this diary. My use of other manuscript material has been made possible by the generosity of the Dukes of Portland and Marlborough, the Marquesses of Downshire and Cholmondeley, the late Earl Stanhope and Sir Richard Hamilton. I was able to draw

xiv   *Acknowledgments*

on the despatches of Friedrich Bonet because Dr Harry Dickinson most kindly put a microfilm of these manuscripts at my disposal.

Dr G. L. Harriss, Librarian of Magdalen College, Oxford, and Miss Jane Isaac of the Lichfield Joint Record Office both helped me to establish important facts about Sacheverell's early career from the papers in their care; while Mr Clyve Jones of the Institute of Historical Research did some fine detective work on the Doctor's later years at Highgate. I am most grateful to them, as indeed I am to all those who have assisted me at various times: to Mr Christopher Harley, Professor H. L. Snyder, Professor Austin Woolrych, Miss A. Green of the Berkshire Record Office and Dr Anne Whiteman; to the Rev. Kenneth Twinn of Dr Williams's Library, the Rev. Gordon C. Bolam of Nottingham and the Rev. Peter B. Godfrey of Sheffield; to Lionel Glassey, Oliver Westall, Andrew Compton, Stephen Green and John Beckett; and to the staffs of the British Museum, the Public Record Office and the House of Lords Record Office.

In its final form this book owes much to the wise counsel and judicious criticism of my publishers Eyre Methuen. At every stage it was helped forward by my wife, who coped heroically with all I asked of her, as well as with two enterprising and vociferous young children.

1972   G.S.H.

Dates, Quotations and Abbreviations

All dates in this book, both in the text and in the notes, are given in the Old Style, though assuming the year to begin on 1 January, not on 25 March.

In quotations, spelling and punctuation have been modernised.

The key to all abbreviations used in the notes will be found in the bibliography.

THE TRIAL
OF DOCTOR
SACHEVERELL

PROLOGUE

The trial of Doctor Henry Sacheverell in February and March 1710, for 'high crimes and misdemeanours' against the State, has commonly been seen, first and last, as a political trial. Likewise the whole pageant of events of which the trial was the centrepiece has appeared inseparable in the eyes of later generations from the best known political crisis of the early eighteenth century: that which brought down the Whigs, together with the great duumvirate of the duke of Marlborough and Lord Godolphin, and set up the last truly Tory ministry Britain was to see for a hundred years. A sequence which began in December 1709, when Sacheverell was impeached by the Whigs, and which came to its *finale* in October 1710, when the cause he came to personify formed the platform for one of the most resounding electoral triumphs in British history, is peopled at one point or another by every politician of any note in the land. From beginning to end the noises of a party battle, epic in scale, echo stridently through every scene.

Yet Henry Sacheverell was more than just a Tory zealot and the focus of a party feud. He was an Anglican parson. His chief offence was a seditious sermon preached in an Anglican cathedral. And these circumstances, far from being incidental to his case and to the furore which it aroused, were of the essence of both. It is quite true that the Sacheverell affair could only have erupted from a political society deeply divided by party antagonisms.[1] But it is equally true that the affair was a symptom of the malaise which had stricken the Church of England by Sacheverell's day.

Why was there by 1710 such desperate anxiety about the future of Anglicanism that the prosecution of one young divine should

B

convince at least four-fifths of the clergy (not to mention a majority of the laity) that their Church was in imminent danger of destruction? Why should such anxiety focus on a man who, though admittedly a pulpit demagogue, was otherwise of fairly limited talents, of no special status and of far from saintly character? How could a single sermon preached by such a parson, on the theme of 'false brethren in Church and State', so convulse the political nation as to give rise to a *cause célèbre* of English history: one of the longest state trials then on record, setting the whole kingdom by the ears, 'husband against wife, parent against child, male against female'?[2] Why were the issues involved in this trial of such great moment to the men and women of Queen Anne's England?

These are not easy questions to answer. An acquaintance with the bizarre phenomenon of Sacheverell himself will take us some way towards an understanding of them. But for all his individuality, Doctor Sacheverell is not comprehensible outside the context of the Church whose cloth he wore or of the political *maelstrom* into which he and his Church were drawn. The chapter which follows, therefore, will take the story of the man and the parson as far as the point, in the middle of Anne's reign, when Sacheverell had achieved a local notoriety but not yet a national reputation. The second chapter will then look back, with a broader perspective, as far as the 'Glorious Revolution' of 1688; and it will seek to explain the quandary in which that great constitutional event, and the subsequent ferment of political parties in the nation, placed the Established Church of England over the next twenty years.[3] For out of this quandary and the Anglican reaction to it was born the Sacheverell Affair.

I THE MAN

In April 1706 a canon of Christ Church wrote in evident alarm to an absent Oxford colleague about a sermon just delivered by one Read, Fellow of the House. For more than a year past the cry had gone out from the pulpits of the university city – as from many other churches in the land – that 'the Church was in danger' under the Queen's administration, an administration at this time gradually succumbing to the growing power of the Whigs. But even by Oxford's standards Read's sermon was exceptional.

> It is said at the close he bid them arm themselves against the fiery trial that was now approaching . . . *Fiery trial* is the word, and it is said that Sacheverell has been outdone by one of Christ Church, and no doubt it is at Lambeth before you will receive this.[1]

Christ Church had vied with Magdalen in trumpeting the Church's peril and defying her assailants! Sacheverell himself had been outdone! What manner of man was this young don, who in the very arsenal of High Anglicanism had already made himself and his sermons the gauge by which clerical militancy was measured? Outside Oxford, few as yet knew much about Sacheverell, beyond his name and his reputation as a preacher. Oxford knew – or thought it knew – him well. But even in the university which had bred him there were many who never guessed how unlike that of the orthodox High Churchman was his pedigree, and how unpredictable in many ways were the events which had brought him among them and enabled him to capture the limelight.

*   *   *

On 8 February 1674, in St Peter's parsonage at Marlborough in Wiltshire, a third son was born to the rector, Joshua Sacheverell, and his wife Susannah. Nine days later he was baptised and given the name of Henry. If, as seems possible, the choice of name was an act of family piety, in deference to the child's maternal grandfather, Providence could hardly have devised a more ironic stroke. For evidence exists, uncorroborated but in Sacheverell's day unrefuted, identifying this grandparent with Henry Smith, knight of the shire in the Long Parliament for Leicestershire; and this same Henry Smith had put his hand to Charles I's death warrant in January 1649, had been attainted after the Restoration, reprieved in 1662, and had probably died in prison shortly before Susannah Smith married the incumbent of Marlborough in 1669.*

Whatever he thought of his Christian name, in early manhood Henry Sacheverell became intensely proud of his uncommon family name, supposedly a corruption of the Norman Saute de Chevreuil. The landed gentry at the beginning of the eighteenth century included a small clutch of Sacheverells with estates in the north and west midlands. George Sacheverell, a septuagenarian veteran of

* There is a mystery here. In 1711 Dr Henry Sacheverell's uncle Benjamin, his father's half-brother and a dissenter with a business in London, published a remarkable pamphlet, *Sacheverell against Sacheverell*, in which he reminded his nephew not merely of his Puritan ancestry on the father's side, a fact already widely known, but also of his mother's still more embarrassing connections. In this passage (p.7) he made the astonishing statement (which was never to be contradicted in print by the Doctor or by any of his Grub Street henchmen) that Henry's maternal grandfather 'was one of the regicides of Charles I'.

This skeleton in Sacheverell's cupboard was named, however, as 'John' Smith. But only a 'Henry' Smith is traceable among those who presided – in his case, it seems, as a reluctant, bewildered judge – over the trial of the King. Heir to 900 acres in Leicestershire, he married the daughter of a fellow regicide, Cornelius Holland, and his wife, who died of the plague in London in 1664, is said to have borne him an only daughter. The identification of this daughter with Susannah (b. 1650), the mother of Henry Sacheverell, cannot be positively made, but it is a clear possibility. An alternative explanation might link Susannah with the family of Philip Smith of Baydon, Wilts., M.P. for Marlborough 1641–53. (See *D.N.B.* article on Henry Smith [b. 1620]; M. F. Keeler, *The Long Parliament, 1640–1641*, p. 341; C. V. Wedgwood, *The Trial of Charles I*, pp. 101, 209; G. Yule, *The Independents in the English Civil War*, p. 118. Cf. the statement in John Nichols, *The History and Antiquities of the County of Leicester*, iii, 510, that the regicide's daughter was the *mother*, not the wife, of Joshua Sacheverell: patently absurd on grounds of age.)

If Susannah Sacheverell was indeed a regicide's daughter, or even near kin to a Rumper, we are offered a new insight into one of the more unsavoury aspects of Henry's later life, for which he was much criticised by his enemies, namely his rather shameful neglect of his widowed mother, even in the days of his highest prosperity.

the royalist cause in the Civil Wars, owned a country house and estate at Newhall, Sutton Coldfield, and another manor at Callow in Derbyshire. Robert Sacheverell, a member of Parliament for Nottingham, inherited from his father, the famous Exclusionist Whig, the Nottinghamshire estate of Barton and the nearby Derbyshire manor of Morley. His brother William, who married a Sitwell of Renishaw, bought a house at Derby in 1708.[2] With George and Robert Sacheverell, Tory Anglican squires in the standard mould, Henry in his halcyon days was to boast of kinship. With George he was to claim friendship also; and indeed there is every likelihood that his acquaintance with the Newhall branch* went back to his very first years in the ministry, when he found himself in Warwickshire.[3]

But as for the relationship on which he so loved to preen himself, this was tenuous and remote indeed. His great-great-grandfather was a younger son of Hugh Cheverel, lord of the Dorset manor of East Stoke in Elizabeth I's reign, who bore the same arms as the Sacheverells but little other trace of his distant kinship with them. For three generations, moreover, Henry's direct antecedents had been southern clerics, not midland squires; above all, they stood significantly closer to the Puritan than to the Royalist–Anglican tradition. From his student days onwards Sacheverell was always acutely embarrassed by what he called his 'fanatic kindred': like his contemporary Luke Milbourne, a popular preacher of comparable violence, his High Anglicanism contains in its very extremity more than a hint of revulsion from his own tainted stock.[4]

His great-grandfather, John, was the first Cheverel to change his surname to Sacheverell. At the time of his death in 1651 he had been rector of East Stoke for thirty-six years, enjoying a high reputation among the Dorset clergy.[5] Three of his four sons – John, Timothy and Philologus – followed him into the ministry in the 1640s and 1650s, each one as a Presbyterian.[6] And the Anglican reaction at the Restoration was a grievous blow to all three. John Sacheverell, Henry's grandfather, vicar of Wincanton

* George Sacheverell of Newhall (now New Hall) was descended illegitimately from the Sacheverells of Barton and Morley and there seems to have been little love lost between the two branches. Add. MSS 6696, f. 75; Sir G. Sitwell, *Letters of the Sitwells and Sacheverells*, i, 276 and n.

in Somerset and the very model of a zealous, godly Presbyterian pastor, was indiscreet enough to preach a sermon (on Charles II's coronation day, no less) on the text from the first book of Samuel, 'But if ye shall do wickedly ye shall be consumed, both you and your king'. This exploit not merely half emptied his church while the sermon was still in progress, but led to his being burnt in effigy by his own townsfolk. He and his two brothers were all ejected on St Bartholomew's Day, 1662; and for John and Timothy that was not the end of their sufferings in the Good Old Cause. Timothy, who at great personal risk stayed in his Dorset parish of Tarrant Hinton after the Ejection, fitted up a meeting-house in a barn at Winterborn during the brief interlude of Charles II's Indulgence policy in 1672, only to have his own house, and all his books and papers, burnt in reprisal.[7] By that time John was already beyond tribulation. Arrested in an illegal meeting at Shaftesbury within a year of 'Black Bartholomew', he died in Dorchester gaol three years later 'in his chair, speaking to those about him with great vehemence and affection of the great work of Redemption'.[8]

During his third and last marriage John Sacheverell had enjoyed a life-interest in his wife's personal estate, and this enabled him to take a decision whose ultimate repercussions were to affect the lives of many thousands of people. He sent his son Joshua, intended for the ministry, to a university instead of to a dissenting seminary. St Catharine's Hall, Cambridge, made a conformist out of Joshua; so that while his two half-brothers, Benjamin and Samuel, followed the dissenting tradition of the Sacheverells, he and his own family were committed to a future of Anglican respectability.[9] Joshua's was a large family. Six sons and two daughters were born to him and his wife between September 1670 and December 1683, five children following Henry more or less biennially, though two of them died young.[10] St Peter's, Marlborough, was no plum living, and although its rector eventually acquired a Prebend's stall at Salisbury as a welcome supplement, this was no substitute for the private means that would have enabled him to provide a good education for his boys. Henry was clearly the most intelligent of the young Sacheverells; yet his might well have been a calling as prosaic as those of his elder brothers – one apprenticed to a London mercer, the other articled as a clerk to an attorney at

Beaconsfield – but for one stroke of fortune. His godfather was one Edward Hearst, a local apothecary in comfortable circumstances. In January 1684, shortly before Henry's tenth birthday, Joshua Sacheverell died. The oldest of his surviving brood was only thirteen, and his widow had very little to support them with. It must have seemed providential when Edward Hearst and his wife, Katherine, offered to adopt Henry and bring him up as their own son. When the boy moved early in 1684 from the parsonage to the Hearsts' house he took the first step on the road which was to lead him to the Bar of the Lords in Westminster Hall.[11]

Dissent was flourishing in the Marlborough district during the late 1670s and early 1680s, encouraged by the ministrations of a dynamic young Presbyterian preacher named Daniel Burgess, a considerable thorn in the side of the rector of St Peter's. In 1685, when he left the town for good to take charge of a London congregation,[12] Burgess can hardly have dreamt that twenty-five years later his meeting-house would be sacked and his very life threatened by a mob whose battle-cry was 'High Church and Sacheverell'. In his Marlborough days he can have been no more than a name to the young Sacheverell, a name the latter doubtless heard reviled not infrequently during his first year in the Hearst household; for both the Hearsts, High Anglicans of a pious bent, had a hearty dislike of 'schismatics'. It was a great joy to them, Mrs Hearst later recalled, to welcome into their home a boy whose habit it was to be 'always retiring to his private devotions before he went to school'.[13] Henry Sacheverell was sent to the Public Grammar School at Marlborough very soon after his tenth birthday, and under the guidance of the Master, Mr Carr, he took the school's curriculum precociously in his stride. After her husband's death, Mrs Hearst, whom Henry now called 'Mother', lavished all her care and affections on her adopted son; and it was she who arranged to send him to Magdalen College, Oxford – now, under John Hough, its President, high in public esteem after its battle royal with James II. This was at the end of August 1689. A month earlier he had been elected to one of the prized demyships of the college in the 'Golden Election' of 30 July, in which Joseph Addison, Richard Smalbroke and Hugh Boulter were also taken on to the Foundation of forty Fellows and thirty Demies. Henry Sacheverell was not quite fifteen and a half.[14]

Of Sacheverell's first spell at Oxford, the five years he spent there as an undergraduate and as a junior graduate, scant evidence survives. The bare landmarks are preserved in the College Register: the award of the degree of Bachelor of Arts on 30 June 1693, and of the Master's degree on 16 May 1695. He is known to have struck up a warm friendship with Addison; in fact, Magdalen tradition has it that they roomed together. A strange attraction of opposites: but it brought Sacheverell to the notice of an important clerical family, and for Addison there was benefit too. It was at Sacheverell's suggestion that he wrote his verse 'Account of the Greatest English Poets', and it was to his friend, 'dearest Harry', that he addressed it.* Most probably Addison visited Wiltshire with his friend during occasional vacations (he was a Wiltshire man by birth himself).[15] If so, it was to the Hearst house at Wanborough, not to Sacheverell's mother's home, he went; for soon after the Revolution the relict of the late rector of Marlborough, having subsequently married, and buried, a second reverend husband,† was admitted by the good will of the new bishop of Salisbury, Gilbert Burnet, to the *Collegium Matronarum* – a genteel retreat recently established for clergymen's widows in the quiet of that cathedral city. Here she lived out the remaining thirty years and more of her life, troubling either Sacheverell's conscience or his pocket but little in all that time.[16]

Mrs Hearst has left a distinctly strained picture of Sacheverell in his undergraduate days: the picture of a young man as respectful, dutiful, sweet-tempered and thoughtful in his relations with her as any natural mother could wish. A later panegyrist was to write how, from the moment he took up his demyship, 'he behaved himself with an exact deportment to the rules of his college and the statutes of the University'. But all the impressions of his formed character by his late twenties, as well as a few surviving fragments of evidence from Oxford itself, tempt one to qualify these testimonials. There are foreshadowings of the turbulent, passionate, arrogant young don of the early 1700s, first in a lively episode at Magdalen, when the fifteen year old student worked off

---

* Published in 1694, the poem begins with the couplet:
> Since, dearest Harry, you will needs request
> A short account of all the Muse-possest

† Anthony Tate, vicar of Preshot near Marlborough.

a fit of fury on the college cook by belabouring him with a shoulder of mutton, and likewise in the curt entry in the Vice-President's Register for 31 January 1693 (his final year as an undergraduate) which records his admonishment by the Vice-President of Magdalen and three deans, *propter contumaciam et contemptum* towards the Dean of Arts.[17]

Meanwhile there is no hint of a spectacular academic career, either as an undergraduate or later in the Faculty of Divinity. Indeed, although John Hough, now bishop of Oxford, ordained him deacon on 18 May 1695,[18] his progress towards final ordination in 1697 was not as smooth as his *amour propre* demanded. When he first presented himself to William Lloyd, bishop of Lichfield and Coventry, armed with a testimonial from the dean of Lichfield, there was a celebrated altercation. Lloyd testily complained of Sacheverell's bad Latin, objecting to the grammar of a number of his sentences. Sacheverell, who as a student had developed a fair talent in Latin verse and had had several poems published, would concede no error. With complete self-assurance he proceeded to quote grammatical authorities to justify himself. One account even credits him with the assertion that "'twas better Latin than he [Lloyd] or any of his chaplains could make'. The bishop, by then understandably in high dudgeon, despatched his secretary to his study for books that would disabuse this cocky young Oxonian; but when even this failed to budge him, Lloyd (whether with or without an unsuccessful *viva voce* in divinity is not clear) refused to ordain him, 'and set him a time of study to be better prepared'.[19]

By then Sacheverell had been away from Oxford for some time. His first foothold on the rung of preferment was a modest one: a chaplaincy in the household of Sir Charles Holt, just outside Birmingham, combined with the curacy of the local parish church of Aston during the illness of the incumbent. As a Warwickshire J.P. before the Revolution, Sir Charles had been a noted baiter of the Birmingham dissenters. However, it seems that he found Sacheverell's character less congenial than his views, for when the Aston living fell vacant soon afterwards he passed over its curate in favour of Walter Hollier* – a rebuff the more galling, in that Hollier himself had only been second choice to the brilliant if

---

* Hollier was still in possession when Sacheverell revisited Aston Hall in triumph in 1710.

unorthodox Cambridge scholar, William Whiston.* Years later Whiston was to recall a conversation with Holt's mother-in-law, the pious Lady Clobery, which throws an illuminating shaft on Sacheverell at the age of twenty-two.

> My Lady Clobery, talking one day with me about the matter, happened to enlarge upon the reasons she and Sir Charles had to be averse to him. So much I fully remember she said: 'that Sir Charles knew him too well to give him Aston; that his behaviour was exceedingly light and foolish, without any of that gravity and seriousness which became one in holy orders; *that he was fitter to make a player than a clergyman;* that in particular, he was dangerous in a family, since he would among the very servants jest upon the torments of Hell'.[20]

No longer needed at Aston, and in serious danger of unemployment, Sacheverell now enjoyed his greatest piece of luck since his adoption in 1684. The living of Cannock, in neighbouring Staffordshire, became void. The patrons and the appropriators were the dean and chapter of Lichfield; and the dean of Lichfield was none other than Dr Lancelot Addison, father of Henry's Magdalen intimate, and a High Church Tory with intemperate views which had made something of a stir in the Convocation of 1689. Sacheverell's nomination to the curacy, which carried a 'competent stipend', soon followed; and in September 1697 a new application to the bishop, this time supported by a firm letter of recommendation from Hough of Oxford, and a rigorous three-day examination at Eccleshall along with other candidates for orders, at length persuaded Lloyd of Sacheverell's worthiness.[21] That autumn the young man moved to Cannock as a fully ordained priest of the Church of England.

Sacheverell's sojourn at Cannock is the most shadowy period of his career. A cure of souls, as such, had little appeal for him. To relieve the boredom of ministering to the bucolic majority of his congregation, for whom he was accused of showing 'his over-

---

* Fellow of Clare Hall since 1691, only a year after he had taken his first degree, he was in 1703 to succeed Newton in the Lucasian Chair of Mathematics at Cambridge, and seven years later was to lose that Chair for publishing an heretical (Arian) treatise. He turned down the Aston offer mainly because it would have disqualified him from his Fellowship. See also p. 266 below for a later *contretemps* between Whiston and Sacheverell.

bearing contempt',[22] he indulged his taste for convivial society, dabbled in local crypto-Jacobite politics, and embarked on a quite protracted love affair with a neighbouring gentlewoman, which cooled on his side after the lady's father had 'protested against the match, and declared he would not give them a farthing, living or dying'.[23] This apart, his main legacy to Staffordshire was his growing reputation for preaching, and in particular a sermon which he preached at Lichfield, possibly in 1700 – the first of his sermons to achieve some notoriety. It was never printed, and the only clue to its content is that a prosecution of the preacher for seditious libel was threatened, though in the end it was dropped 'in disdain [it was subsequently said] of meddling with an obscure country curate'.[24]

If Henry Sacheverell was still 'obscure' in 1700, he was not to remain so for long. It must have been clear to him by now that, with little bent for scholarship and even less for the pastoral life, the only way he could make a mark in the ministry was by preaching. Outstanding preachers were not common in the Church of England by the beginning of the eighteenth century. Even in an age of declining congregations* they could still fill churches and impress influential patrons. In time Sacheverell might aspire to a pulpit in London. But meanwhile there could be no better stamping-ground for him than Oxford. It was natural that during his ministry in Staffordshire he should take whatever opportunities occurred of reminding the Fellows of his old college of his existence; and his Lichfield exploit can have done his cause no harm with them. At all events, when they had a vacant fellowship to fill in July 1701 it was Henry Sacheverell whom they elected. He had been in orders for six years and he was now twenty-seven years old. The choice may not have been a predictable one; but it was not outrageous. Whatever else Magdalen acquired in 1701, it was not a nonentity. Joseph Addison once remarked that the senior common rooms of Oxford, as he remembered them as a young Fellow in the late 1690s, were full of men who were really dead, though they pretended not to be.[25] Henry Sacheverell, at least, was very much alive; and when he came back to Oxford he did so as a man fully determined to make an impression and to do so quickly.

* For this, see p. 25 below.

He was an imposing, arresting figure. Tall and brawny, he moved with the fluency and grace of the big man whose frame is not merely powerful but finely proportioned. His face had good, strong features – most women clearly thought it handsome – but his naturally high colour was so easily worked upon by excitement, anger or wine that the general impression was 'of a livid, rather than a ruddy complexion'.[26] What men noticed first about Sacheverell, at close quarters, were his eyes. They were large and protuberant – words such as 'staring' or 'goggling' recur in contemporary descriptions; yet at the same time they seemed opaque and lifeless. They detracted but little, however, from the utter assurance of the man's bearing. Both in the pulpit and out of it Sacheverell carried himself like a man wholly convinced of his own inherent superiority to the greater part of his fellow-mortals. Even his dress reflected this; the quality of his cloth and linen was that of a well-to-do gentleman. For a clergyman his tastes were considered foppish (years later he was to startle a visiting female parishioner by receiving her in what she described as 'a very rich and gaudy Indian night-gown with gold flowers, as if he had been some young lord'). But 'a good assurance, clean gloves, white handkerchief well managed, with other suitable accomplishments', as Sarah duchess of Marlborough remembered in later years, were all part of the necessary accoutrements in which he decked out his ego. So was his voice – strong and invincibly confident. But it was his expression and his general carriage which spoke most eloquently of the man's unquestioning self-confidence. They were 'assertive', 'audacious', at best. At worst, and all too frequently, 'he had a haughty, insolent air, which his friends found occasion often to complain of'.[27]

The character behind this imposing front was singularly unattractive. One searches in vain for evidence of anyone who knew Sacheverell as an Oxford Fellow in the days before his impeachment enabled him to pose as a martyr, and who genuinely liked or admired him. Later sympathisers have sometimes suggested that all the unfavourable reflections on him were retrospective, inspired after his impeachment by party malice or by donnish jealousy.[28] This is simply not true. When Sacheverell was awaiting his trial in January and early February 1710 he made a number of attempts to extract from the Vice-Chancellor, William Lancaster, and the heads of colleges a joint testimonial to his good life and behaviour. He failed humiliatingly, being forced to settle in the end for a few lines of commendation from the President and Fellows of Magdalen.[29] But just as significant as the fact of his failure, and laying bare one palpable reason for it, is the whole tone of the letter in which Sacheverell made his final demand.[30] Such is its self-consequence, and so gross the discourtesy it reveals towards the writer's academic superiors, that it would defy credence if it could not be authenticated beyond all doubt. Such phrases as 'I shall think myself most barbarously used to be denied such a piece of justice from a body of people I now represent, and whose interest so much depends on the success of my cause'; 'I desire no remora may be made in this necessary matter, and without excuse or prudential reserve, I hope I shall be not disappointed'; 'I am amazed I have been thus long put off' – all speak more eloquently than any contemporary comment of the unenviable personal reputation Sacheverell had earned in Oxford by 1709.

Not that contemporary comment, and comment wholly un-clouded by Whig bias, is lacking. From an entry in the diary of the arch-Tory, Thomas Hearne, for 1 August 1709, soon after Sacheverell had moved to Southwark and before he had delivered either of the two sermons which were to bring down the wrath of the Whigs upon his head, it is strikingly obvious that the writer's own impressions of Sacheverell, like those of many fellow-Oxonians, were already indelibly formed.

> There recently appeared a poem, elegant and clever, composed, it is said, by a young man once of Jesus College, the title of which is *The Description of Hoglandia* [Hoglandiae Descriptio]. Briefly but uncommonly well it touches on the pride, ignorance and depraved character of the same Henry Sacheverell, S[acrae] T[heologiae] P[rofessor] of Magdalen College.

Before proceeding to describe his preaching, Hearne (never a man to mince his words when criticising a university colleague) dismissed him personally with devastating economy as a noisy, presumptuous wine-soaker.[31]

Long before 1709, in fact, Henry Sacheverell had been marked out as one of the more unsavoury of Oxford academics. The university was not unused to hard drinkers; but even Oxford buzzed for a while in 1706, after Sacheverell and another Fellow of Magdalen had gone from a Thanksgiving service in St Mary's to a drinking bout in Lord Henry Somerset's rooms in Christ Church, and had finished the day by falling into a saw-pit, 'from whence they were delivered in a very nasty pickle after much struggle'.[32] He was a quarrelsome colleague, given to violent rages, overbearing towards equals and disrespectful to senior Fellows.[33] Local tradesmen no less than fellow-academics found him a mean and vindictive opponent. In 1710 that assiduous muckraker William Bisset had no difficulty in nosing out for inclusion in *The Modern Fanatick* a number of discreditable incidents involving Sacheverell and some of his humbler local creditors, stories which were later verified by reliable sources in Oxford.[34] One man who stood up to him was a glover named Ryley, who sued him for a debt of £5 after having been repelled from Sacheverell's rooms in Magdalen by a barrage of language more appropriate to a Billingsgate porter than a clergyman. Some years later Hearne took the opportunity of asking Ryley

> (nobody else being present) whether the story relating to him and inserted at the end of Bisset's book . . . were true? He said 'twas exact and true in all its circumstances, except in that which specifies the number of oaths the Dr swore. He says that he cursed and swore at a very strange rate; but as to the number of the curses and oaths he cannot be positive. The time when the thing happened was a little before the Queen came to Oxford.*

The sequel was equally revealing of the man's ill nature.

> Sacheverell being enraged at Mr Ryley for the prosecution (which was managed very successfully by Mr Houghton, the attorney), it makes Mr Ryley think that he was the more zealous against him when the matter of discommuning [excommunicating] came to be considered. Dr Sacheverell was one of the Delegates in that affair. . . . *I am very hardly dealt by* [Ryley told his friends at the time]. *I had no hand in the affront (if so be there was an affront) put upon the University. Mr Sacheverell has been my enemy. I could have done him a disservice, if I would*

---

* Queen Anne paid her only visit to Oxford at the end of August 1702.

have turned informer, by making him pay for his curses and oaths. But I leave him to his own conscience.[35]

Henry Sacheverell's conscience was more iron-clad than most: but there were some vulnerable chinks in its plating. Scarcely any of his books and papers are now extant – they were mostly destroyed, on his own instructions, after his death – but one fortuitous survivor is a little manuscript volume, clearly dating from his Oxford days, headed 'Prayers & Devotions for my Particular Use in the Daily Worship and Service of God'.[36] In one prayer, *Petition*, there is an unexpected glimpse of Sacheverell's view, before God, of his own character. It shows him fully aware of some, at least, of the faults which others saw in him, and of one other, sexual lust, which was less remarked upon.[37]

O! Thou that knowest the secrets of all hearts, and discernest the naked infirmities of our nature . . . do Thou vouchsafe to strengthen me with a double portion of Thy blessed Spirit and Grace where Thou findest my weakness most requiring, to restrain me from those sins which Thou knowest me to be more prone and inclinable to, either by the power of any vicious custom or the natural corruption of my constitution. Purge my mind of every evil thought and sinful desire, suppress and stifle the very first motions of an unjust concupiscence or affection, curb the violence of my passions, and subdue every inclination to thy Holy Will & Command. Give me such a diligent watchfulness over my heart & tongue that no temptations may prevail upon either, to be guilty of an immoral thought, or an indecent expression . . .

Later in the same prayer Sacheverell spared a modest thought for his temporal career. Nothing could have been more restrained: stipulating only 'a moderate portion of health and subsistence', he begged in addition no more than 'a contented satisfaction in all the circumstances Thou shalt be pleased to place me in'.

Fiercely ambitious though he was, Sacheverell must have felt at the start of 1709, looking back over seven years as a senior member of the University, that the Almighty had not taxed his peace of mind too severely. Oxford had given scope to his capacities as well as indulging his love of good living. And to do him justice, he had more to offer Oxford than prowess in the pulpit. He was a vigorous working member of his college, seeking responsibility and most probably discharging it competently.[38] For one thing, he was an active and authoritative teacher. In July 1703, slightly less than a year after his Fellowship had been confirmed (following Magdalen practice, his original appointment had been probationary), he was elected to an endowed lectureship, and by 1709 many a score of students had passed through his hands as Public Tutor. In addition, from 1703 he was College Librarian; in 1708 he was appointed Senior Dean of Arts; and in the following year gave up the Librarianship to become Bursar. He was busy, too, in the wider field of the University's administration.[39]

Most gratifying to his self-esteem, however, was the receipt of a Doctorate of Divinity in July 1708. Whether his Magdalen colleagues were equally gratified by such an incongruous award at the tender age of thirty-four to a man with no serious scholarly reputation, is open to doubt.* "'Tis well known', Bisset observed, 'his aim was to take place [i.e. precedence] of his seniors in the College, several of whom (about 12) his vanity has put to the same great and needless expense; from whence he has got the name of Doctor-driver'. And the charge was not far wide of the mark, for no fewer than nine other Fellows of Magdalen did indeed take the same degree on the same day, plainly determined that Sacheverell should not steal a march on them.[40]

If his doctorate could be said to recognise anything, other than his teaching ability, it can only have been his reputation as a preacher. Something of this reputation had preceded him to Oxford, and there it must have been confirmed with remarkable rapidity. Otherwise a very junior Fellow of little more than ten months' standing would hardly have been singled out by the then Vice-Chancellor, Roger Mander, to deliver the University Sermon preached on 10 June 1702; for this was the Fast Day appointed by

---

* Sacheverell was qualified in a technical sense to 'take up scarlet', having taken the intermediate degrees of M.A. and B.D., having 'gone through the several . . . exercises and number of years which the University requires as necessary qualifications for the doctorate', and having paid the fee appropriate to his case – possibly in the region of £50. ([Charles Lambe] *A Vindication*, pp. 29–30). Oxford did not insist at this time on the evidence of a major piece of original scholarship. But it is ironical that she had denied a D.D. to the learned William Nicolson, bishop of Carlisle, in 1702, and that one of the leading Anglican theologians of the late seventeenth century, George Bull, was fifty-two before the University so honoured him. See MS. Ballard 4, ff. 61, 101–3.

1*a* Henry Sacheverell, 1710, by A. Russell, mezzotint engraved by J. Smith

1*b* Magdalen College, Oxford, 1675, engraved by David Loggan

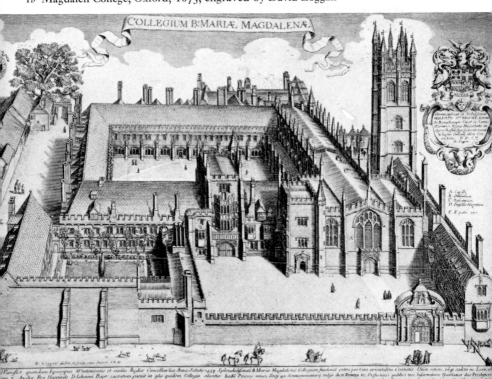

2a The parish church of St Saviour's, Southwark, from a drawing of 1737, published 1739

2b The parish church of St Andrew's, Holborn, 1754

the Queen for invoking the blessing of Heaven on her arms in the great new struggle with France which had just begun. It so happened, however, that when Sacheverell mounted the pulpit of the church of St Mary the Virgin to expound his text from the Second Book of Chronicles, 'If Thy people go out to war against their enemies . . . Then hear Thou from the Heavens their prayer',[41] he did so as a figure who had already, and in this self-same church, achieved notoriety. Preaching there in May on what was to become over the next few years one of his favourite themes, the common interest of the Church and the secular power, he had laid hold of the opportunity to flay the dissenters, and more especially the occasional conformists* and their Whig protectors, with a quite startling ferocity. He had ended that sermon with some of the most provocative words heard in Oxford for many a day, recommending all true Anglicans not to 'strike sail to a party which is an open and avowed enemy to our communion', but rather to 'hang out the bloody flag and banner of defiance'. The printed version of the sermon, *The Political Union*,† which appeared in Oxford about 18 June,[42] marked out Henry Sacheverell for the first time as a reinforcement to be reckoned with on the side of the High Church–Tory controversialists. It even earned him a small London readership. Daniel Defoe, for one, took note; and fastening with relish on the Oxford sermon's melodramatic conclusion, dubbed its author 'the bloody flag officer'. When Defoe's famous parody, *The Shortest Way with the Dissenters*, appeared at the end of the year, its sub-title contained a tongue-in-cheek acknowledgment to 'Mr Sach—ll's sermon and others'; and by this time John Dennis had already published a more direct reply, aptly called *The Danger of Priestcraft to Religion and Government*.[43] By the lights of Grub Street, as well as by those of Oxford, Sacheverell had arrived.

The summer of 1702 was a period of intense activity for Magdalen's new champion of the Church Militant. The country was going to

* The acutely controversial issue of 'Occasional Conformity' is discussed below, pp. 35, 39–41.
† Its full title was *The Political Union: A Discourse shewing the Dependance of Government on Religion in General: and of the English Monarchy on the Church of England in Particular*, and one of its joint-publishers, appropriately, was Henry Clements, who just over seven years later was to resume his partnership with Sacheverell, to their mutual satisfaction and enrichment.

C

the polls for the third time in eighteen months, and now that Anne had succeeded William III the Tory star was high. By the time *The Political Union* was on sale in the Oxford bookshops, Sacheverell already had another shot not merely in his locker but in the breech. On 29 July his former tormentor, that spry old prelate William Lloyd of Worcester, who had been stamping his diocese tirelessly in the Whig cause, protested against the slanders perpetrated against him in a recent publication entitled *The Character of a Low-Church-Man*. Although the pamphlet did not bear Sacheverell's name, half Oxford already knew it to have come from his pen.[44] Ostensibly it was an election tract. But Sacheverell had a personal as well as a political motive in writing it. Consumed with ambition and already thinking of Oxford as a springboard to further advance, he was openly on the look-out for a wealthy and influential patron. He had already dedicated the printed version of his Fast Day sermon to the High Tory peer Lord Weymouth, known protector of the Nonjuring Bishop Ken. Now, in *The Character of a Low-Church-Man*, he took up cudgels on behalf of the Tory knight of the shire for Worcestershire, Sir John Pakington of Westwood. Pakington was a rich landowner of Jacobite sympathies who had recently been pilloried in a pamphlet which Sacheverell, like many others, wrongly attributed to the baronet's most strenuous adversary, Bishop Lloyd.[45] Sacheverell's riposte became a minor best-seller.* And it deserved some success; since in twenty-four pungent pages, as well as lambasting Lloyd and lionising Pakington, its author contrived to rehearse the full range of his political and religious ideas in a style inimitably his own. It also contained an omen; for on the very last page the clergy currently electing a new Convocation were warned to be on their guard against 'false brethren' within the Church.

Pakington, whose election campaign manifestly benefited from the appearance of *The Character*, did his best to repay the debt. After the last English and Welsh constituencies had polled in August 1702 the Tories were cock-a-hoop. With 323 seats captured against 190 by the Whigs,[46] they had gained their most emphatic victory since the Revolution. It was virtually certain now that Robert Harley, the 'New Country' leader who had

---

* *The Character of a Low-Church-Man* went through three editions in 1702, one of them in Dublin, was reissued in 1706 and again in 1710.

twice in the past eighteen months been elected Speaker by Tory
votes, would fill the Chair for a third term. Who would be the
Speaker's chaplain? This was not a question to trouble the politicians overmuch, but it was of great interest to any young divine
seeking an entreé to the centre of influence and patronage in the
capital, the more so since the chaplaincy was a recognised stepping-
stone to preferment. On 1 September, therefore, Henry Sacheverell
presented himself at Witley Court in Worcestershire, the home of
Harley's brother-in-law, Thomas Foley, armed with a letter of
recommendation from Pakington.

> His character [is] as great in the University of Oxford [wrote
> Sir John] as his relations in the House of Commons, whom I
> am confident you have often heard mentioned there with great
> respect . . . I desire the favour of your letter to Mr Harley in
> Mr Sacheverell's behalf, who in every respect will acquit himself
> like an honest, ingenious man, and I am sure the House will be
> so well satisfied with him as to do all they can for his promotion.

It is not at all surprising to find Sacheverell already plying his
family name for all it was worth, though rather more so to realise
how easily he appears to have conned Pakington into accepting his
close connection with the great William Sacheverell. More
puzzling at first sight is the complacency with which Foley, a
Presbyterian by birth and education though now a nominally-
conforming Anglican, endorsed his suit. 'I am a stranger to him,
farther than this letter', he admitted, 'but if he answers the character he must needs be a very worthy person'. Presumably he knew
nothing as yet of Sacheverell's new reputation as the sanguinary
scourge of the dissenters. Harley, who had numerous contacts in
Oxford, cannot have been so ignorant. The 'flag officer' was one of
the last men in England he would have dreamt of appointing as
his chaplain: when he did make a new choice in 1703 it fell on an
Oxonian of a very different calibre, William Stratford.[47]
For Sacheverell, after this disappointment, it was to be six and
a half years before another opportunity occurred of cutting a
figure in London. Throughout this time, however, he contrived to
keep himself at least in the corner of the public eye by consoli-
dating his reputation both as a fiery preacher and an unquenchable
controversialist. Of the dozens of sermons he preached in Oxford

in these years, only two were printed: a turgid discourse on presumptuous sins delivered at St Mary's in September 1707, exceptional only for its total lack of political content, and the more characteristic Assize sermon of March 1704,[48] with its emotive revival of the 'Political Union' themes of 1702. The printing of the Oxford Assize sermon, as well as provoking at least four direct replies, brought from Defoe the further acknowledgment that 'Mr Sacheverell of Oxford has blown his second trumpet to let us know he has not yet taken down his bloody flag'.[49]

Yet it was one of his many unpublished Oxford sermons which in the long run was to be the most significant of all. It was preached at the height of that 'Church in Danger' campaign of 1705–6 to which Read of Christ Church, as we saw, made a spectacular contribution, and into which Sacheverell threw himself with his customary energy and lack of inhibition;* and we know of it only from an entry in the diary of Thomas Hearne for Sunday, 23 December 1705:

> This morning preached at St Marie's Mr Sacheverell of Magdalen College, upon In Perils amongst False Brethren, in the prosecution of which words he did with a great deal of courage and boldness show the great danger the Church is in at present (notwithstanding the Parliament has voted to be in none) from the fanatics and other false brethren, whom he set forth in their proper colours.[50]

Much later, Hearne was to turn back to this entry and add a note to it: 'This is the very sermon that he preached afterwards in London, November 5th 1709, before the Lord Mayor; for which he was impeached and punished'.

But we cannot hope to understand even why Sacheverell came to deliver the London sermon, still less why he was impeached for printing it, without first taking a searching view of that Anglican Church which he and thousands of his brethren were convinced stood embattled and imperilled: without examining the problems which taxed it, the divisions which rent it, and the hostile forces which – in the eyes of those whom Sacheverell came to represent – encompassed it about.

---

* In particular he co-operated with John Perks to produce *The Rights of the Church of England Asserted and Proved* (London, 1705).

II THE CHURCH

1. *The Anglican Dilemma*

The episcopal Protestant Church, with its Prayer Book and its royal supremacy, which had emerged from the English Reformation in the sixteenth century, and which in the mid-seventeenth century had triumphantly survived the years of Puritan ascendancy, enjoyed rare unity and prosperity after the Stuart Restoration of 1660, and more especially after 1673. However, in the spring of 1687, when the Papist King James II launched in real earnest his attack on the Church's hegemony, there began three years of grave difficulty and distress for all sincere Anglicans; and their plight was paradoxically unrelieved by James's precipitate flight to France in December 1688, which left his subjects with little practical alternative but to settle the crown on his Protestant daughter Mary, and his Dutch nephew William.

The most immediate bequest of the 1688 Revolution to Anglicans was political: their involvement, actively or passively, with rebellion against James called in question their cherished principle of a divinely-ordained authority in the State, and broke down that special relationship with the monarchy which was their greatest strength. Just as embarrassing in its consequences as the political dilemma was a crucial feature of the settlement which followed the Revolution: the failure to solve the other problem of the hour, that of the Protestant dissenters, by embracing them in a more comprehensive State Church; and the establishment instead of what soon came to be called 'the Toleration'. Even by themselves, these two problems would have been enough to demolish the clerical unity of the 1670s and the earlier 1680s.

Most Anglican clergy in Charles II's time accepted unquestioningly that as well as being spiritual pastors it was their business to serve the monarch, as head of both Church and State, in every possible way. This they did, in part, by commending a strictly hierarchical view of society, a view based on the Christian obligation of obedience. Above all, however, they took every opportunity to preach from their pulpits the Divine Hereditary Right of Kings, together with the obligation that lay on all Anglicans to eschew resistance to a lawful sovereign and passively to suffer even the illegal exactions of a tyrant. Imagine the effects on such a church and such a philosophy of the events of 1687 to 1689: not merely of James II's attacks on Anglican supremacy, but of his panic flight, which crippled the efforts of Anglican leaders to preserve the regal authority intact in negotiations with William of Orange.[1] Then, the rejection in the House of Lords of the proposal for a Regency, to be exercised by William in James's name – the expedient on which Archbishop Sancroft of Canterbury and most of his diocesans had come to pin their hopes, 'thereby to salve their oaths'.[2] Finally, the accession of a Calvinist Dutchman and his coronation in April 1689 by the rebel Bishop Compton. These were traumatic experiences. They reduced to tatters the whole Anglican concept of an indissoluble religious link between the altar and the throne. Passive Obedience, Non-Resistance, Divine Right: had not the events of May 1688 to April 1689 made a mockery of all three? How could the Church remain untouched by so blatant a denial of its political creed?

That it could not hope to preserve even outward unity was very soon apparent. The imposition on the clergy of sacred oaths of supremacy and allegiance to William and Mary, albeit oaths obligingly trimmed by Parliament, led in 1690 to open schism in the Church. In the twenty years which separated the secession of the Jacobite clergy and the trial of Sacheverell, there existed in effect two Anglican churches: the official, Established Church and the small, ostracised but none the less influential church of the Nonjurors. The tragedy of the schism went far beyond its physical extent.* The loss of quality was far more serious; for no church could lightly have shrugged off the banishment of men of the

---

* Only four per cent or so of the parish clergy were involved, while three of the nine prelates who could not 'come up to the oaths' died before or soon after their administration, so that they would have had to be replaced in any case.

reputation of Sancroft, Ken and Frampton. But most damaging of all was the influence which the martyrs' crowns of the Nonjurors and their skilful publicists gave them subsequently over the mass of conforming clergy.

Their psychological advantage was considerable. For to say that nine-tenths of the Anglican clergy 'conformed' after the Revolution tells us nothing of the contortions of conscience and the mental reservations which conformity for the majority involved. Nor does it convey the anguished irresolution of those designed to fill the sees of the deprived bishops: least of all the torments of Tillotson, who obeyed the long-delayed summons to Canterbury with a heavy heart after eighteen months of prevarication, 'telling his Majesty he would with greater cheerfulness have received his command to have gone to the Indies'.[3] It was after 1702, however, when a new oath was imposed on the clergy requiring them to abjure all allegiance to 'the pretended Prince of Wales',* that the vulnerability of many churchmen to Nonjuring propaganda was most painfully exposed. This Whig-inspired Abjuration oath slammed the door to official reconciliation with the Nonjurors which the accession of James II's daughter, Anne, had narrowly opened;[4] and Henry Sacheverell was but one among hundreds of Anglican clergy who succumbed the more readily thereafter to the calculated revival of Divine Right and Non-Resistance tenets by Jacobite writers such as Charles Leslie.†

Among the concomitants of the Revolution, however, was one of graver import to the Church than the loss of the Nonjurors. This was the final failure of English Protestants to reach agreement on formulae for 'Comprehension'. The Toleration bill introduced into Parliament in 1689 was not at first intended to apply to all dissenters; only to an irreconcilable minority who could be expected to reject reunion with the State Church even on the most liberal terms. Since 1660 periodic attempts had been made by Anglicans of goodwill, among them responsible laymen such as Daniel Finch, earl of Nottingham, to work out schemes for a *modus vivendi* with moderate Dissent. Their purpose was to reconcile most of the Presbyterian ministers ejected from Church livings in 1662, along

* i.e. Prince James Edward Stuart, son of the late James II, recognised as the rightful King of England by the French in 1701.
† See pp. 33–4 below. Also Burnet, v, 436–7, for the influence of Leslie's *Rehearsal*.

with their flocks,* and if possible to accommodate the more flexible of the Congregationalists or Independents.[5] The achievement of a common Protestant front in the face of James II's catholicising policies, and the express undertakings then given the nonconformists by Anglican leaders, appeared by 1689 to have created the most favourable possible climate for reconciliation. Fair weather, however, rapidly turned to foul; and the prospects of Comprehension, first damaged in Parliament, were finally shipwrecked in Convocation.

Among the reasons for this sorry failure was the enforced withdrawal of the Nonjurors from a scheme of which Sancroft had initially been a leading sponsor; for this made it easier for the enemies of Comprehension to stigmatise its Anglican supporters indiscriminately as Whigs and Latitude men, prepared to sell out the dearest treasures of their inheritance to a swarm of 'fanatics'. Nothing could have been further from the truth. The thirty members of the 1689 Commission on Prayer Book reform were men of learning and representative of many shades of opinion in the Church; and the changes they proposed in order to appease the Presbyterians were few and modest.[6] But this cut no ice with the Convocation elected in an atmosphere of singular militancy in the autumn of 1689, and an assembly from which much had been hoped proved so intractable that both King and bishops were soon agreed on one thing – the need to put it to sleep and keep it asleep.

Thus it was that the Toleration Act, which had passed through Parliament quite easily in the spring of this year, was left to do a job for which it was never designed: a hastily-drafted measure, as frigid, as limited and as short-term in conception as its title suggests – 'a bill for exempting their Majesties' Protestant subjects dissenting from the Church of England from the penalties of certain laws' – was fated by the end of 1689 to apply to perhaps four times as many people as the Baptists, Quakers and other 'scrupulous consciences' envisaged in the bill's preamble.

The net result of the wreck of Comprehension and of the achievement of 'Toleration' in this oblique and fortuitous manner was to damage the Church in many ways, quite apart from the personal animosities aroused. Six or seven hundred moderate congre-

---

* Sacheverell's great-uncles had been but three among some 1,800 victims of 'the Great Ejection'.

gations which had no legal existence before 1689, many of them ministered to by men who would have been an asset to the ranks of the parish clergy, were allowed henceforward to flourish outside the pale, in lawful competition with the Establishment. Less foreseeably, Englishmen were now at liberty, in practice, to interpret the new freedom to attend conventicles as a right to stay away from *any* place of worship; and it is clear that ordinary people did precisely this in increasing numbers in the 1690s. Bishop Lloyd's first visitation in his new diocese of Worcester in 1699 revealed that by then the curate of Queenhill had no congregation at all, 'no not upon a Sacrament day, but returned home without saying service'.[7] Most serious of all, a whole generation of churchmen was to be dogged by the uncertainty surrounding this 'Toleration' so adventitiously granted in 1689. Radical disagreements, or plain confusion, over the Act's implications lent more bitterness than any other issue to the faction feuds among Anglicans from the late 1690s down to the Sacheverell trial. And by so doing they did much to deprive the Church of the measure of common conviction which it needed to combat not merely apathy in the lower ranks of society, but intellectual criticism from the upper ranks.

The 1690s in England saw the advance of rationalism to a pitch of self-confidence which made it intellectually the most powerful force of the day.[8] Many Anglican clergy themselves fell under the spell of Locke and Newton. Unfortunately, from the well-intentioned endeavours of conforming Anglicans to buttress the Christian faith by reducing its essential dogmas to the simplest intelligible minimum (which was Locke's purpose), it was but a short step to Deism and to the total rejection of all 'revealed' religion. When, as Atterbury wrote, 'all mysteries in religion have been decried as impositions on men's understandings'; when, as a noted Oxford preacher deplored, 'the infinite knowledge and wisdom of God himself must not be allowed to understand and reveal anything but what the scanty mind of man . . . may be able to comprehend';[9] then the way was open for Deists such as John Toland[10] to achieve widespread publicity for their own essentially non-Christian positions.

Yet even Deism seemed almost respectable when compared with the flow of sceptical, blasphemous or downright atheistical litera-

ture on to the London bookmarket,* encouraged by the effective
end of press censorship in 1695. It was no surprise to the clergy,
'whom all malcontents have ever thought lawful game',[11] that
they should be the first sufferers from the new freedom. But the
sheer audacity of their critics did appal them, and their consternation was all the greater because the challenge to their spiritual
authority from without was paralleled in the 1690s by a loss of
control within the gates. This was the peak period in England of the
influence of the Socinians, anti-Trinitarians whose thought cast
into doubt, and occasionally openly denied, the divinity of Christ.
It was a source of scandal to thousands of Church of England
parsons that the chief distributor of Socinian tracts, Thomas
Firmin, was the personal friend of Tillotson and Tenison, successive Primates, and a pillar of an Anglican congregation in the
City, and that their most prolific author, Stephen Nye, was rector
of a living in Hertfordshire.[12]

Rightly or wrongly, devout Anglicans believed they were living
by the 1690s in a thoroughly reprobate age, as well as in an age of
irreligion and heresy. The standard of public morals was widely
deplored and the church courts (to which 'dilatory and expensive'
were the kindest epithets the bishop of Salisbury could apply)
were as ineffective in raising it as they were in enforcing church-
going. Later in the period Tory preachers were to claim a monopoly
of concern for the moral and spiritual plight of the nation; but the
truth was, anxiety on this score pervaded the whole Church.
Among the London clergy in the early 1690s there was no more
vigorous crusader against vice than Tenison, the future Whig
Primate. In January 1707 Charles Trimnell, soon to be made
bishop of Norwich by Whig influence, told the House of Commons from the pulpit of St Margaret's that God's mercies to the
country in the present war had been bestowed 'notwithstanding
the vice and irreligion that, like a pestilence . . . now rages among
us'. It was a Whig prelate, too, who soon afterwards recalled to a
St Paul's congregation which included the Queen herself the fate
of Sodom and Gomorrah.[13]

In that same sermon in 1708 Bishop Fleetwood put his finger
on what was, in a sense, the most demoralising of all the Church's

---

* 'There are few atheists', Burnet commented later, 'but many infidels, who are indeed
little better'. *Own Time*, vi, 387.

problems: the clergy's loss of public respect in the years since the Revolution in the face of a barrage of anti-clerical literature. 'Priestcraft' had become one of the dirty words of the age. Fleetwood's own word, 'contempt', which he used to describe the general attitude towards the ministry, had come to be repeated, dirge-like, with uncanny regularity in the private and public utterances of the clergy and their friends.[14] By 1709 there can be no doubt that the self-confidence of the Anglican clergy was at a low ebb and that belief in their own mission was wavering.

A more prosperous Church, materially, would have found it easier to hold on to its self-respect. But the Church of England went into the post-Revolution era already poor, and getting poorer. True, there were coveted prizes still to be had by the fortunate or the influential: lush dioceses such as Durham, Winchester or Ely, or parish livings as fat as Liverpool, Warrington, or Sedgefield in Durham (reputedly worth £1,200 a year). But in general the clergy's poverty, as Davenant observed in 1704, was 'scandalous'. Even the hierarchy was not untouched: for able divines, enjoying influential and profitable City benefices, or comfortable deaneries, might well recoil at the thought of 'promotion' to such arid sees as Oxford, Bristol or St Asaph's.[15] Essentially, however, poverty was a parochial problem. The governors appointed to administer Queen Anne's Bounty in 1704 considered £80 per annum a fair reward for the average incumbent; yet they found that 5,082 livings out of the 9,180 charged for clerical taxation yielded less than this, and that 2,122 of them brought in less than £30.[16]

'Impropriations' remained the economic bane of the Church in 1700, as they had been in 1600. After the dissolution of the monasteries there took place over a period of years a massive transfer into lay hands of the major revenues of many of the best benefices in England. By the late seventeenth century in a total of 9,913 parishes there were 3,845 'churches impropriate'.[17] But while impropriations were a grievance of long standing,* taxation more

---

* Two cases taken from the diocese of St Asaph illustrate the cost to the clergy of this catastrophe (still denounced by a few intrepid spirits as a national act of sacrilege). The income of the parish of Oswestry was over £400 a year and that of nearby St Martin's nearly £300. But by the time Lord Craven, the impropriator, had taken his rake-off, the vicar of Oswestry was left with between £30 and £40 and the incumbent of St Martin's with barely £20. A. T. Hart, *William Lloyd*, p. 75. For contemporary protests, cf. Lansdowne MSS. 987, ff. 240–1; Lansdowne MSS. 1024, f.

severe than had ever fallen on the clergy – the price of two wars of unprecedented dimensions fought between 1689 and 1713 to safeguard a Protestant Church and Succession – was a new affliction, one which in these years reduced many a bare competence to little more than a pittance. Clearly, as long as the wars lasted the traditional abuses of pluralism and non-residence, which made the 'poor curate' of £15 or £20 a year an all too common phenomenon, would continue to defy reforming prelates.[18]

After the passing of the Toleration Act the Church was made increasingly aware of one other disabling inheritance, a further penalty of its established status. Its basically medieval parish structure was far too inflexible, unresponsive at many vital points to population growth and ill-adapted to meet the challenge of Dissent after 1689 in the suburbs of London, in the textile and metal-working towns, and in many of the ports. To divide an ancient parish and build a second church where one had stood before needed an Act of Parliament; whereas all the dissenters needed to erect a conventicle was a group of well-to-do tradesmen and a licence. While old cathedral cities were often over-endowed with parish churches, sometimes to the point of embarrassment, many expanding urban areas were left hopelessly denuded. Gloucester's 4,750 inhabitants, for example, had ten churches, and Lincoln, 'an ancient, ragged, decayed and still decaying city', still had thirteen;[19] yet Taunton, twice the size of Gloucester and the queen of the Somerset clothing towns, had only two, and Leeds was in a comparable plight. The building of Manchester's second church, St Anne's, was only authorised by Parliament in 1708 and completed in 1712, by which time the population of the town was probably around 10,000 and of the parish well over 30,000.* Even the worst provincial black spots were favoured, however, by comparison with some of the mushrooming London suburbs, where, as Swift observed, 'the care of above thirty thousand souls hath been sometimes committed to one minister, whose church could hardly contain the twentieth part of his flock'.[20]

---

207 (Kennett's diary, 15 March 1710); H. Sacheverell, preface to *Fifteen Discourses of William Adams* (1716); Robert Nelson, *The Life of George Bull, Late Bishop of St David's* (1714), pp. 431–5.
* Birmingham and Liverpool, both expanding just as rapidly, had to wait even longer for their second churches, as did Sheffield.

2. *The Church Divided*

It was not her problems alone, however, which made the post-
Revolution situation so tragic for the Church and so significant
for the nation. It was the fact that the Anglican response to the
dilemma was such a deeply divided one. Symptomatic of this
division, and mainly responsible for perpetuating it for over a
decade before Sacheverell exploded on the scene, was the cleavage
of the Anglican clergy into High Church and Low Church parties.

These parties already had antecedents of a kind before 1689. In
the 1680s, as Tenison of Canterbury would later remind his
brother of York, 'I was thought a much higher Churchman at St
Martin's [in-the-Fields] than you at St Giles's'. But the distinctions
then understood by such terms were relatively limited and amic-
able. They mostly involved matters of discipline, liturgical practice, vestment and ritual. Even as late as 1695, when William Wake
deplored the fact that Lord Carberry had 'set up for a High
Churchman', he explained himself by adding: 'He bows at going
into the chapel and at the name of Jesus . . . lets his chaplain say
grace; and seems to mind little in his family more than that they
strictly conform to the Church services and ceremonies'.[21]
Despite the ill effects of the Comprehension issue in 1689, the
hard division of the clergy into rival factions remained for several
years thereafter more a danger to be apprehended than an irrevocable fact. Tory parsons might carp at the early Williamite
bishops; but they could not in their hearts feel that the Church
was in genuine danger in the hands of men who had been mostly
hand-picked by Lord Nottingham, whose devotion to the Church
no one could doubt. Equally important in holding the ranks
together was the influence of Queen Mary, who prudently discharged the responsibility for ecclesiastical policy which her
husband unloaded on her.[22]

The turning-point came in 1694. Mary died, in the prime of
life; and thousands mourned, with Burnet, the loss of 'our chief
hope and glory on earth'.[23] In the same year the decision was taken
to promote to Canterbury Thomas Tenison, rather than the more
strictly orthodox Bishop Stillingfleet of Worcester. Not that there
was any immediate capitulation to the Whigs in the field of preferments, such as the bulk of the clergy feared. But as the nucleus of

a powerful ecclesiastical opposition took shape, and above all once the dissidents discovered a focus for their opposition in an organised campaign for the recall of Convocation, so the 'great moderation' (as one contemporary fairly put it) with which Tenison 'governed the Church for three years' began to crumble under pressure.[24] If there were no clearly-defined parties at the beginning of the Convocation controversy of 1697 to 1701, they certainly existed before it was over. Rarely can an ostensibly academic disputation have aroused such violent animosities or left such scars on personal relationships. One of Tenison's lieutenants in the fray, Archdeacon Nicolson,* remarked in May 1700, after reading the abuse heaped on him by one anonymous cleric, 'if there should happen to be a majority of his kidney [elected to a Convocation], I'd as soon hope to have our Church's peace established by a Convocation of English bull dogs'. And the stormy events of 1701, when the Church's representative assembly was at length reconvened, fully justified his apprehensions. By 1702 the High and Low Church parties had consolidated in and out of Convocation with their labels firmly attached, in much the form they were to retain for the rest of Queen Anne's reign.[25]

'God forgive them who have coined and applied these opprobrious distinctions'. So said Francis Atterbury, with more than a touch of self-righteousness. Clergy and laymen alike would go on deploring 'this invidious distinction, tending to set us at enmity'.[26] But from now on they could never ignore what were plain facts of life. The facts obtruded at every turn. In Convocation from 1701 to 1707 there was a protracted struggle between the bishops in the Upper House and the High Church majority in the Lower, for it soon became plain to the latter that no High Church programme could ever be carried through unless the Lower House could assert a right to sit independently, ignoring adjournment orders from the Primate.[27] In the House of Lords party voting by the bishops became the order of the day, the moderate High Churchmen of the early 1690s – Patrick, Hough, Moore and Cumberland – being forced, in defensive reaction to Highflying

* The main controversialists were Wake, Gibson and Kennett on the 'Low' side, Atterbury and Samuel Hill for the 'High' party, with Wake and Atterbury providing the heaviest artillery. 'I now press on myself to an end of my work', wrote Wake in February 1701. 'The world expects it, and Mr A [tterbury] has took effectual care to provoke me to it'. MS. Ballard 3, f. 36.

attacks, into the Low Church–Whig camp. Worse still was the situation in the dioceses, where party rivalries brought such bishops as Nicolson, Burnet, Lloyd and Trelawney into a state of near-open war with their cathedral and parish clergy. Even Hough of Lichfield, who was relatively fortunate in this respect, had occasion to complain in the Lords 'of the opprobrious names the clergy gave their bishops and the calumnies they laid on them, as if they were in a plot to destroy the Church'.[28]

Other manifestations of a divided Church were just as disturbing. By Anne's reign Church preferments were too often viewed and discussed in terms of party ambitions, successes and failures: Wake's appointment to Lincoln and Trimnell's to Norwich were as much deplored by High Churchmen as the elevation of Hooper to St Asaph and Blackall to Exeter were applauded. At the same time a running battle was waged through the press, where the Low Churchmen found the fluent, vitriolic pen of Benjamin Hoadly, Rector of St Peter-le-Poor, more than a match even for the polemics of Atterbury and murderously effective against the less flexible weapons of Blackall.* The extreme positions adopted by this 'thin, meagre, sour fellow',[29] and the fact that to a majority of his fellow-clergy he seemed nothing less than a satanic traitor to the cloth, proved an embarrassment at times even to those whose causes he championed. Hoadly was mocked as a cuckold and had his physical deformities jibed at by infuriated opponents; but at least he was spared the fate of one of the most noted lay pro-tagonists in the Low Church interest, the newspaper editor John Tutchin, who died after a savage beating at the hands of a Tory mob in 1707. In the brutal world of early eighteenth-century contro-versy, however, Tutchin was denied even the posthumous consolation of being recognised as a martyr for a cause. 'The fellow, indeed, had an honest, dry drubbing', conceded the Reverend Charles Lambe, 'just as much as he deserved and no more; but

* Hoadly, two years Sacheverell's junior (b. 1676), made his name in a controversy with the nonconformist Edmund Calamy in 1703–5, and with a sermon before the Lord Mayor in 1705 for which Bromley in the Commons accused him of 'preaching rebellion'. He engaged in a protracted duel with Blackall in 1708–9 over obedience and the right of resistance. Of his tilts with Atterbury at this time, Bishop Nicolson (not entirely unbiased) wrote that 'Dr Hoadly . . . has been formerly much too hard for his adversary of Bridewell'. See also E. Calamy, *Historical Account of my own Life*, ii, 20.

he was furiously poxed, as the surgeon who dissected him will witness, or else he would have lived, thrived well and mended like a walnut tree after a beating'.[30]

Clerics who conducted their quarrels with so much license in print were not likely to keep them out of the pulpit. And so it proved. The least edifying of all the spectacles presented by a Church divided into High and Low factions was the prostitution of the pulpit, particularly in Queen Anne's reign, to blatantly party ends. Henry Sacheverell's crime of 1709 was but the offence of hundreds of his fellow-divines writ large.

The issues which sustained all this controversy are best understood as integral parts of two incompatible solutions to the Church's manifold problems. From the later years of King William onward, it was the choice between those two fundamentally different remedies which often determined whether a clergyman gravitated to the High or Low pole. A great majority[31] still yearned for the closest possible return to the pre-1687 position, when Church and State had worked in harmony within a regime in which uniformity and unquestioning obedience to authority were the watchwords. At the very least, Atterbury argued, good churchmen should be concerned with 'keeping up the present ecclesiastical constitution in all its parts', down to the last canon and rubric, 'without making any illegal abatements in favour of such as either openly or secretly undermine it'.[32] High Churchmen also envisaged a traditional reliance on political means, not merely to restore the *status quo* but to effect any serious programme of reform.

In complete contrast, the minority who came to be branded as Low Churchmen saw the best hope for the Church in the acceptance of two unpalatable truths. The first was that the Church had only survived in 1688 by turning its back on its old political principles; and that this was a fact to be lived with, not swept under the carpet. The second was that the Church in 1689 had, in effect, been partially disestablished. In consequence, instead of looking to the State to work new miracles on its behalf, the Low Church clergy were prepared 'to accept the place in English society of a basically voluntary body':[33] allowing some latitude within its own pale; welcoming Toleration; seeking to re-establish the Church's declining influence by concentrating not on political activity, nor on the revival of ancient claims, but on furthering its

3a Henry Compton, Bishop of London,
by Sir Godfrey Kneller

3b Gilbert Burnet, Bishop of Salisbury,
c. 1690, copy after John Riley

3c 'The Church in Danger', 1709: Ben Hoadly, Latitudinarian rector of St Peter-le-Poor,
penning his second Answer to the Bishop of Exeter, while the Devil removes his (prospective)
mitre and staff. Dutch engraving

4a 'The Church in Danger', 1706: impression of an inn sign put up at Stoke by Naland, Suffolk. The amused and delighted spectators are dissenting pastors

4b 'The Church in Danger': a Presbyterian meeting-house erected in Friar Gate, Derby, in 1698

social mission, its pastoral and evangelising work, and its charitable endeavour.

Given this direct antithesis of approach, three areas of conflict between the clerical parties naturally assumed exceptional importance: the Church of England's relationship with the monarchy and the State; its relations with society in general, especially the nature of its moral responsibility; and its attitude to Dissent.

A basic political issue was whether the Church's relation with the State should be an Erastian one, in which the bishops accepted the subordination of the ecclesiastical to the civil power, and the clergy in their turn accepted their own subordination to the bishops as the representatives of the Crown, or whether it should be based on a genuine alliance of equal partners, as many High Churchmen still fondly believed to be possible. Bolder claims still were being canvassed by 1710 among some of the younger High-flying parsons: claims to a substantial measure of clerical independence, owing something to Atterbury's campaign on behalf of Convocation but more to the influence of Henry Dodwell and the Nonjurors. Such views seriously alarmed moderate Anglican leaders, who feared they would further discredit the Church at a time when its standing was already precarious enough.[34]

A remarkable fact is that the resuscitation of the theories of Passive Obedience and Non-Resistance among High Churchmen, which was to be in many ways the most vital issue of the Sacheverell trial, was a late development in the controversy over the Church's political role. Ritual lip service had been paid to these notions since the Revolution in sermons preached on 30 January, the anniversary of Charles I's martyrdom. Yet that shrewd observer Arthur Mainwaring, member of Parliament and journalist, detected the beginnings of a true revival no earlier than 1704–5, the years when most of the original High Tory ministers of Queen Anne were squeezed out of the Cabinet. And it was two sermons preached as late as 1708, Blackall's before the Queen and Atterbury's before the Corporation of London, which caused the first considerable fluttering in the Whig dovecotes.[35] After that, Highflying preachers seemed increasingly bent on convincing the Whigs that they were out to play the Pretender's game by casting doubt on the validity of the whole post-1688 Establishment. But even so, the lines of demarcation across this particular battlefield were still

D

not drawn with perfect clarity. Atterbury's doctrine, for instance, was subtle enough to take account of the Revolution, in contrast to the standard line taken by crypto-Jacobite parsons which was to draw a veil over the Revolution and pretend it had never taken place. On the other side, the many Low Churchmen who extolled Hoadly's justification of rebellion, advanced in 1709 in response to Blackall, must have been uneasily conscious that it went beyond what most of them could privately accept.[36]

As regards the Church's relations with society in general, all were agreed on the need to dispel the widespread ignorance of the Word; to raise the general level of literacy to facilitate evangelism; to restore respect for the moral laws of Christianity. But here agreement ended. By 1702 the Low Church party was already convinced of one thing: that these tasks were beyond the power of the clergy themselves and that the work of moral reformation, in particular, was far beyond the resources of the church courts, which High Churchmen hoped to reinject with life. Clerics must take into partnership committed, philanthropic Anglican laymen – yes, and dissenters as well, if need be – and work with them through voluntary, self-supporting organisations to make the Christian presence felt in society. It was therefore no coincidence that the Anglican charity school movement should have owed so much to the fund-raising sermons of Low Church parsons;[37] nor that the voluntary societies which had sprung up by 1702 – for the Reformation of Manners, for the Promotion of Christian Knowledge and for the Propagation of the Gospel – should have been as warmly espoused by the Low Church divines as, by and large, they were cold-shouldered by the High.[38] Over the Reformation of Manners, in particular, the two sides were decisively split.* Burnet lauded the reform societies to the skies; and Fowler of Gloucester claimed that 'our whole bench have never done the 40th part of that service and honour to our Church that these Church of England laymen have done'. Yet their work was gravely suspected by High Churchmen, who regarded it as a dangerous invitation to the encroachment of Dissent.[39]

---

* The earliest of the many societies for the Reformation of Manners (which brought moral misdemeanours to the attention of the magistrates and instituted Common Law actions against adulterers, swearers, brothel-keepers and so forth) was founded in 1691.

Dissent was the problem which most persistently troubled the post-Revolution Church and most grievously divided it. Out of the uncertainty which had enveloped the so-called 'Toleration' since its freakish inception arose a whole crop of contentious questions. At bottom there was a choice for Anglicans between an insistence on the letter of the Act of 1689 and a charitable interpretation of its spirit. Should the dissenters be accorded freedom to develop their own schools and academies, which the Act had neither allowed nor disallowed? Should the Presbyterians be conceded some vestige of the civil rights which would have been theirs under Comprehension? And if so, should those who were prepared to do so be allowed to qualify for office through the growing practice of 'Occasional Conformity' – taking the Anglican sacrament once a year to satisfy the 1673 Test? Low Churchmen, with no illusions about 'the fry of enthusiastical people' but hoping and believing that leniency would reconcile a new generation of Presbyterians to the Establishment,[40] answered all these questions in the affirmative; and while such Anglicans represented only a small minority of the clergy at large, their voice was strong enough on the Bishops' Bench to be influential. Other voices, however, demanded that the Toleration be stringently limited to the explicit terms of 1689 and that the remaining preserves of the Established Church be jealously guarded. And behind these voices lurked the hope that a Toleration which arguably was never meant to be permanent would be abolished altogether when the opportunity presented itself. Such were the High Church specifics for the disease of Dissent; and they were endorsed by over eighty per cent of the parish clergy, as well as by the two universities, the training-grounds of the Anglican ministry.

It was hardly surprising that the two prescriptions should have been so much at variance, for each side started from quite different premises. First there was the question of terminology, one which was to play a significant part in Sacheverell's trial. The curt preamble to the Act of May 1689 had begun: 'Forasmuch as *some ease to scrupulous consciences*[41] in the exercise of religion may be an effectual means to unite their Majesties' Protestant subjects'; and the Act's frigid title* was in line with this. Before many years were out, therefore, the bolder High Anglicans affected to deny that the

* See p. 24 above.

law had ever created a 'Toleration', as such, as opposed to an 'Indulgence' or 'Exemption'.* Secondly, there was total disagreement over the most material facts of dissenting numbers and dissenting growth. The Low Church prelates were never able to substantiate their claims that the end of persecution had led by Anne's reign to widespread secessions from the nonconformist ministry, and to a reduction of twenty or thirty per cent in the total number of dissenters.[42] But neither could High Churchmen convincingly sustain their case that a laxly-interpreted 'Toleration' had opened the floodgates to an engulfing tide of sectaries. The truth, not surprisingly, was somewhere between these two extreme views.

Staunch Anglicans were understandably despondent at the number of licences for conventicles taken out by virtue of the Toleration Act, almost 4,000 in two decades; yet they were wrong to see this as evidence of a wholesale spawning of new congregations.† There was also a tendency for many High Church parsons to exaggerate the national growth of Dissent on the basis of their own parlous local situation. There is no question that in certain areas of growing population nonconformity did make striking progress between 1689 and 1709. In the London suburbs, where Swift believed there were 'at least three hundred thousand inhabitants . . . whom the churches would not be able to contain,

---

* Although the terms 'Toleration' and 'Toleration Act' had come into public currency by 1702 (e.g. in Anne's speeches to Parliament, 1702–9), even Whigs had often referred in earlier years to 'the bill of Indulgence' or 'the bill of Exemption' (see *Parl. Hist.* v, 263–6; Burnet, iv, 16). These were distinctions which by the time of the Sacheverell affair were to assume an importance which no one in the early 1690s could have foreseen; but they were there from the start.

† By one clause of the Act every dissenting meeting-house, in order to be legally recognised as a place of worship, had to be formally licensed either by a J.P. or by a bishop. 3,901 licences for both permanent and temporary buildings were issued to all denominations between May 1689 and the end of 1710, more than two-thirds of them after December 1690. But the vast majority of new licences issued after the initial spate of 1689–90 came in response to the needs of existing congregations: either because they wished to move from one temporary meeting-place to another, often on a change of minister, or because they had built a permanent structure in place of their former temporary one. It is perhaps more enlightening that by 1710 only 333 permanent structures had been licensed, though it is known that others were built, and somehow contrived, with the connivance or by the negligence of local magistrates, to flourish unofficially. See E. D. Bebb, *Nonconformity and Social and Economic Life*, Appx. I, p. 174; A. Brockett, *Nonconformity in Exeter, 1650–1875*, p. 53.

if the people were ever so well disposed',[43] there were roughly twice as many conventicles as churches and chapels of ease by 1711. In areas where industry was being stimulated by war there were several towns (or swollen parishes, such as Halifax) where the meeting-houses quickly came to outnumber the churches. There were also many others whose imposing new conventicles were better attended. Sheffield's Presbyterian chapel was a typical case. Opened in 1700, a stone's throw from the old parish church, and soon catering for close on 1,200 'hearers', it testified publicly – like many such buildings in growth areas – to the prosperity of nonconformity as well as to its strength.[44] In the older textile areas, too, there were ominous signs, as there were in the flourishing western ports of Queen Anne's day. Taunton's Presbyterians had the biggest single nonconforming congregation in England (2,000), while Bristol counted almost a third of its population of just over 20,000 as regular attenders at Baptist, Presbyterian and Quaker meetings.[45] On the other hand, the alarmists overlooked the many counties in which the seed of Puritanism had fallen on stony ground and had yielded by 1700 but a sparse harvest. Cornwall's population of over 100,000 contained only one dissenter to every hundred inhabitants, while in Lincolnshire a correspondent of John Evans, compiler of a semi-official census of dissenters in 1715, could find only ten congregations, numbering 1,762 'hearers', in the whole of that sprawling county.[46]

In retrospect, there are sound reasons for believing that Dissent did experience after the Revolution a moderate, steady growth: that the number of its congregations, Quakers apart, increased from 940 in 1690 to around 1,200 in 1716;[47] and that the average size of individual congregations in many towns probably rose. It is even possible to calculate that, including foreign Protestants,[48] there were very nearly half a million dissenters in England and Wales by 1715. But while this may have represented an increase of 100,000, or even slightly more, on the total at the time the Toleration Act was passed, it was hardly the landslide which High Tory propaganda regularly sought to convey. There is a still more important fact to be borne in mind. Highflyers and Tories invariably described dissenting progress in terms which suggested a grave threat to the whole Establishment from some great close-knit conspiracy. The truth is, neither before the Revolution nor after it was Protestant Dissent an entity, with a common plan of campaign or a capacity for united action. Some co-operative experiments there were, at least among the major denominations, Presbyterians, Congregationalists and Baptists. But Puritanism had always been fissiparous, and essentially it remained so.

Of course, the growth of Dissent was not to be measured solely in quantitative terms. The assertiveness of the dissenters in both the educational field and the civil field was something about which all contemporary Anglicans were sensitive and most High Churchmen increasingly resentful. So far as the dissenting academies were concerned, the paranoia of Oxford and Cambridge absurdly exaggerated the threat to the Anglican monopoly of higher education. Sir John Pakington told the House of Commons in 1705 that, in his view, one of the gravest dangers to the Church, as well as to the universities, was

> the great increase of dissenting schools and seminaries all over the kingdom, in which great numbers of our youth are poisoned with principles which make them disaffected to the Church, and considering the strict union between Church and State, I may say to the monarchy too. I take them to be nurseries for rebellion.[49]

The same cry had been raised in Convocation during 1701, and it rang from many a pulpit. Yet the cool statistics of modern scholarship[50] have cut much of this contemporary scare-mongering down to size. There may have been thirty academies in existence by 1714. Yet a score or so were already in being before the Toleration Act was passed;* and whether under Queen Anne these institutions ever catered for more than five or six hundred students in all, at any one time, is doubtful. Admittedly, they trained a new generation of dissenting ministers, and thereby played a vital part in that 'propagation of schism' which even Low Churchmen viewed with some concern. But their pupils in Anne's reign also included a future archbishop of Canterbury and a future bishop of Durham,[51] while many prominent layment who studied

---

* Anglicans often forgot the number of academies which had to close their doors between 1689 and 1710 – at least twelve, including the celebrated establishment at Stoke Newington which had nurtured Defoe and Samuel Wesley – while remembering the new foundations which had opened, especially those of great repute like Manchester, Tewkesbury, Moorfields or Warrington.

under nonconformist tutors became respectable conformists in later life. When Henry Sacheverell attacked the seminaries in 1709 for teaching heresy and atheism, and debauching the youth of the nation, he was not to know that within eight months he would be prosecuted by two of these 'debauchees' representing the Commons – Sir Peter King and Sir Joseph Jekyll – and defended by a third, Sir Simon Harcourt, soon to become Lord Chancellor of England.*

The civil encroachments of the dissenters, through the loophole of Occasional Conformity, lent stronger support to the High Anglican case. Yet even here there was gross exaggeration. Practising dissenters so rarely penetrated the upper reaches of the government service that it caused an outcry when John Shute was made a Commissioner of Customs in 1709. The county commissions of the peace, too, were only peripherally infiltrated, and in the House of Commons thoroughgoing dissenters were surprisingly few.[52] But in the municipal corporations, and therefore in the electorate, it was a different story. Occasional Conformity did not begin with the Toleration: but after the passing of the 1689 Act it steadily became more obtrusive and more complacent.[53] How much more became startlingly apparent in 1697, when the Lord Mayor of London went for two Sundays running in procession, preceded by the City sword-bearer, to Mead's meeting-house, 'a nasty conventicle' which was kept in a hall 'belonging to one of the mean, mechanical companies'.[54] His action fleetingly caused great scandal; but it was its implications in electoral terms, in some seventy or eighty parliamentary boroughs, which caused the lasting alarm. The 'occasional men' were a force to be reckoned with not only in limited corporation boroughs† but in every borough where the corporation had the decisive voice in 'modelling' the electorate: in most freeman boroughs, for example, it was the councillors who nominated to the freemen's roll. When, in addition, Presbyterian mayors were able to use their powers as returning officers to send up to Westminster opponents of 'the Church interest', in defiance of the polling figures,[55] it is not hard to understand why clergymen

* King was educated at Exeter Academy, before going to Leyden; Jekyll was a student at Islington, and Harcourt at Shilton, in Oxfordshire.
† i.e. the nineteen parliamentary boroughs where the right to vote was in the hands of the 'select number', the mayor, aldermen and common-councillors.

and M.Ps alike were clamouring by Anne's reign for stern remedial legislation.

Yet even on this issue the Church was not at one. To High-flying parsons Occasional Conformity was at one and the same time an 'abominable hypocrisy', a political enormity and an invidious imposition on incumbents.* The Low Church party, however, while recognising that the practice was sometimes abused both for selfish and political ends, would not condemn it in principle. No doubt the pragmatic arguments that swayed the politicians, and for a time even Queen Anne herself, had some influence with moderate bishops – in particular, the necessity of preserving Protestant unity during a war against the power sheltering the Catholic Pretender. But their main argument was that a practice which Anglicans when abroad regularly followed, in foreign Protestant churches, could not morally be illegalised at home.[56]

The conduct of the bishops in Parliament, when bills against Occasional Conformity were sent up to the Lords in three successive sessions from 1702 to 1704, led to their further disastrous loss of caste in the eyes of the clerical rank and file. On the first occasion,[57] few bishops were ready to oppose the bill root and branch; but the bench was divided almost equally under its two archbishops, Tenison and Sharp, over the Whig amendments which led to the bill's ultimate paralysis, and it was the bishop of Oxford's change of sides which proved decisive. When the second bill was rejected outright in December 1703, fourteen bishops now voted against it and only nine for; and the Reverend Humphrey Whyle was 'ashamed to think that fourteen bishops should be thought to vote against the apparent interest of the Church of England'. By 1704, the wild attempt of the extreme Tories in the Commons to force the third bill past the Lords by 'tacking' it to the Land Tax bill, on which vital war supply depended, soured even Bishop Nicolson, who since 1702 had been held firmly to the Sharp party on this issue. When the Commons had just reached their historic decision against 'the Tack' on 28 November 1704, Nicolson records how 'when the coaches began to move, I sent out

---

* A parson could be sued under the Test Act for refusing the sacrament to a parishioner without lawful cause, and yet he was obliged by canon law to exclude 'notorious schismatics' from the altar rails.

my servant to enquire how things went; and he presently returned with a lamentable story that *the Church has lost it*. . . . With sub-mission [the bishop added] I am of a contrary opinion'. But in one sense he was wrong. Whatever had happened to this grievously divisive bill in 1704, the Church, in its now distracted state, was bound to be the loser.[58]

3. *The Politicians and the Clergy*

The bitterly-fought campaign over Occasional Conformity sig-nalised how in the second decade after the Revolution, religion and politics were still as closely involved with each other as they had been at any time since the Reformation. But it also illustrates how the nature of that involvement had changed since 1688, as parties gradually developed inside the Church of England which, wittingly or not, became the ecclesiastical counterparts of the Whig and Tory parties in the State; so that from the last year or two of King William's reign the fortunes of all four parties, Whig, Tory, High Church and Low Church, became closely interlocked.

Understanding this entanglement is vital to the story of Henry Sacheverell. Without it the post-Revolution Church would still, no doubt, have produced its Sacheverell. An incendiary sermon might even have been preached in St Paul's in 1709. But whatever notoriety and censure such a sermon brought upon the preacher, it is improbable that in a political world in which religion had little part it would have resulted in his being brought to trial before the most solemn court in the land, or that it would have made his name a household word among several million people.

Divisions on religious issues had played a central part in the genesis of political parties in England in the later years of Charles II. Those who came to be called Tories had backed to the full the claims to exclusive authority advanced by the restored Church, rejecting the claims of the dissenters to freedom of worship and civil rights. Likewise they had embraced the political theory of Anglicanism and the high religious concept of monarchical right and authority; and this they staunchly upheld against the powerful movement of the years 1679–81, aimed at excluding by law the King's Catholic brother James from the succession to the throne. On the other hand, the first Whigs had favoured a measure of toleration for the dissenters, who backed them strongly in that same Exclusion struggle; and as an intrinsic part of the logic of their political position, both then and in 1688, they rejected the religious view of the basis of monarchy in favour of the secular view that kingly authority rested on consent, or as John Locke argued, on a man-made contract; and that if that consent were forfeited, or if that contract were broken, then the obligation to obey the sovereign was dissolved.

As far as the politicians were concerned, the events of November 1688 to May 1689 should logically have laid to rest these contentious issues of religious principle. In the failure of the Tories to rally to the defence of James II, the Lord's Anointed; in the parliamentary settlement both of the Crown and of the succession, by-passing the legal heir; and in the passing of the Toleration Act, those Tory convictions which had proved too much for the Exclusionists seemed to have been thrown on the political scrapheap by men who, at the moment of truth, preferred their liberty, their property and their Protestantism to their ideology. The passage twelve years later in a Tory-dominated Parliament of another succession act, this time in favour of a Hanoverian family absurdly remote from that hereditary line the Tories had once held so sacred, may appear to confirm that the contest of the lay parties had become wholly secularised.

Yet such was far from being the case. Within a decade of the Glorious Revolution religion had begun to embroil the party politicians once again; and the reason for this lay essentially in the sickness of the Church of England, and in the propensity of each clerical faction in turn to look to rival groups of politicians to administer its medicines. The initiative in this process came logically from the High Church–Tory side, and it was not until 1701, the year that the Whig leader, Lord Somers, 'dined publicly at my lord of Canterbury's, which was the first time that ever he did so', that Tenison and his Low Church allies finally committed themselves, in desperate self-protection, to the 'Junto',* the spearhead of the Whig power-politicians.[59]

High Churchmen, looking for a future for the Church in the past, knew their aims to be unattainable without the full support

---

* The name given to the association of Lord Somers, Halifax, Wharton, Sunderland and Orford.

of the State. As long as William III lived, they could not expect
that support from the Crown, as of old. William was known to
dislike the sacramental test for office-holders; he had sanctioned
the abolition of episcopacy in Scotland; he connived at Occasional
Conformity and the spread of dissenting academies. Once Queen
Mary was dead, High Churchmen knew that there was never a
chance that the King's position as Supreme Governor of the Church
would be an effective guardianship.[60] And so, since they could not
look to the Crown, they had to put their trust in Parliament. And
there their only hope lay in a prolonged period of Tory supremacy.
Only from their old allies, the Tories, could they hope for acts
illegalising Occasional Conformity, suppressing dissenting seminaries, resuscitating the moribund Church courts so as to revive
their discipline over the laity, financing church-building from
public funds, and restraining the freedom of the press to pour
out heretical or anti-Christian literature.

Consequently, well before Queen Anne came to the throne in
March 1702 there had already been sealed a tacit compact between
the Tory gentry and power-politicians on the one hand and the
Highflying clergy on the other: an unwritten compact, but one
whose terms were clearly understood. For their part, the Tory
politicians were pledged to press in the first place for the recall of
Convocation; and having succeeded (in 1701) in making this the
price of their support for King William's administration, they then
undertook to maintain the closest ties they could between the Lower
House of the Canterbury assembly and the Lower House of Parliament. In the bitter Convocation dogfights of the next few years the
extremist clergy were firmly supported by the earl of Rochester
and Sir Edward Seymour, the most partisan of the High Tory
chieftains, and by their henchmen in the Commons.[61]

But this was only the beginning. Tories were encouraged by
the clergy to proclaim their Church's danger from the housetops.
In Parliament a climax was reached in December 1705, with the
defeat of motions made by Rochester in the Lords and by Bromley* and Seymour in the Commons, that *the Church of England
was in danger* under Godolphin's middle-of-the-road administration.[62] In the constituencies the message of this crude party slogan –
so easy to spread (a shrewd foreigner observed) and so hard to

* William Bromley, M.P. for Oxford University.

eradicate – was even more effective; and at the General Election of 1705 it was largely instrumental in the re-election of a high proportion of the 134 notorious 'Tackers'* (one of whom had a banner carried before him in his campaign showing a picture of a steeple crumbling and falling, a token of what the electors could expect if they returned his Whig rival).[63] Finally, Tories were expected to try to repel the danger to the Church by legislative action; although after the failure of the third Occasional Conformity bill they were never strong enough, before 1710, to attempt any major controversial measures, and had to be content with lending their support to useful bills designed to improve the economic status of the poorer clergy or to improve parochial libraries.[64]

In return for this backing, the bulk of the 9,000-odd parish clergy threw their whole weight behind the Tory cause in Election after Election from 1698 onwards. 'It was never known that the parsons were so busy', wrote one of the duke of Devonshire's agents after the 1702 Election; and balefully he added, 'I wish they may not one day repent it'.[65] They were indeed formidable electioneers. For one thing, in most English counties they presented a block of anything from 100 to 400 clerical freeholders, often ready to ride to the polls in squadron order to demonstrate their solidarity in the Tory interest.† Also, by the very nature of their office they were the most effective canvassers any party could possess. But above all, they were prepared to use their pulpits shamelessly for electoral ends: as did the clergyman who preached before the burgesses of Durham just before the city election of 1708, whose text

> was the -th verse of the 12th chapter of the 1st of Samuel, and the words, they say, by hard straining he perverted into the management of elections, on which his whole discourse ran, lashing all those who opposed Mr Conyers, concluding that damnation would be their future lot if they did not repent of

---

* See p. 40 above.
† Many examples will be found in W. A. Speck, *Tory and Whig: The Struggle in the Constituencies, 1701–1715* (1970), pp. 24–5. Tory clergy were also willing to travel far in the cause. In May 1705 Rev. L. Blackburn wrote to William Wake: 'I have it from Exon but the last post that Sir R. Vivyan [M.P. Cornwall] has written to Exeter that if there be any want of clergymen to oppose my Lord [Bishop Trelawney] there, he will come up himself for that purpose at the head of 80 of 'em from Cornwall'. Wake MSS. Arch. W. Epist. 17, misc. i, letter 97.

such an heinous sin as the attempting to reject so true and trusty a member of the Church.[66]

But the High Church clergy did not confine their pulpit-politics to election times. The bolder spirits among them chose to vent their fears, and too often their turbulence and malice, by making 'the Church in danger' a regular feature of their sermons. They strove to convince their congregations that the Church not only was in danger, but without drastic action must fall into the direst peril, from the dissenters, from the new intellectual forces unleashed against it, and above all from the enemy within the gate – from those black sheep, the Low Church bishops and the Whig or moderate politicians. In the view of that shrewd Scot, Alexander Cunningham, this brand of fire-raising, quasi-seditious sermon, confined in William's reign to a small group of conforming clergy, mostly ill-disguised Jacobites, spread with extraordinary rapidity in the early and middle years of Anne; 'so that at length the distemper which had seized them diffused its contagion among almost the whole body of the inferior clergy'.[67]

Indeed, to understand the mounting resentment of the Whigs and of Queen Anne's moderate 'managers'* under the sting of these attacks, and its extraordinary culmination in December 1709, we have to accept that such attacks were widespread as well as damaging. A few fireballs might attract particular notice, as much by their flamboyant style of preaching as by the brazen content of their sermons: the wild, itinerant Irishman, Francis Higgins; Tilly, and Read, as well as Sacheverell in Oxford; Whalley Lambe, Welton, Hilliard and Milbourne in London. By and large, these men gave their audiences what they expected to hear: the crowd which regularly flocked to listen to Luke Milbourne, for example, and the susceptible women who sat mesmerised by the Celtic charm and oratory of Higgins, would have been astonished to hear their idols preaching Peace on Earth, Goodwill towards Men. But these were no freaks. They were in numerous company. When Lord Poulet reached Devon in the spring of 1705 he found that the 'clergy preach nothing but the Church being now in the greatest danger, and the bishop himself is often named in their

* i.e. Lord Godolphin (Lord Treasurer, 1702–10), the duke of Marlborough (Captain-General, 1702–11) and Robert Harley (Speaker of the House of Commons, 1701–5, and Secretary of State, 1704–8).

pulpits as an enemy to the Church'; while Godolphin, returning to London the following autumn already smarting under the libellous attacks in the High Church pamphlet, *The Memorial of the Church of England*, 'heard of several insolences of the clergy which are really insufferable and next door to open rebellion'.[68]

Godolphin was no Whig, and neither for that matter was the bishop of Exeter. All the same, as 'moderates' – by now a word of bitter opprobrium in the High Church vocabulary – they came in for their share of abuse. But whereas these and other betrayers of the cause provoked 'the odium of the priests',[69] it was the Whigs who inspired fear. And it is fair to say that although the High Church parsons made a terrible bogy of the Whigs (the bulk of whom were, after all, conforming Anglicans),* there was some basis for their apprehension. It was undeniable that whenever the Whig leaders achieved political influence they struggled to secure the highest preferment for moderate or latitudinarian divines;† that the dissenting vote was cast even more solidly for the Whigs in elections than that of the parish clergy for the Tories; and that Whig votes in the Lords had killed all the first three bills against Occasional Conformity and had threatened even the Queen Anne's Bounty bill.[70] Above all, it was common knowledge that within both the leadership and the ranks of the party there did exist among nominal Anglicans a definite anti-clerical element, intolerant of 'priestcraft' (that vogue word of the day), sceptical, freethinking.

But here it was hard to say which came first, the chicken or the egg. Obviously pulpit politics alone did not make freethinkers out of the members of Lord Sunderland's‡ circle: to John Gellibrand, for example, all clergy were 'vermin'.[71] Likewise the mildest diet of sermons would not have made a pillar of orthodoxy out of Sir Joseph Jekyll, or out of Lord Coningsby (who, arguing once with a Tory about the Pretender and vehemently protesting that he 'always was against the father and will be against the son', was smartly answered, 'aye, my lord, and against the Holy Ghost too');[72]

---

* See John Toland, *A State Anatomy of Great Britain* (1717), p. 16. Archbishop Sharp candidly admitted in 1705 that he did not believe the Whig party 'meant any harm to the Church'. *The Life of John Sharp* (1825), ii, 133-4.
† There were the examples of Tenison in 1694, of Talbot in 1699, Wake in 1705 and Trimnell in 1707.
‡ Charles Spencer, 3rd earl of Sunderland, one of the lords of the Whig Junto in Anne's reign.

neither would it have made a believer out of Sir Richard Gipps, who began his canvassing in the Whig interest at Totnes by 'singl[ing] out the parson of that place to prove to him that there was no God'.[73] At the same time, the animosity which scores of Whig politicians had come to feel by 1709 towards the 'black coats' was sharpened beyond estimation by the extent to which they had suffered, electorally and in their political prospects, at the hands of these turbulent priests. The greatest danger to the Church, Coningsby told the Commons in 1705, came from the pulpits themselves.[74]

It is striking how each wave in the 'Church in Danger' campaigns of the post-Revolution period began to rise towards its crest at a period when the Whigs were either firmly in control of the government or were threatening to seize control. This was true of the first wave, which began to gather momentum in 1697. It was true of the second wave in 1704–5, which was scarcely more than a premonitory swell when a future Tory M.P. exclaimed to the archbishop of Dublin: 'the Whigs expect to be established, and then God preserve the Church of England'.[75] And it was true of the third and most mountainous wave, which reached its height in the years 1709–10, when the Whig Junto was more firmly entrenched in office than it had ever been.

Rumours were rife in 1709 that the government intended to repeal the Test Act, thus throwing all public offices open on equal terms to Anglicans and Nonconformists, and to break the clerical hold over the universities. Despite the Junto's ostentatious efforts to scotch the Test Act scare, these rumours spread dismay through manor house, common room and parsonage.[76] From the start of the year the salvoes thundered out afresh from the London pulpits. On 15 January at the Mercers' Chapel a savage attack was made on the advocates of 'Moderation', which (the preacher observed) 'had enriched more knaves and made more fools than any word in the Holy Scripture'. Soon afterwards the vicar of St Paul's, Covent Garden, taking as his text, 'Fools make a mock at sin', warned his congregation that they were in mortal sin if they made light of the present danger to the Church.[77] And in May there arrived in Town from Oxford the man who was destined – though few guessed it – to be 'their chief gunner'.[78] His name was Henry Sacheverell.

III THE PREACHER & THE SERMON

Since the day in December 1705 when Sacheverell had preached against 'false brethren' in the university church,* he had been enjoying increasing access to pulpits outside Oxford.[1] By 1709, in fact, John Dunton was to see him as the Anglican Don Quixote: 'I call him *errant*, because he wanders about, like the crack-brained Don of Mancha, in quest of imaginary giants and monsters that would ravish or eat up his Dulcinea, his ideal mistress (what he calls the Church), and runs raving mad about he knows not what'. In July 1706 he had turned up at Leicester to harangue the judges on the midland circuit: a 'good and ingenious' discourse, thought the Tory Baron Price, though he 'could not forbear giving the dissenters and occasionalists a flirt, as most of them do'. At that stage, his most celebrated Assize sermon, that at Derby, still lay three years in the future; it belonged to the crucial months after his removal to Southwark. But shortly before that move, in the first week of January 1709, he went up to London from Oxford, and on a bitter winter's day on which the Thames was frozen from bank to bank, preached at St Paul's for the first time.[2]

Reading his sermons today, in their cold and blotchy print, it may seem hard to understand exactly why Sacheverell was the strikingly successful preacher that contemporary evidence assures us he was. His sermons are usually structurally sound, though with a tendency to be over-elaborate in their organisation; but his language, thought exotic even by his admirers in his own day, would be quite intolerable to twentieth-century ears and tastes. A Warwickshire parson who knew him personally once wrote of

* See p. 20 above.

'what beauty and easiness of language he expresses himself in common discourse'.[3] But there was little of beauty and still less of ease in his pulpit language. Sacheverell scarcely ever painted in tints or half-tones. His canvases were emblazoned with vivid splashes of primary colours: blacks and whites and scarlets. There was a uniform lack of restraint. His phraseology could be strikingly luxuriant, but too often it was garish, exaggerated, even grotesque. Not even the expounding of reasonable moral precepts could inhibit it. Thus, in discussing the sin of prejudice he defined it, at one point, as a '[blind] resolve to be ignorant, and become such perverse bigots as to stick to the first crude and indigested notions that arise from the fumes of lust or the heats of a disturbed and whimsical brain'.[4] Expatiating on the abuse of 'conscience', he lamented how in his own day 'this sacred name' had been

> played upon, to the foul dishonour of God and the disgrace of religion; which nowadays is made the Pharisaical and Puritan cloak, like Samuel's mantle, to amuse the witch and cover the devil and consecrate all infidelity, injustice, pride, lust, avarice and ambition, and the most execrable vices of Hell with the holy title of Conscience; which, in sad truth, is nothing but the vizor-mask of cousenage, knavery and hypocrisy.[5]

Once launched on a theme, be it political, theological or ethical, he could within a minute whip himself up into a frenzy of invective. He was incapable of disagreeing without being intemperate and showing his total lack of humility; incapable of criticising without being offensive. Thus the ideas of the Anti-Trinitarians or other deviators from strict orthodoxy within the Church of England were 'in truth . . . nothing but frenzy, and the lunatic productions of distempered heads'.[6]

A subtler and more sensitive man would have known how to cultivate restraint at least in some parts of his sermons, in order to highlight others of genuine effect. There was, for instance, in the University sermon of 1707 an extraordinary passage in which he contemplated the sinfulness of

> the old debauchees, who when they are grown maimed and emerit in the Devil's service, are left impotent and vanquished by their beloved wine and women, when the act of vice has

E

quite forsaken their decayed and rotten constitutions, rejoice to
view its commission in others, enjoy it at second-hand . . .
call up the ghost of their departed sin, and are perhaps more
lascivious in their thoughts than they were before in their
practices.[7]

But what appears in isolation a memorable sentence is in context
almost submerged in the turbulent sea of imagery and tautology
in which it finds itself. Sacheverell did not seduce his audiences
with words; he bludgeoned them with metaphor and epithet,
delivering the blows in such bewildering profusion that the wonder
is that all his hearers were not regularly reduced to insensibility.
Burnet, for once, erred on the side of understatement when he
wrote that Sacheverell's sermons, and indeed all his writings, lacked
'chasteness of style', and that 'all was one unpractised strain of
indecent and scurrilous language'.[8] George Ridpath, the Whig
journalist, referred to his 'starched, pedantic oratory, which is as
far from good language as a painted strumpet is from a real
beauty', and Dunton could discern no merit at all, save 'his in-
comparable talent at railing in fluent and refined Billingsgate'. Not
far wide of the mark was the observation of one of the Court wits
during the Doctor's trial in 1710, that 'he did not know how the
Lords would deal by him; but if he were to be tried by a jury of
grammarians and critics he could hope for no mercy!'[9]

How, then, did he make such an impact, even on academic
audiences? In an age of extremism there were, of course, many
among his listeners, both in Oxford and in the provinces, who were
very ready to lap up his opinions, howsoever they were couched:
for whom, indeed, his very impudence added spice to the occasion.
It is quite clear that, in addition, he commanded attention by
personal magnetism in the pulpit, where physique, dress, passionate
intensity of manner, histrionic gesture, and above all, voice, all
played their part. Even Hearne, writing many years later, had to
concede that 'he was a bold man and of a good presence, and delivered a thing better than a much more modest man, however
preferable in learning, could do'.[10] But the voice was the key to the
whole performance. It was, wrote Cunningham, his 'greatest
excellency': finely modulated, and as White Kennett conceded
after hearing him read prayers, 'audible without noise or any

harsh grating accent to impress the close of a sentence upon the ears of the congregation'.[11] It was all the more deplorable in the eyes of Low Churchmen that so beautiful an instrument should regularly be put to such a discordant use.

Analysing Henry Sacheverell's opinions on matters of Church and State, as he expressed them in the pulpit and in print between May 1702 and August 1709, one conclusion is inescapable. The actual views expressed in the crucial sermon of November 1709 which led to his impeachment were, in the main, either a repetition or a logical development of themes he had been expounding in pulpits up and down the land since his Lichfield escapade almost a decade before. Nor would they have come as a great surprise to anyone who had read *The Character of a Low-Church-Man*, *The New Association*[12] or *The Rights of the Church of England Asserted*. In his political theories; in his attitude towards the problem of Nonconformity in all its manifestations; and in his conviction that the Church was being attacked or undermined from many other quarters, as well as by its dissenting foes, Sacheverell's mind had been running along deep grooves ever since his mid-twenties. They were the predictable grooves of the extreme High Churchman.

Thus the bedrock of all his political and politico-religious thinking was his assumption that the inter-dependence of Church and Crown was crucial to both, and fundamental to the English constitution. This had been the central proposition of his first known Oxford sermon in May 1702: 'that religion is the grand support of government, that the peace, happiness and prosperity of the secular and civil power depends upon that of the spiritual and ecclesiastical'; 'both . . . sharing the same fate and circumstances, twisted and interwoven into the very being and principles of each other'.[13] He likewise accepted without question that there existed a natural alliance between the Anglican clergy and the gentry, in and out of Parliament, to uphold this union and that the two universities had a major responsibility to cement that alliance.[14] All round him Sacheverell saw men intent on threatening, if not destroying, the sacred links between the civil and the ecclesiastical power: and few of his congregations were left in doubt of the awful consequences of such intentions. Once the links were broken the road to republicanism, and even to regicide, would be open once more. With scant regard to history but a clear appraisal of the prejudices of the Tory gentry (and their sons), he taught that 'Presbytery and Republicanism go hand in hand'; he recalled that 'they were the same hand that . . . at once divided the King's head and crown, and made our churches stables and dens of beasts'; and he enquired 'what can be the meaning of those justifications that are now everywhere published of that horrid rebellion, both out of the Press and (to its eternal disgrace) out of the very pulpit . . . but to prepare the nation to act over the same bloody tragedy again ?'[15]

On a more recent rebellion, that of 1688, and a more recent king, William III, Sacheverell's sermons and writings were understandably more reticent. The first he studiously circumnavigated whenever he could, though the judges and Grand Jurors at Oxford in March 1704 must have presumed that he included it in a sweeping condemnation of 'all that series of rebellions from its odious and never-to-be-forgotten era of transcendent villainy in the year Forty-one', in which were to be found 'the same Jesuitical principles, like a plotter in masquerade, only changing the name, but carrying on the same machinations and wicked practices in Church and State, to the subversion of our constitution in both, down to this present day'. King William he aspersed by innuendo, and kept his true feelings for his friends in Warwickshire, Staffordshire and Oxford, who were well aware that for Sacheverell the day of the King's death was 'the most joyful day he had seen in thirteen years'.[16] His views on rebellion in general, and on the central issues of Resistance and Obedience, were, as one would expect, those of the Carolingian Church, blinkered and untransmuted, as though James II and the Glorious Revolution had never been. In *The Character of a Low-Church-Man*[17] he defied anyone to search the Homilies, liturgies or canons of the Church of England to find 'any limitations or exceptions' to the Anglican doctrine of Obedience, any mention, for instance, of obedience being due only to a *legal* government. Passive Obedience was 'an absolute duty; let the consequences of it be what they will . . .'.*

---

* Curiously enough, not one of Sacheverell's printed sermons dealt with the Passive Obedience or Non-Resistance until an ambiguous reference in his Derby sermon in August 1709. But this, one suspects, is adventitious. It is inconceivable that he balked these issues in the pulpit; although it will be recalled that the full-scale

That one of Sacheverell's most celebrated sermons was on *The Nature and Mischief of Prejudice and Partiality* must have struck even his sympathisers as uncommonly ironical. The very sermon in question [18] was impregnated, as are the great majority of his publications of the years 1702–9, with an absorbing, unwavering hatred of Puritans and of all forms of Dissent. He made no distinction between one brand of Dissent and another. To him they were indistinguishable in their perniciousness; and the only distinction that mattered was that between the Church of England, on the one hand, and 'all that confused swarm of sectarists that gather about its body' on the other. The most poisonous of his calumnies was that there existed an unholy alliance, in aim and perhaps in action, between Dissent and Popery. He began to spread this poison from the pulpit of St Mary's in May 1702, and he was still busily making the same insinuations in the summer of 1709.*

From his hatred of dissenters stemmed four of the recurrent themes of his preaching and propaganda: his rejection of 'the Toleration' in any but its most narrowly-circumscribed sense; his call for the extirpation of dissenting academies; his unremitting campaign against the Occasional Conformists, 'these crafty, faithless and insidious persons' who 'to qualify themselves for a paltry place, can slyly creep to those altars they proclaim idolatrous';[19] and his uncompromising opposition to Comprehension or to any latitude of practice designed to accommodate nonconformity.

Sacheverell was ever warning that, though the Church in 1689 had been mercifully delivered from the schemes of the Comprehension men, they or their apostles were still at work, ready to abolish the Church's fences – even the Test itself – 'to make way for all men of a free and unbounded persuasion to enter'.[20] True churchmen, for their part, were fully justified in asserting their 'legal rights and privileges' to the full, without being accused of persecuting tender consciences. Liberty of conscience, he warned

revival of Non-Resistance preaching among the Highflying clergy was still a relatively recent phenomenon in 1709.

* *Political Union*, pp. 22, 24; *Derby Assize Sermon*, p. 15. 'Who would have imagined,' he asked his audience at Derby Assizes, 'that two or three Jesuits in masquerade crept into a conventicle should sow those schismatical seeds of faction and rebellion that in a few years should rise to that prodigious degree as to be able to grasp the Crown, contend with the sceptre, and not only threaten but accomplish the downfall of Church and State?'

the gentlemen of Leicestershire, was an ensnaring shibboleth: it was no better than a cloak 'to disguise the most fatal and devilish impostures'.[21] But sometimes the Church was powerless to protect its rights without the assistance of the civil power. So it was, he argued, with 'those illegal seminaries that are planted up and down in several parts of this kingdom, as 'twere so many schismatical Universities set up in opposition against the Established Church and these royal fountains of its learning' [Oxford and Cambridge]. They were spawning-grounds of heterodox and atheistical opinions, of 'lewd books and seditious libels'; and he warned that if the legislature did not intervene, the academies would 'propagate a generation of vipers that will eat through the very bowels of our Church and perpetuate their dissension to posterity'.[22] One can imagine his incredulous fury, therefore, at the failure of Parliament to pass draconic laws against his particular bane, Occasional Conformity – 'this amphibious conformity', as he called it in his Leicester sermon. He could not conceive how 'our wise legislature' could continue to leave both Church and State in 'the power of such double-dealing practical atheists . . . who can betray and sell their Saviour for money, and make the Blessed Body and Blood of his Sacrament the seal and sanctuary of the worst of iniquity!' Such was its obsessional hold on his mind that even in one of his rare non-political sermons, in which he compiled a catalogue of the deadliest sins of calculated self-interest, including lying, fornication, adultery, perjury and murder, he unhesitatingly ranked equal with them in heinousness 'that quintessence of fanaticism, Occasional Conformity'.[23]

Sacheverell's hopes that the Church would find the new Jerusalem with the accession of Anne[24] soon turned, like those of so many other High Churchmen, to deep and growing unease. Throughout the years 1702 to 1709 he sounded the alarm bell not only of the Church's danger but of the danger to religion itself. As well as advertising repeatedly the menace of the dissenters, he warned against three main sources of peril. Most insidious were the activities of the traitors within the gate. 'These temporising hypocrites', 'these associated malignants', 'these shuffling, treacherous Latitudinarians' he detected in large numbers not only among Low Church clerics, but among the moderate Tory laity, and above all among the Whigs. When *The Character of a Low-Church-Man* was

written in 1702 the Whigs were in eclipse and Sacheverell castigated them unmercifully as 'a base, treacherous and undermining
set of fellows', 'these public blood-suckers that had brought our kingdom and government into a consumption'. After the party came
back into royal favour in 1705 and 1706, he had to sheath his claws
to some extent, and it was not until 1709, at Derby, that he was to
throw all caution to the winds in his reflections on men in power.[25]

The Church was further endangered by the moral degeneracy of
an age 'sunk in the lowest dregs of corruption'. Before the judges
both at Oxford and Derby he condemned the growth of 'fashionable' blasphemy and profanity, and intemperately denounced the
wickedness of those 'great men' (among the Whigs, he plainly
implied) who corrupted the principles of young gentlemen of
fashion; especially through clubs – 'these cabals for propagating
sin'. Like so many High Churchmen, however, he would not concede for a moment that lay societies for reformation of manners,
these 'mongrel institution[s]', prying officiously into men's lives,
'wherein every tradesman and mechanic is to take upon him the
gift of the spirit', were the right answer to the problem. The only
solution was to return to the 'ancient, primitive discipline of the
Church'.[26]

The third great threat to the Church, the intellectual threat,
was inevitably traced by Sacheverell to the same sources as the
other two: Whiggery, latitudinarianism, 'fanaticism'. Of the be-
setting sins of the age, none was more dangerous both to the Church
and the State, in his mind, than its intellectual arrogance: for this
was the mother of heresy, of rationalism, and ultimately of atheism.
'The children of this world', he told the gentlemen of Leicestershire, 'are taught to be wiser in their generation than the Children
of Light'. In the blindness of their spiritual and intellectual pride,
they seemed to assume that the freedom of worship the State had
granted to persons of real scruples should 'empower Deists,
Socinians and Atheists to revile, ridicule and blaspheme our most
holy Faith and Church at their pleasure, with impunity'. Sacheverell's campaign against the intellectual danger, and particularly
the peril of the printed word, reached a shrill crescendo at Derby in
August 1709. 'It is an epidemical evil', he declaimed, 'a national
calamity, an everlasting plague, that has slain its thousands and its
ten thousands'.[27]

On these recurring themes Henry Sacheverell had for almost a
decade spouted forth in defiance of Authority. Authority had thus
far ignored him. But thus far 'his favourite, itinerant sermon', as
Abel Boyer so shrewdly described it, had merely been peddled
around the provinces from Oxford; it had not been flaunted before
the seat of Authority itself. When at length it was, Sacheverell could
be ignored no longer.

The consistency which marks his public utterances after 1701
entitles us to assume that Sacheverell genuinely believed the substance of his High Church gospel, however synthetic much of the
froth may have been. But depth of conviction and a compulsive
need to spread the message and persuade others of its validity
were not the principal motives which inspired him; assuredly
they did not account for his self-chosen brand of incendiarism.
He was an exhibitionist. More than that, by exploiting his one
exceptional talent he was 'resolved to force himself into popularity and preferment'.[28] Popularity, of a kind, he had achieved
before 1709, though largely through preaching to the converted.
Preferment, however, had eluded him. He passed his thirty-fifth
birthday in February 1709 with only his college offices to show for
seven years of pulpit-drumming. Meanwhile the sun of prosperity
shone as never before on Whigs, 'moderates', dissenters, and all
he hated most.

It was at this point that one of the two chaplaincies at St Saviour's
Church in Southwark fell vacant. Southwark had the thickest
concentration of breweries in London by the early eighteenth
century, and it was one of the wealthiest of its brewers, a suspected
Jacobite named John Lade,* who in March 1709 invited Henry
Sacheverell to offer himself as a candidate for the post at St
Saviour's. The church which is now Southwark Cathedral, but
which in the eighteenth century served the two densely crowded
parishes of St Saviour and St Margaret-on-the-Hill, was the

---

* Lade had taken the Abjuration oath in 1702 in a frankly cynical way, admitting to a
  fellow brewer, the Whig M.P. Charles Cox, that 'the Jacks . . . should never be able
  to do anything if they . . . did not take all the oaths that could be imposed'. Later,
  as member for Southwark for much of the period between 1713 and 1727, he changed
  his political coat, becoming first a 'Whimsical' Tory and then a Whig. Blenheim
  MSS. D.1–32: Cox to J. Gellibrand, 24 Feb. 1705; *The History of Parliament: The
  House of Commons 1715–1754* (1970), ii, 195.

largest medieval parish church still surviving in the London area. Founded in the twelfth century and rebuilt at the start of the fifteenth (not altogether successfully, since the roof of the middle aisle fell down in 1469), it stood just across the Thames, almost immediately to the south of London bridge.* Its incumbents were thus very close to the ecclesiastical heart of the country, even though technically outside the diocese of London. Since the Reformation its rector's tithes and dues had been in the hands of a lay impropriator; and, as another legacy of the sixteenth century, the two chaplains who shared the cure were still chosen by the votes of the vestry, a corruption of the Presbyterian method of popular election which Doctor Sacheverell so despised.[29]

This fact in no way inhibited Sacheverell from closing with Lade's invitation, which he had been more than half expecting for almost a year. On the contrary, he canvassed, campaigned and preached for the vacant place with a verve which would have impressed the elders of Edinburgh. 'None is so much talked of as he all over the Town', observed a brother clergyman: 'I suppose we shall have him very speedily the subject of de Foe's *Review*, in which he has formerly had the honour of being substantially abused'. The greater the publicity, the more Sacheverell revelled in it – all too conspicuously for the peace of mind of his Southwark backers, who at one stage sent him back to Oxford to cool off.[30] Fortunately he had some sage counsellors. His most prominent sponsor outside the parish was Lord Weymouth, whose patronage he had courted years before.† He also enlisted the powerful support of a former Secretary of State, Sir William Trumbull, through the latter's nephew, Ralph Bridges, chaplain to Bishop Compton of London.[31] Early in April he went to the House of Commons to solicit the two Oxford University members, William Bromley and 'Shoe-Strings' Whitlocke; but the former excused himself on the ground that two members of his own college, Christ Church, were in the running, and Whitlocke's coldness was not unexpected, since at the University election in 1705 Sacheverell and the other Fellows of Magdalen had done their best to unseat him.[32] At Trumbull's suggestion the Doctor also approached the

* It was still popularly called St Mary Overy, or Overrie, i.e. the church of St Mary over the river.
† See p. 18 above.

Lord Mayor of London, Sir Charles Duncombe, who gave him his blessing but declined his request for a prestigious appointment as one of the Spital preachers.[33] The previous mayor, Sir William Withers (a Tory, like Duncombe) was found to be already engaged to back the claims of a clergyman named Watson who, a few years before, had been his chaplain as Prime Warden of the Fishmongers.[34]

The competition was certainly hot, and the opposition to Sacheverell, personally, unexpectedly strong. Among a string of candidates Sacheverell's chief rival by common consent was a Cambridge man, Dr Gouge, enjoying the powerful backing of Arthur Annesley, the senior member for Cambridge University, who ranked close to Bromley in Tory standing. The news that the Bloody Flag Officer was storming the ramparts of the metropolis seriously alarmed Tenison, gout-bound at nearby Lambeth; and there soon pulled together a strong, if motley, opposition party, comprised (according to Bridges) of 'the Archbishop, the Fanatics and the Christ Church men (wondrous conjunction)'. The dissenters, he added, 'give out that if they can keep him out this time, they shall for ever keep him from coming into the City'.[35]

But they did not keep him out. At one time the proliferation of candidates had seemed likely to postpone the final choice until midsummer. But the outsiders, including Watson, gradually dropped out; Gouge, though the worthier divine and scholar, made a poor showing in the pulpit;[36] and by 25 May Ralph Bridges was writing to tell his uncle that at the election the previous day their candidate had been voted into the chaplaincy by a large majority – 19 votes out of 28. The Doctor himself celebrated his triumph in a characteristic way by carousing in a 'club' at the Mitre Tavern in Fenchurch Street, 'and there, at the head of a great number of inferior clergy, boasted very much of [his] success . . . reflected very barbarously on his competitor Mr G[ouge]', denigrated Tillotson and Stillingfleet as 'two of the dullest writers in the Church of England', and scoffed at Stillingfleet's *Origines Sacrae* of 1662 as a work containing 'ten thousand and ten thousand times ten thousand errors'.[37]

The news that Archbishop Tenison was reported 'much troubled' at his victory must have delighted him. It certainly brought amusement to Sir William Trumbull in Gerard Street:

Bitter things are good for the stomach [he reflected]; and so I hope his Grace's health will not be impaired by this disgrace, having never heard his admirable constitution to have ever been oppressed by anything, besides a surfeit of black-pudding.

Among the messages of congratulation which reached Sacheverell in the course of the next few days was one from Trumbull. 'I heartily wish you may from this low foundation rise still higher, to be a support and ornament to our Established Church, which I doubt not will prevail notwithstanding all discouragements it has been under'. About the old statesman's private response to the news of his protégé's success there were already, however, uneasy reservations. 'Well [he told his nephew], I hope our friend Dr Sacheverell will take great care of his conduct, and consider how much difference there ought to be between the humility and conversation of his life in London and the pride and arrogance of Christ Church [*sic*] in Oxon'.[38]

Now that Sacheverell at last had access to some of the most influential pulpits in the land, he was the last man to be deterred by 'humility' from using them. The priest who complained in the following December that greater efforts should have been made to keep 'that unquiet man' out of London, since 'it was obvious to think what a firebrand he was like to prove in that place, where there is such a store of combustible matter', may have been wise after the event. Yet he was unquestionably right. Sacheverell's Southwark sponsors (not to mention Lord Weymouth or those other City Tories who, rumour had it, supported the invitation) did not lure him to London with the intention that he should confine his preaching either to moral homilies or to the parishioners of Southwark.[39] By midsummer 1709, when the Doctor's old acquaintance George Sacheverell, currently High Sheriff of Derbyshire, invited him up to Derby Assizes, he already had the bit firmly between his teeth, and on 15 August he duly harangued the judges and Grand Jurors in that pleasant and growing town on a text from Paul's first Epistle to Timothy: *Neither be partaker of other men's sins.*

The Derby sermon contained enough vintage Sacheverell to satisfy an old Oxford man in the audience that London had not changed the leopard's spots.[40] It also earned the approbation of the backwoods gentry in the Grand Jury, who formally requested the Doctor to print it. But in itself it was no more volcanic than the earlier Assize sermons of 1704 and 1706, and hardly more likely than they to attract special attention from the Whig leaders, especially in the middle of a long parliamentary recess. The dedication which Sacheverell subsequently drafted, to be affixed to the printed version, was a different matter. It smacked of sedition; and one paragraph, especially, could only have been the work of a man prepared to press his luck to the limit:

> Now, when the principles and interests of our Church and constitution are so shamefully betrayed and run down, it can be no little comfort to all those who wish their welfare and security to see that, notwithstanding the secret malice and open violence they are persecuted with, there are still to be found such worthy patrons of both who dare own and defend them, as well against the rude and presumptuous insults of the one side as the base, undermining treachery of the other, and who scorn to sit silently by and partake in the sins of these associated malignants.[41]

It was some time, however, before these words saw the light of day. John Stephens, the Oxford bookseller who had published the last two Sacheverell sermons to appear in print, had gone bankrupt in June 1709,[42] and it was well into September before the Doctor sought out Henry Clements in his recently acquired premises at the Half-Moon in St Paul's Churchyard, and offered him the publication of the Derby address with no charge for the copyright. Clements was later to recount how Sacheverell brought him a copy of the original in his own hand and corrected the proofs of the quarto edition of 750 copies himself; how he allocated complimentary copies to each of the Fellows of Magdalen, to the High Sheriff and to each member of the Grand Jury; and how he instructed his publisher to send small consignments to booksellers at Derby and Lichfield. Clements also had Sacheverell's permission to bring out an octavo edition, and of these he later admitted to have run off 'about 12,000'. But the whole process of publication, in contrast to what was to happen in November, was leisurely, and it was not until 27 October that *The Communication of Sin* appeared on sale in London.[43]

The 27th was a Thursday. On the following Saturday, 29 October, *The Post Man* announced, 'Sir Samuel Garrard, baronet, Lord Mayor elect for the year ensuing, took possession of his office with the usual solemnity'.[44] For the third Michaelmas running – a strange freak at a time when the wealthy business interests of the City contained a heavy preponderance of Whigs – London had elected a Tory as its chief dignitary, for the simple reason that recent conventions of aldermanic precedence required it. And as befitted a pillar of the Grocers' Company,[45] Garrard was no milk-and-water Tory. He was an extreme zealot, who as member of Parliament for Amersham had been one of the 'Tackers' of 1704.[46]

Among the Lord Mayor's first duties in his term of office was to invite a preacher to address the City Fathers at the annual service held at St Paul's Cathedral to celebrate one of the most emotive public holidays in the year, the Fifth of November. It was a day doubly sacred to the Whigs: as the day of Gunpowder Treason, and as the glorious day on which William of Orange had landed at Torbay to deliver the country from Rome and from arbitrary government. Yet this was the occasion for which Samuel Garrard, with singular perversity and mischievous intent, decided to put into the most famous pulpit in the very heart of the citadel of Whiggery Dr Henry Sacheverell. He later claimed that the new chaplain of St Saviour's was known to him by reputation only, that he had never met him and had never heard him preach before he went to St Paul's on Guy Fawkes's Day.[47]

Sacheverell had waited years for such an opportunity as this. Now that it had come he was in no mood to waste it. Brooding on the tribulations of the High Church parsons and the Tory squires, held in subjection (as he saw it) to an alien regime, which paid lip-service to the interests of the Church and the gentry but in fact cared nothing for either, it seemed to him that the words of St Paul in chapter 11 of 2nd Corinthians had never been more apposite: 'in peril among False Brethren'. And naturally he recalled how almost four years earlier, at the height of the previous 'Church in Danger' campaign, this very text had supplied the charge of one of the most explosive of his St Mary's sermons. This sermon had the additional advantage – particularly appealing to Sacheverell – of being almost totally irrelevant to the present occasion. To the 30th January anniversary it might have been reasonably germane.[48] But what the City merchants, bankers and 'moneyed men' were accustomed to listen to on the Fifth of November were broadsides against the evils of Popery, followed by encomiums on the Revolution and all the benefits it had conferred on the fortunate English. However, as John Dunton later remarked of Sacheverell: 'every day and every subject are alike to him, for whatever be the doctrine (in season or out of season) railing and slander must be the application'.[49] So be it: he would come not to praise the Revolution, but to bury it under a torrent of invective against his familiar bugbears.

As Sacheverell took the old sermon out of his drawer, dusted it off, sharpened it up and above all made some very pointed additions to it, was he acting as a completely free agent? At Sacheverell's trial General Stanhope was to label the defendant unforgettably as 'an inconsiderable tool of a party'. By the summer of 1710 it had become part of the Whig gospel that Sacheverell had entered St Paul's the previous November under orders. Some Whigs went further and assumed that the orders were not merely general but particular. Arthur Mainwaring, for instance, alleged that there was 'one minister of State in particular [the Lord Treasurer, Godolphin] whom he was *strictly commanded* to defame', and that other hand-picked victims for character-assassination were the archbishop of Canterbury and the bishop of Salisbury.[50] Unfortunately, there is no firm evidence either to prove or disprove these assertions: Sacheverell's letters and papers, and nearly all his unpublished manuscripts, were destroyed after his death.[51] All one can say with certainty is that this man lacked neither the audacity nor the recklessness to do everything he did on his own initiative, and with his own self-advertisement foremost in his mind. It may be significant that he was so delighted with his own handiwork after revising his draft that he bragged of his intentions to his Southwark cronies and other acquaintances, proudly spelling out half-veiled references to the uninitiated.[52]

Services had been held in the peerless new cathedral of St Paul's for almost twelve years by November 1709; but scaffolding still cluttered the chancel, as craftsmen completed the vaulting mouldings, while outside, the work still went on to perfect

Wren's masterpiece, though as the German traveller, Uffenbach, sadly noted, 'it is already so black with coal-smoke that it has lost half its elegance'.[53] At the east end, beyond the organ screen, a congregation of more than average size gathered in the early afternoon of Saturday the 5th. There were some thirty clergymen in the choir (and at least three of them left first-hand accounts of the occasion).[54] In the remaining stalls, and in the galleries above them, though the number of notables was reduced by the fact that Dean Stanhope was preaching before the Queen at St James's, the ranks of the corporation and civic dignitaries were swollen by an unusual number of Jacobites and Nonjurors. Many of them sat together 'on the Doctor's left-wing', headed by John Lade 'and his Southwark myrmidons'.[55] Whatever prior notice they had had of the entertainment in store, they can hardly have anticipated anything half as extravagant as the event they were to witness that autumn afternoon before they went out again through the great west doors to their coaches, their chairs and their dinners.*

During the prayers and hymns which preceded the sermon Doctor Sacheverell sat with his fellow-clergy. He offered the Thanksgiving prayer himself, significantly with 'not a word of the two great mercies of the day'. But otherwise he remained half-oblivious of the service, locked away in a private world, working himself up into the mood of frenzied anger and near-hysteria which an Oxford audience would at once have recognised as presaging a storm. His immediate neighbour, never having seen him before and 'little suspecting him to be the Bloody Flag Officer', was utterly astonished 'at the fiery red that over-spread his face . . . and the goggling wildness of his eyes', and even more taken aback when, on his cue, 'he came into the pulpit like a Sybil to the mouth of her cave' – the very picture of con-centrated ferocity.[56] There, from his canopied height, for fully an hour and a half[57] he thundered away with every battery against the whole range of his favourite targets. 'David Jones', observed another fascinated parson, calling to mind the most spectacular pulpit-eccentric of his acquaintance,[58] 'is a soft, mild preacher in comparison to this'. The Reverend John Bennett was still more

---

* Dinner was normally taken in mid-afternoon at this time. White Kennett referred to Sacheverell's sermon as one 'preached at noon-day'. *True Answer*, p. 18.

appalled. 'I could not have imagined if I had not actually heard it myself, that so much heat, passion, violence and scurrilous language, to say no worse of it, could have come from a Protestant pulpit, much less from one that pretends to be a member of the Church of England'. In a cathedral, of all places, he found it peculiarly shocking. Indeed, in view of what happened after it was printed, it is worth recalling that what struck the St Paul's congregation most forcibly about the sermon itself was less the content than the stunning vehemence and vulgarity of the language. 'I fancy', said one Whig, 'he has bankrupt all the oyster-women, porters, watermen, coachmen and carmen in Town to make up his collection'.[59]

Only by stripping away layers of superfluous verbiage and most of the abuse and the bombast, and reconstructing the sermon a good deal more cogently than it was delivered on the day can we readily come at the substance of it; yet it was this, after all, for which the Doctor was brought to book.[60] At the start it took Sacheverell under three minutes to dispose of the Gunpowder Plot and the Papists; and even here, by bracketing 5 November with 30 January as days of equal significance in the English calendar, he was able to brand the dissenters as being no less abhorrent than the Guy Fawkes's Day conspirators, and thereby work in a pet theme of old – the 'confederacy in iniquity' between 'the Popish and Fanatic enemies of our Church and government'.[61] Having made his few token nods in deference to the occasion, he deserted the main business of the day completely and at once introduced his major theme of the peril to Church and State from the False Brethren in their midst. Just as St Paul (or so he confidently claimed) had considered the treachery of such false brothers more grievous than all the physical sufferings he had undergone as Christ's disciple, so Sacheverell premised that the manifold dangers which threatened the Church of England at this time stemmed even more from its 'pretended friends and false brethren' than from its open and acknowledged enemies. Indeed he saw much in her present deplorable circumstances which paralleled the condition of the Church of Corinth in St Paul's day: 'her holy communion . . . rent and divided by factious and schismatical impostors; her pure doctrine . . . corrupted and defiled; her primitive worship and discipline profaned and abused; her sacred orders denied and vilified; her priests and professors (like St Paul) calumniated, misrepresented and ridiculed; her altars and sacraments prostituted to hypocrites, Deists, Socinians and atheists'.[62]

The rest of the sermon fell into three parts. First he set himself to identify the villains of the piece, to cut away their camouflage and reveal them in their true colours. The False Brethren within the Church herself comprised two groups. In one group were the propagators of heterodox or heretical doctrines: the Unitarians, with their 'execrable, exploded heresies'; the revisionists of the Church's formal articles of belief (a plain allusion to Burnet of Salisbury, whose *Exposition of the Thirty-Nine Articles* had been attacked by High Churchmen in the Convocation of 1701); and the Lockean rationalists – 'whosoever presumes to recede the least tittle from the express word of God, or to explain the great credenda of our Faith in new-fangled terms of modern philosophy'.[63] The second group of ecclesiastical Judases, denounced with equal bitterness, were those concerned with modifying the discipline and worship of the Church. Here Sacheverell raked a wider field: those who strove to make the Church more latitudinarian by tearing down 'the exterior fences [designed] to guard the internals of religion'; those who put the widest interpretation on Toleration, denying that schism was sinful and taking 'all occasions to comply with the dissenters both in public and private affairs, as persons of tender consciences and piety'; and those who derided the Church for its 'priestcraft'.[64]

On the other hand, there were False Brethren in the State who were no less pernicious. Sacheverell identified them as the advocates of constitutional innovation, and in particular all who tried to shake the twin ideological pillars upon which English government stood: 'the steady belief of the subject's obligation to absolute and unconditional Obedience to the Supreme Power in all things lawful [and, by implication, to *passive* obedience in things unlawful], and the utter illegality of Resistance upon any pretence whatsoever'. But even Sacheverell appreciated that on the Fifth of November, of all days, something more was required than this bald restatement of traditional Anglican theory; and so at this point he had made what proved to be the most crucial of all his additions to the original script of 1705.

F

Our adversaries think they effectually stop our mouths, and have us sure and unanswerable on this point, when they urge the revolution of this day in their defence. But certainly they are the greatest enemies of that, and his late Majesty, and the most ungrateful for the deliverance, who endeavour to cast such black and odious colours upon both.

And there followed three sentences which remained very confused in the minds of the congregation until they were able to scrutinise the sermon in print, but the gist of which appeared to be that for Whigs to cite the events of 1688–9 in justification of their rebellious principles was to insult the memory of the Revolution itself, of the Convention Parliament and of William III. However, before his listeners had time to recover their breath Sacheverell had returned to the clergy, those who added injury to insult by denying the tenets of their own Church* and using either pulpit or press to uphold a subject's right to resist and depose kings. Hoadly was not mentioned by name, but the inference was inescapable. The continued expression of these 'villainous and seditious principles', whether by clergy or laity, called for concerted action by those in authority – government, Convocation and Parliament – 'to whose strict justice and undeserved mercy' the preacher committed them and their authors.[65]

It was hardly to be expected that Sacheverell would let any political sermon go by without lashing out at dissenting academies and Occasional Conformity. And by doing some violence to the rules of logical development he contrived to do so at this point. For both these abominations, he argued, encouraged the spread of False Brethren in the government: the former by providing establishments where 'all the Hellish principles of fanaticism, regicide and anarchy are openly professed and taught', the latter by enabling potential rebels to entrench themselves in office and wheedle themselves into royal favour.[66]

And so the Doctor came to the second part of his argument.

---

* These tenets Sacheverell purported to reinforce at this point by a mischievous and quite irrelevant reference to Burnet's youthful book of 1673, the *Vindication of the Church of Scotland*, which later was to figure in the trial. He 'played particularly and expressly [remarked the Reverend D. Evans] upon the bishop of Sarum: whom he hoped was no great friend to Popery, he said', while implying 'he was half channelled over'. *Remarks and Collections*, ii, 304; to Hearne, 10 Nov. 1709.

Here he undertook to lay before his audience 'the great peril and mischiefs of these False Brethren in Church and State', by demonstrating 'that they weaken, undermine and betray in themselves, and encourage and put it in the power of our professed enemies to overturn and destroy, the constitution and establishment of both'.

The great threat to the Anglican Church which he conjured up was that it would steadily lose all distinctive character and be transformed into a 'heterogeneous mixture' of persons united only by their Protestantism (and Protestantism, the congregation was reminded, was only one aspect of the Church of England). Carried away by the horror of this vision, he at once forgot his Protestant criterion, and in the next breath was envisaging 'this spurious and villainous notion, which will take in Jews, Quakers, Mahometans and anything, as well as Christians'. The Church's internal enemies had several times in living memory attempted to achieve this end by Comprehension schemes. Now the same men were using the mines of 'Moderation and Occasional Conformity' to blow up the defences of the established order: having failed to 'carry the Conventicle into the Church, they are now resolved to bring the Church into the Conventicle'. If this 'spiritual legerdemain' succeeded, the effect, he prophesied, would be not merely to destroy the Church's own identity, but to make the dissenters contemptuous of it and thereby encouraged in their separation, and to produce an Erastian climate in which most men became so unconcerned about questions of belief as to fall prey to 'universal scepticism and infidelity'.[67]

As to the State, his main obsession remained the threat from the occasionally-conforming dissenters, despite his fear of those quasi-republican, nominally Anglican Whigs whom he had previously identified as the False Brethren. No true lover of the constitution, civil or ecclesiastical, could feel secure while inside the walls there sheltered these potential traitors, who had been so successful in advancing their religious indulgence into a civil right that they had *filled* the government (no less!) 'with its professed enemies'.[68] Sacheverell permitted himself at this stage a few polite noises about the 'Indulgence' of 1689 itself: but assured as he was 'that the old leaven of their forefathers is still working' in the present generation of nonconformists, he surprised no one when he asked of this 'brood of vipers': 'whether these men are not contriving and plotting our utter ruin, and [returning to the Whigs and Tory 'moderates' at last] whether all those False Brethren that fall in with these measures and designs do not contribute basely to it?' Recklessly he ploughed on, dragging up as he went the sixty-year old spectre of '49. 'I pray God we may be out of danger, but we may remember the King's person was voted to be so at the same time that his murderers were conspiring his death'.[69]

Entreating the patience of his hearers (as well he might, since he had now been in spate for over an hour), Sacheverell turned at the third stage of his argument to the sinfulness of false brotherhood, and argued that for three reasons it deserved to be stigmatised as a heinous and 'prodigious' sin. In the first place, for all Anglicans holding office in Church or State it was a betrayal of pledges taken under oath – a renunciation, in effect, of allegiance to the ruler who was head of both. In the second place, false brotherhood held out to the world an appalling example of hypocrisy and of the subordination of principle to material gain: especially (he hinted, as broadly as he could possibly have done) when that example was being currently set by men of high reputation and status. Not for the first time Sacheverell confused the issue by blurring the distinction between Low Church clerics, bartering their Anglican birthright for the sake of preferment, and the Whig or renegade Tory politicians, ready to betray their Church for political ends; but two of the phrases he now used were, to say the least, startling, however they were interpreted. First, he referred to the 'vast scandal and offence' it must give 'to see men of characters and stations thus shift and prevaricate with their principles', like the disciples when Christ's life was at stake. Then, more pointedly still, he quoted the Book of Psalms in condemnation of what he called 'the crafty insidiousness of such wily Volpones'. For some years 'Volpone' had been an uncomplimentary nickname for the Queen's first minister, the earl of Godolphin.[70] Even for Sacheverell effrontery could scarcely have gone further than to link this word, with every appearance of malice aforethought, with a scathing denunciation of the sinfulness of False Brethren in high places (especially as Godolphin, the ex-Tory who had now thrown in his lot with the Junto, was regarded by many Tories as the worst kind of apostate); and then,

almost at once, to foresee no other prospect in the hereafter for any
False Brother than to take 'his portion with hypocrites and
unbelievers, with all liars, that have their part in the lake which
burns with fire and brimstone'.

Having left his False Brethren 'in the company they always keep
correspondence with',[71] only his peroration remained. What lessons
were his audience to draw from this massive exposé of iniquity?
They must, first and last, stand firm to those 'fundamental principles' on which Church and government were founded. They must
close ranks, presenting 'an army of banners to our enemies', and
must therefore hope that the False Brethren themselves 'would
throw off the mask, entirely quit our Church of which they are no
true members, and not fraudulently eat her bread and lay wait for
her ruin'. And to encourage them to do so the higher clergy must
do their duty in excommunicating and anathematising the offenders
– 'and let any power on earth dare reverse a sentence ratified in
Heaven'.[72] (At this moment of drama he swung round in the pulpit,
not for the first time, to rake the clergy's stalls, in one of which sat
Nathaniel Gower, vicar of Battersea, a convert to the Church from
Presbyterianism; and 'levelled his arguments and anathemas most
virulently against him, and the whole tribe of 'em: in so much
that all the congregation were shaken again at the terror of his
inveterate expressions'.)[73]

For the Church Militant a protracted battle must lie ahead,
'against principalities, against powers, against the rulers of the darkness of this world, against spiritual wickedness in high places'.
The struggle would be bitter and painful, 'because her adversaries
are chief and her enemies at present prosper'. But it must be
waged, in the knowledge that 'there is a God that can and will
raise her up, if we forsake her not'. Thus, defiant and martial to
the last, Sacheverell came to his final invocation:

> Now the God of all Grace, who hath called us into his eternal
> glory by Christ Jesus, after that ye have suffered a while, make
> you perfect, stablish, strengthen, settle you. To Him be glory
> and dominion for ever and ever. Amen.

Whenever official sermons were delivered before the corporation
of London the custom was for the Lord Mayor to invite the

preacher to dine with him after service. As the mayoral coach pulled away from the cathedral precincts that afternoon and moved through the City streets, to the accompaniment of some cheering from a crowd which had gathered,[74] a conversation took place between Garrard and Sacheverell of which both were later to give very different accounts. Garrard's public version, however, subsequently received little credence (he had his own very good reasons, as we shall see, for obscuring the truth). What happened can be reconstructed to a large extent from Sacheverell's own words, uttered to the Commons on 14 December when he was first brought to the Bar of the House to answer for his conduct. The Lord Mayor, after first thanking the Doctor for a fine sermon,

> said he hoped he should see my sermon in print. I told him, No! there would be no order of the court of Aldermen; they would reject it, as they had done a late sermon of the Dean of Carlisle's.*

And Sacheverell added that he was afraid he had 'spoken some bold truths which might displease some people'. Garrard, however, was positively euphoric: he would undertake to propose to the court of Aldermen that it should vote its thanks for the sermon; and if the formal order for printing was denied,

> No matter. I will send a printed copy to every alderman who is against the printing of it.
> Well, said I, I shall take it for a greater honour to print it by your Lordship's command than by an order of the court of Aldermen: *to which I thought his Lordship consented.*[75]

Thus encouraged, Sacheverell left Garrard's home that evening in high fettle, resolved if necessary to cock a snook at the City Fathers. His ebullience soothed some of his fellow Highflyers with whom he ended the day convivially in a favourite tavern. Greeted on his arrival with anxious enquiries, and gloomy talk of a possible prosecution, he is said to have assured them bracingly, 'I fear not. I only wish that the Dean had been in his stall. I

* Francis Atterbury. This was the sermon on Passive Obedience preached at the election of Sir Charles Duncombe as Lord Mayor in October 1708, during which the preacher accused Hoadly of sedition. See p. 33 above, and Lansdowne MSS. 825, f. 8.

would have thrown my Volpone directly in his face'. The point of doing so would not have been lost on those present; for since 1707 the dean of St Paul's had been Dr Henry Godolphin, the former Provost of Eton and the prime minister's younger brother.[76]

When the court of Aldermen met on the following Tuesday morning, 8 November, it was exceptionally well attended. The presence of twenty-one aldermen and the Recorder, however, out of a maximum complement of twenty-six was not necessarily a tribute to Sacheverell, even though half London was already chuckling over the jest of the moment, that 'St Paul's was on fire a Saturday'.[77] The main business before the court that morning was to determine a disputed election for an aldermanic vacancy – quite enough in itself to account for the high attendance. Indeed, the immediate impact which Sacheverell's tirade had on many of the London businessmen over whose heads he fulminated can be over-dramatised. These dignitaries had to sit through so many sermons on public holidays, on fast days, or thanksgiving days, that many developed a faculty for passing into a self-induced coma and allowing the flood of words from the pulpit to flow over them: to the many Whigs among them, the occasional ranting, High-flying parson was one of the crosses they were required to bear in discharge of their public responsibilities. These considerations are worth bearing in mind: for they lend credibility to those few pieces of contemporary testimony, especially that of the Dutch agent, l'Hermitage, and of the Scots diplomat, Alexander Cunningham, which suggest that when the court turned to the Sacheverell item on its agenda its repudiation of the sermon was not quite a foregone conclusion.

When Garrard made the formal motion of thanks, and also moved that the preacher be invited to print his sermon, he probably knew that a number of his colleagues had either not heard or not grasped some of its more flagrantly provocative passages; he knew that giving thanks was regarded as a matter of course; and naturally he was just as aware as l'Hermitage that the invitation to print (despite the recent solitary precedent of Atterbury) was an almost automatic compliment on solemn or ceremonial occasions, 'however little the sermon might be approved'.[78] For the first time in the Sacheverell affair, though not for the last, the course of British politics and perhaps of European history hinged on a decision that could conceivably have gone the other way; for a Whig Parliament would never have concerned itself with a sermon printed with the official blessing, however negligently bestowed, of the Whig aldermen of London. Cunningham's information – more circumstantial than that of any other source – was that the first motion, for returning thanks, actually passed,* and that the second might well have followed, on the nod, but for the fact that a handful of Whigs who *had* listened, most intently, to the preacher, and who took the strongest exception to what they had heard, were determined to make the court aware of its responsibilities in the matter, both to the City and to the government. Two men, Cunningham heard, took the lead: Sir Peter King, the Recorder, generally considered one of the three most brilliantly gifted lawyers in a House of Commons resplendent with legal talent,† and another M.P., Sir Gilbert Heathcote, Governor of the Bank of England and uncrowned king of the Whig monied interest. Heathcote, in particular – forthright, pugnacious and on close terms with Godolphin[79] – was the very man not merely to chivvy his brother aldermen into refusing permission to print the sermon, which they did in the end by a large majority, but to insist (as Cunningham claims he did) 'to have Sacheverell called in question for it'. The attempt to do so there and then, by a resolution censuring him and banning him from preaching in future before the corporation, was effectively blocked by the sudden adjournment of the court by Garrard. But it is not hard to believe that it was Heathcote, backed by King, who thereupon brought Sacheverell's exploit plainly to the notice of the ministry and of the scores of Whigs who were now arriving in town for the beginning of a new session of Parliament, due to open on the 15th.[80]

All the same, if the offending sermon had remained unprinted it is highly unlikely the matter would have gone any further. Some of the Doctor's friends, with no more knowledge of his intentions at this stage than the Whig aldermen, were positively relieved by the court's decision, believing that publication could only harm the High Church cause; and William Bisset was prepared to fore-

---

* On the other hand John Toland insisted that '*both* those motions were rejected with indignation' (*Toland's Reflections*, pp. 10–11), and Narcissus Luttrell, normally well informed on corporation affairs, also heard that thanks had been refused. *Brief Historical Relation*, v, 510.

† The other two were Sir Simon Harcourt and Sir Thomas Parker.

cast in print on 12 November that 'if he should do it of his own head . . . (for all his boasted courage) many passages will be left out, or put in a new dress from what they were delivered in'.[81] Both friend and foe misjudged him. Throughout the week of the court's meeting Sacheverell was preparing his effusion for the press. He composed what Burnet styled 'a flaming epistle [to put] at the head of it', preceded by a dedication to Garrard which began with the startling words: '*By your Lordship's command* this discourse ventures to appear in public, in contempt of all those scandalous misrepresentations the malicious adversaries of our Church have traduced it with'. He did make some cuts; but they were few, and there is no convincing evidence that they involved any vitally incriminating passage.[82] This is not to say he courted prosecution. On the contrary, he embarked on publication fairly confident that he would not be prosecuted, for he made no secret of the fact that he had shown his manuscript to three different lawyers, and bragged that they had 'cleared' it in respect both of common law and civil law.[83]

Thus fortified, about a week after the service in St Paul's (as Henry Clements later recollected) Sacheverell arrived at the Half-Moon, delivered the revised manuscript to his publisher and gave his instructions. Fifty copies were to be sent to booksellers in Oxford, Lichfield and Derby; 150 to be delivered to the Doctor himself; the rest of the first edition (of which Clements ran off 500)* to be sold on the London market. The type-setting, the personal correction of the proofs and the final stages of publication took up the best part of a fortnight.[84] So it was not until Friday, 25 November, that *The Daily Courant* carried the following advertisement: 'This day is published *The Perils of False Brethren both in Church and State*: set forth in a sermon preached at the Cathedral Church of St Paul on the 5th of November 1709. By Henry Sacheverell, D.D.' In point of fact, some copies had already been on sale the previous day; for Ann Clavering, sister-in-law of the Whig Lord Chancellor, Cowper, was just sitting down to write to her brother in time to catch the Thursday post to Durham when (as she told him) 'the learned, bold and pious Mr Sacheverell's sermon came about, so that I could not forbear laying out that two pence and sit down and read it'. Two days later she

* Some in quarto at 1s, the rest in octavo at 2d.

cheerfully admitted, like the good Whig she was, 'I've got no further than what I might have bought for three farthings'. [85]

The first edition was no more than a sighting shot. The real barrage hit London on 1 December when Clements brought out the first printing of the second edition. The facts, as he explained them to the Commons two weeks later, were

> that after [the] publication of the first edition, the Lord Mayor sent for Clements, and he went to him; and the Lord Mayor asked where Dr Sacheverell was, and having the sermon in his hand he read to the word 'command' in the Dedication and then asked Clements how he knew that he had commanded the printing of it (or words to that effect), and seemed angry. To which Clements answering, he supposed the Dr would answer it himself, the Lord Mayor said he wondered the Dr should say it was printed by his command, but if it had been said 'at his pleasure or desire' he should have been pleased with it; and that the Lord Mayor's chaplain was then present.
>
> That Clements said he told the Dr the same day what the Lord Mayor had said, at which the Dr seemed much surprised, but the same afternoon went to the Lord Mayor, and afterwards ordered more of those sermons of the 2nd edition to be printed with the word 'command', and the word 'Barrt' added [after Garrard's name in the dedication].*
>
> Of this 2nd edition he printed 1,000 [in 4to] and betwixt 35,000 and 40,000 of those sermons in 8vo. That these sermons were printed by Dr Sacheverell's order and that Clements gave him nothing for his copy. [86]

Henry Clements, who knew a good thing when he saw one, brought out a further printing of the second edition, at 6*d* per octavo copy, on 3 December. [87] Then, as the pirates inevitably moved in, Clements moved out, content now to sit back and count the guineas as they rolled in from one of the most successful minor publishing *coups* of the century. Before the year was out four pirated editions had already appeared, one of them put out by H. King at the bargain price of 1*d*. In all, eleven English editions, including those of Clements, were published within the course of

* See p. 92 below.

a few months, quite apart from translations into French, German and Dutch.

Obviously the belief that about 40,000 copies altogether had been printed and dispersed, which stemmed from the estimates of the Whig Managers at the trial and which filtered *via* Burnet into the history books,[88] was well wide of the mark. The number circulating in Britain alone before the end of the trial cannot have been very far short of 100,000.[89] As a short-term best-seller *The Perils of False Brethren* had no equal in the early eighteenth century.

The printing of the sermon – both its circumstances and its sheer volume – made it certain that the Sacheverell affair would be no mere nine days' wonder. More than that, it had a vital bearing on the decision to proceed against the preacher. 'I suppose [wrote the bishop of Carlisle, from his distant diocese] that the causing of a seditious sermon to be printed and published changes the nature of the transgression'.[90] Indeed it did. It was not only that in this case the printing was unauthorised, an insult to the Whig majority in the court of Aldermen, which included several influential parliamentarians. Much more important was the astounding fact that by the middle of December about 50,000 copies were already being read and handed about. A sermon which had originally been heard by a few hundred people was now going to be read, at the most narrowly conservative estimate, by at least a quarter of a million men and women, in other words by a number equal to the whole electorate of England and Wales. The dissemination of the poison would be nation-wide and on a scale far beyond the scope of a normally successful pamphlet. In these circumstances, could government or Parliament, in their own interests, remain indifferent either to the sermon or to the preacher?

IV THE DOCTOR IMPEACHED

25 NOVEMBER 1709 TO 12 JANUARY 1710

'Upon the whole, I think,' wrote Defoe in his *Review*, 'the roaring of this beast ought to give you no manner of disturbance. You ought to laugh at him, let him alone; he'll vent his gall, and then he'll be quiet'.[1]

For a fortnight and more after the first appearance of *The Perils of False Brethren* a significant number of Whigs, while not necessarily agreeing that the sermon should be altogether ignored, took the view that both it and its preacher should remain beneath official notice. The Whig clergy, especially, argued that Sacheverell had made himself so vulnerable both by the extremity of his notions and the wildness with which he had expressed them that he could be cut down most effectively with his own weapons, the pen and the printing press. Some months later a Shropshire parson named Fleetwood was to recall how 'when I first came to town, it was between the preaching of his sermon and his being impeached for it: and I believe I may safely affirm there were not ten men of sense and character in all the city but did absolutely condemn that discourse as a rhapsody of incoherent, ill-digested thoughts, dressed in the worst language that could be found'. It was only when the preacher was prosecuted, he found, that 'the sermon mended strangely'.[2]

Certainly there were many High Churchmen, especially those of the cloth, whose first reaction had been to draw back their skirts. 'I'm sure such discourses will never convert anyone', wrote one of them, 'but I'm afraid will rather give the enemies of our Church great advantage over her: since the best that her true sons can say of it is that the man is mad; and indeed, most people here think him so'. Bishop Compton's chaplain, who had so warmly espoused Sacheverell's cause in Southwark, was frankly embarrassed at the publication of *The Perils of False Brethren*: 'for I lay it down with myself as a maxim', he told his uncle, Trumbull, 'that the more politics any sermon has in it, the worse it is'.[3] As for the reaction of the Low Church and Dissenting controversialists, it was compounded of a measure of anger, of even more contempt, and of complete confidence that the Flag Officer could be routed without undue difficulty, partly by force of argument and partly (and some thought, most effectively) by ridicule.

Argument in plenty was available within three days of the sermon's publication. George Ridpath, later to achieve some fame as a political journalist by his courageous editorship of *The Flying-Post*, brought out *The Peril of Being Zealously Affected, but not Well*, a highly professional, detailed, and at times devastating piece of demolition. Hard on its heels came two other pamphlets in a more ironical vein, *The Best Way of Answering Dr Sacheverell* and *The Cherubim with a Flaming Sword*. On 10 December Defoe ignored his own counsel and entered the fray.[4] But by then Sacheverell had already drawn upon his head the fire of the formidable Dr White Kennett, rector of St Mary Aldermary, next to Hoadly the most telling marksman in the Low Church ranks. Kennett's *True Answer* scored unerringly on target after target, exposing Sacheverell's biblical ignorance, his inconsistencies and absurdities, and the 'fustian and bombast' of his style. The ridicule here was no less sharp for being urbane: 'indeed I have tired myself more than I can do you [he told the 'Alderman of London' to whom his pamphlet was addressed] by searching a place that affords nothing but what is offensive to any senses that are in a right order. You laid it upon me, but I hope one such penance is enough for a man's life'.[5]

The early exchanges in the great Sacheverell pamphlet war of 1709–10 justify to the hilt the claim of the Whig author of *High Church Display'd* that 'the Doctor and his party were entirely routed in those paper-skirmishes'. Indeed Henry Sacheverell at first found so few champions, and those few so reluctant to engage openly, that more than six weeks had elapsed and no fewer than eleven tracts had appeared since the preaching of the sermon before its first direct defence was published.* After Christmas there was a remarkable transformation, as apologists almost fell over each other in the scramble to get their copies into the eager hands of London's printers and booksellers. By then, however, they had the strongest incentive to action: for the 'cherubim' had been disarmed of his flaming sword, and was in the custody of the Serjeant-at-Arms of the House of Commons. We must now see what circumstances, persons and arguments combined to put him there, by elevating his sermon from a 'brazen-faced banter' (as it was first described in the press, on 12 November)[6] to a 'high crime and misdemeanour' demanding the attention of the highest court in the land.

Historians have done less than justice to the Whigs over the impeachment of Sacheverell. Their proceeding against him has been regularly depicted (save by Trevelyan, who showed more understanding of their problem) as an act of the grossest political folly and myopia. In particular, their prosecuting him by the portentous method of impeachment, making a massive public spectacle of the trial of a relatively insignificant hothead in order to provide a forum for a full-scale vindication of 'Revolution principles', has been made to seem rash, arrogant, even stupid. This condemnation of the Whigs is based on almost total misunderstanding of their motives and aims, and a serious misjudgment of the political calibre of their leaders.

The men holding political power in Britain in the winter of 1709–10 were not fools. Their decision that Sacheverell and his diatribe could not with safety be left simply to the attentions of Low Church pamphleteers, however sharp their hatchet-work, was a response to one undeniable fact. At the end of more than a decade of political exertion in the Tory cause by the great bulk of the Anglican clergy, one of these parsons had preached a sermon in the heart of London which, on any reasonable construction, was seditious in implication and which was undoubtedly seditious in intent.[7] The content, the manner of its delivery, the circumstances of its subsequent printing, the insolent defiance of its 'Epistle

* This was William Beck's *Dr Sacheverell's Vindication*. It contended, as the Doctor had done, that the dissenters were potentially as rebellious as ever. 'Mr Burgess may thump his cushion till he beats the skin off his knuckles before he makes the understanding part of mankind believe that lies are true'. I am indebted to Dr W. A. Speck for this information.

Dedicatory' – all were deliberately provocative and inflammatory. Moreover, *they did inflame*. However hostile the reception of the sermon among 'men of sense and character', there were early and disturbing signs that Sacheverell might develop very rapidly into a dangerous demagogue. On 5 November he had been cheered away from St Paul's. On the last Sunday in the month there were astonishing scenes in and round the church of St Margaret's, Lothbury, when he went there as visiting preacher. Not only was the church itself packed to suffocation, but a great crowd milled about outside threatening to pull down the doors and break the windows for a chance to hear the High Church champion.[8] With copies of the St Paul's sermon circulating in every coffee-house and many a tavern by early December, and selling daily in their hundreds, even Whig parsons began to doubt whether a mere paper victory over Sacheverell would serve the purposes of either the party or the Church.[9]

Within a day or two of the printed sermon coming on sale it was being closely scrutinised by the law officers of the Crown, by a number of leading Whig Q.Cs and judges, and more ominously, by members of the 'Cabinet Council'.[10] Earlier in November the last Tory had been removed from the Cabinet to make way for Lord Orford of the Whig Junto to come in as First Lord of the Admiralty. This meant that among the thirteen Cabinet ministers there were only three who were not recognised Whigs; and they – Godolphin, the Lord Treasurer, Marlborough, the Captain-General, and Queensberry, the Scottish Secretary of State – could now by no stretch of the imagination be classed as Tories. They represented 'the Court': but a Court which by this stage of Queen Anne's reign seemed to many observers so closely tied to the Whigs as to be almost indistinguishable from them.* The vast majority of the non-Cabinet offices were also by this time secure in Whig hands; and among these junior ministers were the Attorney-General, Sir James Montagu (younger brother of Halifax of the

---

* The rest of the Cabinet consisted of four Lords of the Whig Junto – Somers (Lord President), Sunderland (Secretary of State for the South), Wharton (Lord Lieutenant of Ireland) and Orford; two of the Junto's closest allies, Cowper (Lord Chancellor) and Devonshire (Lord Steward); and four more moderate Whigs, Henry Boyle (Secretary for the North and the only commoner), Newcastle (Privy Seal), Somerset (Master of the Horse) and Archbishop Tenison of Canterbury, an infrequent attender.

Junto), and the Solicitor-General, Robert Eyre, one of the more moderate group of 'Treasurer's Whigs'. If Sacheverell was prosecuted at Common Law, they would be expected to lead that prosecution. But the Whig party at this time was stiff with legal talent. In the Cabinet were Cowper and Somers, present and past occupants of the Woolsack, the two greatest names in their profession; and in the Commons there were at least four more distinguished lawyers, in addition to Montagu and Eyre, entitled to be consulted about Sacheverell's case. They were Sir Peter King, who had first roused the court of Aldermen; Sir Joseph Jekyll, Somers's brother-in-law and a judge on the Welsh circuit; Nicholas Lechmere, Q.C., the client of Wharton; and Sir Thomas Parker, Queen's Serjeant, and as member for Derby a likely auditor of the August Assize sermon. Looking at the St Paul's sermon with professional eyes, and not simply with the eyes of party zealots, what did the Whig lawyers see?

They saw, for the most part, a typical Sacheverell effusion. Much of what he had said, on topics which had been his hardy annuals for almost a decade, was offensive; almost all of it was couched in language more violent than any but a tiny handful of Highflying divines would have dared to use; but it was hardly the sort of matter to justify his being accused of seditious libel in the courts, or being brought to account in Parliament. So it was with his latest blasts against the advocates of Comprehension, against the occasional conformists, who over the years had suffused his blood vessels more than any other group of his fellow-mortals, and against dissenting tutors: all were deplorable – but predictable and unpunishable. And yet in two ways Sacheverell had gone significantly further than ever before. He had done so most glaringly in his choice of occasion, place and time. But likewise in what he had said, as well as where and when he had said it, he had at certain points gone beyond all tolerable bounds in the eye of any self-respecting Whig government. In no previous printed work had he slighted the Glorious Revolution in the pointed way he did at St Paul's, both by neglect and innuendo. Never before had he so openly extolled the doctrine of Non-Resistance, which every Whig abhorred, nor come so close to challenging the authority of Parliament, especially in respect of the Toleration Act and the resolutions of December 1705 declaring the Church to be in no danger.

And never before, in print, had he attacked a leading minister of the Crown as self-evidently as at St Paul's he had attacked Godolphin. Finally, in his passion for the whole metaphorical apparatus of the Church Militant, he had seemed to invite an accusation that he was inciting sedition, if not open violence, against those currently in authority, whom he had made synonymous with the false brethren betraying both Church and State.

The main problem for the government, as the Whig lawyers saw it, was that in some of these places Sacheverell had been cleverer and more calculated in his excesses than his own friends had given him credit for. The legal advice he himself had taken had not been carelessly given. Once the sermon was under the microscope it transpired that at a number of crucial points he had chosen his words carefully enough, or inserted enough studied ambiguities or contradictions to make it uncertain, to say the least, that he could be convicted of sedition *on words alone.** In addition, and paradoxically, it appeared that the hazards of a prosecution in the court of Queen's Bench would be increased by the fact that where Sacheverell's cunning was insufficient to shield him, he had a fair hope of being able to shelter behind his muddled thinking and defective logic. Even his turgescent style might protect him.[11]

In consequence, even where the Doctor seemed most vulnerable – in his treatment of the 1688 Revolution, his attacks on the Toleration, his vilification of individuals – he was very far from being wide open. It was already being said that Sacheverell had 'preached against the Revolution'. Yet a striking thing about the sermon was how very little the Revolution figured in it anywhere. And nowhere in the crucial five sentences which did refer to it could he be shown to have directly and specifically condemned it. In the case of the Toleration, he had used the term with an extraordinary looseness, leaving it open to debate whether it was the 1689 Act itself he was condemning or the subsequent abuse of it; and any defence counsel worth his salt would point out that on the solitary occasion on which he did unmistakably allude to the Act, it was to say that he intended in no way 'to cast the least invidious reflection upon it'. Everyone knew this was a brazen lie. But could the lie be proved? Finally, it was transparent that Sacheverell had

* It should be borne in mind that by normal Common Law practice the most favourable construction would have had to be placed on his words.

G

not libelled any member of the government or of the bishops' bench in words that could possibly sustain a prosecution on those grounds alone. Even the notorious reference to Godolphin was slyly masked by the use of the plural 'Volpones'. It was all very well to say, as Burnet did in his *History*, that 'the Lord Treasurer was so described that it was next to naming him'. But it is instructive that only one of the Commons' Managers at the trial was to refer to the Volpone allusion, and that without comment; the only peer who did so later in the House of Lords, Burnet himself, was deemed to have committed a great *faux pas*.[12]

As well as listening to the considered opinions of their friends of the long robe, the ministers also took counsel of some of their allies in lawn sleeves. 'I was then in my diocese', notes Burnet, 'so I had no share in the deliberation';[13] but the Primate, Wake of Lincoln and Trimnell of Norwich were all available for consultation, and one possible alternative to a Common Law action was for the government's clerical friends to secure Sacheverell's prosecution in an ecclesiastical court for breaches of canon law.[14] Wake, at least, believed such a court to be more appropriate in this case than Parliament.[15] There were, however, two overpowering objections. One was the notorious ineffectiveness of the consistory courts. The other was that whereas, as chaplain of St Saviour's, Sacheverell's diocesan was Sir Jonathan Trelawney, bishop of Winchester, the offending sermon had been preached in the territory of Compton, bishop of London; and for that matter, neither prelate from the ministry's viewpoint was a credible agent of retribution.

One other course was suggested to the government as an alternative to that eventually taken, one which we know to have been favoured by Eyre, the Solicitor-General, and by some other members of the Commons.[16] The proposal was to make use of Parliament, rather than the courts, but without invoking the protracted ritual of an impeachment. There would be no difficulty about bringing Sacheverell to the Commons' Bar on a charge of showing contempt for the express resolution of the House in December 1705, declaring the Church in no danger. A straight, cut-and-dried party vote would then do the government's business: the sermon would be burnt and the preacher incarcerated. With hindsight it is easy to argue that not accepting this advice was the most serious mistake ever made by the ministers of 1708–10. Yet the reasons marshalled against it seemed perfectly sound at the time. If the Whigs were going to proceed against Sacheverell at all, an element of publicity had to be one of the main objects of the exercise.[17] Moreover, once the offender was released from the custody of the Serjeant-at-Arms at the end of the session (and being in the Serjeant's custody scarcely implied durance vile for a man of means), that was the end of the matter. Punishment by the House would certainly be swift and assured – but far from drastic. It would not be the deterrent, the 'exemplary punishment', on which the Whig ministers found their supporters increasingly set.[18] A Commons' vote could not suspend the Doctor from any of his priestly functions; it could not bar him from all further preferment; still less could it unfrock him. But a Lords' vote, on a charge of high crimes and misdemeanours, could do all this and far more: it could inflict a swingeing fine, confiscate his goods, even imprison him for life.

Above all, it must be borne in mind that the choice of parliamentary courses open to the Whigs was not necessarily between Eyre's 'short way' and the flamboyant, emotive public spectacle into which the trial eventually degenerated.* To do justice to the political judgment of the men responsible for the decision, few if any of them had any thought of such a spectacle at this stage. A hearing at the Bar of the House of Lords, lasting perhaps three days, and in the presence of an audience almost purely parliamentary – this is what 'impeachment' meant to its original advocates. Had they only been able to achieve this goal, and certainly had they contrived in doing so to avoid the crippling delays which in the event enmeshed the whole proceedings, their decision might well have been thoroughly justified.

It is impossible to say with utter certainty either when or how this decision was taken, at the highest level.† One can be virtually sure on whose initiative it was taken; but not of the motives of several of those involved in it. Such are the accidents of history that they have conspired to deprive us at this point in the Sacheverell

---

* A vital point. See also pp. 110–13 below.
† It is beyond question that it *was* taken at the highest level, and primarily on its own merits. The contention of the Scottish member of Parliament, George Baillie, that 'the Court went into the proposal of prosecuting him to amuse the Parliament and to divert them from other designs' (Register House, G. D. 158. HMC. 2123: to Lord Marchmont, 24 Dec. 1710), does not bear close examination.

affair of the kind of testimony which would be wholly authoritative.* Because of this, the account that follows has had to be built
up – here and there by inference and a calculation of probabilities –
out of the fragmentary and often unsubstantiated evidence which
has survived.[19] It is more than a tentative hypothesis, but at some
of its seams at least, it is less than watertight.

We must remember, to begin with, that the solid front which the
Godolphin ministry at this time presented to its opponents, and to
the world, concealed some serious fissures. All was not well between the 'Court Lords', Godolphin and Marlborough, and the
Junto Whigs. The latter had never accepted as more than a temporary necessity the interposition of intermediaries or 'Managers'
between themselves and the fount of all influence, the Crown; and
they continued to aspire to a total monopoly of power. There were
also personal animosities. Halifax, not yet back in the Cabinet,
disliked Godolphin and coveted the Treasury; and Somers's relations with Marlborough had been very strained for some months,
since he and Lord Chancellor Cowper had helped to scotch the
duke's first attempt to get life tenure of his Captain-Generalship.[20]

While the members of this uneasy coalition were taking their
legal soundings on the Sacheverell sermon, their own dispositions
towards the most extreme course open to them, impeachment,
were becoming plain. Lord Godolphin, who combined an anti-
clerical bias with a strangely thin skin when his own loyalty to the
Church of England was called in question, was so touched on the
raw by the personal reflection in the sermon that for once in his
life he was scarcely capable of cool political judgment. This made
him easy game for the two leading Junto advocates of impeachment, Wharton and Sunderland, whose motives were mixed. They
unquestionably aimed 'in a parliamentary way [to] fasten a brand
of indelible infamy on that enslaving tenet' of Non-Resistance, and
at the same time a brand of Jacobitism on all who spoke and voted

* I have in mind particularly the destruction by fire in George II's reign of Lord
Somers's papers, and the uncharacteristic silence on these questions – for reasons
which are largely freakish – of the two most important collections of political papers
which have survived from the early eighteenth century, the Blenheim manuscripts
and the Harley papers. For example, the sickness of his son and other family
business prevented Robert Harley, for the only time in his long career as a member
of the House of Commons, from attending the beginning of a parliamentary session;
so that the most receptive of all the Tory grapevines was temporarily out of action.

in its support.[21] But neither were they blind to the political advantages that would accrue from committing Godolphin publicly to the parliamentary prosecution of an Anglican parson; for this seemed certain to cut his last line of retreat to the Tory party and therefore isolate him in preparation for his removal, when the time was ripe.

Marlborough's early reactions to the printing of the sermon are more difficult to deduce, but it seems probable that at first he occupied an intermediate position – resentful of Sacheverell's insolence, sympathetic to Godolphin, but unwilling to present the Whigs with a gratuitous opportunity to make party capital out of a parliamentary trial in which 'Revolution principles' were bound to receive maximum publicity. Finally, there were the hesitant and the doubters. To begin with it is likely that they included Cowper, on the grounds of judicial propriety; they certainly included Somers, who had stronger reservations on the same grounds as well as questioning the political wisdom of an impeachment, and also Henry Boyle, whose instinct was to let the whole matter subside as quietly as possible.

During the first week in December, before the key meetings took place which were to determine the issue, two developments were in progress. One was the private proselytising going on among Cabinet ministers themselves, not without effect, as Sunderland reported to the duchess of Marlborough:

> I found by Mr Boyle's manner of talking this morning about the business of Sacheverell's sermon that Lord Marlborough and Lord Treasurer had spoke to him; for he talked of it with another sort of warmth than ever I heard him.[22]

Somers succumbed less easily, however much he may have shared the wish of his Junto colleagues to embarrass Godolphin.[23] More important in his case was another kind of pressure to which he, Cowper, and indeed all the Whig ministers were now being exposed – pressure from below. Strong feelings were manifestly building up among their supporters in favour of drastic parliamentary action against the Doctor and all he stood for. White Kennett was not alone in being aware of this swelling protest from the rank and file of Whig M.Ps and peers, goaded beyond endurance by the stabs of a whole black-coated army over the past seven years. Wherever there was latent anti-clericalism, it burst to the surface. Even courtiers as canny as James Brydges became convinced that neither the Queen nor the constitution would be safe until 'a stop [was] put to the liberty some gentlemen of his coat take in their pulpits'.[24]

It is doubtful whether ministers could have ignored such feelings, even if they had wished to do so; especially since the reports reaching them from their 'understrappers' in the Commons, as well as their own observations in the Lords, suggested that the situation at Westminster was ideal for exploiting their parliamentary majorities against the Highflying cause with crushing effect. In the Upper House Tory peers, apathetically marshalled by a Lord Rochester who seemed to Arthur Mainwaring 'very dejected and old', were doing little more than go through the motions of opposition in a chamber which on most days was much less than half full. In St Stephen's Chapel Tory morale was even lower. As the government's business was steam-rollered through the Commons in record time, the average attendance of members dropped from around 200 in the middle of November – in itself exceptionally low – down to 120 in the last few days of the month, of which barely a third were Tories. Had Harley been there to encourage them, things might have been different, for earlier in November he had been full of schemes for thwarting 'those heathen magicians', the Junto. But urgent family concerns kept him in Herefordshire, and without him Bromley and other Tory chiefs seemed quite unable to put heart into their meagre forces. Little wonder most Whig commoners felt so cocksure about launching an impeachment, with their adversaries (in Mainwaring's words) 'so broke in the House of Commons'. The only fears were that the Whigs themselves might be too *blasé* to attend, a contingency which the Junto's Sir Joseph Jekyll had in mind on 3 December, when he 'made a very warm speech upon the members not coming to Town and attending the great and important service of the nation'. By the 8th their numbers were already up to 250.[25]

Although the men who took the final decision to impeach Sacheverell were Cabinet ministers, the Sacheverell affair was never formally discussed in the Cabinet. In none of the surviving Cabinet minutes of Secretary Sunderland is it as much as mentioned.[26] Since it was essentially a political decision, and technically only within the competence of the House of Commons, it could not have been thought a proper matter to debate before the Queen in full Cabinet. One of the most remarkable features of the whole affair, in fact, was how well-kept a secret the proposed impeachment was: the shocked reactions of the Tories when it was first broached in the Commons are proof of this. The reason why secrecy was successfully preserved must lie partly in the location of two vital ministerial meetings. On or about 8 December there was a gathering of unusual importance round the convivial table of the celebrated Whig Kit-Cat Club, assembled on this occasion at the house of the wealthy financier Sir Henry Furnese, M.P. for Sandwich.* Marlborough attended this meeting, 'admitted extraordinary' to membership, and concurred with the general feeling of the meeting in favour of impeachment.[27] Three leading members of the Cabinet, however – Godolphin, Orford and Boyle – were not Kit-Catters;† so that another and more formal ministerial meeting had still to be held before the government hounds in the House of Commons could be let loose upon their quarry. In the interests of secrecy, no better place could have been found for it than the offices of the Secretaries of State at the Cockpit, where the same ministers regularly met once or twice every week in their capacity as the committee of the Cabinet Council, *alias* 'the Lords of the Committee'. This camouflage would explain both Alexander Cunningham's near-contemporary reference to the matter being 'laid before the Council' and the fact that Sunderland never minuted the meeting.

The only account of this second meeting to survive is in Cunningham's own pages. Yet it is so extraordinarily detailed, especially on the contribution of Somers to the proceedings, that it is hard to believe that it is not substantially accurate, or that Cunningham was not 'fed' with the information subsequently by the Lord President, who by the summer of 1710 was set on vindicating his own role in the Sacheverell affair. In the main, therefore, we must let Cunningham tell his own story.

* The membership and importance of the Kit-Cat Club as an element in Whig political organisation is discussed in my *British Politics in the Age of Anne*, pp. 297–8.
† Godolphin was a member by November 1711 (Oldmixon, p. 479) but it is probable that he had only recently been admitted. Newcastle, Lord Privy Seal, was also a member, but had not yet come up to town.

When they were all of opinion that the sermon deserved a censure . . . the duke of Marlborough proposed that Sacheverell should be prosecuted; 'lest', said he, 'such preachers as these should preach us all out of the kingdom'. They all agreed to the duke of Marlborough's proposal: but still there was a question among them in what court he should be tried for so great an offence; neither were they all inclined to proceed vigorously . . .

The main alternatives had by now narrowed themselves down to two: impeachment, of which Sunderland now stood forth as the principal advocate, and an ordinary prosecution in the Queen's Bench. In the end, the doubts which the law officers had raised, as to whether a prosecution at Common Law for seditious libel could be sustained, proved decisive with the waverers. But not before Somers had delivered himself of a speech which his friends can only have regarded as equivocal.

After considering the opinions of some others my own judgment continues much the same as it was formerly. I said many years ago[28] . . . that good laws ought to be provided, lest such men as this should some time or other kindle a flame to the destruction of our country, our religion, our property and our allies: and this evil, I said, was of such a nature that unless ye provided against it, it would be in vain to have recourse to prosecutions.

He then turned to the risks involved in impeachment. He clearly did not envisage the massive movement of public opinion which in the event took place: what concerned him was the possibility of a substantial erosion of the government's majority in both Houses, especially by deliberate absenteeism in the Lords. At one point he addressed himself plainly to Godolphin.

Order a charge to be drawn up against the offender; but still take care not to consult your passions or affections more than your own dignity and usage. We are all of us liable to passion: and no man looks upon the injuries done to himself as small ones. For my own part, indeed, I look upon those which Dr Sacheverell has done to the ministry to be very great; but in the punishment thereof, let no hatred, revenge, anger or passion interpose, for where these take place the mind does not easily discern the truth.

The Lord President's concluding advice to his colleagues was, in effect, this. Impeach this man, provided you can be sure of carrying through Parliament a sentence that matches the magnitude of the crime; otherwise 'I think it best to make use of that method of process which our laws have provided'. Of the rest of the meeting Cunningham tells us only this. 'This opinion, which tended to clemency, was not agreeable to the duke of Marlborough's friends, and especially to the earl of Sunderland. The Lord Somers therefore came over to their sentiments . . .'[29]

After the lengthy cogitations of the past two weeks, events suddenly moved with startling swiftness. The decisive meeting of ministers may have taken place on Monday, 12 December. It cannot have been later, for as Ralph Bridges learned from two stunned Tories in the Commons:[30]

> On Tuesday in the afternoon, the House full and all in a calm, on a sudden up starts J[ohn] Dolben, son of a worthy Archbishop,[31] and holding the lately printed sermons of Dr Sacheverell in his hand, which were marked with a pen in the most exceptious places, moved the House to take into consideration those two seditious pamphlets as libels upon her Majesty and her government, and delivered 'em on the Speaker's table.[32]

Spencer Cowper, brother of the Lord Chancellor, rose at once to second him, and the whole House buzzed while the Clerk, in his flat monotone, read out the Epistle Dedicatory to the Derby sermon and the various marked paragraphs from *The Perils of False Brethren*. Dolben, who sat for Liskeard and was generally reckoned a 'Lord Treasurer's Whig', now moved that the House should vote the two books to be 'malicious, scandalous and seditious libels, highly reflecting upon her Majesty and government, the Protestant Succession as by law established and both Houses of Parliament'. He and Cowper were supported by King, Jekyll and Walpole, by the Junto men George and Sir James Montagu, and by three Treasurer's Whigs in the ministry, Boyle, Coningsby and Smith. One of the Whig spokesmen 'particularly named my Lord Mayor as accessory to the crime'; and John Smith, the Chancellor of the Exchequer, moved an amendment adding the phrase 'the late happy Revolution' to Dolben's catalogue of what Sacheverell had 'highly reflected' on.

Against this concentrated barrage the return fire from the astonished Tories was desultory and unconcerted. The two members for Oxford University* spoke up briefly for Sacheverell, as did Arthur Annesley, John Hungerford and a prominent Tory lawyer, John Ward: 'but very sparingly', Sir John Percival noted from the gallery, 'none of them excusing the paragraphs, but desiring only that the matter might be referred to the Committee of Religion, or else to one appointed on purpose [a Select Committee], who might read the sermons at length; or else they did not think they could pass a fair judgment'. Whitlocke protested that 'at the rate the House proceeded they might pick sentences here and there out of the Bible to censure'; but only Annesley had the spirit to take the war to the enemy. He upheld Passive Obedience as orthodox Anglican doctrine (if the Whig bishops 'had now changed their minds' about this, he said, 'they would do well to set the laity right again'), and he argued that whatever the situation five years earlier, the Church was patently in peril now – if only from the opening of new conventicles in market towns and the recent stifling of Convocation.

When the vote of censure was carried with a great shout of 'aye' there came at once from the Whig benches cries of 'impeach! impeach!' 'The House was in such a ferment', Bridges was told, 'that nothing would serve them but to order my Lord Mayor to attend in his place and expel him the House (from whence he was then absent); and all they could be brought to by Mr Bromley, Mr Annesley, etc., that night was to respite the impeachment of the Doctor', until the morrow. He and his publisher, Clements, were both ordered to attend at the Commons' Bar at 12 noon.[33]

On the morning of Wednesday, 14 December, Henry Sacheverell made the first of his many journeys to Westminster as a marked man. And almost overnight, it seemed, the black-coated ranks had begun to close behind him. William Lancaster, Oxford's Vice-Chancellor, bore him to the Palace Yard in his coach and went with him into the Court of Requests in Westminster Hall to await his

* See p. 57 above.

summons. Over a hundred other clergymen thronged the court, some there out of curiosity but most of them – those who 'thought themselves attacked in the person of their brother' – to lend moral support.[34] By midday, in a crowded chamber which included Garrard, sitting uneasily in his place, the Commons had worked down their order paper as far as 'the Doctor's business',[35] and White Kennett, craning from the gallery, 'heard Mr Dolben begin, after reading the order of the day, with commending the proceedings of the House in the matter yesterday and answering what had been then professed of the dangers of the Church'; and heard him conclude that, since it was clearly the feeling of members that they wished to go further than the censure passed the day before, he would move that Doctor Sacheverell be impeached, in the name of the Commons of Great Britain, of high crimes and misdemeanours.

Then the Lord Coningsby said there were some things to be done in order to the said impeachment, to call in the bookseller and the preacher. It was moved to call in the Doctor, and he was brought to the Bar with the Officer and the mace before him.

The Speaker said: Dr Sacheverell, I am to ask you whether you own these two sermons that are in your name. I will send 'em down to you, and [you must] give the House an account of what you know of 'em.

After some prevarication by the Doctor over the edition of the Derby sermon, 'a little pirated copy',

the Speaker said: Pray Doctor, look upon the Epistle Dedicatory before the Assize Sermon and see if you can disown it. The Doctor . . . read some part of it, and then said: 'This is agreeable to what I did write and give to be printed to my bookseller'.[36]

It was Sir Richard Onslow's next question from the Chair, however, which brought expectancy to the bewigged faces along the Whig benches. Turning to the dedication of the St Paul's sermon he asked: 'Dr Sacheverell, did my Lord Mayor command you to publish this sermon?' The Doctor's answer came pat. 'In the strict sense of the word *command*, he did not; but in the common acceptation of the word, as the desires of superiors to their inferiors are said to be *commands*, he did *command* me, for he did desire and press me to print it'. When Onslow required him to amplify this, Sacheverell retailed the full story of his first conversation with Garrard on 5 November.* But he also told how

> when I came to bring two printed copies to his Lordship, then indeed he did seem to be altered, and told me I should not have said *by his command*. I told him, my Lord, if your Lordship be afraid or ashamed to stand by the truth, in the second edition now in the press I will leave out the whole dedication. No, says my Lord, you shall leave out nothing; you should rather put in somewhat, for I am a baronet and you have left out that title. So in the second edition, Mr Speaker, I put in the word 'Baronet'.

All eyes were now on Garrard, whose neck (as Peter Wentworth remarked) now seemed very much 'in the collar'. But Sacheverell, whose air throughout had been positively jaunty, was not the man to give up the centre of the stage easily. Having finished his evidence he pulled out a paper from the hat he was holding in his hand and blandly embarked on what was obviously a prepared speech. The Speaker hastily checked him – his instructions from the House were to ask questions, he said, not to hear any speech – and ordered him to withdraw and await the members' further pleasure.[37] Here was Garrard's chance to earn those glowing testimonials to his 'undaunted resolution' which Sacheverell had bestowed in his Dedication on 'so bright an ornament' to the Church. Alas, his courage proved embarrassingly short. He knew that the least he could expect if he admitted the truth of the Doctor's account was the loss of his seat, and that he might well spend his Christmas in the Tower. At first, therefore, he remained mute, despite the beguiling invitations of his opponents. Eventually 'in respect to his Lordship', Kennett tells us, 'Mr Smith moved and insisted that the company in the gallery should withdraw. So we were all turned out but the members'. Only then did the Lord Mayor stand up in his place and, in a strained voice that seemed close to panic, told the House 'that he would deal as plainly as the Doctor had done; that he protested he never saw him until that 5th of November in the pulpit; that he carried him home, as the custom is, to dinner; but as to the printing his sermon, he did not command it, nor order it, nor so much as desire him to do it'. After so categorical a denial,

* See p. 70 above.

made 'upon his honour', the Commons had little option but to accept his word. Garrard had escaped, though only to become the butt of the Town wags and an object of contempt to both parties. Years later it was still regarded as a polite insult in London to call a man a 'bright ornament'.[38]

Meanwhile, before the Commons' vote that would set the whole complex machinery of impeachment in motion, there was the formality of a debate to be gone through. But first Sacheverell was allowed to say his piece. Called in a second time, he was asked by Onslow if he had anything further to offer the House. Out again came the paper from his hat, and this time he was permitted to read it uninterrupted. The statement was brief, and barely apologetic.

> Mr Speaker: I am very sorry I am fallen under the displeasure of this House. I did not imagine any expressions in my sermons were liable to such a censure as you have passed upon them. If you had been pleased to have favoured me so far as to have heard me before you passed it,* I hope I should have explained myself so as to have prevented it.[39]

The debate which followed, and went on well into the afternoon, was in the main a recapitulation of the previous day's arguments. Predictably it was said that this was a case for a Church court or for the Queen's Bench. Other Tories argued that if, as rumour had it, the judges and the Queen's counsel had been consulted and had declared that a prosecution at Common Law could not be sustained, 'they thought it was very unreasonable, by an impeachment in Parliament, to make a man a criminal that by the law of the land was innocent'. But by this time every Whig member had the picture clear. Highflying clergymen had sheltered too long behind their cloth and behind the unwillingness of courts to convict for libel on the basis of innuendo. If Parliament alone could bring them their just deserts, then Parliament must do so; for come what may, as Sir Stephen Lennard was heard to say exultingly, in a moment of naked political emotion, they were going 'to roast a parson'. The very next day Sir Stephen had a stroke while walking in Drury Lane and died immediately. It seemed to many offended Tories a particularly speedy manifestation of divine retribution.[40]

---

* This statement had evidently been prepared as a comment on the vote of the previous day.

When the question was put there was no division; and Paul Jodrell, the Clerk of the House, recorded in his Journal, with customary economy

> *Resolved* That the said Dr Henry Sacheverell be impeached of high crimes and misdemeanours.

> *Ordered* That Mr Dolben do go to the Lords, and at their Bar, in the name of all the Commons of Great Britain, impeach the said Dr Henry Sacheverell of high crimes and misdemeanours, and acquaint the Lords that the House will, in due time, exhibit articles against the said Dr Henry Sacheverell.[41]

This he could not do immediately, since on Tuesday the Lords, being short of business, had adjourned themselves until the 15th. But now that Sacheverell was in the custody of the Serjeant-at-Arms, a committee could be appointed to draw up the articles of impeachment, and to it seventeen leading Whigs were now nominated. Nine were lawyers; indeed the core of the Articles Committee was one of the most distinguished combinations of lawyers ever assembled to do a job of work in the Commons. It was made up of two future Lord Chancellors, one future Master of the Rolls, four future judges, one budding Attorney-General and one ex-Solicitor General. Of the rest of the committee, only Dolben and Lord William Powlet were not of ministerial rank.*

Its members were already preparing to leave for their first meeting, and 'the House was in great confusion, it being late, and every one expecting immediately to rise', when Anthony Henley, M.P. for Weymouth, seconded by Sir Joseph Jekyll, decided that this red-letter day for the 'High' Whigs ought to end on an appropriately high note. In an atmosphere of 'great ferment', as Sir John Percival witnessed it,

> Mr Henley took that opportunity to tell the House that in such licentious times as these it was not sufficient to punish offenders that write against the Constitution, but they ought to distinguish those that writ serviceably for it; and therefore he would make them a motion if they would give him leave. Being ordered to go on, he moved that her Majesty might be addressed to confer

---

* Even Powlet was a minor placeman. For the full composition of the Committee, see p. 97 n.* below.

some ecclesiastical dignity upon the Reverend Ben Hoadly for his excellent defence of the Constitution; which was agreed to with a great noise.

The two pro-Hoadly resolutions which were then carried[42] were patently unconcerted and unprompted by the government. In fact, when their import was digested there was head shaking among some ministers, concerned lest the sympathy of Queen Anne, that staunch, conservative Anglican, should be alienated at the very start of the Sacheverell prosecution. Even 'by some in the gallery', Percival observed, 'it was thought odd . . . that the Queen should be addressed to reward a man for writing against the bishop of Exeter's [Blackall's] sermon,* which very sermon she approved and ordered to be printed'. 'At best it was an unconsidered and un-mannerly thing', wrote a Scottish member soon afterwards, 'and I believe they themselves think so now'. Queen Anne certainly thought so when the address was belatedly presented to her by Secretary Boyle, and her chilly reply was seen by some, even then, as a straw in the wind.[43]

So far this month noble lords had been sprinkled very thinly along the benches of their chamber in the Palace of Westminster. Even on 15 December, with the promise of rare game, there were only sixty present when John Dolben, with a large supporting cohort of members, arrived at the Lords' Bar formally to impeach Henry Sacheverell. After promising the Lords that particular articles would be sent up to them in due course, Dolben added that the Doctor was in the custody of the Serjeant-at-Arms, ready to be handed over to Black Rod at their Lordships' convenience. In fact, Sacheverell had been taken after his commitment to the lodgings of the Commons' Messenger in Peters Street, Westminster, where his friends and sympathisers proceeded to make things remarkably comfortable for him. On his very first evening a hamper of claret and a purse of 50 guineas arrived from the High Tory duke of Beaufort. Other handsome presents followed and so did a stream of visitors, mostly clerics and lawyers, but also such prominent Tory figures as Leeds, Rochester and Buckingham. The 'prisoner's' only ground for petitioning the Commons on the 17th to allow his

* See pp. 31 and 33–4 above.

release on bail – 'that he may have an opportunity of making his defence' – was thus doubly shaky: it was not only that he could consult in Peters Street with whomever he could persuade to visit him; there was also the obvious objection that until the precise charges against him had been formulated by the Articles Committee no defence was possible. When the House rejected his petition on the day before Parliament rose for the Christmas recess, the Tories for the first time ventured a division; but the fact that they mustered a mere 64 votes is a fair indication of just how dead a duck many of them still felt the Doctor and his cause to be.[44]

But if the Tory politicians appeared to lack stomach for a fight, this was not so of the Highflying clergy. On the first Sunday after the impeachment, 18 December, the ramparts were already manned in many parts of London. The 58th psalm, with its theme of Divine vengeance on the ungodly ('Break their teeth, O God, in their mouths; smite the jaw-bones of the lions, O Lord') was sung for Sacheverell's benefit at St Margaret's, Westminster, and in several other churches. Other parsons preferred the subject of Christian tribulation. While the Doctor consoled himself with a comfortable dinner and good French wine, Charles Lambe preached in his place at St Saviour's on the merits of suffering, a theme echoed by Richard Welton at Whitechapel and Samuel Hilliard at Lothbury.[45] Canon Stratford of Christ Church* had news from London that even 'those whom he has used brutally' were forgetting their resentments and joining the long queue of Sacheverell's visitors: 'so solemn a prosecution for such a scribble', he forecast, 'will make the Doctor and his performance much more considerable than either of them could have been on any other account'. 'In this one man', agreed a west-country parson, 'the House of Lords must encounter with a legion'; and the Reverend Ralph Bridges had no doubt why. 'Nobody in a black gown that has any sense thinks that this matter will end in the impeachment of one single clergyman. There's a new Test designed for us all'.[46]

The two bishops most nearly concerned, Compton and Trelawney, spent an uneasy Christmas, despite their Toryism. Compton as yet held his hand; but the bishop of Winchester, hearing that Sacheverell had arranged for the firebrand Francis Higgins to deliver the afternoon sermon at St Saviour's on the first Sunday

* See pp. 3 and 19 above.

in 1710, sent the other Southwark chaplain, Thomas Horne, post-haste to Peters Street to say that the bishop 'wondered at his imprudence in appointing such a preacher as Mr Higgins, whom his Lordship would not suffer to preach within his diocese; and if he did not take care to provide men of a better character to supply his lecture, the bishop himself would take that care'. Sacheverell gave way under protest.[47] He was busy at this juncture composing a public appeal to the Queen for clemency.[48] But few of his friends could yet believe that he would escape his cross. One Sacheverellite vicar was so obsessed with the parallel of Calvary that he prepared a sermon to be preached before Garrard on the text from St Luke describing Simon Peter betraying the Master.[49] And Bridges lamented that his friend was 'most certainly doomed and condemned to ruin before his trial, which will only be a formality'.[50]

However, the duke of Marlborough, for one, was not now so sure. It was confidently reported early in January, not as rumour but as fact, that he had lately

> asked my Lord Wharton, what should they do? or how far should they proceed? for, says his Grace, I've continual solicitations from all the Church Party, and the whole body of the inferior clergy espouse his interest; and [the duke] seemed to express some apprehensions of carrying things too far. To which the Lord Wharton answered in a very rough manner: Do with him, my Lord? Quash him and damn him.[51]

But although Wharton and his friends succeeded in keeping their Court colleagues up to the mark, the stresses between them were discernible under the surface. They were, for instance, one factor which made the preparation of the indictment against Sacheverell such an unexpectedly protracted process.

Although seventeen members were appointed to the Articles Committee on 14 December, one of the original nominees, Robert Walpole (no doubt because of pressure of work at the War Office), took no part in its discussions.[52] The sixteen active members represented a remarkably fair cross-section of the Whig parliamentary party, and this very fact demonstrated the impressive unanimity of the Whigs in support of the impeachment.* But it

* The members (lawyers italicised) were: the Attorney-General and Solicitor-General (*Sir James Montagu* and *Robert Eyre*), Henry Boyle, Sir John Holland (Comptroller

H

also complicated the already difficult task of formulating the charges. The chief sticking-point was the part to be played in the indictment by Sacheverell's alleged attack on 'Revolution principles'. This crucial article was to lie at the very heart of the conflict between Whig and Tory philosophies during the Trial, and was to embarrass the Whig managers because, by highlighting the issue of Resistance, it laid them open to a charge of disloyalty to the reigning Queen. The Paymaster of the Forces, no lover of the Junto, was later to allege that Sacheverell would never have been impeached at all for 'a Billingsgate, nonsensical sermon'* if the Whig hierarchs had not been set on paving the way by a judicial decision for the passing of a new law – one which would give statutory authority to the subject's right to resist in certain circumstances. There is little convincing evidence to support his allegation.[53] Yet we do know that Sir Joseph Jekyll, who shared Somers's reservations about the impeachment and saw its purpose as a limited one, 'thought the article for vindicating the Revolution the only thing worth contending for'.[54] Lechmere, on the other hand, eager as he was to see Non-Resistance doctrine outlawed, was so powerfully swayed by his patron, Wharton's, determination to bring Godolphin to an irreparable breach with the High Tories that he was anxious to widen the indictment to include articles of a specifically religious nature, especially a charge of attacking the Toleration. The ex-Tories Marlborough and Godolphin, for their part, would have been happy to see the charges restricted to sedition and preaching the Church in danger: they were naturally chary of identifying themselves too closely with a 'Hoadleian' view of Resistance which had still to be reconciled with orthodox Anglican teaching.† And there were men in the Committee who stood close enough to them to press their case. Coningsby, indeed, was later to claim that 'I opposed to the last moment making his preaching for Passive Obedience and Non-Resistance one of the articles', and that it was 'my Lord Somers, my Lord Halifax and

---

of the Household), Spencer Compton, John Dolben, *Nicholas Lechmere, Sir Joseph Jekyll, Sir Thomas Parker, Sir Peter King*, Lord Coningsby, Lord William Powlet, John Smith, *Spencer Cowper, William Thompson* and *Sir John Hawles.*

* Cf. Brydges's view of the sermon at the time, p. 86 above.

† 'In the time of the trial', Lord Dartmouth later wrote, 'the earl of Godolphin asked me if I did not think they were all gone mad to fall foul upon the doctrine of the Church of England as well as [upon] the doctor'. Burnet, v, 443n.

my Lord Sunderland who crammed this article down our throats'.[55]

The eventual outcome of all this wrangling was a victory for those who wanted as broadly-based a charge as possible. A further delaying factor was the Committee's decision to frame not merely four articles but a most elaborate, ambitious preamble to those articles, exceeding in length all of them combined.* Significantly it was this preamble, more than the articles, which was subsequently challenged in the Commons, and many hours of previous discussion must have been spent over its exuberant phraseology. So although the Committee had its first meeting on 14 December, was convened with some regularity until the 23rd, and then met every day after Christmas at Jekyll's house,[56] it was not until 3 January that John Dyer, the newswriter, heard that its work was completed.

However, the substance of the charge remained a well-kept secret for several days, and neither the Tories nor Sacheverell himself had any real inkling of its content until Parliament reassembled on Monday, 9 January, and John Dolben, after making his formal report from the Committee, laid the articles on the Table. When members were able to peruse them at leisure they found that Sacheverell was to be charged with sedition and subversion, both against the present Establishment and the Protestant Succession, on four grounds. In the first article it was alleged that in his St Paul's sermon he did

> suggest and maintain [*suggestion*, it appeared, rather than assertion, was to be the recurring *motif* of the whole document] that the necessary means used to bring about the said happy Revolution were odious and unjustifiable; that his late Majesty, in his Declaration, disclaimed the least imputation of Resistance; and that to impute Resistance to the said Revolution is to cast black and odious colours upon his late Majesty and the said Revolution.

In the second article the main charge was of suggesting and maintaining that the legal Toleration was 'unreasonable, and the allowance of it unwarrantable', and of aspersing as a 'false brother' anyone who defended 'Toleration and liberty of conscience'. Thirdly, Sacheverell was accused of falsely suggesting and assert-

* For the full indictment, see appendix A, pp. 279–82 below.

ing, with seditious intent, that the Church of England was 'in a condition of great peril and adversity under Her Majesty's administration', and with making the malicious insinuation that those who voted the Church out of danger in December 1705 'were then conspiring the ruin of the Church'. Lastly there was the broad charge that the defendant had in various ways defamed the Queen's administration: by suggesting that it 'tend[ed] to the destruction of the constitution'; that it included 'men of characters and stations . . . who are false brethren', undermining the constitution themselves and enabling others to destroy it; and that the Queen and all in authority under her were guilty of 'a general maladministration'. Combined with this accusation was a general charge of sedition: that Sacheverell 'as a publick incendiary' had stirred up the Queen's subjects 'to arms and violence'. And the fact that the Doctor had mangled a number of Old Testament texts, most likely through a combination of ignorance and slipshod scholarship,[57] enabled his accusers to add, with relish, that he had perverted Holy Scripture to achieve his ends.

In conclusion, the Committee had declared, on behalf of the Commons, their readiness to prove that 'the said Henry Sacheverell . . . did abuse his holy function, and hath most grievously offended against the peace of her Majesty, her crown and dignity, the rights and liberties of the subject, the laws and statutes of this Kingdom and the prosperity and good government of the same'; they prayed that he 'may be put to answer to all and every the premises'; and they called for 'such proceeding, examination, trial, judgment, and *exemplary punishment*' as was consonant with law and justice.

Members had been streaming steadily into London during the past few days, among them Robert Harley who had arrived from Herefordshire *via* Oxford on the 6th or 7th; so that when the Commons came to give its final consideration to the articles on the 11th there were almost 370 present, a vast increase in attendance since before Christmas. It was soon apparent that in the past three weeks the Tories had been reinforced in morale as well as in numbers. In recapitulating the Committee's handiwork, the Clerk had read only as far as the end of the preamble when an opposition member rose to move that the report be recommitted. From then until dusk fell and candles were brought in, the Commons were locked in the longest and most heated of all their debates on the Sacheverell affair. Harley spoke first, and at length, for the motion: Bromley, Annesley and Ward all distinguished themselves in support. They dealt not merely with the preamble but with the very general nature of the articles, criticising their 'looseness' and demanding that the House be told on which specific passages they were grounded. Boyle, Smith, Lechmere and Thompson replied, rhapsodising on 'Revolution principles' but declining, for tactical reasons, to be drawn into particulars.

But it was Harley's speech which aroused most interest. In discussing the preamble he was sharp and effective, 'and in particular . . . insisted on leaving out the word *seditious*, alleging a fatal precedent in the reign of King Charles I in the prosecution of Prynne, Bastwick and Burton'. Sedition, he said, 'was no law word'. He hoped the House 'would take care to preserve the honour and dignity of impeachments'. He then, however, went on to state his own position on the issues raised by the sermon and the impeachment; and at once he slipped into his most elusive and equivocal vein. As Cunningham relates, Harley condemned pulpit licence in general and described the St Paul's sermon as 'a circumgyration of incoherent words without any regular order'; but when he had finished 'the members observed that Mr Harley had in his speech made use of such a circumgyration of incoherent words as he himself had before condemned in Sacheverell, so that the House could not certainly discover from his expressions whether he spake for him or against him'. The truth was that Harley, the ex-Presbyterian who had always favoured limited Toleration, could never condone clerical excesses: but, with his eye firmly fixed on the overthrow of the administration, he had to be poised tactically to take advantage of the forces which the anti-clerical extremism of the Whigs now threatened to unleash. At this very juncture, he was preparing to exploit an event of yet unsuspected importance, the death of Lord Essex, to make his first bid since his fall, two years earlier, to recover his initiative at Court.* But a flexible tactical position in Parliament was important to him too.

The outcome of this particular day did not much concern him. The gale of Whiggery was still blowing too strongly to be resisted in the Commons, as he well knew. That the Tories would lose their

* See pp. 113–16 below for the crisis over the Essex regiment.

motion for recommitment by 232 votes to 131; that the articles would then be approved; and that they would be carried to the Lords next day by Dolben – all this was now unavoidable. What concerned Harley was what happened from now on. If it should turn out that the Whigs had sown the wind only to reap the whirlwind, and if not merely the Whig supremacy but all those moderate political values to which Harley himself was committed should prove to be threatened by that whirlwind, then he must somehow contrive to ride it.[58]

V THE DIE CAST
12 JANUARY TO 26 FEBRUARY 1710

Since John Dolben had first appeared before them on 15 December the peers had been little more than interested spectators of the Sacheverell case. They had, to be sure, set up an Impeachment Committee under Wharton's chairmanship, which had made a leisurely investigation before Christmas into the procedures followed in a chain of seventeenth-century cases from Bacon to Somers.[1] But their real work did not begin until Thursday morning, 12 January, when Dolben made his second visit to their Bar, carrying the engrossed articles. As soon as these had been read and Dolben and his numerous escort had departed, the Lord Chancellor instructed one of Black Rod's deputies, David Davis, to locate Dr Sacheverell and take him out of the custody of Mr Serjeant Wibergh. This he did so swiftly that Sacheverell was whisked away from Peters Street without paying his fees for a month's confinement. By midday he was a prisoner of the House of Lords.[2]

A number of notables, absent in December, had taken their seats since the Recess: Newcastle, Devonshire and Somerset of the Cabinet; Lord Chamberlain Kent ('the Bug'); Archbishop Sharp of York and the bishops of Durham and Salisbury. Even the duke of Leeds, who, as Danby, had been impeached himself more than thirty years before, had come up from Yorkshire – no mean feat in January for a man of nearly eighty – prepared to fight his last fight for the Church of England. Although their numbers would almost double again before the end of February, the peers' chamber was nevertheless quite comfortably filled[3] when Sir David Mitchell, Gentleman Usher of the Black Rod, conducted the Doctor for the first time to their Lordships' Bar.

After first kneeling, then standing – at Cowper's direction – to hear the charge read over, the prisoner 'was asked by the Lord Chancellor [the clerk records] "what he had to say for himself?" ' Sacheverell, as always, had plenty to say for himself. He made four requests: first, for a copy of the articles; secondly, for sufficient time to prepare his Answer to the charges; thirdly, for permission to employ counsel to conduct his defence; and fourthly, for bail. The first and third requests were granted at once. After brief discussion of the second, he was ordered to 'put in his Answer . . . in writing on Wednesday, 18 January, at 11 o'clock', which the Tories thought 'very hard, considering the charge is all general'. Bail, the prisoner was told, could not be granted until it was properly applied for, by written petition.[4]

The petition duly followed next morning, presented by Lord Rochester. In it, Sacheverell pleaded flimsily that the month he had spent in custody had been 'to the great prejudice of his health', and with more justice, that for all that time he had been kept 'wholly ignorant of the proceedings preparing against him'. To stand bail for him he proposed his Vice-Chancellor, Dr Lancaster, and Dr Richard Bowes, Fellow of All Souls. One wonders with how much genuine enthusiasm that 'old smooth-boots', Lancaster, had offered himself. As Hearne's nickname suggests, he was notoriously pliant, reluctant to offend those in power whatever their party, and he was particularly obsequious to the duke of Marlborough. It seems that he was doing what he felt the honour of the University required of him, rather than carrying a torch for Sacheverell or for the Highflying cause.[5] The Lords were not concerned with his enthusiasm, however; only with whether, 'all debts paid', he and Bowes were worth £3,000, the sum for which each of Sacheverell's sureties would be liable if he absconded. When Wharton's committee had satisfied itself on this score the Doctor was released on bail on Saturday morning, his own recognisance being fixed at £6,000.[6] The news was round London by nightfall, and next day the Whigs had a sobering preview of the measure of popular excitement which the case had aroused. So dense were the crowds which converged on St Saviour's in the expectation that the Doctor would preach there, that it was said 'the parishioners could not get near their seats, till a stratagem of reporting that Dr Sacheverell preached at Newington carried the mob thither'.[7]

In fact it was Richard Welton, the Jacobite rector of White-chapel, who filled the bill at St Saviour's this Sunday.* Sacheverell, not surprisingly, was busy with his Answer. He was also consulting at his new lodgings in the Temple with his conclave of clerical counsellors, among whom Francis Atterbury was now believed to be the key figure, and with some of his legal advisers. The learned counsel he had so far enlisted, subject to the Lords' approval, were of the highest calibre. It had been no secret ever since Christmas that Sir Simon Harcourt, the former Attorney-General who had resigned from the ministry along with Harley and Henry St John in February 1708, had agreed 'to govern the cause'; and Sacheverell must have counted it a stroke of the greatest good fortune that one of the most sought-after advocates of his day – who had also, in Arthur Onslow's opinion, 'the greatest skill and power of speech of any man I ever knew in a public assembly'[8] – had been turned out of the present House of Commons by the Whigs in the scandalous Abingdon election decision, and was therefore not only free but eager to act against the Commons' own Managers. Two other lawyers whom Sacheverell had provisionally retained[9] had no such political axes to grind: indeed Serjeant John Pratt was a decided Whig, and Robert Raymond reputedly a very mild one. They were both, however, outstanding barristers. Raymond became Solicitor-General in the next ministry, and both he and Pratt were to preside over the King's Bench under the Hanoverians. Sacheverell's most recent capture was Constantine Phipps, whose performance in this trial was to earn for him the Lord Chancellorship of Ireland.

The most acute political minds among Sacheverell's advisers, Atterbury's and Harcourt's, must certainly have appreciated by mid-January that time was of the essence both to his cause and their party's. The longer the trial could be postponed, and the longer thereafter it could be spun out, the more likely did it seem that the powerful currents of opinion already discernible would become a spate. It was far from certain that this would disturb the normal pattern of voting in the House of Lords sufficiently to lead

---

* See p. 45 above. Welton was one of the most controversial of all the London divines, who caused a scandal four years later by having a portrait of White Kennett painted on his Whitechapel altarpiece in the role of Judas. See the article on him in *D.N.B.*; G. V. Bennett, *White Kennett*, pp. 127-31; and p. 274 below.

to the Doctor's acquittal: but at this stage it seemed the only hope. Immediately after the weekend, therefore, Sacheverell submitted a second petition to the Lords, seeking further time to put in his Answer to the articles, as they were 'very long, general and uncertain . . . and were drawn by the Committee of the Honourable House of Commons with such secrecy' that he had no knowledge of them until the 12th. He could not have chosen a more fortunate time for his purposes. For on the 15th the duke of Marlborough had gone dramatically out of town to Windsor Lodge, absenting himself from the Cabinet and threatening resignation after a dispute with the Queen. His action at once plunged Court and ministry into a ferment, putting all else for some days out of mind. In such an atmosphere the House of Lords was content on 17 January to accept Sacheverell's plea that it was 'utterly impossible' for him to meet the deadline, and to allow him a further week, until Wednesday, the 25th. In so doing, however, it was taking, almost absentmindedly (as Burnet recognised), one of several crucial steps which 'concurred to delay the proceedings' and play into the hands of the High Church Tories.[10]

The Lords also agreed on the 17th to the four counsel Sacheverell had retained. By the end of this week, however, two of them had had second thoughts and parted company with their client. The occasion, if not the whole cause, of the rupture was the Answer to the articles. Pratt and Raymond favoured a short answer, as non-committal as possible, leaving counsel the maximum field for manoeuvre during the trial. Sacheverell was more intent on causing a stir. He insisted on dealing with every point, many at inordinate length, and would make no concessions of any kind: and unfortunately for his counsel, when the Doctor took his draft for vetting to Archbishop Sharp, the latter refused point blank to look at it.[11]

Its very first words were captious and disrespectful: 'The said Henry Sacheverell saving to himself all advantage of exception to the said articles for the generality, uncertainty and insufficiency thereof'. On the point of Resistance he was totally unrepentant, averring 'the illegality of Resistance on any pretence whatsoever to be the doctrine of the Church of England, and to have been the general opinion of the most orthodox and able divines from the time of the Reformation to this day'. It was a doctrine 'taught in that university whereof he hath been for more than twenty years a member'; and 'often with public approbation of each House of Parliament preached and printed, and in terms of greater force than any used by the said Henry Sacheverell'.

But if this doctrine be declared erroneous, and it should please God that he should suffer for asserting it, he trusts that God will enable him to show his steady belief of this doctrine by a meek and patient resignation to whatever shall befall him on that account.

On the Toleration he was equally inflexible, acknowledging that an Act of 'Exemption' had passed in 1689, which he had explicitly accepted in his St Paul's sermon, but affirming 'that upon the most diligent enquiry he has not been able to inform himself that a Toleration hath been granted by law'. In the same vein he wrote on for page after page, sometimes shrewdly, sometimes provocatively; pausing before refuting the 'several charges of a very high and criminal nature' in the fourth article to

observe with comfort that . . . in this 4th article he is not accused of maintaining or asserting, but barely of suggesting what is therein contained; and he humbly hopes that bare suggestions or insinuations, could they with any colour or probability be made out, as he is fully satisfied they cannot, will not under the most mild and gracious government . . . be adjudged sufficient to involve an English subject in the guilt and punishment of high crimes and misdemeanours.[12]

Sacheverell was reported to be astonished when Pratt and Raymond sent their servants to him on 21 January to return their fees and 'excuse themselves from further serving him'.[13] But it is clear that not even the value of the brief could reconcile either to an Answer so incautious, 'without either submission or common respect', and so constraining to counsel. (What Harcourt thought about it we can only speculate; he had to balance political against legal considerations, but both he and his auxiliaries often found it an embarrassing incubus during the trial.) Also, by the 21st the further question of publicity had arisen. Neither Pratt nor Raymond can have approved of the flagrant intention of the Doctor and his Tory cabal to use the extension granted by the Lords to appeal

to opinion 'without doors' by publicising their case in advance.
There were a number of emotive passages in the Answer which had
been penned with this in mind, as for instance:

> Hard is the lot of the ministers of the Gospel, if when they
> cite the Word of God in their general exhortations to piety and
> virtue, or in their reproofs of men's transgressions . . . the several
> texts and passages by them cited shall be said to have been by
> them meant of particular persons and things, and shall be con-
> strued in the most criminal sense, and be made by such con-
> struction one ground of an impeachment.

Such titbits as this were not intended only for the Lords. The
Doctor had finished his Answer well before the 25th. As the author
of the pamphlet *High Church Display'd* took note, it 'was first
handed about in manuscript, then printed privately, and at last sold
publicly to incense the people and prepossess them in his favour,
before there were any proceedings upon it. The Parliament took no
notice of this, though certainly they might have done it to the
Doctor's disadvantage'.[14]

The delivery of the Answer shortly before one o'clock on the
25th was a propaganda exercise in its own right. An anonymous
broadsheet which appeared soon afterwards describes the scene
vividly.[15]

> An hour before Dr Sacheverell made his appearance in the
> Court of Requests . . . hardly was any person there. But presently,
> upon his appearance, the said Court . . . was filled with clergy-
> men, gentlemen, and several officers in new scarlet clothes,
> adorned with gold loops and buttons, and a vast number of men
> of no mean rank soon filled up the place.

Waiting for his summons, the Doctor held court like a great
minister at his *levée*. Then he was gone – for an age, it seemed. The
reason lay in the bulky roll he carried under his arm, eighteen
'presses' or sheets of parchment stitched together[16] which took the
Clerk three-quarters of an hour to read through. At the end the
Lord Chancellor asked the author if he had anything to add.
Coolly, defiantly, Sacheverell answered, 'I will abide by my
Answer'; he signed it and left the chamber. As he re-entered the
Court of Requests a greater crowd than ever surged round him, and

he departed for the Temple like a conquering hero. 'The people gave three great huzzas, as many in Westminster Hall, as many in the New Palace Yard. Then the Doctor took coach, and 50 or 60 coaches followed after the Doctor's'.[17]

Belatedly the government peers were themselves becoming conscious of the time factor and realising that it was not on their side. They sent down the Doctor's monstrous manuscript at once to the Commons, instructing their messengers to request its return '*with convenient speed*'.[18] But the Commons had a long day's business before them, and they put off the reading of the epic until the morrow, following this order with a fierce Whig resolution 'that such members of this House who do absent themselves without the leave of this House are to be reputed deserters of their trust and neglecters of that duty they owe to this House and their country'. On the 26th they referred the Answer to the Articles Committee for consideration and report, giving them leave 'to meet at such times and places as they shall think fit'.[19] The 26th was a Thursday. The Committee met at Jekyll's house the next day, but adjourned without decision. Despite fresh evidence of anxiety in the Lords on the 28th,[20] the weekend and the first part of the following week slipped by. Eventually it was not till the Thursday, 2 February, that Dolben was able to make his report from the Committee. Why this was so remains a baffling mystery, unless there were sharp differences of opinion on tactics which took several sessions to resolve; for the 'Replication' was neither long nor detailed, and the very terms in which it was couched demonstrated that a majority of the Committee's members were now just as conscious of the need for speed as their noble friends. There were many things in the Doctor's Answer, Dolben explained, which were 'foreign to the charge of the Commons, unbecoming a person impeached, and plainly designed to reflect upon the honour of the House of Commons in this proceeding; for which they might demand your Lordships' most immediate justice'.

But the Commons being sensible that the nature of the crimes whereof he stands impeached, and the necessity of bringing him to a speedy and exemplary punishment, require that all occasions of delay should be avoided; and not doubting that your Lordships will, in due time, vindicate the honour of the Commons and the justice of their proceedings, the Commons do aver their charge against the said Henry Sacheverell . . . to be true.

They would be ready to prove that charge 'at such convenient time as shall be appointed for that purpose'. When the Whigs moved that the Committee's short paper should be accepted as the Replication of the whole House, Opposition spokesmen fought it, on the ground that it merely asserted the Answer's inadequacy without demonstrating it. But their thrusts were coolly sidestepped by men who knew by now that they would be required to manage the impeachment when the trial began and were not willing to uncover their armoury or to squander ammunition unnecessarily. They certainly did not need to do so to convince the current House of Commons, for the Replication was easily approved by 182 votes to 88, and on the 3rd it was duly sent up to the Lords along with the Answer.[21]

In the course of the Sacheverell affair there are two days, February the 3rd and 4th 1710, which can be seen with hindsight as the fulcra on which the fate of a Parliament and of a government were finely and crucially balanced. Stress has been laid already on the fact that the impeachment of Henry Sacheverell was not from the start an act of suicidal folly. The point is so generally misunderstood that it deserves to be reiterated. The Court and Whig ministers of Queen Anne in December 1709, and the Whig members of Parliament who were their eager collaborators, were no Gadarene swine rushing blindly to their own destruction. The ministers took a considered and calculated decision on the basis of certain assumptions. By the beginning of February things had not gone entirely to plan: some ten days of valuable time had been needlessly lost; the ferocity of the High Church backlash and the level of public interest in the case and of sympathy for the accused had surprised almost every Whig; an unexpected crisis at Court had, as we shall see, caused some alarm. But for all that, the situation remained under reasonable control when Dolben took his message back to the Lords on 3 February. The government's parliamentary majorities remained adamantine. The resolution of its supporters had been if anything stiffened by the defiant tone of Sacheverell's

Answer. The Queen's support was not yet seriously doubted. There was still an even prospect that a swift trial, held without further delay, and above all conducted as the strictly parliamentary occasion which had been all along envisaged, would yield the condign, deterrent punishment which was the prime declared aim of the prosecution. Once that had been effected the alarm and anger of the clergy could be expected gradually to subside; likewise, and more rapidly, the excitement of the public; and not merely the ministry but the whole Revolution Settlement and the Protestant Succession would be on a firmer footing than before.

Nothing happened on the 3rd to weaken this prospect: rather the contrary. Impatient at the latest delay, the Whig peers went briskly about their part of the business. The House was moved 'to appoint a time for the trial of Dr Sacheverell *at the Bar of this House*'.[22] Godolphin and the Junto lords had already agreed privately on the date and time to be proposed – Thursday, 9 February, six days hence, at 11 a.m.; and the seventy-nine peers present were persuaded without difficulty to accept this proposal. Facilities were to be provided for the Commons' Managers; otherwise no special provisions were envisaged beyond the usual space at the Bar, where a few score members could stand, and the limited accommodation in the Strangers' Gallery. There were points of punctilio involved in this procedure which had caused trouble between the two Houses in the past. But three weeks earlier Arthur Annesley had warned his High Tory friends to hope for nothing on this score: the Whigs, he believed, were 'resolved that no difference on that account shall put off the impeachment's prosecution'.[23]

Disastrously for the Whig leaders, they seem never to have anticipated that a trial at the Bar might *in itself* prove unacceptable to the Commons. Had they foreseen trouble on 4 February, the Country Whig independents whose support was necessary to guarantee the administration its majority in the Lower House would undoubtedly have been canvassed. As it was, the Junto's normally efficient organisation was found wanting: too many Whig backbenchers still had an imperfect grasp of the party's priorities when William Bromley on this fateful Saturday morning made the unexpected move that was to transform the entire situation. It had been concerted between the High Tory chiefs and the Harleyites, and the presence of the biggest Tory attendance of the whole session argues a serious effort to alert the Country Tories. One quite fortuitous circumstance played into the hands of the Tory 'whips'[24] and at the same time left the ministry far more vulnerable than it would otherwise have been. The Third Reading of an important Place bill, a measure which proposed strictly to limit the number of office-holders entitled to sit in the Commons, and which was just the issue to bring country members of both parties flocking to the House,[25] had been fixed for this same day, 4 February. It was a coincidence which did much to determine the outcome of the trial of Dr Sacheverell.

When the Lords' message reached the Commons the first step taken was formally to confirm the members of the Articles Committee as Managers of the impeachment. There were almost 380 members in the chamber when Bromley got up to propose that the Commons should attend Sacheverell's trial *as a Committee of the Whole House*, and that the Lords should therefore be asked to abandon their plans for a trial at their Bar. His case and that of his supporting cast was on the surface an attractive one. Only if the trial was in a large public place could all the members then in town be present. And since, by normal impeachment procedure, the Commons would be required in the end to vote whether or not they would demand judgment on the prisoner, every member, it was argued, had a right and a duty to hear all the arguments. Precedents were cited in support which seemed convincing.

The government spokesmen fought hard to parry this sudden thrust in a debate that lasted for several hours; but their opponents' case, Burnet wrote, 'took so with all the young unthinking members that it could not be withstood', although (he added later) 'the effects it would have were well foreseen'. The Whig leaders were caught in a trap: for on the floor of the House they dared not openly use the two most telling party arguments for rejecting a full-scale public trial. They could not admit that popular feeling was against the prosecution and that time was therefore precious, nor that with opinion running against them they had now far less reason than the Tories to welcome maximum publicity. Bromley and his friends could not own their real motives either – least of all the hope of embroiling the two Houses in a dispute in which the impeachment might founder – but this mattered less. The division at the end of the debate was extremely close, with only 12 votes separating the two sides; and it is plain that at least forty, more likely nearer fifty, Country Whigs must have stayed in their places to vote with the Tories and swell their numbers to 192. It was enough to carry the day.[26]

For the ministerial Whigs there was no option now but to cut their losses. They would not entertain dropping the trial (which is said to have been Godolphin's first reaction to the news of the Commons' vote).[27] But at least they would deny the Tories the satisfaction of seeing an unwholesome squabble develop between the two Houses. When the peers reassembled after the weekend, they had been well briefed. With scarcely a murmur raised in dissent, the Lords bowed as gracefully as they could to the Commons' wishes and despatched the chief Household officers to request the Queen to set in train the preparation of Westminster Hall for a full-dress occasion. On the 8th Sir Christopher Wren, Surveyor-General of the Queen's Works, attended them to make his report and to receive their Lordships' instructions. The die was cast.

The critical setback which the ministry suffered in the Commons on 4 February was the more unsettling because in the past few weeks its position at Court had suffered an equally surprising shock. The first tremors had been felt within a few days of Harley's return to London early in January. Ever since his resignation in 1708 he had been scrupulous in staying away from the back stairs which gave access to Anne's private apartments at St James's or Kensington. Down to the autumn of 1709 he had occasionally offered the Queen unofficial advice; but this had been sparingly tendered by ciphered letters, sent to his intermediary Mrs Abigail Masham, the Queen's dresser and Harley's kinswoman – for she, as all England knew, had supplanted the imperious Sarah, duchess of Marlborough, the First Lady of the Bedchamber, as the Queen's favourite.[28] With the coming of a new year, however, and one in which economic hardship and war-weariness,* as well as the unrest of the Anglican Church, threatened to undermine the administration in public esteem, he had judged the time ripe for renewing his personal contact with the Queen. No sooner had he done so – immediately after his arrival in Town[29] – than a Whig nobleman,

* See p. 177 below.

I

Lord Essex, had fallen critically ill, with a fever popularly supposed to have been 'contracted . . . by hard drinking of bad wine'. Essex held two posts: he was Constable of the Tower and also colonel of a regiment of dragoons. By the time he died on 10 January Harley had a contingency plan prepared for putting the ministry's command of the royal closet to its first serious test.

He had long sought to persuade the Queen that the power and pride of the Marlboroughs was threatening her constitutional authority; and he knew that her confidence in the duke had been shaken by his rash request for a life grant of his supreme command of the army. Harley now managed to persuade her – somehow putting steel into that timorous nature – that the death of Essex was her opportunity to re-assert the royal prerogative of making military appointments. On the 11th Marlborough was flabbergasted to find that, without consulting him, the Queen had already earmarked both Essex's offices: the Tower for Earl Rivers, a malcontent Whig now in league with Harley, and (what seemed a studied insult) the coveted regiment of dragoons for Abigail's brother, Jack Hill – for a junior colonel of infantry, in fact, instead of one of Marlborough's favoured circle of Whig general officers.[30] After two chilling interviews with his sovereign, the duke had retired to Windsor in dudgeon on 15 January, and there, under his wife's abrasive influence, had at once been persuaded to make this incident the touchstone of his whole position in the State, calling on his colleagues to support him in giving Anne a blunt choice between Abigail's removal from Court and his own immediate resignation. His stand was not primarily over the Essex regiment, but (as his secretary, Cardonnel, explained) over 'whether Mrs Masham and her party should have the disposal of all vacancies in the army, and by degrees of everything else'.[31]

The ten-day crisis which followed Marlborough's departure is one that is little known and has never been fully told in all its intriguing detail, which is strange in view of its obvious bearing on the destruction of the Godolphin ministry by Harley later in the year.[32] Indirectly, it affected the outcome of the Sacheverell trial in three ways. The government's failure to make a united front with Marlborough in the stand he took damaged its morale and credibility; Tory confidence received a wholly unexpected boost; and Harley succeeded in exploiting the crisis to persuade other Whig dissidents besides Rivers that an alternative regime was possible in a matter of months, if they would throw in their lot with him. All these factors brought Sacheverell decisive votes, or cost his prosecutors decisive votes, at the final reckoning. There is, for instance, little doubt that Marlborough's disgust at the pusillanimous attitude of most of his colleagues towards his ultimatum to the Queen* powerfully influenced his decision to depart precipitately for the Continent a week or so before the trial opened. With many of his Whig colleagues it was a far from popular decision; but they were willing to support it 'to give a new lustre to him after the cloud he has been under', since the official explanation was his indispensability to the Queen in view of the new peace negotiations being mooted between France and the Dutch. For Marlborough, however, this was little more than a convenient excuse.[33] His absence cost not only his own vote in the Lords but that of the duke of Northumberland, over whom he had great influence, and possibly those of several other Court Tories; and these were to prove vital votes. Of the desertions of the malcontent Whigs in the Sacheverell divisions we shall have more to say later. But the most immediate and dramatic effect of the Regiment crisis was its revivifying influence on the spirits of those Tories from whom the prospect of Court favour seemed to have receded for good. Shortly after Marlborough's withdrawal to Windsor his most zealous supporters among the Whigs began to talk openly of resolving the crisis by securing a Commons' Address to the Queen calling for Abigail's removal. The repercussions of this bold scheme – which was never in fact implemented – were thus described to Lady Nottingham:

> This Address . . . gained so much belief even with her Majesty that 'tis said she sent for several persons of both Houses in her service, declared with great spirit and courage against it and that she should take it as an indignity to herself. . . . And thereupon very great numbers of lords and others have daily attended her Majesty to assure her of their detesting any such proceeding: the Scotch to a man, the duke of Leeds, Ormonde, Beaufort, Rochester, etc. And the Queen took it extremely kind.

* Only Sunderland, and to a lesser degree Wharton and Devonshire, gave him firm support.

... Lord President [Somers], Lord Chancellor [Cowper] and many others did the like. So that observers say they never saw such a turn in their lives.

Even when the Regiment crisis itself had been resolved by compromise, the Whigs could not easily forget the encouragement it had given to the veteran High Tories, 'several of whom were now observed running to Court with faces full of business and satisfaction, as if they were going to get the government into their hands', or 'the access so many new faces have had to the Queen on this occasion'.[34]

In the three weeks which preceded the start of Sacheverell's trial, many Tories naturally managed to persuade themselves that the Queen's demonstration of independence during the Regiment crisis could be taken as a token of her favour towards the Doctor's cause. It is a commonplace of the history books that popular opinion in London was quite convinced of this favour by the time the trial opened, and mob enthusiasm was unquestionably stimulated by this belief. Yet almost all the evidence we have until the trial is well under way suggests that Tory rumour and popular conviction were equally misinformed. Queen Anne had always distrusted and disliked the warmer spirits among the High Church clergy. When Burnet arrived in London after the Christmas recess and had an audience with the Queen, she made no bones about telling him that Sacheverell's 'was a bad sermon and that he deserved well to be punished for it'. Even after the first day of the trial, when she had sampled for herself the excitability of the mob,* her opinion of the sermon and the need to punish the preacher remained unchanged: though her fears for public order, she admitted to her physician, had persuaded her that a mild sentence was desirable. Several pointed gestures during the opening week of the trial – her dining with Halifax of the Junto during her first day in Westminster Hall, or her order to Bishop Compton to dismiss a clergyman named Palmer for offering prayers for Sacheverell in the Chapel Royal – were far more reliable indicators of her true sentiments than the whispers of the Tory rumour-mongers.[35] But they came too late to quench the bush fires of High Church emotion, which spread more alarmingly than ever during that further period

* See pp. 133–4 below.

of frustrating delay for the Whigs while the court was being prepared for a full state occasion.

Once the Commons had decided in favour of a public trial it became clear in a matter of days that even the great medieval carcase of Westminster Hall was not large enough to accommodate more than a fraction of those who were anxious to be present. No trial since 1649 had roused such interest. When Wren was first pressed by the Lords to estimate how long the preparations would take, and urged 'to make what haste he could', he could not promise that the Hall would be ready in less than a fortnight. That he failed to achieve even this was not his fault. By the 10th he had fifty workmen employed day and night on the construction of the special stands (the shopkeepers' stalls against the walls, which catered for suitors and habitués of the law-courts, had already been cleared out, to the disgruntlement and ultimate financial hardship of the vendors).[36] But twice at least he was forced to make quite drastic modifications of his original seating arrangements. By the 14th the bulk of the scaffolding had already been erected, and ministers were already beginning to think of an opening early in the following week; but alas, on the 15th, when Wren appeared before the Lords to make another progress report, he was showered with complaints. Why was there not sufficient seating to allow every peer to introduce up to eight relatives and friends, if he so wished? How were all the ladies who were importuning them for places possibly to be gratified?

> He informed the Lords that the House of Commons took up a whole side, and there was some other place Lord Treasurer had ordered to be left unbuilt, which would save the Queen £300; which was not thought fit to be saved by the Lords, and they gave him orders to make as much room as ever had been usual. Then he told them plainly that the Queen was positive she would have nobody over her head, which made the House laugh coming so pat to what had so lately been the discourse of the Town.

Wren was therefore ordered to create as many additional seats as possible on the peers' and visitors' sides without taking down any of the scaffolds already erected.[37]

His troubles were not over, however. On the 20th the House of Commons, at the instance of some members who suspected the peers of squeezing them out, appointed a committee of thirty-two under Thomas Onslow to inspect the accommodation prepared for Managers and other members. To their intense annoyance they found seating for only 327 members, seventy too few places for the number now in town. Their voluble complaints set the carpenters hastily to work again, and by the 23rd a somewhat mollified Onslow was able to report back that there was now accommodation for 400 M.Ps, in addition to the special stand for the Managers. With this, and an order forbidding any encroachment on their preserves, the Commons rested more or less content.[38]

While this feverish work was in progress, at an estimated cost to the government of almost £3,000,[39] the representation of both sides was being finalised. Sacheverell was hard pressed to replace Pratt and Raymond. It was 13 February before his solicitor, John Huggins, was in a position to complete his team of advocates, and then only with three surprising names: Samuel Dodd, 'an ancient practiser' of the court of Exchequer, mainly known as a commercial lawyer;[40] Duncan Dee, the Common Serjeant of London, a somewhat anonymous figure; and a civil lawyer from Christ Church, Dr Humphrey Henchman, possibly engaged through the good offices of Atterbury. Meanwhile the Commons added four more to their own already formidable squadron of Managers to bring the number up to twenty. Two of them, the witty Harry Mordaunt (an intimate of Wharton) and the distinguished Scottish lawyer, Sir David Dalrymple, never acted: they both fell ill on the eve of the trial. But the others were the two commoners whom the Tories feared and respected above all – Robert Walpole, recently appointed Treasurer of the Navy, and Lieutenant-General James Stanhope, who had been on the way home from his command in Spain at the time the impeachment was introduced, but had since committed himself to it heart and soul.

Having heard Wren's third report on 18 February, the Lords felt able to set a firm date for the opening of the trial. It was to be Monday, the 27th. The atmosphere of London in those frenetic days was something that would be remembered for years. The anniversary of 30 January had been marked by an outburst of pulpit hysteria surpassing anything the capital had experienced

since Charles II's reign, and it set the tone for the sustained in-
doctrination, over the next four weeks, of every London congregation with a High Church parson. A few of the more reckless divines
seemed bent on sharing Sacheverell's martyrdom, especially the
fiery Luke Milbourne, who at his parish church of St Ethelburga
commemorated the judicial murder of Charles I with a Non-
Resistance sermon so offensively blatant that its printing 'in this
critical conjuncture', Hearne was told, 'provoked the Whigs almost
to an outrage'. On the same day Nathaniel Whalley, Fellow of
Wadham, had preached a sermon in Oxford calling on every
minister who was resolved to be true to his calling 'to take up his
cross'. The insertion of public prayers in services 'for the deliverance of a brother under persecution' became so widespread that the
Rector of St Mary Aldermary was affronted in the aisle of his
own church for refusing to follow the fashion; and on the last
Sunday before the trial the minister of St Bride's and several of his
brethren abandoned circumlocution and prayed for Sacheverell by
name.[41]

The women of London, especially, were subjected to other
pressures. Since his release on bail Sacheverell had found time,
among all his other concerns, to sit for the young portrait-painter,
Thomas Gibson; and Andrew Johnson's copy of the painting,
'curiously performed in Mezzotinto', became the model for the
thousands of prints on sale in London by the second half of
February, not only the originals (priced at 1s 3d) but various
counterfeits: they did much to increase 'concern both for the
Church and the afflicted assertor of its rights' among 'the fair and
tender-hearted sex'.[42] The author of *The Officers' Address to the
Ladies*, one of the few Sacheverell pamphleteers to prefer polished
wit to party polemics, would have us believe that ladies of rank (and
for that matter housemaids) were far from being the only converts
and captives.

No love now is to be made without religion and the Doctor.
When we accost our kind shees in the Park, we are whispered,
'are you for the Doctor?'. 'God bless the Doctor', says the
stroller in the Strand, who never prayed for herself in her life.
And for the great ornament and benefit of religion, the Doctor's
name is a ticket which admits you into the best favours of all the

Phyllises in Drury Lane. Strange! how the women love a High-
Flyer.

The booksellers, like the parsons, had no reason to complain at the
postponement of the trial. New pamphlets cascaded off the presses
almost daily. From many of the titles which appeared in February[43]
it was plain that the pamphleteers had now no doubt as to what the
great issues of the trial would be: Obedience, Resistance, the very
legality of the 'late Happy Revolution' and of the present 'Establishment'. In this furious central controversy over Resistance
Anglican Tory propagandists appealed to the past with particular
relish. But the Whigs too drew pertinent lessons from history: most
effectively with *The Proceedings of the Lords and Commons in the
year 1628 against Roger Mainwaring, Doctor in Divinity (the
Sacheverell of those days)*. At a crucial point of the trial, when the
whole prosecution seemed momentarily in danger of collapsing, it
was the precedent of Mainwaring's case which was to prove the
instrument of rescue.

The great majority of those who read and listened to, and argued
over, the outpourings of pulpit and press, had no hope of hearing
the trial itself. For those who had, the last few days before the 27th
were occupied in an undignified scramble for tickets. The absence
in Lincolnshire of the Lord Great Chamberlain, the marquess of
Lindsey, whose responsibility it was to organise State occasions,
permitted enterprising peers to indulge in a ticket racket more akin
to the ritual of a modern Cup Final than to the decorum normally
associated with the Upper House. On the 23rd the House decided
that seven tickets each should be issued, *on personal application*, to
any member '*who will personally appear at the trial*'. But with 'all
the ladies . . . making advances to the lords to get tickets from them
to see and be seen at the trial', a variety of ploys were made use
of to evade the vital provisos and open up the ticket market.*

* The fact that the distribution was in the hands of the Lord Great Chamberlain's
servants in itself encouraged abuses. The House was then cajoled into opening
up a most inviting avenue for sharp practice and collusion by agreeing to a motion
that 'if any lord desires tickets for another lord, they are to be delivered if two
lords do say, "such lord, they believe [*sic*], will personally appear at the trial" ';
and to make certain this gate would not be closed, it proceeded to defeat the sober
proposal 'that every lord who hath tickets do sign and seal such tickets'. One of
Lindsey's kinsmen even complained of 'an attempt to contract my lord's own box
into a narrow compass'.

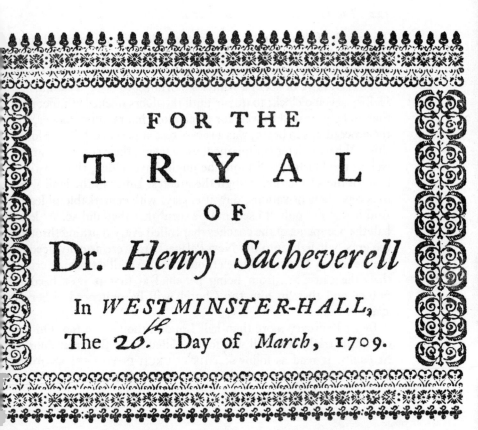

FOR THE

TRYAL

OF

Dr. *Henry Sacheverell*

In *WESTMINSTER-HALL,*

The 20.*th* Day of *March*, 1709.

Ticket of admission to Westminster Hall, 1710, dated 20 March 1709 (Old Style)

The result of this anarchy was foreseeable. When the trial began the scramble for seats among ticket-holders every day was as desperate as the previous competition for tickets had been.[44]

To rise at five or six of a winter's morning; to be at Westminster Hall by seven o'clock; to queue until the doors opened at nine; and then to be prepared to wait for three more hours, often longer, for the proceedings to begin, was a severe test of party zeal. Their lordships, Wharton later complained, were trying their constitutions as well as the Doctor: still more, he might have added, the constitutions of the spectators, though the greatest ladies in the land were to accept their privations, day after day, with remarkable phlegm. And it was not only 'to see and be seen' that they did so. At least half the occupants of the coaches that rolled every morning through the grey half-light into the New Palace Yard were as convinced as the Reverend Maurice Wheeler, once Sacheverell's scathing critic, that 'the cause . . . from being personal at first is now become public' and that 'in him the Church will be sentenced either to stand or fall'.

By 27 February more than half London thought so too. On the eve of the trial a handbill was found nailed on to the great door of St Paul's. It read as follows: THIS CHURCH IS TO LET; ENQUIRE AT THE COMMONS' HOUSE AND YOU MAY KNOW FURTHER.[45]

VI THE CASE FOR THE PROSECUTION

The Commons' House by a quarter past nine on the morning of Monday, 27 February, was, like every other part of Westminster Palace and its environs, a scene of thronged excitement, of babble and of some confusion. Though a private bill was being read for the second time, few present paid any heed to it. Members were streaming in all the time, some to join the chattering groups on the benches, others to cram the gangways or cluster about the Bar. Expectancy and tension were heightened as the Serjeant-at-Arms left the chamber to inspect the low passages connecting St Stephen's Chapel with Westminster Hall; he was making sure that the Constables of Westminster had performed one of their allotted duties, to keep the way clear of loiterers so that four hundred members of his Honourable House could pass through without being incommoded or molested. When he returned, something like quiet fell for the first time since prayers as the Clerk called over the names of the Whig Managers, and one by one* they left to take the places set aside for them in the Hall, in a special enclosure to the left of the Bar facing the throne.

Now came the moment for Speaker Onslow to leave the Chair, as the House resolved itself into a Committee of the Whole for the first of many times while the trial lasted. It had been thought that the Speaker would head the procession out of the Chamber; but instead he bowed to a last-minute motion and made his way to the passage-way below the 'short seats' at the lower end of the House, where by standing up he was best placed to ensure that the solemn, orderly procedure laid down for the exit of members did not degenerate into an unseemly rush. Slowly the Clerk, standing at the

* The lawyers among them were gownless, by an earlier order of the House.

Table and reading from the Return Book, called out every member's name, proceeding in alphabetical order of counties; and in this order they left in pairs. The Scots, much to their annoyance, were relegated to the end, even after the Welsh. But John Aislabie[1] laughed off their protests that Aberdeenshire should have been called first by assuring them that when one of their own countrymen was impeached they should have the precedency with pleasure![2]

Before ten o'clock the last of the Commons had packed on to one or other of the nine terraced benches, each more than 80 feet long, which had been raised on scaffolding down part of the length of the court, on the right of the throne; and Onslow, entering last of all, had taken his own reserved seat in the middle of the front row. While they waited for the peers to robe and come down they had time to take stock of an extraordinary scene. For all the gaunt exterior of Westminster Hall – resembling in Defoe's eyes 'nothing so much as a great barn of three hundred feet long', rising above an uneven huddle of roofs[3] – the inside, under the Gothic grandeur of its massive roof, was a fittingly impressive theatre in which to play out with due ceremonial one of the great political set-pieces of British history. Looking down from the back row of the Commons' benches, high up and quite close to the wall, one could see clearly how in the carpeted centre area of the Hall Wren had created a court very similar in layout to the House of Lords itself: at the upper end of the Hall, the throne, which was to remain vacant throughout the proceedings; immediately below the throne, the Woolsack for the Lord Chancellor, and the two other woolsacks, set at right-angles, for the twelve judges; then the clerks' table. Below that, in the very heart of the court and facing the Bar, were the benches on which the peers were to sit, strictly according to rank, with two benches for the bishops running along their right-hand side, and therefore directly below the centre of the Commons' enclosure.

There, however, the similarity to the Lords' chamber ended. Wren had created not just a court but an amphitheatre. For one thing, above and behind the throne was a platform, and on either side under a canopy was a sizable box. That nearest to the Commons was set apart for the Queen, whose chair could be discreetly curtained off, and for her ladies of the bed chamber: at present it was occupied, in solitary state, by the First Lady, the duchess of Marlborough. That on the farther side of the throne was reserved for the maids of honour. Between the Commons' stand and the royal box was a small enclosure providing twenty-four seats for foreign diplomats. Facing the Commons, across the other side of the court, was a stand which was the exact counterpart of their own.

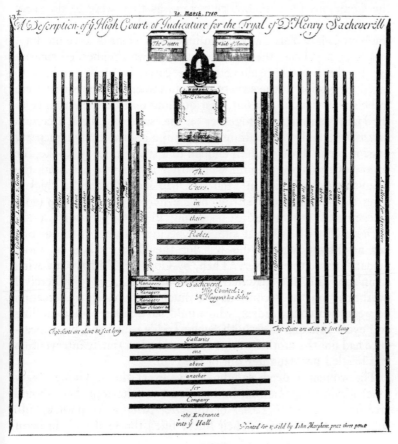

A Description of the High Court of Judicature for the Tryal of Dr Henry Sacheverell, 1710

This and a slightly smaller stand raised at the lower end of the Hall, well below the Bar, provided some eight hundred seats for holders of the Lord Great Chamberlain's tickets. Finally, there were shallow galleries running high along each of the two long walls of the Hall, and designed for ordinary spectators paying from three to five guineas for entrance (though in practice they had to take an overflow of ticket-holders). It was thus possible for about two thousand people in all to hear the trial.*

Every available stand and gallery seat had been taken well before the Commons filed in. Before 7 a.m., as they were to do every morning of the trial, the coaches and chairs had begun to arrive in the New Palace Yard, where contingents of Guards were on duty, and after disgorging their occupants had been shepherded smartly out by the constables along a route carefully predetermined to avoid congestion in the streets.[4] The innumerable hours that were to be spent, day in, day out, first queuing outside the entrance to the Hall, then crowded together on the 'scaffolds', bred a certain *cameraderie* and good humour among the audience, though party passion broke through often enough to disrupt it. Lady Rooke, the widow of the Tory admiral who earlier in the war had sunk the Spanish treasure ships in Vigo Bay, had kindly offered a chicken wing to the gentleman sitting beside her on the first day (cold chicken was the favourite sustaining diet of spectators at the Sacheverell trial), when it suddenly occurred to her to enquire of her neighbour whether he was for the Doctor. 'No, by God, madam', came the answer. 'Then, by God, sir, I'll have my wing again', she said, and snatched it out of his hands. Sir John Percival overheard, on the second day, a much more violent altercation between two young ladies, who would have fallen to hair-pulling and eye-scratching over both Sacheverell's cause and his appearance had not the mother of one of them made a timely intervention and bustled her daughter out of the Hall.[5]

The women, indeed, caught the eye everywhere. Though 'very much afraid lest somewhat in their dress or behaviour there should give occasion to the *Tatler* or the *Observator* to turn them into ridicule in their papers', their finery filled the Hall with brilliant

---

* See *A Description of the High Court of Judicature for the Tryal of Dr Henry Sacheverell* (p. 125). Further information on the interior of the court may be found in detail in the anonymous broadsheet, *The Life, Character and Memorable Actions of Dr Sacheverell* (London, 1710); also in Bonet's despatch of 24 Feb. (D.Z.A. Rep. XI England 35D, f. 122); John Pringle's letter to Sir William Bennett (Ogilvie of Inverquhurity MSS. G.D. 205/4); Sir John Percival's Letter Book (Add. MSS. 47026, p. 9); and A. Cunningham, *History of Great Britain*, ii, 289–90. John Dyer's Newsletter of 11 March and Bonet's despatch of 14 March (loc. cit. f. 92) confirm Percival's estimate that the total capacity of the court, with stands and galleries, was roughly 2,000.

colour. Brisk business in the marriage mart was forecast, as one by-product of the trial; though Ann Clavering, Lady Cowper's vivacious sister, who was up at four every morning for three weeks and never missed a speech, frankly declared herself out of the reckoning as far as the Tories were concerned. Mocked by a High Church lady for being too fiery to get a husband, she proudly declared herself to 'despise all Tories, were their estates never so large; and yet don't despair, for I'm sure the Whigs like me better for being true to my party'. All in all, concluded the writer of *The Officers' Address*, the lover's lot had been complicated, rather than eased, by the trial.

When we dress to court my lady's daughter, the servant is immediately interrogated whether the master be High-Church or Low-Church, and he answers that he does not find that his master goes to church at all. . . . When we describe our restless, waking nights, the fate of amorous eyes, she cries truly, she was up before six as well as we. When we would . . . let her know the thin diet that we lovers are confined to (a kind look being a full meal) she answers that the careless servant put up a nasty black-legged chicken into the napkin, which obliged her to fast the last day of the trial.[6]

Humour, colour, passion, wit, oratory, a clash of arguments to satisfy the keenest intellect; and now and then, sudden drama or searching emotion: Westminster Hall held all these to reward the stamina of every spectator of Dr Sacheverell's trial. One ten-year old boy, unique in having the two most famous grandfathers in the land, had the time of his life. Soon afterwards he was to pen this careful little letter.

Dear, dear Grandpapa, I should have thought it a very great scandal in me to have let Doctor Hare go without sending a letter by him. I wish that there was to be Peace because then there would be no more battles, but if it please God to prolong the wars, may he prosper the arms of her Majesty and protect you. May you ever be fortunate, as at Blenheim, Ramillies, etc. I have been at Doctor Sacheverell's trial every day and am against him.

Your dutiful grandson,
William Godolphin.[7]

The trial's opening on 27 February produced ferment outside, as well as inside, the Hall and the Palace precincts. At nine o'clock a coach of ostentatious and bizarre design drew up outside Henry Sacheverell's lodgings in the Temple. It belonged to young William Newland, a wealthy student of the Inner Temple and eldest son of a Smithfield scrivener, Sir George Newland, who was sitting in this Parliament for the family borough of Gatton.* From Sacheverell's viewpoint Newland's 'tawdry chariot' had one admirable advantage over more sober conveyances: it was constructed very largely of glass, which rendered its occupants startlingly visible to the throng which had already gathered to cheer him to his Calvary. Compared with what London was to experience in the next two or three days the first mob of the trial was vociferous rather than ugly. It was not even particularly large. Some 400 people raucously flanked the cavalcade of eight gentlemen's coaches – Newland's in third position, Harcourt's and Dodd's, among others, behind – which made its way from the Temple to Westminster. Along the route, however, the 'better sort' as well as many more ordinary folk turned out in strength. Exhorted by Newland's hat-waving footmen in their garish yellow-green liveries, most of them raised a cheer, or shouted 'God bless you', 'God send you a happy deliverance', or 'They shall not hurt a hair of your head'. Dozens scrambled for the coins that were tossed out of the leading coaches as the procession rolled along; and 'one Ewen, a carpenter in Blackfriars', with a slip-fielder's eye, congratulated himself on having caught half a crown before it reached the ground.[8]

Despite their slow progress the coaches reached the New Palace Yard well before ten o'clock, the hour fixed by the Lords. As it happened, however, Sacheverell had a long time to wait for his cue. The Lords, contrary to their own orders, had decided to transact business before their adjournment. So it was almost eleven when the head of their solemn procession was first glimpsed from the hall: first the clerks; then the judges; next the peers' eldest sons and peers minor, two by two (they were to sit below the peeresses in the front of the large stand facing the Commons); and then,

---

* The family was staunchly Tory. William sat for Gatton (Surrey) himself, 1710–1738, while his younger brother George was elected a Demy of Sacheverell's college, Magdalen, in 1711. *The History of Parliament: The House of Commons, 1715-1754*, ii, 293.

5 'At Their Lordships' Bar'. Queen Anne in Parliament, *c.* 1710, by Peter Tillemans. This, the first known painting of the interior of the House of Lords, shows how cramped the peers' quarters were, and how few spectators could have witnessed a trial there, either behind the throne or in the new gallery at the window end (not shown)

6a Robert Harley, Prime
Minister, August 1710 to July
1714, attributed to Jonathan
Richardson

6b Sidney, 1st Earl of Godolphin
('Volpone'), Lord High Treasurer,
1702–14, after Sir Godfrey
Kneller

6c ' "A great barn", rising above an uneven huddle of roofs'
Westminster Hall, 1720, from a print in the Crace Collection

behind the Yeoman-Usher of the House and Black Rod, the peers themselves in full ceremonial – 119 of them in all, including fifteen bishops – in strict reverse order of rank and seniority. Bringing up the rear came the Serjeant-at-Arms, bearing the Lords' mace, one of the heralds, and last of all the Lord Chancellor, whose duty it was to preside over 'the Supreme Court of Judicature' which was now to assemble to try Henry Sacheverell.[9]

When the Lords had comfortably disposed themselves on the benches in front of the woolsacks (they, at least, had room to stretch),[10] the Serjeant-at-Arms called for silence and proclaimed

Oyez! Henry Sacheverell, Doctor in Divinity, come forth, save thee and thy bail, or thou forfeitest thy recognisance.

Immaculately gowned, bands crisp and white, and exuding self-confidence, the broad, commanding figure of the prisoner approached the Bar. There he knelt, his five counsel standing at his right hand, and behind them a group of High Church divines, among whom craning spectators could discern the familiar figures of Dean Atterbury, Dean Stanhope and Dr Robert Moss, all three of them chaplains to the Queen. Bidding Sacheverell rise, Cowper opened the proceedings by directing the Clerk to the House to read out to the court three documents: the articles of impeachment, the prisoner's Answer to the articles and the Replication of the Commons. As the Clerk embarked on this marathon* there was an unexpected diversion for the audience: Duchess Sarah left her box and found herself a space to sit at the end of one of the Commons' benches, next to the Managers' stand: a pointed gesture, perhaps, from the *ci-devant* favourite to demonstrate her still-uncompromising Whiggery and her unqualified support for the prosecution; but an embarrassing one for her friends, not least because it encouraged less notable spectators over the next few days to follow her example, with the more straightforward motive of finding a seat, somehow, somewhere, in that grossly overcrowded arena. As a result the Commons, and more especially their Serjeant-at-Arms and the Deputy Clerk, were involved in a ten-day running battle with the public to keep the House's already straitened accommodation clear of 'strangers'.[11]

---

* It occupied more than an hour.

K

When at length the Clerk had finished, the Lord Chancellor for the first time addressed the Managers. 'Gentlemen of the House of Commons, you may proceed with your evidence'. The Managers, however, had decided to leave over until the second and third days of the trial their detailed prosecution of the charge. On this opening day they had deputed their Junto spearhead, Montagu and Lech-mere, to expound the nature of the charge in general and to clarify the reasons for the impeachment. The Commons, the Attorney-General began, were not only concerned to prove the actual mis-demeanours of the prisoner as laid out in the four articles; they intended to demonstrate the defamatory, subversive, seditious motives behind them. The motivation of the Doctor's crime was their justification for proceeding against him by the awesome processes of parliamentary impeachment; and Montagu did not attempt to conceal that it was not Sacheverell alone whom the Commons were bringing to book.

> My Lords . . . when they considered of what import it was to the nation, how much it concerned the very being of our con-stitution, to . . . put an end to such sort of seditious proceedings as the Doctor, and some others of his brethren, have been lately practising in divers parts of the kingdom, they could not think otherwise than that it was a matter fit for the Grand Inquest of the Nation to take notice of.

He reminded the court of the circumstances of the two offending sermons: both delivered on public occasions; both distributed 'with more than ordinary application' after printing; and one the most perverse misuse of a day set aside to thank God for two transcendent acts of Divine deliverance from Popery and tyranny. It was bad enough that on a Fifth of November Dr Sacheverell 'should in a great measure pass by both the businesses of the day and entertain his audience with a long harangue of the deplorable condition the Church was in' – not from her avowed enemies, the Papists, but from 'her pretended friends' and from the dissenters. It was worse still that when the preacher was not ignoring the great work begun on 5 November 1688, he was depicting it in black and odious colours by 'lay[ing] down a general position, *that it is not lawful, upon any pretence whatsoever, to make Resistance to the Supreme Power*'; and this 'Supreme Power', Montagu insisted, 'by other passages, he explains to be the Regal Power'.* The Commons would argue that in maintaining this position, the Doctor had both vilified the late King and cast the most damaging reflections on the present Queen. 'For was there any occasion at that time to be so earnest to cry down Resistance and preach up Passive Obedience? Can anyone pretend to say there were any symptoms of discontent throughout the nation, in any parts thereof?' Of course not. Did it not, therefore, 'savour of some wicked design to be talking so unseasonably of this subject'?[12]

Both the tone and content of the opening speech were relatively restrained. The Whigs looked for more potent stuff from Montagu's adjutant, Nicholas Lechmere. His delivery may not have satisfied the captious, for he 'read without taking his eye off the paper, with graces and gestures peculiar to himself';[13] but what he had to say had cogency and bite. The unknown Tory diarist, whose recently-unearthed comments on the whole trial are so enriching, recorded sourly that 'Mr Lechmere . . . gave himself liberties, both in his expressions and principles, not consistent with that solemn occasion'.[14] In short, he achieved the first objective of a disciple of Lord Wharton's: to get under the skin of his opponents.

Although Lechmere's commission was to explain to the court the general grounds on which all four articles had been framed, his overriding concern was to justify the formulation of the first article. He served notice that the Managers were ready to take up the gage thrown down in recent weeks by High Tory propagandists, and if necessary stake the success of their whole prosecution on Article I, and in particular on vindicating that right of Resistance which was the bedrock of Whig ideology. 'Your Lordships . . . will soon perceive that all parts of the design of the prisoner centre in that'.[15] What is more, recalling the long argument which had gone on in the Articles Committee about the expediency of prosecuting Sacheverell for preaching Non-Resistance, Lechmere seems to have set out to insure against possible backsliding by his colleagues by enunciating at the outset the most extreme Whig position on these issues. Taking it as axiomatic that 'the nature of our constitution is that of a limited monarchy, wherein the supreme power is . . . divided between Queen, Lords and Commons, though the

---

* *Tryal*, p. 27. The defence counsel, and Harcourt in particular, were to reject this crucial deduction. See pp. 182–3, 187 below.

executive power and administration be wholly in the Crown', he argued that

> The terms of such a constitution do not only suppose but express an Original Contract between the Crown and the people, by which that supreme power was (by mutual consent, and not by accident) limited and lodged in more hands than one; and the uniform preservation of such a constitution for so many ages, without any fundamental change, demonstrates to your Lordships the continuance of such a Contract.[16]

This was arresting enough; but for Tory ears worse was to follow. The anonymous diarist bitterly remarked[17] that he 'laid down a new scheme of his own contrivance for our constitution', namely,

> that whenever the executive power . . . intends anything towards the destruction of the other part of the constitution, the Original Contract (included, as he said, in Magna Carta and all our laws and grants) is dissolved, and then 'tis not only lawful for the people to resist but their undoubted duty. The proof of this assertion was that the glorious successes of her Majesty's arms [since the Revolution] are testimonies from Heaven in behalf of this point of Resistance.*

Lechmere made it quite clear, however, that it was not only to vindicate a general theory of Resistance that the Commons had included the first article in the indictment. They were also determined to vindicate a particular rebellion, 'the late happy Revolution', and the memory of the man who had made it possible, 'our Great Deliverer', William III. 'And upon this foundation . . . they doubt not but your Lordships will, in a parliamentary way, fasten a brand of indelible infamy on that enslaving tenet by which it's condemned'.[18]

These, for one of the staunchest of Junto Whigs, were the main objects of the prosecution. But before he ended he had something pertinent to say in justification of the remaining three articles. Article II had been framed not only with the purpose of vindicating

---

* The diarist did Lechmere less than justice in suggesting this was the only 'proof' he cited. For example, he drew attention to successful acts of resistance to tyranny long before 1688, which God had blessed and made the foundations for new regimes – even in pre-Reformation days, when our ancestors were 'muffled up in darkness and superstition'. See *Tryal*, p. 35.

the Toleration but of reasserting the supremacy of the civil over the ecclesiastical power.* Article III, the 'Church in Danger' article, was in the indictment because Sacheverell's allegations on this head showed contempt of Parliament and slandered the Queen. After dealing most briefly of all with the final article, defaming the Queen's ministers, Lechmere closed by begging 'to draw the scene a little closer', and claiming that it was only by supposing a pro-Jacobite and insurrectionary intention behind the various positions in Sacheverell's sermon to which the Commons had objected that they could impart a *rationale* and a unity to the whole. For Lechmere such intentions were inescapably proclaimed the moment a man took up a basic position which, in effect, denied the legality of the Revolution. 'Your Lordships will find that, in his opinion, the duty of absolute Non-Resistance is owing to him only that has the divine commission to govern; and from thence, your Lordships can't fail of knowing against what Queen, what government, what establishment, he encourages the taking up the arms of Resistance'.[19]

After Lechmere it was the Attorney-General again: this time to ask that the dedication to the Derby sermon, and the whole of the St Paul's sermon, along with its dedication, should now be read. The first day's formalities were entering their final lap. The sermon and the two dedications, notes our diarist, 'were now all muttered (or read) over' by the Assistant Clerk to the Commons. The muttering took an hour and a quarter. By then it was close on three o'clock and the Lords adjourned the court and retired to their chamber to proceed with their own business and to await the arrival of the Queen, who was due about four o'clock to give her assent to five public Acts. Anne had not been in her box in the Hall all day. About half-past three she was helped into her sedan at St James's and set off across the park towards Westminster Palace. To her surprise and consternation she found her chair almost engulfed by a great crowd of people. 'God bless your Majesty and the Church', the cry was raised; from others, 'We hope your Majesty

* Referring to the provocative 'anathema' passage of the sermon, in which Sacheverell had defied any earthly power to reverse 'sentences ratified in Heaven' (see p. 69 above and pp. 145–6 below), Lechmere said: 'The Commons crave leave to observe that the independent power or jurisdiction of the Church, or of ecclesiastical judges, is . . . a violation of the Oath of Supremacy, contrary to the principles of the Reformation, and the doctrine and interest of the Church of England'.

is for Doctor Sacheverell'; and here and there, more ominously, there were shouts of 'No Presbyterians!', 'No meetings!' Little wonder Anne looked subdued when she reached the entrance to the Lords, or that she was distinctly nervous when she saw her physician that evening. She would have occasion to be more so before the week was out.[20]

The trial of Dr Sacheverell lasted for three and a half weeks. For the greater part of this time, in Burnet's words, 'all other business was at a stand; for this took up all men's thoughts'.* A breakdown of those twenty-five days shows that six were spent by the Prosecution in presenting its case – the first four days of the trial (27 February to 2 March) and 9–10 March – while a seventh (and blank) day on the 8th was due to an adjournment at the Prosecution's request. The Defence sprawled over five days (3–7 March), including admittedly a Sunday. No fewer than eleven days, counting adjournments and weekends, were then absorbed by the House of Lords in assessing the evidence which had been presented and in coming to a judgment. But the Commons had still to decide whether or not to demand the execution of judgment, in the light of the punishment proposed; and once they had decided, sentence had to be formally pronounced. This accounted for the last two days of the trial, 22–3 March.

There is no simple explanation of why, on top of all the earlier delays, the proceedings themselves were so protracted. The reasons were manifold. The charge was broad-ranging and highly complex. The representation of both sides was prodigal. Mainly to ensure the maximum breadth of support for the impeachment, the Commons named at least half a dozen too many Managers; and since Sacheverell was carrying at least one counsel more than was necessary, the result on some days was unnecessary repetition of argument. Other circumstances conspired to spin out the trial. There was some deliberate procrastination by the Defence, and

* Burnet, v, 440. The extent to which public affairs as a whole, even routine administration, was suspended for the duration of the trial is attested by many hands. The countess of Lindsey, for instance, was told on 28 February that 'men's eyes and minds are wholly turned upon this affair, so that here is a sort of stop to all business'; while the Paymaster-General, James Brydges, complained on 7 March to his agent in Holland, John Drummond, that 'our bills of money are all in the House and had been passed before this time had it not been for the unfortunate trial of Sacheverell'. H.M.C. *Ancaster MSS.* p. 439; Stowe MSS. 57, II, f. 173.

there were also unforeseen adjournments and delays, due either to serious public disorders or the raising of knotty legal or procedural points. Above all, there was the leisurely nature of impeachment procedure itself. The trial timetable reveals that no fewer than five days were directly attributable to two important differences in practice between impeachments and procedure in an ordinary court of law. The convention that the Commons must demand judgment was one. Much more striking was the fact that in trials by impeachment the Prosecution was granted two bites at the cherry: the Commons' Managers had the right to reply at length to the Defence, and were the more determined on this occasion to exercise their right because of the unexpected necessity of answering not only Sacheverell's advocates but the Doctor himself.

The heart of the case for the Prosecution, however, was reached on the second and third days of the trial. It was then that fifteen leading Whigs attempted to make good each of the four articles in turn. On the long second day they spoke to the first two. On the third day they addressed themselves to the rest of the indictment. And it is this case, presented on 28 February and 1 March, that is so often considered the classic exposition of the Whig creed of the eighteenth century.

Tuesday, the 28th was one of the great days of the trial. Interest was focused for much of the day on Article I, to which no fewer than six Managers – including three of the finest speakers in the House – had been allocated; and as to its importance (Sir Joseph Jekyll reiterated at the start of the day's proceedings) 'your Lordships were rightly told yesterday that the whole charge centres in this article'. In addition, four memorable speeches were made this day, those of Jekyll, Stanhope and Walpole to the first article and that of Sir Peter King to the second. The court assembled considerably later than its scheduled time. Queen Anne, dressed in purple and 'wearing a thin hood over her face', arrived promptly at eleven, having been carried in procession in a purple-covered sedan escorted by her halberdiers.[21] But it was long after eleven when the Lords came down;* so that the Queen, who subsequently

---

* Spectators had been diverted while waiting by the removal of the duchess of Marlborough and a group of other ladies from the Commons' enclosure by the Serjeant-at-Arms, brandishing a newly-minted order of the House. Osborn MSS. 21/22: 28 Feb.

left the Hall for a long time to keep a dinner engagement
with Lord Halifax,* heard less of the proceedings than she
expected.

The case for the first article was opened by Sir Joseph Jekyll,
who spoke for about three-quarters of an hour – with fire and conviction, or with unbecoming heat, according to one's party viewpoint. He set himself to prove his case by evidence drawn not from
the Doctor's actual words but from 'what I apprehend to be the
clear sense and meaning of those passages . . . which maintain this
article'. To refer to particular passages of the sermon, he told the
court, was 'a province which is assigned to another gentleman who
will speak after me', Robert Eyre, the Solicitor-General.[22] In the
event Eyre added relatively little to the substance of Jekyll's case.
His distinctive contribution lay in exposing the weakness of
Sacheverell's Answer. With his rational, restrained method,
eschewing invective, he impressed many on his own side, and it
was said by one Tory that 'the Doctor afterwards thanked him for
using him like a gentleman, which only he did'.[23]

Sir John Holland, Comptroller of the Household, who followed
Eyre, made a short, script-bound, but effective speech, in character
noticeably unlike the lawyers' speeches which had preceded it.
Even more unlike them was Robert Walpole's: the speech of a
natural House of Commons man, but also typically Walpolean,
robust, combative, well-honed, spiced here and there with mordant
humour. To the purist it smacked too much of the debating
chamber rather than the law court (though in point of fact, from the
notes which have survived it is plain that it was most painstakingly
prepared).[24] But while Tories might criticise him for abusive language and for 'aiming at turns and wit, but falling wretchedly
short',[25] he gratified his many Whig admirers in both Houses.[26]
They warmed to him as he scored party points with relish, in a way
no previous speaker had attempted. They loved the blunt vigour
with which he cut away the camouflage – 'the rubbage with which
the Doctor has an excellent talent at puzzling common sense' –
behind which the accused had tried to conceal the plain drift of the
words spoken at St Paul's. Most of all Walpole delighted his own
side with the savage wit with which he turned the prisoner's own

* See Add. MSS. 17677DDD. f. 419 and p. 116 above. Generally the Queen took
dinner during the trial in a small ante-room off the Hall provided for her.

words against him. Parker and Stanhope apart, no one lashed Sacheverell with such severity as Walpole:

> My Lords, I hope your just judgment in this case will convince the world that every *seditious, discontented, hot-headed, ungifted, unedifying preacher* (the Doctor will pardon me for borrowing one string of epithets from him, and for once using a little of his own language), who had no hopes of distinguishing himself in the world but by a matchless indiscretion, may not advance with impunity doctrines destructive of the peace and quiet of her Majesty's government.[27]

With Sir John Hawles's quiet, mannerly, academic and rambling discourse, which followed Walpole's, the Commons' case for the first article lost momentum.* But it more than recovered that momentum with James Stanhope, the last of the six Managers to speak to it. Whereas Hawles had ranged discursively, Stanhope, in 'a remarkable speech, full of manly oratory and delivered with spirit and vehemence',[28] concentrated his attack on a limited but vulnerable front, the intentions behind the relevant parts of the St Paul's sermon. These, he claimed, were downright subversive. What Lechmere had hinted, Stanhope asserted: that 'this Non-Resistance of his was due only to a Prince on the other side of the water'. The speech had ingenuity and learning;† such biting contempt for the accused that the Doctor's composure was visibly shaken and his high colour drained away; and a flow of words the more remarkable because Stanhope spoke with no more than a few notes to guide him. Except for John Smith he was the only Manager to dispense with a prepared script. Perhaps the handsomest of many tributes he earned came from a fellow soldier, General Ross – a true-blue Tory. 'If ever any man was inspired,' he said afterwards, 'Stanhope was'.[29]

One thing which all six speakers had in common was a conscious-

---

* Hawles made too many concessions to endear himself to the partisans on his own side, above all when he gratuitously reminded the Lords that they could not impose a stiffer sentence than the nature of the crime allowed, and added that if they thought fit to lighten it, the Commons would 'acquiesce in and be well satisfied with the same' (*Tryal*, p. 104). These words were to mock him later.

† Atterbury, standing with Smalridge and Moss behind the Bar, must have been nonplussed to hear this cultivated soldier deftly quoting the dean's own Latin sermon *Concio ad Clerum*, in defence of a limitation on the obligation of total obedience to the ruler.

ness of the basic importance of the Resistance issue to the whole
Prosecution case and to the whole trial. Sir John Holland, however,
impressed it most vividly on his audience by putting it in direct
personal terms.

> My Lords, the present consideration is of the greatest im-
> portance; no less than whether so many of your Lordships and
> the Commons of Great Britain who took up arms at the Revolu-
> tion, and were then thought patriots of your country, were
> really rebels; whether our late Deliverer was an usurper; and
> whether the Protestant Succession is legal and valid. All these
> considerations depend upon the lawfulness of the Resistance at
> the Revolution.[30]

Of the three questions, the majority of the Managers preferred to
concentrate on the dangerous *future* implications for Britain of the
recent revival of Non-Resistance teaching and preaching, which as
Eyre said had made such striking progress since the Jacobite
attempt of 1708.[31] Jekyll, Walpole and Stanhope all harped on the
same theme: since sermons and pamphlets devoted to such a topic
could not conceivably have any current relevance under a well-
loved Queen, they must be designed to fulfil a definite future
purpose – in the Pretender's interest. Sacheverell, claimed Stanhope, had given the game away at St Paul's in everything that
followed his references to the Revolution:

> Had the Doctor, my Lords, in the remaining part of his
> sermon . . . shown how happy we are under her Majesty's ad-
> ministration, and exhorted obedience to it, he had never been
> called to answer a charge at your Lordships' Bar. But the tenor
> of all his subsequent discourse is one continual invective against
> the government. Passive Obedience is set down as an indispen-
> sable duty. But 'tis evident by the whole sermon that it is not due
> to Queen Anne or her administration.[32]

'Upon the present question, therefore,' Jekyll had concluded,
'depend our present happiness and future hopes'.[33] But while he
and his colleagues were perfectly agreed on the need to repudiate
the doctrine of Non-Resistance and vindicate both the Revolution
and the Protestant Succession, they were less unanimous (as Lech-

mere had forseen they would be) about how best to make their case, and how far they ought to take it. Both Jekyll and Eyre, for instance, virtually dissociated themselves from Lechmere's sweeping assertions of the previous day by cautiously emphasising that they were not concerned to argue the case for justifiable Resistance in general, but merely the legality of that particular Resistance used in bringing about the 1688 Revolution.[34] Holland went a little further by offering the touchstone of *necessity*: 'the Commons would not be understood as if they were pleading for a licentious Resistance; as if subjects were left to their good will and pleasure when they are to obey and when to resist. . . . But yet they maintain that that Resistance at the Revolution, which was so necessary, was lawful and just *from that necessity*'.[35] Closer to Lechmere, but still aware of the depth of the water, was Walpole.

> I am very sensible, my Lords, of the difficulty and nicety that attends the speaking to this point, and that whilst a loyal subject . . . of the best of Queens is speaking in defence of the necessary and commendable Resistance used at the Revolution, his arguments may be misconstrued and misrepresented, as maintaining antimonarchical schemes. But surely, my Lords, to plead for Resistance, that Resistance, I mean, which alone can be concerned in this debate, is to assert and maintain the very being of our present government and constitution; and to assert Non-Resistance, in that boundless and unlimited sense in which Doctor Sacheverell presumes to assert it, is to sap and undermine the very foundations of our government . . .

Yet, unlike Lechmere, Walpole evoked no 'Contract theory' to justify Resistance, which 'ought never to be thought of but when an utter subversion of the laws of the realm threaten the whole frame of a constitution, and no redress can otherwise be hoped for'.[36]

Boldest and least inhibited of the six was Stanhope. Of his predecessors, only Jekyll had laid down in constitutional terms (as Lechmere had) the circumstances in which Resistance was justifiable, avoiding the controversial word 'Contract', but arguing that all authority rested on law, that law drew 'its being and its efficacy' from *consent*, and that if people were deprived of laws without their consent they had a right to recover them from those who had dispossessed them. But Stanhope went further than this, further in some ways than Lechmere, whose Contract theories he projected on to an international, rather than a purely English, plane.

> I believe one may . . . venture to say that there is not at this day subsisting any nation or government in the world whose first original [i.e. origin] did not receive its foundation either from Resistance or Compact. And as to our purpose, it is equal if the latter be admitted. For wherever Compact is admitted, there must be admitted likewise a right to defend the rights accruing by such Compact.[37]

The odd man out was Sir John Hawles. He alone conceded that there was a Supreme Power in the State to which absolute obedience was always owed. 'But perhaps', said he with nice irony, 'the Doctor and I differ in the persons in whom the Supreme Power is lodged, for the Doctor has not mentioned that matter, either in his sermon or in his Answer to the articles. . . . I'll tell him in whom I think it is lodged,' he went on (and at this moment gave Harcourt, sitting on the prisoner's right, the very cue he was, three days later, so eagerly to follow up). 'I think it is lodged in the Queen's Majesty and the Lords Spiritual and Temporal and Commons in Parliament assembled'.[38]

In his Answer Sacheverell had maintained that Resistance was inconsistent both with the law of the land and the teachings of the Church, and all the Managers were prepared to take issue with him either on one or both of these grounds. On the point of legality Eyre advanced an argument of great subtlety. How could it ever be supposed that laws were made to authorise a despotic power to destroy the laws themselves? Or that they warranted the subversion of that very constitution which they were designed to establish and protect?[39] Stanhope, for his part, had more to say about the attitude of the Church, for he knew that this was bound to be one ground on which the Doctor's counsel would choose to stand, and he hoped to undermine it beforehand. What was important, he stressed, was not 'the opinions of some particular divines, or even the doctrine generally preached in some particular reigns'. It was 'sufficient for us to know what the *practice* of the Church of England has been when it found itself oppressed'. Holland followed the same tack, dwelling particularly on the circumstances of 1688, when 'the true distinguishing characteristic of a Church of England man . . . was wishing that Resistance good luck, and rejoicing at its success'.[40]

However, the charge in Article I could not be sustained simply by proving that a right of Resistance did exist and was justifiably exercised at the Revolution. The charge, we recall, made two specific allegations which needed to be substantiated. Sacheverell had been accused of suggesting and maintaining 'that his late Majesty in his Declaration disclaimed the least imputation of Resistance, and that to impute Resistance to the Revolution is to cast black and odious colours upon his late Majesty and the said Revolution'. All the Managers assumed that the relevant words in the St Paul's sermon could bear no other construction,* and confined themselves to matters of fact. In Jekyll's view, to deny the fact of Resistance in 1688, as Sacheverell had done, was to deny 'a fact as clear as the sun at noonday'. Walpole not only shared the same sentiments but used precisely the same metaphor, and Holland wondered what other word than Resistance could describe the taking up of arms in many counties and 'the desertion of a Prince's own troops to an invading Prince and turning their arms against their sovereign'.[41] Moreover, Jekyll found in the very Declaration of the Prince of Orange which Sacheverell had cited phrases which spoke eloquently of William's intention to resist.†

Given this intention, and the indisputable facts of armed rebellion from within, the libel on the late King seemed palpable. 'He hath charged the Prince of Orange [said Hawles] with an act of the

---

* The full passage in the sermon reads: 'Our adversaries think they effectually stop our mouths, and have us sure and unanswerable on this point [of Resistance], when they urge the Revolution of this day [5 November] in their defence. But certainly they are the greatest enemies of that, and his late Majesty, and the most ungrateful for the deliverance, who endeavour to cast such black and odious colours upon both.

How often must they be told that the King himself solemnly disclaimed the least imputation of Resistance in his Declaration; and that the Parliament declared that they set the crown on his head upon no other title but that of the vacancy of the throne? And did they not unanimously condemn to the flames (as it justly deserved) that infamous libel that would have pleaded the title of Conquest, by which Resistance was supposed?'

† He referred especially to the passage 'wherein his Majesty takes notice that he carried a force with him sufficient, by the blessing of God, to defend him from the violence of evil counsellors, and that he designed that expedition to oblige King James to call a free Parliament'; and also that in which William referred to those subjects of James who had invited him to undertake this expedition and then assisted him in it.

highest treachery, in pretending peace when he actually made war'.[42]

The Prosecution had one more objective at this stage: to use the case for Article I to pillory the Tories as a whole, by exposing the inconsistency between their party philosophy and their current practice. Nothing served better for this purpose than the old issues of Obedience and Resistance, and no two Whigs in the Commons were better equipped to exploit Tory embarrassment than Walpole and Stanhope. Walpole mocked those who 'to recommend themselves to the Queen . . . condemn that Revolution without which she had never been Queen'; who 'to testify their zeal and affection for the Protestant succession . . . invalidate all the laws that have been made for securing that blessing to posterity'. But nothing in the course of the whole trial was more devastating than Stanhope's attack on those many Tories whom he wickedly dubbed 'the Nonjuring Jurors':

> My Lords, if these *Puritans* [the Nonjurors] . . . would confine themselves to their own conventicles, to get money from a few deluded women, it may perhaps be consistent with the indulgence of the mildest of governments to suffer them to enjoy the benefit of that Toleration which is allowed to Protestant Dissenters. . . . But [and here Stanhope brilliantly hoisted the Doctor with the petard of his own language] when they shall come and vent their treasons abroad; when they shall occasionally conform, and take the oaths to the government in order the better to destroy it; when they shall abjure the Pretended Prince of Wales, but not forget him; when they shall invade the pulpits of the true Church of England . . . venting sedition against the best of Queens; it is high time for your Lordships to animadvert upon it, for the honour of those glorious princes who are dead, for the honour of her Majesty, who so happily rules over us, and for the peace and tranquillity of all her subjects.[43]

By the time the Commons had concluded their case on the first article it was already well into the afternoon. At this point came an unexpected manoeuvre for position between the Doctor's counsel, in collusion with a group of Tory peers, and the Managers. The counsel had hopes that they might be allowed to make their defence on Article I before the remaining articles were aired. Why, is not entirely clear: for in the event they benefited from the fact that the edge of Jekyll's, Walpole's and Stanhope's arguments had been blunted by the passage of time and their supercession by a complex of other arguments, differently orientated. But at this stage counsel were possibly more influenced by the fear that they might lose the services of their star, Harcourt, before they were able to open their case at all; for on the 22nd he had been elected *in absentia* at a by-election for Cardiganshire, and although the Tory sheriff had delayed the election itself for a week, and had since contrived to delay the return of the writ, from the moment that return was officially received in London Sir Simon would be disqualified as a member of Parliament from serving his client.

Whatever the motives, the result was the first of several strange hiatuses in the trial. It happened in a curious way, the Lords retiring to their own chamber on a motion of the duke of Buckingham, when London's gifted Recorder, Sir Peter King, was already two minutes into his opening speech on Article II. A short discussion, and a division in which the High Tory peers were swamped by 72 votes to 45, decided the question in favour of the Managers, who were duly authorised by the Lord Chancellor, when the court reassembled, to 'proceed in the method you were in'.[44]

It took rather less than an hour and a half for the three Managers concerned with the second article – King, Lord William Powlet and Spencer Cowper – to present their case. But it was King, speaking for almost an hour of this time, who totally dominated the closing stages of this day. When he sat down, after dissecting the relevant parts of both the sermon and Sacheverell's Answer with clinical care, there was very little left for his two colleagues to do, except dot the i's and cross the t's of what King had said, something which on Cowper's part was elegantly done, but in Powlet's case was almost laughably bungled.

It was very short, and the word heterodox proved something too hard for him,[45] and he was pleased to make use of pathick instead of passive. Nothing could atone for what he said but his shortness, and that he might have a better title to our approbation on that score, he skipped two pages; though 'tis said the connection he happened upon by this mistake was Heterodox Church.[46]

Nothing, however, could erase the impression left by King's performance: measured, restrained, but of the highest intellectual calibre, his was a speech even the most grudging Tory had to admire.

With this part of the indictment the Prosecution had a two-fold task. It had to make good the general charge against Sacheverell, of suggesting and maintaining 'that the . . . Toleration granted by law is unreasonable, and the allowance of it unwarrantable'; and it had to substantiate the series of more specific allegations against him in Article II, each of them stemming in some way from the general charge. In addressing themselves to the general charge the Managers wasted relatively little time justifying the Toleration itself. They preferred to take its great benefits, in the interests of humanity and of national unity, as axiomatic. Nor did they see any reason to apologise for it to the Anglican clergy. King considered the Act of 1689 a monument 'to the glory of the Church of England', not to its decline.[47] More to the point than justifying the Toleration was to make the charge itself stick. And to do this the Managers had to deal at some length with the specious defence predictably attempted by Sacheverell in his Answer, namely, that the Commons had misunderstood his use of terms: that by 'Toleration' or 'liberty of conscience' he had meant 'a universal toleration' and 'a universal freedom of conscience'; and also that he regarded the 1689 Act, which he claimed to approve, as having conferred at most an *indulgence*, to 'truly scrupulous consciences', or even simply an *exemption*, from the penalties of persecuting laws, so that 'upon the most diligent enquiry he had not been able to inform himself that a Toleration hath been granted by law'. King thought it

> almost difficult to be serious in giving a reply to that part of his Answer. . . . 'Tis true the word Toleration is not mentioned in that Act [neither, as both he and Powlet pointed out was the word 'Indulgence'] . . . but everybody knows that the Exemption granted by that Act is commonly called the Toleration, and the Act itself, the Toleration Act.[48]

Neither he nor his colleagues had the slightest difficulty in demonstrating that the term 'the Toleration', meaning the exemptions granted by the 1689 Act, had long since passed into public usage – in Speeches from the Throne, in parliamentary conferences, in the

7a Counsel for the Defence Sir
Simon Harcourt, as Lord
Chancellor, 1713–14, engraved by
J. Simon, after Sir Godfrey Kneller

7b Leading Prosecutor Sir Thomas
Parker, created Lord Chief Justice
in March 1710, by Thomas
Murray, engraved by J. Simon

7c President of the High Court
of Judicature: William, Lord
Cowper, Lord Chancellor, c. 1710,
by or after Jonathan Richardson

7d Leading Prosecutor Robert
Walpole, as Secretary-at-War,
1708–9, by Charles Jervas

7e Leading Prosecutor James
Stanhope, by J. Van Diest

8a Daniel Burgess preaching to his congregation in the Carey Street meeting-house. A Tory cartoon

8b The sacking of Burgess's meeting-house, 1710. The figure of Dammaree, in the livery of the Queen's water-men, is in the left foreground

law courts.[49] They were further able to show that Sacheverell himself had used the term in his St Paul's sermon on several occasions
when it was quite patent that he understood by it exactly what
everyone else did. For instance, after deploring the spread of
atheism, Deism and Socinianism he had added, 'the Toleration was
never intended to indulge and cherish such monsters and vipers in
our bosom'. 'What was it possible for the Doctor to mean in that
place', King quietly enquired, 'but the Indulgence, as he calls it,
granted to dissenters by the Act of 1 William and Mary?' It was,
Cowper suggested, 'a distinction without a difference' which the
Doctor had manufactured.[50]

Having discounted Sacheverell's juggling with terms, it only
remained for the Managers to show that he had 'visibly and
plainly' condemned the Toleration. This was left entirely to the
ingenuity of Peter King; and there was one particularly damaging
sentence in the sermon which he brought out for display. Enlarging
on the villainy of the latitudinarian false brethren within the
Church since the Revolution,* Sacheverell had declared: 'what
could not be gained by Comprehension and Toleration must be
brought about by Moderation and Occasional Conformity; that is,
what they could not do by open violence, they will not fail by
secret treachery to accomplish'. 'Is not this calling the Toleration
an open violence to the Church?' King asked the court; 'that it was
an attempt made to destroy the Church, though the Church itself
came into and settled this Toleration?'[51]

Of the more specific charges in the second part of Article II, it
was the last which mainly occupied the prosecutors and which most
keenly interested their Whig audience, since it opened up the
whole sensitive area of dispute between the Erastian and High Tory
concepts of the Church – State relationship.† Sacheverell was
accused of asserting 'that it is the duty of superior pastors to
thunder out their ecclesiastical anathemas against persons entitled
to the benefit of the Toleration', and of insolently defying 'any
power on earth to reverse such sentences'. On this point Sir Peter
King was able to make devastating play with one of those gratuitous passages in Sacheverell's Answer in which he had recklessly
overplayed his hand, and dovetail it with the relevant words of the
sermon.

* See p. 67 above.   † See p. 33 above.

L

In his Answer[52] Sacheverell had insisted that

> some sentences pronounced by the pastors of the Church are ratified in Heaven; and that some persons exempted from punishment by the particular laws of the land may yet by the laws of Christ be justly liable to such sentence; and that schism, or a causeless separation from [the] Church . . . is a sin, which exposes the persons guilty thereof to the censures of the Church.

In the light of these admissions King reinterpreted for the court the notorious 'anathema' passage in the St Paul's sermon.

> Now what is this but to say, the dissenters causelessly separate from the Church . . . [and] though the law of the land doth exempt them from punishment for this schism, yet for this sin they are exposed to the censures of the Church; those censures, when inflicted, are ratified in Heaven; therefore notwithstanding the law of the land hath given them this exemption, let the ecclesiastical superiors do their duty in thundering out their anathemas against them

– in defiance of any secular authority. The Doctor, he concluded, had not only incited the Church's own hierarchy to undermine the legal Toleration, guaranteed by Parliament and the Crown, but had by implication repudiated the royal supremacy over the Church.[53]

When the third day of the trial opened on 1 March the case against Sacheverell on Article III (the 'Church in Danger' article) took up relatively little of the court's time.* Its management was left principally to William Thompson, who had assistance of questionable value from two junior ministers, Spencer Compton and Lord Coningsby, and from the initiator of the impeachment, John Dolben. 'Lord Coningsby', wrote the anonymous diarist, 'spoke so indifferently, and seemed to have taken so little pains, that some of his friends† said, he spoke like one that expected a change of affairs'.[54] The contributions of Compton and Dolben were both vitiated by an excess of passion and invective. Compton, who at

---

* In the official printed account of the trial it occupies only thirteen octavo pages, compared with twenty-four on Article II and forty-one on Article I.
† In the margin he wrote 'Sir R. T.' – probably Sir Richard Temple.

times 'trembled in every joint and almost foamed at the mouth', so far forgot himself at one stage as to refer to 'the *criminal* at your Lordships' Bar'.[55] Dolben went further. To him Sacheverell was more than a factious, seditious, Jacobitical clergyman; he was the incarnation of Evil, 'an agent despatched from that dark cabal whose emissaries appear in all shapes, and almost in all places'. Even the Whigs winced when, half way through his speech, he abandoned his own article and launched into his personal, quasi-Republican justification of the trial.* Thompson was the least-known political figure of the four – he had entered the Commons as recently as 1709 as M.P. for Ipswich – but he had a clear, methodical lawyer's mind, a refreshingly direct approach and a professional adeptness at marshalling evidence, and he alone concentrated on substantiating the charges by close attention to the Doctor's words. His speech enhanced his reputation and did all that was really necessary on this article.

Not that the Prosecution's task at this stage was unduly exacting (Coningsby ingenuously admitted that he had been given the easiest article to speak to!). The Managers had to prove that in defiance of the votes and resolutions of the two Houses of Parliament, Sacheverell had asserted that the Church of England was 'in a condition of great peril and adversity under her Majesty's administration', and had insinuated that the Members of Parliament who passed these resolutions 'were themselves conspiring the ruin of the Church which they voted to be out of danger'. Even Coningsby had the wit to appreciate that 'the sermon preached by the Doctor at St Paul's . . . from the first word in the title page to the last line in the conclusion, is one false, malicious and seditious assertion that the Church of England was . . . in the utmost peril and danger'.[56] Nor was it any problem for Thompson and Compton to find passages which clearly suggested that the Church's most treacherous foes were to be found within its own gates. The one

---

* Dolben saw it as 'an occasion, in the most public and authentic manner, to avow the principles and justify the means upon which the present government and the Protestant succession are founded and established'; and while there was no need (he handsomely conceded) to teach the present Queen these lessons, 'we hope [he said] the record of this proceeding will remain a lasting monument to deter a successor that may inherit her crowns, but not her virtues, from attempting to invade the laws or the people's rights' (*Tryal*, p. 149). A still worse indiscretion was to follow, as we shall see.

thing that had to be done with some care was to demolish the
Doctor's claim in his Answer, that the votes of 1705 – 'that whoever shall go about to suggest and insinuate that the Church is in
danger under her Majesty's administration is an enemy to the
Queen, the Church and the Kingdom' – had no relevance to the
situation in 1709. Thompson argued that the very words 'whoever
shall go about' implied '[*at*] *any time* during the continuance of her
Majesty's reign', and Dolben that the royal proclamation to which
the resolutions gave rise had never been revoked.[57] A more important commission for the Managers was to use their case to make
a public defence of the Church policy of Whig administrations,
Whig Parliaments and Whig bishops. Here Thompson was at his
most effective, contrasting the facts of the Church's condition in
the present reign and under the present government with the
'seditious murmurs' of the Highflying clergy.

> Is there any invasion or attempt upon the liturgy, even the
> least ceremony of the Church, or any part of the ecclesiastical
> constitution ? Are her revenues impaired or any of her temporal
> rights violated ? No, my Lords. But our royal sovereign has dis-
> tinguished her care for this Church in a more peculiar manner
> than any of her predecessors.[58]

The end of the Prosecution case on Article III was a remarkable
one, producing something near uproar and a protracted break in
the proceedings. John Dolben concluded his speech by envisaging
what would be the country's fate if the Doctor and his like escaped
their due punishment. Anticipating the termination of twenty
years of war, bringing to all Europe its hard-earned fruits, he
declaimed: 'yet we, only we, must be rendered uncapable of the
common blessing, betrayed at home to a perpetual condition of
bondage by such false brethren as are at your Lordships' Bar'.[59]
There was a gasp in the court, then a burst of laughter as Sir
Simon Harcourt was seen making a very low bow in Dolben's
direction. But the Tory peer, Lord Haversham, was not amused.
Immediately he moved that the court should adjourn. Back
in his own chamber, Haversham explained 'that one of the
Managers against the impeachment, having dropped an expression
reflecting upon the counsel who were assigned by [the Lords], he
thought for their own dignity the gentleman ought to be called

upon to explain himself'. For two solid hours this matter was debated (the Queen meanwhile retired for refreshment to her private dining-room). Some hot Tories demanded that Dolben be committed to the Tower for a calculated insult. Wharton, on the other hand, tried to dismiss the whole thing as a slip of the tongue: after all, even Lord Haversham had perpetrated one in referring to the Managers *against* the impeachment (quite deliberate, retorted Haversham – from what he had heard, most Managers were doing their utmost to make the impeachment fail!). Others claimed that it was the clergymen standing behind Sacheverell, not the counsel, at which Dolben had pointed when he was uttering his closing words (and indeed, it is more than likely that Dolben meant the clergy by his innuendo). But even that was bad enough; and in any case the element of ambiguity strengthened the case for requiring an explanation.[60] Westminster Hall was agog when the peers came in again and Cowper called on the member for Liskeard to explain himself. Dolben now committed a far bigger *gaffe* than his previous one, which had at least been deliberate (as he himself admitted later). As a representative of the Commons he should not have offered any explanation without the formal leave of his own House, for to do so was to concede an important point between the two Houses, not only in this but in future impeachments. To the dismay of his friends, however, Dolben lost his head. Our diarist observed that he 'rose, and repeating "my Lords" twice, after a considerable pause, and in a great deal of confusion, said: "I only meant the Prisoner at the Bar";[61] which explanation, though flat nonsense and a lie, was admitted'. He had wriggled off the hook; but it was thought by many when he died suddenly in the early summer, that the humiliation of having lost caste so badly in a chamber where two and a half months earlier he had been a hero had contributed to his end.[62]

Because of the long intermission the Prosecution was not able to open its case on the final article until mid-afternoon. The Managers had long since arranged that the major speech to Article IV should be made by Sir Thomas Parker, Serjeant-at-Law and, by a nice coincidence, one of the members for Derby. In support were to be the Secretary of State, Henry Boyle; the Chancellor of the Exchequer, John Smith; and Nicholas Lechmere. The Whigs had pinned great hopes on Parker, but for several days he had been very much indisposed, and when he got to his feet at the end of the Dolben fracas it seemed at first as if the remaining speakers would be called on to do more than support. He looked ill; he sounded ill (his voice for several minutes was so weak as to be almost inaudible); and he apologised to the court for the effects his sickness would have on his capacity to discharge the commands of the Commons adequately. And yet, well over an hour later he was still on his feet, holding even the hostile part of his audience captive with a display which for intellectual quality and power of analysis can rarely have been matched in any British political trial.* Although Sir Simon Harcourt, opening for the Defence two days later, won far greater public acclaim, it is fair to say that he depended far more than Parker on the spellbinding eloquence of his delivery. Comparing the two contributions in cold print, 260 years after the event, one cannot but consider Harcourt's an exceptional piece of pleading. But for utter mastery of a complex brief, and for the sheer range and penetration of his analysis, Parker's speech is breathtaking. It stands alone.

One result of this extraordinary feat at the time was to render any direct reinforcement more or less superfluous. Consequently the last three speakers assumed a roving commission; and to analyse the Prosecution case on Article IV is in effect to do so in terms of one speech – Parker's.† This final article – described by Parker himself as 'a charge of sedition, under several aggravations' – contained no fewer than six different branches. But the two crucial charges, and (because of Sacheverell's studied ambiguities) the two most awkward to substantiate, were the second and the fifth. The second accused the prisoner of suggesting that there were 'men of characters and stations, both in Church and State' who were false brethren, and who not only themselves undermined the Establish-

---

* The speech of the future Lord Chancellor Macclesfield (which occupies no less than eighteen pages of small print in the octavo edition of the *Tryal*) was rated by two expert witnesses on the Whig side with very different criteria, Walpole and Burnet, as the outstanding one for the Commons. Few on either side demurred. See HMC. *Portland MSS*. iv, 533; Burnet, v, 440; Osborn MSS. 21/22: 1 March ('his speech was looked upon as the best').

† The pity is that in a narrow compass one can do it no sort of justice. To savour it to the full one must read the original from start to finish. In the official *Tryal* it is on pp. 150–70.

ment but encouraged and empowered its professed enemies to destroy it; the fifth charged him, 'as a public incendiary', with inciting the Queen's subjects to 'arms and violence'. We must see briefly how Parker set out to prove these two charges.

Of course he had to concede tacitly that at no single point in the sermon of 5 November had Sacheverell, in so many words, made the specific accusation about men in high places lodged against him in the second charge. He had to argue that the preacher had intended this meaning to be deduced from his words. He drew the court's attention to page 15 of the sermon, where in representing the *perils* of false brotherhood Sacheverell had bewailed the threat which it involved to the whole Establishment in Church and State; while on pages 20 and 21, in emphasising the malign *sin* of false brotherhood he described 'what a vast scandal and offence' it gave 'to see men of characters and stations thus to shift and prevaricate with their principles', to wear their religion 'as loose almost as their garments', and to conduct their public lives by shift and hypocrisy. Since such men were stigmatised as 'false brothers', and the congregation had but a few minutes earlier been told that the greatest danger of false brotherhood was to the constitution, how could they or the readers of the sermon fail to conclude that men in high places, by their unprincipled, hypocritical behaviour, were imperilling the Establishment? The Doctor in his Answer had denied that an accusation could be sustained by linking two passages many pages apart: 'as though [said Parker, mockingly] the false brotherhood he shows the danger of, and the false brotherhood he shows the malignity of, had no relation to one another because twelve pages asunder'. Neither was there anything in the sermon itself to justify Sacheverell's other plea – that his 'men of characters and stations' were identifiable merely with some few magistrates 'of the meaner sort'. On the contrary: 'it is a general arraignment of the government throughout, and as such he must answer for it. And to put this out of doubt, he has told us, page 26, in Scripture words, that "the Church's adversaries are *chief*" '.[63]

Sir Thomas next produced his proofs of the charges of accusing the Queen and her ministers of a general maladministration, and of fomenting destructive divisions among the Queen's subjects; in the latter case underlining more effectively than any previous

speaker the essential inhumanity and total lack of Christian charity
of the prisoner:

> If, with these mistaken opinions, [schismatics] communicate
> with the Church, they are false brethren, and as such to be
> abhorred: and yet if they do not, they are not to be tolerated.
> . . . For though he seems in words to approve of an indulgence
> to consciences truly scrupulous, yet in reality he approves none,
> since he admits not anyone to have a conscience truly scrupulous
> that differs from him.[64]

By the time he reached the article's fifth charge, Sacheverell as an
inciter to violence and rebellion, Parker had the audience in thrall.
His first point was that a sermon so charged with heat and passion
could only have been calculated to raise passions. The people are
called on to show 'the bravest resolution' and 'to contend earnestly
for the faith'. 'In the dedication of the Derby sermon he extols
those who are for maintaining what he calls "forsaken truth" with
their *lives and fortunes*'; and the sacrifice of lives and estates is
again commended at St Paul's. Finally, 'in the dedication of the St
Paul's sermon he seems to avow this design; he pretends not his
sermon to be Christianity, but owns it to be *politics*, not *preaching
peace* but *sounding a trumpet*'.[65]

This led Parker to the most telling part of his speech. 'We say he
has stirred up her Majesty's subjects to arms and violence. He says
[in his Answer] he has declared all Resistance unlawful. Yes – all
resistance to the Supreme Power. But he has never declared Resistance to her Majesty unlawful'. For the sake of argument Parker
proposed to assume that the protestations of loyalty to the Queen
Sacheverell made in his Answer were sincerely meant. If they were,
then the St Paul's sermon contained some inexplicable inconsistencies.

> By false brethren in the text of this sermon were meant those
> who pretended to be Christians but really were not. Dr Sach-
> everell seems so to understand it; and therefore to declare those
> to be false brethren in the Church that pretend to be of the com-
> munion of the Church of England but are not; that live in its
> communion but own not its doctrines and authority. By like
> analogy, false brethren in the State are such that perhaps swallow

the oaths to the Queen, or if they go not so far yet take the benefit of her laws, her courts, her protection, yet deny her allegiance and are for another Prince. A just and well managed reproof of these had been a noble topic for one that pretends all this zeal for the Queen. But *they* are wholly passed by. . . . There is no danger from *them* either to Church or State. . . . This seems strange.

Another extraordinary inconsistency was revealed if Sacheverell's professions of zeal for her Majesty were set beside his insistence on Non-Resistance as a fundamental doctrine in the State.

> One would expect that he . . . would have fallen in so far with the business of the day, and have made so much use of his favourite doctrine as to dissuade from rebellion; and when he had taken notice of these false steps in the administration, that he should have persuaded the people to make proper applications for redress, but to be careful not to let the faults of the ministry cause 'em to forget their duty to the Queen. But there's not the least exhortation to that purpose.
>
> All this seems strange, taking it for granted that the Doctor is sincerely zealous for the Queen. Give me leave therefore to make another supposition. Suppose this zeal is but pretended to the Queen, but really for another, and that he thinks the other is rightful Prince, your Lordships will find all consistent, every expression and the whole procedure exactly just.[66]

And this proposition, with deadly skill and logic, Sir Thomas went on to demonstrate as the key to the paradox.

He had taken so many tricks that an ace was scarcely needed. But he had one up his sleeve, and now he played it. If the court accepted that behind the façade of loyalty to the Queen lay the reality of devotion to the exiled Stuart prince, they might guess what made the preacher 'choose to describe the case of our Church in the words of the prophet in the Lamentations which are in chapter 1, verses 4 and 5 (tho' not truly cited in his printed sermon): "The ways of Sion mourn for a time, and her gates are desolate, her priests sigh and she in bitterness, because her adversaries are chief and her enemies *at present* prosper." '

My Lords, that book was wrote just after Nebuchadnezzar's taking Jerusalem, and the condition of the Jews then, which is thought proper by him to give an image of ours now, was this. They were enslaved; their King in a foreign country, stripped of his crown, and the Prince then reigning was an oppressor, that had no other title but possession and force.*

Thus has the Doctor, out of his 'tender concern for her Majesty's person and government' thought fit to express his sentiments.[67]

The great speech ended on a note of dignity and crushing severity. Many had claimed in recent weeks, said Parker – and none more plaintively than the accused himself – that Dr Sacheverell had been prosecuted *only for doing his duty as a clergyman.*

My Lords, the Commons have the greatest and justest veneration for the clergy of the Church of England, who are glorious through the whole Christian world for their preaching and writing, for their steadiness to the Protestant religion when it was in the utmost danger. . . . But when we consider Dr Sacheverell, stripping himself of all the becoming qualities proper for his order . . . and with rancour and uncharitableness branding all that differ from him, though through ignorance . . . reviling them, exposing them, conducting 'em to Hell and leaving 'em there; then labouring to sap the Establishment, and railing and declaiming against the government, crying to arms and blowing a trumpet in Sion . . . to overthrow the best constitution and betray the best Queen that ever made a people happy – and this with Scripture in his mouth – the Commons looked upon him by this behaviour to have severed himself from all the rest of the clergy.

The Commons for this reason had no fear of discouraging true religion by bringing to justice a priest who had preached sedition and rebellion. They could have no thought of dishonouring the clergy by bringing to punishment a clergyman who disgraced the whole order.[68]

---

* Parker's exceptional textual command over the Bible enabled him to handle with complete aplomb that last branch of the fourth article by which the Doctor was accused of perverting Holy Scripture. See *Tryal*, pp. 162–5, and p. 100 above.

To have to follow Parker was an invidious task, and it says much for John Smith that in an unpredictable, extempore speech he managed to keep the audience's attention.* But by now the peers had been in the Hall for over five hours, most of the spectators for nine, and there was a general feeling that the real business of the day – and the case for the Prosecution – was effectively over. Harry Boyle's few half-hearted generalities were heard with impatience. Outside the coaches were queuing, suppers were waiting, and the London mob was stirring. So although 'Mr Lechmere rose, and with great eagerness begged and prayed to be heard only a few words to the last branch of the last article',[69] their Lordships were not to be persuaded. On Lord Godolphin's motion the court adjourned at six o'clock.[70] Who can have guessed that it would be past two o'clock on the following afternoon when Lechmere was able to resume his speech, and that some of those who heard him then would be counting themselves lucky to be still alive?

* Smith summarised Whig thinking on the Toleration, with its interplay of ideology and interest, as well as anyone throughout the trial.

VII THE NIGHT OF FIRE

The storm that broke over London on the evening of Wednesday, 1 March, and died away in the early hours of Thursday morning had been gathering for weeks. There had been rumblings as far back at least as 25 January. These had grown louder on 27 February, during Sacheverell's first triumphal progress from and back to the Temple and during the Queen's passage through St James's Park. On the 28th they had become too ominous to be ignored. The crowds which surged alongside the Doctor's coach, as it swayed all the way from the Temple Bar down the Strand to Charing Cross, and then down Whitehall to the New Palace Yard, were far bigger than those of Monday. They were also far more aggressive. 'A hired company of butchers' served as close bodyguard; other thugs (reputedly paid thugs) had been brought over the river from Sacheverell's home ground of Southwark; and staves and clubs were in evidence. While the quality saluted the hero from the relative safety of open windows and balconies, the thousands massed on the pavements and in such open spaces as the May Pole in the Strand and Charing Cross found themselves well advised to pull off their hats and halloo when the procession came abreast. The laggards and the recalcitrant found themselves abused and manhandled; and several Whig members of Parliament, caught up in the crowd and declining to make their obeisances, were rudely jostled. Understandably the cavalcade itself was shorter than before; several of the gentry whose coaches had tagged behind on the 27th now found it prudent to leave the centre of the field to the plebs – and of course to the Doctor, who acknowledged all the acclaim with imperial condescension, and from time to time gave his hand out of the coach window to be kissed.[1] His coach, with its footmen egging on the spectators as before, moved at a predetermined crawl, forcing many other vehicles unfortunate enough to be caught in its wake – including the Lord Chancellor's – to follow suit. And when, on entering the Palace Yard, it was actually overtaken by Cowper's fuming coachman, the crowd 'made a very great shout'.[2]

In view of what happened the following day, was the government culpably negligent about taking preventative action? A significant passage which took place in the House of Lords after Tuesday's adjournment of the court may suggest that it was. Some peers were seriously alarmed by what they had seen that morning, and the House was moved 'that Dr Sacheverell might be taken into custody'. After some debate it was suggested belatedly that Black Rod should be sent to enquire if the accused had left the Palace precincts, and if not to require his attendance. But the message soon came back that 'he had been gone some time', whereupon the House resorted to a select committee 'to enquire into the occasion of the disorders by Doctor Sacheverell's coming to his trial'. It was instructed to meet on Wednesday at 9 a.m., and this it duly did in the Prince's Lodgings under the chairmanship of the Junto's ally, Lord Mohun; but on the evidence of the Lords' Committee-Book it only took evidence from one witness before adjourning to allow its members to robe for the procession to the Hall. The committee was not specifically empowered to propose remedies; nor was it instructed to meet with appropriate urgency on Tuesday evening. Had either course been taken, it is just conceivable that Mohun would have had time to present a report to the House on the morning of the 1st.[3]

Even without that stimulus, however, the ministry had enough evidence at its disposal by Tuesday night to have justified its instructing the City authorities and the Lord Lieutenant of Middlesex to call out at least two regiments of the militia on the morrow. Sacheverell's return to his lodgings on the afternoon of the 28th was a replica of his morning journey. A mob estimated in thousands rather than hundreds accompanied him, picking up reinforcements on the way (like the young basketmaker's apprentice, George Gosdin, who ran pell-mell from his work to join them), and of these many hundreds swirled through the gates of the Middle

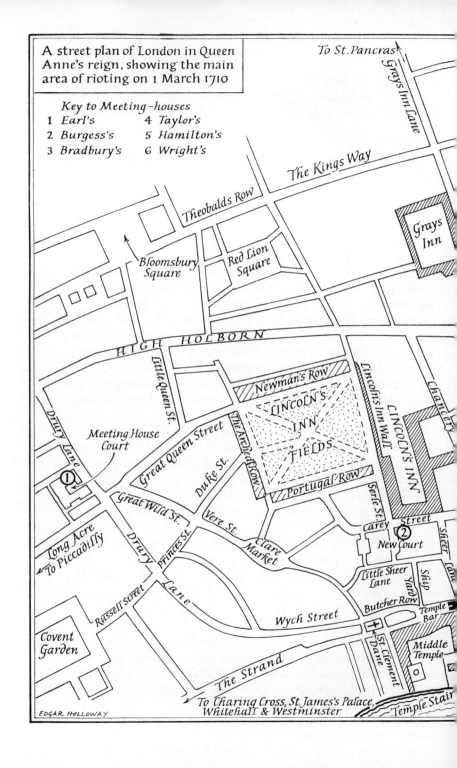

A street plan of London in Queen
Anne's reign, showing the main
area of rioting on 1 March 1710

Key to Meeting-houses
1 Earl's   4 Taylor's
2 Burgess's   5 Hamilton's
3 Bradbury's   6 Wright's

To St. Pancras

Grays Inn Lane

The Kings Way

Theobalds Row

Bloomsbury Square

Red Lion Square

Grays Inn

HIGH HOLBORN

Little Queen St.

Newman's Row

LINCOLN'S INN FIELDS

Lincoln's Inn Wall

LINCOLN'S INN

Chancery

Drury Lane

Meeting House Court

Great Queen Street

Duke St.

The Arched Row

Portugal Row

Serle St.

①

Great Wild St.

Vere St.

Clare Market

Carey Street

② New Court

Sheer Lane

Long Acre To Piccadilly

Drury Lane

Princes St.

Little Sheer Lane

Ship Yard

Russell Street

Wych Street

Butcher Row

Temple Bar

Covent Garden

St. Clement Dane

Middle Temple

The Strand

To Charing Cross, St. James's Palace,
Whitehall & Westminster

Temple Stairs

EDGAR HOLLOWAY

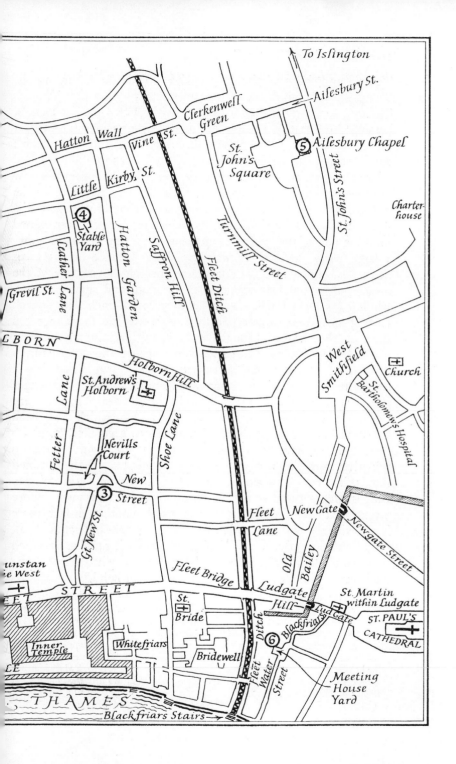

Temple and followed the Doctor right to his door, turning the Temple-walks into a sea of humanity. It was here that Thomas Talboys, a periwig-maker from the parish of St Clement Dane's, passing through the Temple on his lawful occasions (or that, at least, was his story),* 'saw the Doctor put his hat off to the mob'; and it was here he overheard what he described as a public 'Council of War', in which a proposal to demolish Daniel Burgess's new meeting-house, near Lincoln's Inn Fields, was debated by the ringleaders. There was disagreement about whether this should be done there and then, left until the following night, or postponed until the end of the trial; but in the end, by way of compromise, a large party made their way the short distance across Fleet Street and along Sheer Lane to the meeting-house, one of the most opulent and best attended in London, and smashed every window (as Dyer put it) 'as far as they could reach with sticks'. Having moved on to Burgess's private house and there repeated the dose, they broke off for the evening. Within minutes the news had been carried to Leonard's coffee-house; the proprietor, a member of the congregation, rushed out to inform Burgess's son (the pastor himself, it seems, was away from home), and the younger Burgess carried the news to Whitehall and asked Mr Secretary Boyle for protection against the destruction which had been threatened next day. At the same time he saw several other ministers. It should have been plain to them that they could expect no initiative from Sir Samuel Garrard towards raising the Trained Bands. Yet they took no action that night, beyond a promise to Burgess that a guard would be put on his father's premises before 7 p.m. next day. This promise was never honoured. In fact, there is no evidence that the authorities took any genuine action at all until some time after nine o'clock on the following night, by which time flames lighting up the sky left no doubt whatever that the Sacheverell mobs were not only up but out of hand.[4]

* Talboys's evidence – of a conspiracy to pull down the meeting-houses, hatched in the Temple on the 28th – later proved crucial in the convictions of both Daniel Dammaree and George Purchase for high treason (*State Trials*, xv, 552–3, 655). The Defence would have dearly loved to know that there was a deposition in the government's hands by one Thomas Gray, sworn before Robert Pringle on 4 March, that he had been in Talboys's company on Tuesday night and the latter had told him 'he had been at a Council of War and that he was one of the Council wherein it was agreed to send a detachment of the mob to [attack] Dr Burgess his house'. Blenheim MSS. Box VII, 18.

The scenes on Wednesday morning were a repetition of those of Tuesday. The mob following the Doctor was described as 'prodigious', as 'hanging about the horses and the coach like clusters of bees', and as 'treating very rudely all such as did not pull off their hats and say, God bless him!' But by the afternoon, long before the Commons' Managers had finished putting their case in Westminster Hall, anyone on the streets could sense that something exceptional was afoot. The morning mobs had never properly dispersed. Between two and three o'clock there was already so much din in the Strand, in Fleet Street and round the Temple that three bailiffs, dining together at a tavern in Chancery Lane, gave up all thought of further business for the day and decided they could not be better employed than in sitting and smoking their pipes. The crowds milling round Westminster Palace waiting for the day's proceedings to end – some 3,000 of them, according to one foreign correspondent – were entertained with copies of a new broadsheet, hot from the press, about an imaginary prizefight between Hoadly and Sacheverell. When the Queen came out, 'very pensive', she was huzzaed through the Park, but for others there was a less welcoming reception. A number of the Managers were spotted and were 'assaulted and affronted' on their way back to their homes; the earl of Wharton and Lord Chancellor Cowper were both insulted in the streets, and the bishop of Salisbury had dirt thrown in his coach. Worst of all, as Abigail Harley heard, a party of the mob 'caught Dolben, and were going to hang him upon a tree, till he swore he was not Dolben nor a Parliament-man'.[5]

But as on the previous day, the main body of the mob escorted Sacheverell's coach back to his lodgings, where he arrived around half-past six. As they joined forces with the crowds already waiting round the Temple the ferment was indescribable; but it could not disguise the fact that there were many there who knew full well what they were about. They had come carrying crowbars, pick-axes, woodmen's axes and carpenters' tools: they were equipped for action, and it is certain that some – like the two bricklayer's apprentices, William Watson and Ned Hughes – had been enlisted beforehand and had been promised payment for their night's work.[6] Daniel Burgess's Presbyterian meeting-house, square and brick-built, stood in New Court, between Little Sheer Lane and Carey Street. From the neck of the cobbled alley which led from the

M

court into Carey Street one could glimpse several hundred yards away up Serle Street the south-east corner of Lincoln's Inn Fields. It was probably just before 7 p.m. that the advance guard of the mob reached the building, and they found it unprotected. The boy apprentice, George Gosdin, who for the second day in succession had run along with them to see some sport, was there in time to see a man in sailor's garb 'climb up by the door to the window' and break the window.* He was followed through the window by 'another in a light coat and short hair', possibly Rainer, an attorney's clerk, who later admitted 'being one of the first that broke into it'. It was just about seven o'clock when the main body of the mob converged on New Court through Little Sheer Lane, forcing the Widow Newth, on her way from Petty France to visit a house-holder in the court, to cower for shelter in the door of a book-binder's shop, by the corner of Ship Yard. She was later to tell how two boys, who had been out for a lark like Gosdin and had strayed far from home, broke through the crowd from the opposite direction and asked her the way back to Westminster; and how, as she was directing them,

> a gentleman, well dressed and having a blue cloak, came to the boys and with a great deal of eagerness asked them, 'have they got in?'; meaning, as this informant apprehends, whether the mob had got into Dr Burgess's meeting-house. The boys answered, 'yes, and they were pulling the pulpit down'. [Then] a maid servant who lives at the sign of the Fountain in Sheer Lane, knowing this gentleman, called him by his name, to which he replied, 'Who is there, Betty? Have they got in?' 'Yes,' answered she, 'and they say they are pulling the pulpit down'. 'Then', said he . . . with a great deal of joy and snapping his fingers, 'we have done it', and returned the same way he came towards Fleet Street.[7]

The internal demolition of a building as large and well-appointed as Burgess's chapel was no light task. Over the next three and a half hours this splendid building was stripped of everything that was combustible, and of much that was not. Apart from the pulpit, hundreds of feet of pews and matted forms had to be torn up not

---

* This must have been one of the upper, gallery windows. The downstairs windows had presumably been boarded up since the previous night's attack.

only on the ground floor but in the three capacious galleries: the ubiquitous Edward Orrell, a dissenter who covered the site of almost every riot and fire this night in an attempt to identify some of the participants, found twenty to thirty at work on the pews alone on his first visit to Burgess's about eight o'clock. Scores of others were busy unhinging the great doors, pulling up floor boards, ripping down the gallery rails, the panelling and the wainscoting, and dismantling the casements. It was man's work, and bystanders were not welcome. 'I went in several times [said Orrell], till some of them that were pulling up the boards swore at me, and said, Damn him, what does that lazy fellow do? And I believe they took me for a spy'. (Orrell retreated, but not so hastily as another observer, Captain Jackson of the Trained Bands, whose anxious face so quickly gave him away that there was a rush to throw him over the gallery and he had to run for his life.)[8] There were hazards for the rioters too: some were cut by glass, and one, to the horror of young Gosdin, who was standing only a yard and a half away from him, was struck down and killed instantly by a falling casement.

The largest working parties were employed in continuous relays, carrying the heavy timbers out of the chapel, down Serle Street, and over the fencing into the Fields, where a great pyramid began to take shape. In this first part of the evening, before great numbers of auxiliaries came along – many at first out of idle curiosity – and began to pick themselves in, the evidence of prior planning was unmistakable. 'There were pullers down and there were carriers', one of the mobsters later admitted; and there were those responsible for building the bonfire as well.* By soon after eight the great pile was alight, and for the next three hours it blazed up into the March sky, so that Londoners in their hundreds were drawn to the flames like moths from all over the city's western parts, and a pawnbroker named Francis Morgan even came over in his nightgown from Southwark. By nine o'clock, before the first party of secessionists broke away to find new targets further east, there were probably three thousand people at Burgess's or in the Fields.

* Blenheim MSS. Box VII, 18: Sarah Sawery's deposition. Sir David Hamilton, the Queen's Physician, wrote in his journal how 'when she [Anne] heard of the order in which the mob moved in pulling down the meeting-houses, each acting their proper part, some pulling down, others carrying away, and some burning, and all this so quickly as an argument of its being designed beforehand, she seemed greatly concerned'. Panshanger MSS. Hamilton Diary, *sub* 27 Feb.

The wild scenes round the fire seemed more akin to fantasy than reality. Those of the 'carriers' who had the lighter burdens to bear – cushions, candlesticks, vestry chairs and small planks – performed a kind of ritual dance round the blaze before hurling on their fuel. Conspicuous in the garish light was a tall man wearing the uniform of one of the Queen's watermen. Daniel Dammaree was his name, a comparative latecomer on the scene who had spent the early part of the evening getting quietly tight at the Bell tavern in Water Street, but now emerged as a born cheer-leader who 'excited the mob very much in their proceedings . . . pull[ed] off his wig and halloo[ed], and seemed mightily to be rejoiced'. Unfortunately for him he was conspicuous, especially when he carried from the meeting-house the great brass sconce that held the main branch of candles, 'went about hallooing for Sacheverell, and went round the fire two or three times, and then threw it in':[9] but for the Grace of God and a change of ministry, his enthusiasm would have led him to be hanged, drawn and quartered.

From time to time some very special offering was brought to the sacrifice: there was a bedstead, torn from under a terrified woman who with her three children had been found by the mob in the vestry; and there was the famous pulpit itself, dismantled earlier but preserved more or less intact for an hour and a half 'with intention [the ringleaders boasted] to have burnt Dr Burgess in it', could they only have found him.[10] (It was afterwards said that Burgess had escaped by climbing out of a back window of his house, and that he found nearby asylum in the house of a friendly Catholic.)[11] Predictably, there was a good deal of unashamed plunder as well as destruction: three of the chapel's candlesticks and a psalm book, for instance, were found next day buried in a garden in Clerkenwell. But one item not to be concealed under anybody's coat, the splendid japanned grandfather clock, was burned with the greatest ceremony of all:

> Whilst each lined pew, and matted form
> That kept the Saints' posteriors warm,
> Long occupied by pious dames,
> Were now consuming in the flames;
> The faithful clock, which oft before
> Had pointed to the pudding hour,

And told the Preacher many a time
When pig and goose were in their prime;
And when the listening Saints and Sinners
Were ready for their coarser dinners;
Was now advanced upon a rail,
Near neighbour to the flaming pile;
That as the hand with leisure turned,
The mob might see how fast it burned.[12]

To all this the mob chanted their unending, deafening accompaniment of 'High Church and Sacheverell'. 'Such as joined not in the shout were insulted and knocked down' – even a soldier, an injudicious sightseer on leave from the 2nd Foot Guards, was forced to pull off his hat and cheer. There was no point in arguing, for as the indictment against Dammaree was later to state, many of the rioters were 'armed and arrayed in a warlike manner, that is to say with colours flying, swords, clubs and other weapons'. By now, however, the mob had already begun to split. About ten o'clock the roaring of another great bonfire, in Holborn opposite the top of Fetter Lane, announced that the centre of operations was moving east. The first target here was the Independents' meeting-house in New Street, standing roughly mid-way between Fetter Lane and Shoe Lane, which had been served since 1707 by the ablest Congregational minister – and one of the stoutest Whigs – in London, Thomas Bradbury.* The leading detachment from Lincoln's Inn Fields reached it before 9.30, in the van being William Watson, the bricklayer's apprentice, who shortly before had been on Burgess's roof stripping off the tiles, and who now 'was the first that got into [Bradbury's] which he did at the window, and bid the rest follow him'.[13] By soon after ten, when Captain Orrell arrived in Fetter Lane after recruiting his strength at Leonard's coffee-house, there were already 'abundance of people, a great mob, carrying the materials from Mr Bradbury's . . . into Holborn'.

When I had stood there a little time, says I to my friend, let us go into the meeting-house; I will see; it may be I may know

---

* This meeting-house had been made famous under James II and William III by its great pastor, Stephen Lobb. For it, and Bradbury, see Walter Wilson, *History and Antiquities of Dissenting Meeting-Houses in London* (1808–14), iii, 420–1, 450–1.

somebody there. I went through a dark passage and narrow entry. When I came in, Lord have mercy upon me, said I, it is all down. I turned back to my friend, Mr Hawkins: this is destroyed, said I . . .[14]

In Holborn, where the bonfire half blocked the road, there was pandemonium. It was one of the two main thoroughfares into and out of the City, and coaches and chairs moving in either direction were at serious hazard. Many were stopped; few of their occupants escaped without lighter purses. Gentlemen soon found that the most acceptable answer to the yells of 'God damn ye, are you for Sacheverell', was a shilling or two to drink the Doctor's health. One rioter alone, Harman Smalt, confessed himself eight shillings the richer for an hour or so's piracy in Holborn. By half-past ten, the mob there was estimated at five or six hundred; and several of the bystanders on its fringes noticed that its captain appeared to be a man in a footman's green livery who bore aloft in triumph one of the curtains from Bradbury's chapel hoisted on a pole, which he called his High Church standard. This livery was to endanger the life of another footman, Francis Willis, whose mistress, Mrs Miles, sent him out from her house in Grevil Street to find out the cause and whereabouts of the fire she could see from her window. Being a countryman by birth, he lingered longer than he should have done, for as he told the anxious enquirers when he got back to the house, 'he never saw a mob in London before'. When, towards eleven o'clock, the main body of the rioters made off up Leather Lane to begin sacking another meeting-house, Mr Taylor's, he could not resist following them; for he knew the place well – it lay discreetly concealed in a yard, in the hinterland embraced by Leather Lane, Little Kirby Street and Hatton Garden – and no doubt, poor fellow, he thought he would have a better tale to tell. Perhaps in the flush of excitement he picked up the odd board or two and carried them to the fire. At all events he was spotted by a neighbour in Little Kirby Street, and on mistaken identity (for he wore a blue livery, too easily mistaken in the firelight for a green) he was later put on trial for his life.*

Christopher Taylor's Presbyterian meeting-house, built when

---

* Willis was the only one of the three men charged with High Treason to be acquitted. Sir Thomas Parker's summing-up (he was by then Lord Chief Justice) was an eminently fair one. See *State Trials*, xv, 614–52.

times were hard for dissenters, was better protected than most. Access from Leather Lane to the stable-yard in which it was situated was barred by a pair of formidable gates. This was a circumstance which caused not only frustration to the rioters but alarm to Henry Bendish, a Treasury official living in Hatton Garden; since 'the back door out of his gardens [was] the only back door of the houses in the Great Street that goes into the Yard where the great door of the meeting-house is, and the mob found so much difficulty in breaking open the great gates leading into the said yard that he and his family apprehended they would demand passage through his house'.[15] When the attackers did at last break through it took about 150 men, 'as hard at work as they could be', to gut the chapel; and three separate bonfires in Hatton Garden to consume its contents.

The Hatton Garden mob was in an ugly mood. The builder of the meeting-house, who had the misfortune to live close by, was pulled out of his bed and dragged off to the fire. A bribe earned him reprieve and in the end they 'only burnt his night cap, that he might never forget the danger he had been in'. Another to be terrorised was a magistrate's clerk named Robert Culbridge, who was slipping out of his lodgings to inform his master when he was recognised. In a moment he was cornered, and threatened that his brains would be knocked in if he did not pull off his hat, cry God bless Doctor Sacheverell, and hand over every penny he had in his pocket. By now it was approaching midnight; word had almost certainly come from Drury Lane that the troops were out and engaged there; those 'persons in good dress that had the mien of gent' and had at first directed operations in the Gardens had mostly left; and once again the mob split – some heading for St John's Square in Clerkenwell, to wreck the meeting-house of Mr Hamilton, the rest determined to broach the City itself and begin the work of destruction there in Blackfriars.[16]

Theirs were not the only thoughts that had turned Citywards, as Captain Orrell had learned when he made his way back for the last time to Lincoln's Inn Fields. It was then almost ten-thirty, and the great fire was beginning to burn lower. But the mob seemed as big as ever, and the ringleaders who had remained to finish off Burgess's (by now the chimneys were down) were ready for fresh game. Someone had been distributing papers among the throng bearing the slogan: 'Down with the Bank of England and the Meeting-Houses; and God damn the Presbyterians and all that support them'.[17] But the order of priorities was a matter of dispute. Orrell 'heard some asking, which was the Lord Wharton's house? Others said, St James's: no, said others, the City, the City, the Bank: damn them, says another, we will have all the meeting-houses down'.[18] Before long the prospect of golden guineas at the Bank – Whig guineas, too – and of firing more Presbyterian tubs *en route*, was to draw many away down Fleet Street towards Newgate and Ludgate; but the first and bigger movement was in the other direction. In evidence at the Old Bailey on 20 April Orrell was to tell how about half-past ten (as near as he could guess) he and Hawkins

> walked down that row [bordering the Fields] where Sir Francis Child's son's house is and went towards my Lord Chancellor's house.* . . . When I was there I halted a little, and observed a small body of the mob detached from that fire; they run after one another cross the fields. I observed a pretty tall man at the head of them. I kept my eye on that party. In the middle of the field they grew stronger, and then they divided themselves: some went towards the arch, but more towards Powys house. I went towards those at Powys house, and there I saw Dammaree, in the Queen's livery with his badge; and there they held a council of the mob. . . . God damn it, says Dammaree, we will have them all down. Some were for going into Wild Street. Damn it, says another, that is a hen-roost; the other [Earl's in Drury Lane] is worth ten of it. . . .
>
> Some of them turned off towards Wild Street, and others towards Powys house. Dammaree and the mob with him, went through Queen Street, and once in ten or twelve yards, he turned about: Huzza! Why don't you come on, boys, to Drury Lane? God damn them, we will have them all down. . . . In this manner, he led them on from Lincoln's Inn Fields to Drury Lane, but I never saw him afterwards.[19]

Jabez Earl's meeting-house stood in a court off the west side of Drury Lane, a little above the junction of that street with Long Acre. The mob made short work of it. 'A little fellow with a pick-axe', Orrell observed, was first to the door, but was making little

* This apparently stood near the S.W. corner of the Fields.

progress when a burley sawyer, one Henry Sanders, strode up wielding a hatchet, and pushing aside both him and a woman who was screaming in terror that her sister was in the house and would be killed, he was heard to bellow: 'God damn you, don't you know how to break down a meeting-house door!' With the third stroke of the hatchet he split it open and the rabble poured through. They concentrated at first on what was most readily portable – the clock, cushions, chairs, a pile of manuscripts out of Earl's private room – and yet another fire was soon blazing at the end of Long Acre. Then they began to demolish in earnest. It was now almost eleven, and already the crowd in Drury Lane had swollen to well over a thousand, with reinforcements still flooding in. Among them came the indefatigable William Watson, who had already this night stripped many of the tiles off Burgess's roof and with an iron crowbar had personally demolished every chimney at Bradbury's. But now, as he told his friends with no little pride the following day, he 'was so tired with what he had done before that he could not meddle with nothing [in Drury Lane] but was forced to content himself with being a looker-on; but he hollowed and laughed with them, for there was such havoc, he never saw such pastime in his life'.[20]

For four hours since seven o'clock the Sacheverell mobs had rampaged unchecked, the constables and watch being utterly powerless to control them. And they were far from having exhausted their impetus. Some of the revellers in Drury Lane were already planning to pillage Lord Wharton's house and Jack Dolben's. Others were talking of destroying Hoadly's church and house, and still others of heading for the City, to pull down Salter's Hall and Shower's meeting-house and, above all, to join in the plunder of the Bank,[21] when quite suddenly, the sound of horses' hooves clattering down Great Queen Street and Wild Street dispelled these rosy visions and gave notice that for the rioters in the west end, at least, time had run out.

It has often been said that it was only when the Whig directors of the Bank, convinced that mobs were bearing down on Mercers' Lane, made panic pleas for protection that the government at last bestirred itself and called out the troops.[22] In fact, evidence survives which tells a quite different story. Throughout the first part of the evening the earl of Sunderland, lord of the Junto and

Secretary of State for the Southern Department, was at work in his office at the Cockpit in Whitehall. It must have been around nine o'clock that two coaches – those of the Lord Chancellor, Cowper, and the Lord Privy Seal, Newcastle – deposited their flustered owners at his door. Both ministers had had a clear view from their windows of the conflagration in the Fields. They told the Secretary quite frankly that they believed their own houses were in danger. Mr Burgess, junior, was also on his doorstep for the second night running, frantic (as well he might be) for his father's safety as well as for his property.[23] There could be no more procrastination. Sunderland took chair for St James's Palace and sought an immediate audience with the Queen. He was in an unenviable quandary. The militia could not now be raised in time; there were not a great many regular troops readily available, and such as were available were either on guard duty at the palace itself or on stand-by at Whitehall. The consequences for him and for the whole government would be unthinkable if the guard should be withdrawn from St James's, and then part of the mob should evade it, as could easily happen in the confusion, and sack the palace. Anne, however, seems to have resolved the difficulty herself. Although at the first news of the riots she was said to have been 'seized with a paleness and trembling', she soon took control of herself and put both her horse and foot guards at the Secretary's disposal. He was still a worried man, and put to the Queen the danger of leaving her own person unprotected; but Anne's reply (Boyer tells us) was simply that 'God would be her guard', and she gave him her positive order.

Thus armed, he hurried back to the Cockpit where he must have arrived at about the time Bradbury's bonfire was being laid in Holborn. The forces at his disposal were detachments from the 3rd troop of Horse Guards (the earl of Arran's), most of them at St James's, from the 2nd troop of Horse Grenadiers (Lord Crawford's) and from two companies (Hubbard's and Turner's) of the 2nd Foot Guards, the Coldstream. Recruiting the services of young Burgess as a messenger he hastily penned and addressed a note to 'Brigadier Tatton or the Commanding Officer of Her Majesty's Foot Guards'. It informed him simply that a riotous mob was pulling down Burgess's meeting-house and threatening further mischief, and conveyed the Queen's order that you send such a detachment of the Guard under your command as upon the information of Mr Burgess's son, the bearer, you shall judge sufficient for suppressing them, and that you use your utmost endeavours to have the ringleaders secured, that the Justices of the Peace may take informations against them.[24]

Tatton, however, was not to be found. The senior officer on duty was an infantry captain, inappropriately named Horsey, to whose subsequent loquacity we owe virtually all we know of the celebrated interview to which he was summoned in Sunderland's office. The earl

ordered him to mount immediately, and go and disperse the mob. The captain making some scruple to obey this order, unless he were relieved [by some more senior officer], alleging 'he was the Queen's bodyguard and must be answerable for any accident that might happen', he was told it was the Queen's express command; and both the earl and Lord Chancellor representing the danger of delays, he acquiesced upon a promise that the Secretary should give him his orders in writing.

Sunderland gave the captain his word of honour that he should have them next morning, and with this the officer had to be satisfied, though as he told Edmund Calamy, 'he ventured his neck by going upon verbal orders, without anything in writing to warrant his march till the work was over'.

But there still remained the question of the degree of force that was to be used. 'Am I to preach', Horsey enquired, 'or fight the mob. If I am to preach I desire some better speaker may be sent along with me. If I am to fight, fighting is my trade and I will do my best'. To this the Secretary's answer was that he must use his own judgment and only resort to violence if absolutely necessary. One order, whispered in the officer's ear as he left the room, was more precise: it was to 'send a party to the Bank, which the Captain did accordingly, and sent thither a corporal with six horse grenadiers'.[25] It was surely because he had no time to draft careful written instructions that Sunderland counselled restraint on Horsey. For when, some hours later, he began to organise reinforcements, commanding the duke of Bedford to call out two regiments of the Middlesex militia, and likewise instructing General Withers and the duke of Argyll to hold 'constantly in readiness' the 1st Foot Guards and the 4th troop of Horse Guards, he specifically enjoined that if their troops 'meet with any resistance from the mutinous rabble, they are even to fire upon them if other means are judged insufficient to quell them'.[26]

As things turned out, thanks to the soldiers' superb discipline, the Sacheverell riots were suppressed without a shot being fired and with relatively few casualties among the mob – perhaps fifty all told, from sword or sabre cuts.[27] From this point of view, it was just as well that time was frustratingly lost at the start of the operation because Horsey ordered the three units first to rendezvous in Whitehall and then to move towards Lincoln's Inn Fields together, at the pace of the infantry. For had the cavalry, alerted and mounted very soon after ten o'clock, ridden straight from St James's along Piccadilly, Long Acre and Great Queen Street to the Fields, they must have arrived there to find some 3,000 rioters in a large open space, much more difficult to disperse than perhaps half that number in the narrow confines of Drury Lane. As it was, it was about eleven when the first units, marching up from the Strand, reached the southern boundary of the Fields. By then those round the fire and in New Court were to be numbered in scores rather than in thousands. Despatching the Foot Guards and Grenadiers to deal with them, Horsey took the Life Guards at full trot towards the arch, and towards the noise and the glow of the fire beyond, ordering the Grenadiers to follow as soon as it was clear that the situation in the Fields was under control. A short cut through Wild Street, pointed out by Edward Orrell (who else?) who was now solicitously examining the meeting-house there for signs of damage, and within a few minutes the troopers were among the mob, riding in file, and using their chargers and occasionally the flat of their sabres to move them back from the fire.

To begin with, it was not at all easy. From the end of Long Acre to the meeting-house door the street was thick with rioters, and at first they could only be pressed back against the two sides of the street where at the rear they packed under the bulks. As the guards rode up to them they would retreat 40 or 50 yards, and then re-form as soon as the troopers' backs were turned. It was only with the coming of the Grenadiers under Serjeant Sutherland that the mob were broken up into groups of 50 or 100 and at length put to flight. But this was not before Captain Hensbrough of the Horse Guards had been almost run through by the sword of a bailiff named George Purchase, who, as an ex-trooper himself, had enough professional know-how even when mad drunk to know that the only way for a mob to overcome heavily-outnumbered cavalry was to get behind the horses and unseat the riders.[28] Fortunately for all concerned, there were not enough rioters able to follow his example or willing to share his determination that 'God damn them, he would lose his life in the cause!' Horsey gave the order 'to cut him to pieces', but Purchase somehow escaped down Long Acre. Some twenty minutes after the first trooper had ridden into Drury Lane the action was over.

The riots, however, were not, and more than three hours of hard activity still lay ahead of the soldiers. The infantry was still mopping up and making a few arrests round the Fields. The rest rode up Drury Lane and then headed east along Holborn, apparently at Orrell's urgent insistence: 'Gentlemen, says I, it is better to have all the meeting-houses destroyed than the Bank, pray let us go thither'.[29] When they reached the bottom of Leather Lane they came on the scene of the Holborn fire. There were still enough rioters on the street to force Captain Horsey to detach part of his cavalry to deal with them and to clear up Hatton Garden as well. It was no simple task to flush out the warren of alleys and courts between Holborn and Fleet Street and not surprisingly there were casualties here among the mob. Meanwhile the main body of Horse Grenadiers pressed on towards the City gates. It was as the tireless Captain Orrell guided them to the short cut down Fleet Lane that he heard from bystanders that the Hatton Garden mob (or part of it) had gone not to the Bank but to Blackfriars. By now it was turned midnight.

'I headed them in the Old Bailey', Orrell said later, 'and run before, and got the gates open [at Ludgate], and told them the Queen's guards were coming. I showed them the way to the meeting-house, and there they met the mob pulling it down'.[30] It was as well the Guards had Orrell for their vade-mecum that night, for City folk afterwards said that their timely arrival was a 'great deliverance'. The Blackfriars meeting-house of Samuel Wright stood in an intensely congested area, hemmed in on all sides by

other houses and shops; so not surprisingly it seemed providential
to those with memories of the Great Fire that the troops rode up
to the meeting-house door at the moment when the mob had
already 'cut the pews and galleries into pieces and put straw, rushes
and links under them', and when three other parties of rioters were
on the point of being despatched from Blackfriars, one to Shower's,
one to Nesbitt's chapel in Aldersgate Street, and the third to the
Bank. Here resistance was stiffer than in Drury Lane. One
resolute group made a stand near Fleet Ditch, where a Guards
captain was wounded, and the troopers had to use their sabres in
some earnest. Though there were no fatalities, they 'made a great
havoc'; and it was almost an hour before the streets were cleared
and the prisoners (among them John Pittkin, taken on Fleet Bridge,
still protesting 'that Sacheverell was much in the right of it')
were handed over to the constables.

One large pocket of rioters remained, in Clerkenwell. There part
of the Hatton Garden mob, incited by a professional gambler and
reputed Papist named Corbet, had arrived not long after midnight
and had soon begun putting to the torch in St John's Square the
contents of Hamilton's meeting-house, which had formerly been
the private chapel of Lord Aylesbury's town mansion. The St
John's riot was shamelessly abetted by gentlemen directing
operations from their coaches, as well as by some of the well-to-do
Tory residents of the area,* and it involved serious violence, as
well as arson. Burnet, whose windows overlooked the square, tells
how one man was dragged from the meeting-house and thrown
about until his leg and arm were broken, and how later another 'was
killed before my door; his skull was cleft with a spade'.† Burnet's
own house was threatened and the walls of his neighbour, Sir
Edmund Harrison, one of the leading Presbyterians in London,
were just being scaled by a party seemingly intent on mayhem
when, at almost two o'clock in the morning, Serjeant William
Sutherland led the 2nd Troop of Horse Grenadiers into the Square
and put the rioters to rout.[31] By 3 a.m., though a few arrests were

* Among those who plied them with money was the formidable Mrs Snell, whose
prejudices were so open and avowed that, as her maid remarked, she 'frequently
called her Presbyterian bitch (tho' she knew [I] went to the Church of England)'.
Blenheim MSS. Box VII, 18: Elizabeth Andrews's deposition.
† This because he protested against the mob's tearing down the Queen's arms, which
hung over the communion table in the chapel, and throwing them into the fire.

still being made, an uneasy quiet had at last settled on the capital, a quiet disturbed only by the tramp of the Foot Guards patrolling the streets, and by the beating of drums in the City where an emergency meeting at the Guildhall, to which the Lord Mayor was summoned at the absolute insistence of some of his fellow-aldermen, had at last produced the order which brought the members of the Trained Bands from their beds.[32]

Not until the end of the trial, however, did London fully return to normal after its night of fire and violence. On Thursday, the 2nd, all day and all night, the Guards patrolled the streets. Though they had to disperse thirty louts in Lincoln's Inn Fields just before midnight, the government was satisfied by the 3rd that the situation was sufficiently under control for the troops to be ordered back to quarters. But for the next three weeks companies of the militia and the Trained Bands remained constantly under arms and posted at key points to deter further disorders. In this they were entirely successful. Tory householders complained loudly of the £10,000 which it cost to keep the militia on foot;[33] but in truth they, like every man of property in the metropolis and every politician, had had a fright they were not to forget for many a year. 'This confusion', wrote Lady Wentworth, 'seems to me to be like the beginning of the late troubles, I having lately read Baker's Chronicles'.[34] Even Sacheverell himself, no doubt conscious that the violent insurrection of his supporters was 'an odd way of defending passive obedience and non-resistance',[35] was prevailed on by his friends to abandon 'his triumphal car', and after the great riot he travelled to and from the Hall comparatively chastely, first in a sedan chair with drawn curtains, then in a hackney coach, his escort reduced to a few score youths.[36]

The authorities naturally invoked legal as well as military deterrents to keep the city quiet. Within a week nearly a hundred suspects were in prison as a result of the informations laid before more than a dozen hard-worked magistrates. But although bills of indictment were found against three persons for High Treason and against thirty more for riot, the rioters escaped with relatively moderate fines[37] and the two men convicted of treason – Dammaree and Purchase – were later reprieved and pardoned. More frustratingly for the Whigs, they had to admit that few of the real ringleaders had been caught and above all that not one of the many men 'in gentlemen's habits' who, as scores of witnesses agreed, had been prominent at almost every focal point of the riots, was brought to justice. The Whigs were convinced at the time, and always remained convinced, that the Sacheverell riots had been in some measure planned and organised and that some prominent London Tories – even some in the Doctor's *entourage* – bore a heavy load of responsibility. Their own ministers showed this in the wording of the Proclamation drafted by the Privy Council on 2 March, in response to an uncompromising address carried in the Commons earlier that day; for it promised that 'all such rioters, traitors, rebels, and *all their accomplices, adherents, abetters and advisors* shall be forthwith proceeded against according to the utmost severity of law'.[38] But although their suspicions were not without foundation,* they could never be proved. Meanwhile they could only hope, as Nicholas Lechmere said in Westminster Hall on the afternoon after the riots, that as the Sacheverell trial itself was resumed, 'the rebellion that had been raised and that high treason that was committed, the last night, by those persons who abet the prisoner', would not deter the peers of England from bringing the insurrectionary-in-chief to justice.

---

* It is beyond the scope either of this chapter or of this book to analyse the surviving evidence – much of it of great interest – bearing both on the organisation and the social composition of the Sacheverell mobs. I propose to discuss this in a separate paper.

Note on the Economic Background to the Sacheverell Riots

It is often thought that prevailing economic conditions had an important
bearing on the riots of March 1710. Without doubt, the past year had been a
hard one for the ordinary people of London. Dear bread, the legacy of a disastrous harvest in 1708, had pressed hard on the straitened purses of the poor
the country over. A dismally wet summer and early autumn in 1709 offered
no relief from the dearth, and a 'pinching' winter lowered morale still further.[39]
A successful end to the war, or failing that, another Blenheim or Ramillies to
cheer, would have made hardships much easier to bear. But here, too, 1709
was a year of frustration: the Hague peace talks collapsed in the spring, and
in the autumn the Pyrrhic victory of Malplaquet left a costly 'butcher's bill',
further inflated by Tory propaganda. The popularity of the Whig ministry
with 'the meaner sort' must therefore have sagged in any event (for then, as
now, governments were blamed almost as much for developments outside
their control as for those within it). But in London the labourers and poorer
artisans had an additional grievance against their governors in 1709: the arrival,
at the government's invitation, of over 10,000 destitute refugees from the
Palatinate, and the temporary settlement of most of them in or around the
capital, where they attracted a great deal of private bounty and presented a
source of cheap labour to employers.[40]

It is obviously tempting to establish straight links between all these circumstances, most of all the economic plight of the London poor, and the wave of
popular disorder which suddenly broke over the capital in the first week of the
Sacheverell trial. And yet the evidence will not really justify doing so. A connection there was, no doubt, but it was not that of direct cause and effect. It
may not be conclusive in itself that the mobs who rampaged through the streets
of London and Westminster on the first two days of the trial shouted 'High
Church and Sacheverell' rather than such slogans as 'No War', 'No Foreigners'
or 'No more dear bread'; or that those who burned, pillaged and terrorised on
the third day attacked meeting-houses, not corn merchants' warehouses or
workshops. What is much more striking is that in close on a hundred depositions made before the J.Ps of London, Westminster and Middlesex after the
riots, by those who had witnessed the disorders and who had participated in
them, and likewise among all the abundant testimony given at the subsequent
treason trials, there is not one solitary allusion to empty bellies or empty
purses – indeed not one reference to material discontents of any kind. What
these men and women evinced were religious prejudices, crude political
passions, and above all sheer hooliganism, drunken or merely wanton.

It is clear that the Godolphin ministry already stood low in common esteem
at the beginning of the winter of 1709–10; low enough to be extremely vulnerable to the repercussions of just such an unpopular policy as the impeachment of Henry Sacheverell turned out to be. Because politicians in the early
eighteenth century rarely allowed such considerations – even when they were

N

aware of them – to influence important political calculations,* this unpopularity had had little or no effect on the arguments about whether the Doctor should be prosecuted, and how. But in any case, by February 1710 much of the discontent of six months earlier was little more than residual. Grain prices were now under control; nearly 6,000 Palatines had already been settled either in the provinces or in Ireland, and plans were well in hand to transplant a further 3,000 to New York; and Marlborough's sudden departure for the Continent had revived fresh hopes that peace might not, after all, be too long delayed.

In short, we must take the Sacheverell riots very much for what they were in appearance: violent demonstrations of sympathy for a priest under persecution, of anger and fear for a Church thought to be in danger, and of fury against those 'fanatic' thousands in their midst who appeared to prosper from their nonconformity, and who were believed (for had not the Doctor himself assured the world of it?) to have their tentacles everywhere from the Bank of England to the Queen's Cabinet table.

If it seems strange that most of the rioters lived not in the City proper with its thick carpet of parish churches, but in the neglected suburbs, so that it is a fair deduction that the majority never went to any Anglican service and had known little or no religious instruction, we need not trouble ourselves unduly with theorising about the reasons. Knowing how difficult it is at times to penetrate the minds even of the highly literate classes of a past society, let alone those of the inarticulate masses, we should perhaps be content in this case to allow the facts – which are in the main surprisingly clear – to tell a reasonably straightforward story.

---

* Significantly they showed some sensitivity in an Election year, even to the reactions of 'the common people'. But under the normal workings of the Triennial Act the next General Election was not due until the summer of 1711.

VIII THE CASE FOR THE DEFENCE

The fourth day of Sacheverell's trial, Thursday, 2 March, was entirely overshadowed by the events of the previous night. With the Commons acrimoniously debating, and the Lords urgently investigating the activities of the mob, it was two o'clock before the court was in session,[1] and by three o'clock it was adjourned. The Queen never appeared at all. Lechmere's summing-up for the Prosecution took only half an hour, and its hectic tone and occasional incoherence reflected the frayed nerves and tempers prevailing on both sides in the aftermath of the riots. When the speech was finished, Cowper invited the accused's counsel to open their defence. But Harcourt, who had been taken ill that morning, apparently with some form of influenza, was resolved on delaying tactics.

> My Lords, there having been already three whole days spent by the gentlemen of the House of Commons in maintenance of their charge, and this day being so far spent, I am bound in duty humbly to represent to your Lordships that it will be impossible for us to go through the very first article so as to finish in any reasonable time. My Lords, we humbly expect your Lordships' commands.

To this appeal, which can only have been made in the knowledge that the Cardigan return was still being judiciously delayed, many peers responded at first with calls of 'go on, go on'. But when Harcourt calmly persisted in asking for a firm decision, Lord Abingdon successfully moved the adjournment.[2]

'All people's expectations are fixed on Sir Simon Harcourt', wrote Abigail Harley that night to her nephew Edward, to the accompaniment of the militia drums outside her window; 'and everybody desires to hear him'.[3] Queen Anne was no exception, and she was watching attentively from her box when the Lords came down into the Hall soon after noon on Friday. Harcourt was an advocate of immense experience who in twenty-six years had already made a fortune at the Bar. But his defence of Sacheverell on the first article of the impeachment was the most difficult assignment of his career. He had not only to vindicate his client against the charge of condemning Resistance, and therefore of questioning the legality of the 1688 Revolution, King William's title and the Protestant Succession; he had also to vindicate his party – to wipe off the smears of Jacobitism and somehow to reconcile those seemingly glaring illogicalities in its ideological position since the Revolution which the Whigs had stripped naked on the first two days of the trial. Simply in itself this was taxing enough (as he said himself, 'his speaking was like dancing upon the ropes: if he slipped, he was sure to break his neck; they watched his words so').[4] For a man still so ill that he was allowed to have a doctor – the famous Radcliffe – sitting at his side throughout the day, it was truly daunting. It was of great help to him, however, that he was no rigid High Church Tory of the old breed, but one who had learned in association with Harley, his political mentor for many years, a suppler political philosophy which made it possible for staunch support of the Church of England and frank acceptance of the consequences of the Revolution to go hand in hand. He may not have flattered himself that he could thoroughly convert the bulk of his party to his philosophy. But he could at least apply it to the not inconsiderable task of saving Henry Sacheverell from his own folly.

The impact which Sir Simon made at the time, on the court and spectators alike, was remarkable. For almost two hours he held the floor, 'and so well that had there been no watches none had thought the third part of the time spent; no heat or indecent language, [but] gave everything a noble turn with mighty force of reason'. George Smalridge, stationed with Atterbury and Moss behind the Bar, thought that never in his life had he heard 'such a winning persuasion, such an insinuation into the passions of his auditors'.[5] As for the 'force of reason', the power and versatility of his argument

is less overwhelming in print than the rhapsodies of contemporaries
lead one to expect. But on this two comments should be made. One
is that the official version of the speech, printed by Tonson,[6]
probably bears no very exact relation to what Harcourt said in
court. He had a prepared script: but he first discarded several
pages of it, believing that his strength would not be equal to
delivering it all, and then, once on his feet and with the adrenalin
flowing, added extempore more than he had left out.* But however
excellent the matter, it was primarily the manner of Harcourt's
pleading, and above all the quality of the language, which created
the sensational impression on those not accustomed to his silver
tongue. 'His speech you will see in public,' Smalridge wrote next
day to his friend, Arthur Charlett; 'but you will not be able to
conceive half the pleasure from reading it as we did from hearing'.
Those who knew him already as 'the most eloquent lawyer of the
whole profession'[7] had some inkling of what to expect. But the
rest were spellbound by his soft, beautifully-modulated voice, 'the
cadences, and the strength, the justness and the beauty of the
expression'. Our anonymous diarist, glowing with both party
pride and professional appreciation, thought it could 'with modesty
be said that it at least equalled anything we yet know of the Grecian
or Roman oratory'.[8]

There were three distinct charges embodied in Article I. An
extraordinary feature of the opening speech for the Defence (and
one that most auditors, hypnotised by the speaker's eloquence, did
not appear to grasp) was that Harcourt concentrated over-
whelmingly on the first of these charges. Sixteen out of eighteen
pages in the printed version are devoted exclusively to justifying
the Doctor's stand on the general illegality of Resistance, while
at the same time trying to clear him of having condemned the
Resistance practised in 1688 in the case of the Revolution. The
other two charges were based on Sacheverell's eccentric claim that
King William himself had 'disclaimed the least imputation of
Resistance' at the time of the invasion, and that therefore (in the
Commons' version of the preacher's argument) 'to impute Resistance to the Revolution is to cast black and odious colours on his

---

* This explains the puzzling fact that the printed version, eighteen octavo pages in
   length, could not possibly have taken two hours to deliver – read as it stands it would
   have been no longer than Parker's speech on 1 March.

late Majesty, and on the said Revolution'. Since it was impossible
to deny that Sacheverell had said the former, and very difficult
to argue that he had not implied the latter, it is understandable that
Harcourt chose to skim as lightly as he could (in 'but a word or
two', as he himself admitted) over the two passages in the St
Paul's sermon which threatened to dislodge the keystone of the
defence he proposed to erect. It was his intention to depict
Sacheverell as moving in the mainstream both of Anglican teaching and constitutional law, in that he had condemned Resistance
as a general rule while *tacitly* acknowledging that there were exceptions to the rule – of which the Revolution was the prime example in recent history. Such a plea could only succeed if attention could be distracted from the uncomfortable fact that the
Doctor had, not very ambiguously, declined to accept that the
events of 1688 constituted 'Resistance' at all. Harcourt's tactics
were thus extremely shrewd. The very fact that he had to adopt
them must appear in retrospect a serious flaw in his case; but his
art was such that, on the day, he was able to carry them off with
a high degree of success (though his evasions did not escape the
vigilance of those Commons' Managers who were to have the last
word).

Of this art, his opening gambit – perfectly calculated to surprise
and excite – was a fine example. Taking it for granted that by 'the
necessary means' mentioned in the first article the Commons had
principally in mind the resistance of James II's subjects to their
King, he submitted that

> of this Resistance the Doctor has made no mention in his
> sermon. He has indeed affirmed the utter illegality of Resistance
> on any pretence whatsoever to the Supreme Power; but it can't
> be pretended there was any such Resistance used at the Revo-
> lution. The Supreme Power in this kingdom is the Legislative
> Power, and the Revolution took effect by the Lords and Com-
> mons concurring and assisting in it.* Whatever, therefore, the
> Doctor has asserted of the utter illegality of Resistance, his
> assertion being applied to the Supreme Power can't relate to
> any Resistance used at the Revolution, and consequently can't

---

* This, of course, was part fiction. Some peers and some former members of the
House of Commons assisted William, but not *initially* in their legislative capacity,
since no Parliament was in being in November 1688.

be an affirmance that such . . . 'necessary means' were odious and unjustifiable.[9]

Of all the Managers, only Parker and Hawles (Harcourt claimed) had expressly considered the implications of Sacheverell's use of the term 'the Supreme Power' rather than 'the Crown' or 'the Executive Power'; and neither had given him the benefit of the doubt, although Hawles, he gently reminded the court, had generously conceded that if the Doctor *had* meant the Legislature 'he should not have differed from him'. Other Managers had suggested that Sacheverell's 'Supreme Power', to whom Resistance was utterly and invariably illegal, was neither the Legislature nor the Executive but the Pretender. But 'this is diving into the secrets of his heart, and searching into his thoughts, which God alone knows'.[10]

Harcourt's drift now became clear. The Commons could not agree among themselves as to the accused's precise meaning. If such doubt existed, surely the law of England was 'more merciful than to make any man a criminal' – let alone a minister of the Gospel – 'by construing his words against the natural import of them in the worst sense'. After all, he blandly enquired of the cynical faces on the Commons' benches, what grounds were there in Doctor Sacheverell's personal conduct over two reigns for placing the worst construction on his attitude to the Revolution and the post-Revolution Establishment?

> He has taken the Oath of Allegiance, signed the Association, and took the Abjuration. 'Tis a miserable case any man is in if, after he has taken the Abjuration, the utmost which is required, he shall still be told, he has indeed abjured the Pretender, but hath not yet forgot him. . . . What satisfaction is it possible for him to give?[11]

Eminent historians of late Stuart England have written that Harcourt's speech 'put the classic case for the new Tory school', advancing 'doctrines which in the mouth of a Whig would have been condemned as Republican'.[12] But the truth is, Harcourt's highly ingenious redefinition of the old Tory doctrine of Non-Resistance – that it was resistance to the Crown-in-Parliament and not to the Crown alone that was never to be justified – was so far from being the core of his case that in print it occupies no more than the first page and a half of the speech. Aware that Sacheverell himself had not so much as hinted at so subtle and plausible an argument, either in his sermon or, more significantly, in his Answer, his leading counsel rightly concentrated on trying to vindicate his client on the assumption of an altogether more orthodox interpretation of the Non-Resistance theory. As he put it: 'I am not altogether without hopes but that I shall be able to satisfy even the gentlemen of the House of Commons, *whether that expression be understood of the Legislative or Executive Power*, that he is an innocent man'.[13]

On the first day of the trial, he recalled, the Prosecution had insisted that Sacheverell had expressly referred to the Revolution as a case not to be excepted from the general rule that resistance was utterly illegal. This allegation he would not accept. Dr Sacheverell, like the Apostle Paul, had remained silent about the exceptions.* But the Prosecution would argue that 'if in no case whatsoever 'tis lawful to resist, 'twas then unlawful at the Revolution' and that such a doctrine must be a slavish doctrine. 'An unlimited Passive Obedience and Non-Resistance' (Sir Simon disarmingly agreed) was 'a slavish notion'. But

> My Lords, Dr Sacheverell does not contend for it. . . . There is but this small difference between the gentlemen of the House of Commons, who think this expression so highly criminal, and the Doctor, who still conceives it to be otherwise: whether, when the general rule of obedience is taught, the particular exceptions which *may* be made out of that rule are always to be expressed; or whether, when the general rule is laid down, the particular exceptions which *might* be made out of that rule are not more properly to be understood or implied. I humbly apprehend, my Lords, that extraordinary cases, cases of necessity, are always implied, tho' not expressed, in the general rule. Such a case undoubtedly the Revolution was. . . . To point out every such case beforehand is as impossible as it is for a man in his senses not to perceive plainly when such a case happens.[14]

---

* *Tryal*, p. 183. Harcourt's argument, briefly, was that because the reference to the Revolution came between twenty and thirty lines after the assertion of the general doctrine, the connection between the two had been wrongly implied. A glance at the sermon demonstrates that this argument was invalid.

This was ingenious. But his audience could be forgiven a malicious speculation as to whether Sir Simon considered his client out of his senses, since he was so far from perceiving plainly that the Revolution was a 'case of necessity' justifying Resistance that he had gone out of his way to deny that Resistance had taken place in 1688 at all!

As if to discourage such speculation, Harcourt moved swiftly on to the main section of his speech, and on to his safest ground. He would attempt to demonstrate that the Doctor's assertion of Non-Resistance doctrine *in general terms* was 'warranted by the authority of the Church of England', just as it was 'agreeable to the law of England'. To demonstrate that the Church had always stood unequivocally behind this doctrine, Sir Simon (as that distinguished Church historian, Burnet, readily conceded) 'opened a great field'.[15] He first went back to the Henrician Reformation, quoting 'The King's Book' of 1543. He made great play with the Homilies, showing how the original three Homilies of Obedience of Edward VI's reign had received no less than six reinforcements under Elizabeth dealing with disobedience and wilful rebellion, while at the same time pointing to the 35th Article of Religion which required all ministers to read the Homilies 'diligently and distinctly' to their congregations.* Now came the leading question. 'My Lords . . . is it criminal in any man to *preach* that doctrine which 'tis his duty to *read*?' particularly since

> the rubric of the office appointed for the Fifth of November by the late Queen [Mary] of blessed memory directs the clergy on that day, if there be no sermon, to read one of these Homilies against rebellion. Since the Doctor chose rather to preach than to read a Homily on that day, how could he better comply with the command of her late Majesty than by preaching the same doctrine . . . ?[16]

But Homilies apart, the readings which the Defence would submit to the court on the following day would, Harcourt promised, prove

---

* High Church clergy were much addicted to the Homilies. 'Let our adversaries be as sharp and satirical upon the Homilies as they please,' one of them wrote, 'this I dare venture to say, that they will be esteemed and valued by posterity, especially by persons of the best understanding, when dissenters' sermons . . . shall either lie buried in dust or be utterly destroyed'. W. Nicholls, *A Defence of the Doctrine and Discipline of the Church of England* (2nd edn, 1715), p. 329.

beyond doubt that this very doctrine had been preached by the most orthodox and ablest divines in the Church since the Reformation.

> We shall beg your Lordships' patience to lay before you some passages out of the learned writings of several reverend Fathers of our Church, of nine archbishops, above twenty bishops, and of several other very eminent and learned men. That your Lordships may not think this doctrine died at the Revolution, I shall humbly lay before your Lordships the opinions of three archbishops and eleven bishops made since the Revolution. [And not sparing the blushes of seven bishops present, he proceeded to read the roll-call.] . . . Are the same words coming out of their mouths to be received as Oracles of Truth, but spoke by the Doctor fit for Articles of Impeachment?[17]

There were weaknesses in the later stages of Harcourt's speech. His attempt to show that Sacheverell's words on Obedience were in full accord with the law of the land[18] was learned but strained; and about the second charge in the article, the slander against William III, he would say little more than that the passage in the sermon, though obscurely expressed – 'I must confess, I can't easily comprehend him myself' – would hardly justify an impeachment. The most he could do with the third charge was to show that Sacheverell had not explicitly *said* the words in the accusation: he did not deny that he had *suggested* them. But he had no intention of ending on a lame, defensive note. His closing words were a ringing denunciation of those Whigs who professed to be out to stifle all politics from the pulpit, and yet at the same time connived at the activities of those 'new preachers and new teachers' whom the Doctor had boldly castigated, those Hoadleans who used the pulpit to promote republicanism and defend regicide. As for the Doctor himself,

> He is not the person he has been represented; he hath no disloyal thoughts about him. Sure I am he would rather die in her Majesty's defence. We shall show your Lordships that there are such as run most vile comparisons between the Revolution and the most execrable murder of King Charles the First,

and can find no better difference between them than this abominable distinction, of a *Wet Martyrdom* and a *Dry One*.*

Virtually all that remained of Friday's five-hour sitting, after Harcourt's tour de force, was taken up by the case of the four supporting counsel against the first article. Samuel Dodd and Constantine Phipps both made long speeches – Dodd's far too long for the Queen, who abandoned him 'about three o'clock . . . [and] went to dinner, had eighteen dishes of meat on her table, and sat two hours', almost till the adjournment.[19] Neither Dodd nor Duncan Dee had a voice fit for the Hall or the occasion, and even of their audible arguments few rose above the mediocre. Henchman made one distinctive (though disconcerting) point crisply and well, but then subsided. Only Phipps succeeded in dispelling the general atmosphere of anticlimax. Here indeed were lucidity and logic; more than that, astringency and wit and, in flashes, marked originality. He 'behaved himself [thought our diarist] with Sir Simon Harcourt's resolution, and only fell short of him in his delivery and language'.[20] However it may have sounded to his listeners, Phipps's contribution reads scarcely less well than the vaunted performance of his principal.

The efforts of the supporting counsel to add fresh weight to points already made or anticipated by Harcourt were not conspicuously helpful; although Phipps, in following up Harcourt's ingenious equation of 'the Supreme Power' with 'the Legislative Power', and quoting Puffendorf, did insist that what Sacheverell had asserted from his St Paul's pulpit was the utter illegality of resisting the *laws* made in due constitutional form by Crown, Lords and Commons.[21] Rather more effective were their attempts to patch up a few of the holes in Harcourt's very threadbare defence against the third branch of Article I. In fact, Phipps, by careful attention to the text of the sermon, put up the most plausible case possible against the charge

> that the Doctor does suggest and maintain that to impute Resistance to the Revolution is to cast black and odious colours upon his Majesty and the Revolution. In answer to which I must beg leave to take notice that the words of the sermon are

---

* These closing words of Harcourt's speech (*Tryal*, p. 196) were an unveiled, and well understood, reference to Defoe's *Review*.

here transposed and misplaced. For . . . what he *says* is no more than that to justify the calling the sovereign to an account for high treason, and the dethroning and murdering of him, by [appealing to] the Revolution is to cast black and odious colours upon both. And is there anybody that has any respect for the Glorious and Happy Revolution . . . can say less?*

When the later speakers did venture away from the tracks pioneered by Sir Simon they occasionally had something of real value to offer. Unfortunately the coordination of their efforts left something to be desired. Harcourt's central argument on Resistance – that the Revolution represented a spectacular exception to an accepted rule, and that no Anglican divine could have been expected to mention such an exception while enunciating a basic precept – had, to be sure, been dutifully echoed by Dodd and Phipps.[22] But how disconcerted they must all have been when Humphrey Henchman, odd-man-out in this company of Common lawyers, cleverly deduced from one passage of the Guy Fawkes's Day sermon which had so far been ignored on both sides that the Doctor *had* made the exception (or at least deduced the exception) in the case of the Revolution.

If nothing will satisfy the gentlemen of the House of Commons but an exception, an exception they shall have, and that out of his own mouth. It is in the 10th page, and [at] the beginning of that very paragraph where the whole foundation of this accusation is laid. But I don't well know whether I may venture to mention it, lest it should subject him to a prosecution in the spiritual court or the censure of his diocesan [a shrewd dig!] . . . The clause is this . . . *The constitutions of most governments*

---

* *Tryal*, p. 209. We must judge for ourselves. In his sermon Sacheverell had referred to the teaching of 'our new preachers and politicians' that the People had the power invested in them 'to cancel their allegiance at pleasure and call their sovereign to account for High Treason against his supreme subjects, forsooth! nay, to dethrone and murder him for a criminal, as they did the Royal Martyr, by a judiciary sentence'. Then, after two sentences of comment, rather than fresh argument, he had continued, in those incriminating words which everyone now knew by heart: 'Our adversaries think they effectually stop our mouths, and have us sure and unanswerable on this point, when they urge the Revolution of this day in their defence. But certainly they are the greatest enemies of that, and his late Majesty, and the most ungrateful for the deliverance, who endeavour to cast such black and odious colours on both. How often must they be told that the King solemnly disclaimed the least imputation of Resistance in his Declaration . . .'

differing according to their several frames and laws upon which they
are built and founded, it is impossible to lay down any one universal
rule as the scheme and measure of obedience that may square to
every one of them. My Lords . . . he is not here for bringing all
things to his own rule, but every government must . . . be
governed according to its own rules. But he goes on. *Only this*
maxim in general I presume may be established for the safety,
tranquillity and support of all governments, that no innovation
whatsoever should be allowed in the fundamental constitution of
any state, without a very pressing, nay unavoidable necessity for it.

Nobody would deny that the Revolution was just such a case of
unavoidable necessity. But many, Henchman added, would think
it very strange 'that this exception should stand so very full and
plain in the very front of that paragraph from which the learned
Managers have chiefly drawn this accusation, and yet never be so
much as once taken notice of by them. Passages at a much greater
distance have been connected in order to accuse him'.[23]

Even the ponderous Dodd was able to make something of this
last point. Phipps observed that the phrase 'the necessary means'
used to bring about the Revolution, which figured in Article I,
was not even mentioned anywhere in the sermon; and got a laugh
when he added, 'I at first doubted whether I had the right sermon;
for I could no more find that sentence in the Doctor's sermon at
St Paul's than one of the learned Managers* could find a text of
Scripture, quoted by the Doctor, in his Bible'.[24] After Harcourt's
speech, however, the most memorable moment of Friday's proceedings came when Phipps tilted at the Contract theory of monarchy.

When the Original Contract was made, that learned gentleman
[Lechmere] did not think fit to inform us.† Was it before Magna
Charta [*sic*]? If so, why not comprised in it? . . . I never met
with it in any of our law-books, in my little experience. I never
heard it urged in any court before. Was it before the statute of
the 25th of Edward the Third? I never knew it pleaded to any
indictment for High Treason, nor objected to enervate or take
off the force of that statute. . . . And therefore, till the Legis-

---

* William Thompson.
† See pp. 131–2 above, and cf.[pp. 140.

lature have declared what the Original Contract is, and deter-mined what act of the Supreme Executive Power shall amount to a dissolution of that Original Contract and discharge the sub-jects from their allegiance, I must beg pardon if I think that as to Resistance in general, the law stands still upon the foot of the 25th of Edward the Third, and that all Resistance, except in the case of the Revolution, is still treason within that Act.[25]

This was able pleading. On the morrow, however, there was a surprise in store for Phipps about the Contract.

The last day of the week, Saturday the 4th, was set aside for the readings in which Harcourt had promised abundant justifica-tion for Sacheverell's doctrine of Obedience. Those who had fore-cast a dreary ritual, with the clerks droning out interminable extracts from long-forgotten books and sermons, were proved quite wrong. Friday evening must have seen a managerial council, followed by the burning of midnight oil in several Whig houses. Fortunately a number of obliging hints dropped by Harcourt and Phipps had given the Managers advance notice of some of the sources on which the Defence was proposing to draw; and a few hours of feverish research ensured that the first week of the trial would not come to an end with the Doctor's counsel holding the floor undisputed.

However, after the court met in the early afternoon the Clerk to the Lords was allowed to proceed from a reading of The King's Book of 1543 and the Homilies, through passages from Overall, Foxe's *Martyrs* and Jewel's *Apologia*, all condemning Resistance, until he reached Hooker's *Laws of Ecclesiastical Polity*. Reading from page 470 of the edition of 1705 the Clerk had reached the words, 'be subject not for fear but of mere conscience, knowing that he which resisteth them purchaseth to himself condemnation', when General Stanhope got to his feet with an interjection which made the whole Hall buzz.

> STANHOPE. My Lords, since Hooker's *Ecclesiastical Polity* is before your Lordships, and they have read that part, I pray that from page 444 to the latter end of page 446 may likewise be read.
>
> DODD. We submit it to your Lordships whether it is proper to break into our defence . . .

JEKYLL. My Lords, the indulgence of the Managers to let the
Doctor's counsel go into this evidence is very great . . . But
surely, as they have called this witness, for so I may term the
book they were reading, we may be at liberty to cross examine
that witness . . .
PHIPPS. My Lords, we submit to it.

Hooker on the origin of sovereign authority, which the Clerk now
dutifully read, was hardly the sort of material which the Doctor's
counsel would have hand picked; and Phipps, in particular, cannot
have relished the reminder in one remarkable passage that the
Contract was not without the most respectable Anglican pro-
genitors.*
More fireworks were to follow, though only after the Whigs had
had to stomach in silence matter of a more recent pedigree, including the ultra-reactionary 'Oxford decrees' of 1683. Phipps
then called for two extracts from Archbishop Sharp's sermon to the
House of Lords, preached on 30 January 1700. As read, they were
a model of High Anglican orthodoxy. But Sharp himself, sitting
behind the judges, must have known how selective they were;
and so did the Treasurer of the Navy, as the official account tells
us.

WALPOLE. My Lords, I presume the counsel have offered all
they think proper to offer out of this sermon. But that your
Lordships may have a specimen of the candour of the Doctor's
quotations, I pray the Clerk may now read the two next
paragraphs of that sermon, and that he read them as distinctly
as he did the others.
CLERK (reads). 'But then, after I have said this, care must be
taken that this general doctrine be not misapplied in particular countries. Though Non-Resistance or Passive Obedience be a duty to all subjects and under all governments,
yet it is not to be expressed in the same way in all places. . . .
As the laws of the land are the measures of our active
obedience, so are also the same laws the measures of our

* *Tryal*, pp. 231–3. Hooker, among other things, had written that 'albeit we judge it
a thing most true that kings . . . do hold their right in the power of dominion, with
dependency upon the whole body politic over which they have rule as kings, yet . . .
the case of dependency is that first Original Conveyance when the power was derived
from the whole into one' (and so forth).

submission; and as we are not bound to obey but where the laws and constitution require our obedience, so neither are we bound to submit, but as the laws and constitution do require our submission'.

WALPOLE. Before we part with that sermon, I desire one paragraph more may be read; it begins with these words, *If indeed a preacher.*

CLERK (reads). 'If indeed a preacher should in the pulpit presume to give his judgment about the management of public affairs, or to lay down doctrines as from Christ about the forms and models of kingdoms or commonwealths, or to adjust the limits of the prerogative of the prince or of the liberties of the subjects in our present government; I say, if a divine should meddle with such matters as these in his sermons, I do not know how he can be excused from the just censure of meddling with things that nothing concern him . . .'[26]

With Jekyll constituted watchdog-in-chief, the Managers contrived several other shrewd interventions before the afternoon was over. But for the audience the highlight came when, with predictable maliciousness, the Defence claimed to vindicate the doctrine of Obedience from the pen of Burnet of Salisbury, quoting his *Vindication of the Authority of the Church and State of Scotland* of 1673 and his Guildhall Sermon of 1689. While these readings were in progress the bishop was seen 'sneaking from his place to deliver the Managers a book of his own out of his bosom [in point of fact, another copy of his *Vindication*], and directing them to call for a passage to contradict himself!' This Sir Peter King did, with as straight a face as he could muster in the circumstances.[27] When the hoarse-voiced clerks had finished their five-hour stint in the early evening, and the court adjourned for the weekend, neither side can have considered the day wholly ill-spent.

For many Monday, 6 March was until the last hour or two the most disappointing full day of the trial. The Cardigan writ had at last been returned, a scandalous twelve days after the election, and it was clear that Sir Simon Harcourt would take no further part in the proceedings.* Friday's performance had been 'his *Vox Cygnea*', Smalridge sadly acknowledged; 'and [we] shall hear him no more'.[28] Phipps and his colleagues were now concerned with the second and third articles, the 'Toleration' and 'Church in Danger' articles. And it soon became apparent that, except for occasional flashes of individuality from Phipps himself and from Henchman, there was not much they could do beyond repeating and elaborating what Sacheverell had already said, in self-exculpation, in his Answer. Thus with Article II they followed the expected line that since the word 'Toleration' was unknown to the *law*, as opposed to convention, no legal Toleration could be said to exist and the Doctor could not therefore be justly accused of declaring it 'unreasonable' and 'unwarrantable'; and likewise that his one fleeting, specific, statement at St Paul's, that he intended no 'reflection on that Indulgence which law has given to consciences truly scrupulous', deserved to be given far more weight than 'innuendoes' and 'strained inferences'. Counsel's problem was to find some agreed interpretation of the word 'Toleration' that would fit the variety of contexts in which the Doctor had used it – most of them defamatory – without leaving some flank exposed to a criminal charge. It was really insoluble. Dee and Dodd[29] took the easy way out, by echoing the already-discredited argument in the Answer.† Only Phipps attempted something more sophisticated, positing that where the Doctor had condemned 'Toleration' he had had in mind dissenters not legally entitled to official indulgence, especially Unitarians and the 'multitude' who attended conventicles not licensed under the Act.[30] Phipps's ingenuity got the better of him, however, when he took one of the passages which the Managers had used against the Doctor and tried to use it for him. It was the passage *what could not be gained by Comprehension and Toleration, must be brought about by Moderation and Occasional Conformity*. 'Does this suggest the Toleration to be unreasonable', he asked, 'or the allowance of it unwarrantable? It rather excuses it from having hurt the Church'.[31] Here was a sorry tangle. For not

* He had, in fact, been absent from court on the 4th. On the 7th he took his seat in the House of Commons, introduced by Robert Harley and Sir Thomas Mansel, who between them had engineered his election. See Dyer's Newsletter, 7 March; *Evening Post*, 4 March; Blenheim MSS. B II–4: Sir Humphrey Mackworth to Marlborough, 19 Jan.

† See p. 107 above.

only was Phipps conceding, in effect, that Sacheverell had used the word 'Toleration' promiscuously, and that here it was to be equated with the 1689 Act; he was also ignoring what the Prosecution had already pointed out, that the Comprehension bill and the Toleration Act of the 1689 Parliament were both stigmatised in the sermon, nay in the very next sentence, as 'open violence' against the Church, in contrast to the 'secret treachery' practised since.

The Doctor's counsel were also in difficulties when trying to explain against whom (if not the dissenters) their client had urged Anglican leaders 'to thunder out their ecclesiastical anathemas', and exactly what sentences 'ratified in Heaven' he had defied the civil power to reverse. Dee and Phipps flatly contradicted each other on this, while Dodd, floundering hopelessly, could only suggest that 'the discourse is general, and not determined to any persons . . . but properly intended against irreligion'.[32] In the end it was left to Henchman, the expert on canon law, to combine a defence of Sacheverell which did not shirk his true meaning, with a striking exposition of the High Church position on the claims of spiritual as against temporal jurisdiction.

> My Lords . . . thus much I hope I may say without offence: that the spiritual power of Church pastors is not derived from the civil magistrate, but from God; that one branch of that power is the censuring of notorious offenders and excluding them from the Communion of the Church . . .
>
> We are told by the learned Manager that in case any ecclesiastical judge should inflict an illegal censure of excommunication, the temporal courts may and would soon give relief by sending forth a prohibition. But your Lordships will consider that there is a wide and manifest difference betwixt an excommunication founded upon a prosecution in the ecclesiastical courts and the pronouncing censure purely spiritual. The external coercive jurisdiction of ecclesiastical courts being derived from the laws of the land may [be] and is frequently by those laws restrained. But such restraint does not hinder the pastors of the Church from exercising the spiritual power of the keys, which they derive not from the laws of the land but from the institution of Christ.
>
> And therefore, tho' it be provided in the Act of Exemption

[of 1689] that persons taking the oaths and making the declaration in that Act mentioned shall not be prosecuted in any ecclesiastical court for not conforming to the Church of England,
yet it is not by that Act expressed or intended that Nonconformity to the Established Church should no longer be
looked upon as schism, or that separatists may not, by the pastors
of the Church, be pronounced schismatical.[33]

As Trevelyan so truly said, 'Sacheverell may have been a mean
man, but the debate he aroused was no mean argument.'[34]

The case which Sacheverell's lawyers put forward against the
'Church in Danger' article was little more than a peg on which to
hang a further – and this time deliberately sensational – series of
readings, that 'black catalogue' as the Tory diarist described them.
For the remainder of the session on the 6th the court wallowed in
the reading of 'those horrid blasphemies', which the Managers,
on the submission of William Thompson, tried unsuccessfully to
block as 'immaterial . . . for the prisoner's defence'. That they
tried was hardly surprising; for apart from the grotesque parade
of printed blasphemy, the audience was regaled, as Abigail Harley
related, with books 'full of base reflections upon the Queen and her
family, one passage that she had no more title to the crown than
my Lord Mayor's horse'. 'None of common understanding', she
reflected, 'but must think the Church, and State too, in danger from
such christened heathens if suffered to go on without notice
taken of them'. And the Queen, as well as 2,000 others, heard it
all.[35]

When the peers took their places at noon on the following day,
Tuesday, the Defence embarked without much conviction on the
unenviable task of refuting the hydraheaded charge under Article
IV which Sir Thomas Parker had so brilliantly maintained. Dodd,
who opened as usual in Harcourt's absence, was pathetically
banal.[36] Phipps was sharper; but even he was reduced to such
extremities as claiming that Sacheverell's notorious reference to
*men of characters and stations that shift and prevaricate with their
principles* was simply 'a charge upon them in their private capacity,
and does not charge them with any misbehaviour in their stations'.
With equal optimism he suggested, despite what Parker had said,
that because the references to 'men of characters and stations' and

to false brethren 'undermining and betraying . . . the Constitution' were separated by seven pages, the connection between them in the charge was a fictitious one, fabricated by the Commons. But as it happened, these palpable shortcomings were to make only a very limited difference to the impact of the case for the Defence. For the final word on 7 March was not to rest with the lawyers. This, of all the days of the trial, was to be Henry Sacheverell's day. If his counsel had had their way he would not have spoken until after the Managers had replied; but when Dodd made this proposal, at the conclusion of the case against Article IV, Sir Joseph Jekyll tartly replied, on behalf of his colleagues, 'that if he has anything to say for himself, now is his time, before the Commons reply; the Commons claiming it as their right to speak last'. There was no point in Dodd appealing to the Lord Chancellor, and he knew it. 'My Lords,' he said, 'we submit to it. Doctor, go on'.[37]

Dr Sacheverell had already made the lot of his lawyers doubly difficult by taking the composition of his Answer into his own hands in January. We make take it for granted that his counsel would never have allowed him out of his chair on 7 March had they not known that, for once in his life, he had been persuaded that his own deathless prose was not the ideal recipe for the occasion. The work of composition was generally thought to have been put in commission. The wittiest thing the Whigs could find to say about it afterwards (and for them it was no joking matter) was that it was a good speech, 'but made by the University of Oxford'. John Oldmixon was more specific: 'the speech which his brothers, Doctors Atterbury, Smalridge, Freind and Moss made for him, with the help of Harcourt and Phipps'. Others gave the whole credit to Atterbury. The Reverend Thomas Carte was possibly the only well-informed judge of style in England who, on examining the speech at leisure afterwards, could still say: 'I can't but think it his own . . . though I am satisfied Dr Atterbury and Smalridge perused it before he spake it'.[38]

The shrewdly-judged bid for the sympathy of his audience which Sacheverell made in the first two minutes of his speech announced from the start that the bombastic fire-eater of St Mary's and St Paul's had given place, for the occasion, to a far more adroit and sensitive orator. He had only been persuaded to speak at all, he said, out of grave concern for the dignity of the Holy Order to which he belonged and the doctrines of his Church.

For, my Lords, it has been owned by some of the Managers for the Honourable House of Commons that, though I am the person impeached, yet my condemnation is not the thing principally aimed at. I am, it seems, *an insignificant tool of a party, not worth regarding*. The avowed design of my impeachment is, by the means of it, to procure an eternal and indelible brand of infamy to be fixed in a parliamentary way on all those who maintain the doctrine of Non-Resistance, and to have the clergy directed what doctrines they are to preach, and what not. And therefore, as insignificant as I am in myself, yet the consequences of my trial . . . are of the highest moment and importance.[39]

What Sacheverell had to say thereafter was directed to three ends. In the first part of his speech he delivered his own protest against the methods the Commons had used to frame and prosecute their charges. In the second part he commented briefly on each of the articles. The last section he devoted to a personal apologia, declaring his intentions in preaching the St Paul's sermon, asserting his loyalty to the Queen and her government, and laying bare, with an uncanny combination of emotionalism and art, the thoughts and feelings of a wronged priest under persecution.

His initial protest was especially effective because he did not limit it to the Managers' method of 'piecing broken sentences, and conjoining distant and independent passages, in order to make me speak what I never thought of'. He spoke of the consistency with which the most invidious constructions had been placed on any words of his capable of more than one interpretation. He deplored the fact that 'to aggravate my guilt, I have been accused not only for what I am supposed to have said but for what I am allowed *not* to have said' as if 'my silence itself were criminal'. And subtly he asked, whether there could be 'a clearer indication that I am not guilty of having asserted what I am charged [with] . . . than that so many hours learning and eloquence have been employed in proving me to have said it'.[40]

When the Doctor began to address himself to the first article it was apparent that he had not trimmed his sails wholly to order. He was still unrepentant in his refusal to accept that Resistance had taken place at the Revolution, leaving his interpretation of 'Supreme Power' deliberately ambiguous. And he neither endorsed nor rejected his lawyers' plea that the justifiable Resistance of 1688 was the tacitly accepted exception to the High Anglican rule of universal obedience. 'I expressed this doctrine in the same general terms in which I found it delivered by the Apostles of Christ'. It was not 'applicable to the case of the Revolution, the Supreme Power not being then resisted'.[41] Turning to the Toleration article, he again protested his sincerity in approving the indulgence granted in 1689 to men of 'truly scrupulous conscience'. But he did not deny having 'blamed, and perhaps with some warmth and earnestness blamed, the abuses which men of *no conscience* have made of the Legal Exemption'; and he insisted on the classic Anglican position that schism itself, 'notwithstanding the Indulgence', remained a sin in the eyes of God.[42]

Sacheverell stood by his monitory words from St Paul's pulpit that the Church was in danger. He reminded the court that in that pulpit he had warned, in words unheeded by the Managers, against 'the Roman Catholic agents and missionaries that swarm about this great City'; but he rested his case, in the main, on the growth of irreligion:

> I hope I may say without offence that the Church may be in peril from other causes, without any reflection upon her Majesty's government or any contradiction to . . . the resolution of both Houses of Parliament four years ago. If the Church be in danger when the Christian religion is evidently so, I hope it will be thought no crime to say it has scarce ever been in greater danger than it is now, since Christ had a Church upon earth.[43]

On the fourth article he lingered longest, and here for a while the old fires burned strongly as he threw a series of challenges back at his prosecutors:

> After all that has been said by the learned Managers of the Commons, what Minister of State, I beseech your Lordships, have I been proved to reflect upon, directly or indirectly? Where and how do I, by any suggestion, charge her Majesty or those in authority under her with a general maladministration? . . . How

is it possible I should stir up the people to arms and violence, when I am endeavouring to convince them of the utter illegality of Resistance . . . ?

And in response to Parker's suggestion that this last seeming inconsistency could be reconciled by supposing it was only Resistance to a rightful king across the water that was condemned, he proceeded, calling on God as his witness, passionately to repudiate the Pretender and proclaim his undeviating loyalty to Queen Anne since the day of her accession.[44]

So the Doctor came to the final part of his speech, his personal apologia. Here every phrase was carefully shaped, every inflection of his voice theatrically controlled, with a single object in mind: to play upon the emotions of his hearers. The opening was breathtaking in its sense of drama – and in its audacity. His prosecutors had claimed to have penetrated behind his words to his secret intentions.

> I call the Searcher of Hearts to witness in the most solemn and religious manner, as I expect to be acquitted before God and his Holy Angels at that dreadful tribunal before which not only I but all the world . . . must appear, to be acquitted or condemned, that I had no such wicked, seditious or malicious intentions; that there is nothing upon earth I more detest and abhor; that my designs were in every respect directly contrary.[45]

After pledging himself in florid rhetoric to the Protestant Succession, which there had been 'no occasion in either of my sermons to take notice of', he moved towards the calculated, yet intensely moving, climax of the whole speech. It was a plea that the Lords, his judges, would take into consideration all that he had already suffered and deem it 'sufficient punishment for one who has offended against no law yet in being'. He begged them to consider that his good name, 'which is to all men dear, but much more so to those whose whole capacity of doing good in the world principally depends upon it', had been scarred whatever the final judgment; and to bear in mind, 'not the least of my sufferings, that I have been for so long a time debarred from taking heed to that flock over which the Holy Ghost hath made me an overseer'.[46]

Seeking their Lordships' compassion on what he averred was his greatest humiliation, 'the public manner, the length and solemnity of my trial . . . by which means I am made a gazing-stock, both by reproaches and afflictions, and a spectacle to the whole world', he finally entreated them to take into account that whatever he had said at St Paul's, he had only done his bounden duty as a priest of the Church of England. And what could be harder than to be 'punished in this world for doing that which, if we do not, we shall be more heavily punished in the next'.[47] Appropriately, then, he ended his speech not as the prisoner at the Bar but as the man of God, with humility, compassion and forgiveness in his heart; praying 'for the Queen my sovereign, for your Lordships my judges, and for the Commons my accusers; most earnestly beseeching Almighty God to deliver all orders and degrees of men amongst us from all false doctrine, heresy and schism, from hardness of heart, from contempt of His word and commandment, from envy, hatred and malice, and all uncharitableness'.[48]

For an hour and a quarter two thousand people had sat transfixed as the Doctor, 'with a fine accent and the most agreeable voice [our diarist thought] that ever I heard', savoured every meticulously chosen word.[49] His tutors had looked to him for a performance; and he had given the performance of his life. The last ten minutes of his speech were delivered amid some of the most extraordinary scenes ever seen in an English court. Women everywhere wept and sought for their handkerchiefs; many sobbed uncontrollably (to the fury of Ann Clavering, who swore that 'nonresisting ladies' like Lady Granville and the duchesses of Grafton and Shrewsbury, 'had they that moment become widow . . . could not have acted a more hypocritical part'). Arthur Mainwaring was not altogether surprised that Sacheverell, with 'his lungs and actions', should wreak such havoc on the softer hearts. But he and many others were astonished to see that the faces of hardened veterans of thirty or forty years of political campaigning, among them Leeds, Rochester, Guernsey and Nottingham, were also running with tears. Nottingham, himself a noted orator, was not given to enthusiasm; yet he wrote that evening that Sacheverell's was 'the most glorious harangue that I ever heard or read in any author, not excepting Tully'.

In the ranks of Tuscany feelings, understandably, were more

mixed. There had to be admiration for the sheer art of the man; and Sir Peter King so far forgot his Manager's responsibilities in the ardour of the moment as to own as generously as Nottingham that 'it was a speech of the finest oratory that he ever read or heard in any language, and delivered as well'. On the other hand many were visibly shaken at what they could only believe to be the awesome hypocrisy of Sacheverell's spine-chilling appeal to 'the Searcher of Hearts' to bear witness to his innocence. One peer later told how he sat expecting a thunderbolt from Heaven to strike the Doctor dead. Lady Sunderland – 'the little Whig' of Kit-Cat fame – is said to have wept not out of sympathy, but at hearing God's name taken so publicly in vain. Miss Clavering, for her part, felt no urge to cry, except perhaps with rage. 'A parson I never loved,' she told her brother, 'but now I've so great an abhorrence to them that, were it not for a few bishops, I should think the imps of Lucifer had put on that habit to destroy us'.[50]

The most striking tribute paid this day to Sacheverell was the wordless tribute from the Managers' stand. When the Doctor had taken his seat the Lord Chancellor stood up and was heard to ask the Managers, 'are you ready to proceed with your reply'. Spectators watched, fascinated, as 'Sir J. Jekyll first, Mr Lechmere second, and then a third of the Managers rose, looked in a great deal of confusion, and gaped as if they would speak, but said nothing. So after a considerable pause, one of them (I think Lechmere) stooped down and spoke softly to Lord Wharton. Lord Wharton rose, went into the middle of the House, and moved to adjourn'.[51] Since the morrow – the anniversary of the Queen's accession – was a holiday, the adjournment gave the Managers almost two days to recover themselves and deliberate on what lines their reply ought to follow.

The Prosecution began its reply shortly after one o'clock on the afternoon of Thursday, the 9th. It was entrusted entirely to the lawyers, with the understanding that Stanhope was available, if needed, to support Sir Thomas Parker.[52] Jekyll, Eyre and Lechmere were nominated for the first article, King and Cowper for the second and Thompson for the third. To Parker was allocated not only the fourth article but the summing-up. The reply was long, comprehensive and scrupulously detailed. It spread over two days and must have lasted in all for close on seven hours.* The general tone throughout, in contrast with much of the original Prosecution case, was intellectual or firmly legalistic rather than polemical. Very occasionally passion or personal animosity broke through the judicial calm. Lechmere could not resist a few pugnacious blows or tasteless taunts at Harcourt and Phipps. Parker, who on Friday made the longest speech of the whole trial, at the last forsook his erudition and wit, and allowed his abhorrence of Sacheverell, the man, to spill over. But these outbursts were heavily outweighed by ingenious and closely documented argument and by a general restraint, particularly towards Sacheverell himself. In fact, there was a clear agreement that until Parker's final harangue there should be the minimum of reference to Sacheverell's speech and a heavy concentration on the arguments of his counsel.

These arguments were devastated. Those who imagined that the prosecutors would be more than temporarily disturbed by the emotional impact of the Doctor's oratory were soon disabused, as in masterly sequence Jekyll, King, Thompson and Parker took apart the case for the Defence brick by brick, until at the end there was very little, even of Harcourt's work, left standing. Yet exceptional though it was as an exercise in judicial demolition,† it may be doubted whether it had a great deal of influence on the outcome of the trial. There is a sense, not quite of irrelevance, but certainly of anti-climax about these two days. Through every speech there was an unmistakable feeling that professional skill, vigour, supremacy in argument, no longer counted for much: the Prosecution had missed the tide.

However, there are a few highlights in the Managers' reply which it would be unjust to leave unnoticed. The first came when Jekyll in his marathon opening speech asked the court to look back at the previous century and a half for some indication of 'the sense of the nation' on the point of Non-Resistance. He instanced the help given by Elizabeth's government to the Northern Netherlands in resisting Spain, by James I to the Palatines, resisting the authority of their Imperial suzerain, and by Charles I to the Rochellois, and the popular support these efforts had attracted. And he drew a particular moral from the revolt of the Netherlands. The Anglican

---

* It consumes 98 pages of the official account.
† As such, it repays reading from beginning to end. See *Tryal*, pp. 351–447.

clergy, at the very time they were reading out to their congregations the new Homilies against Resistance, gladly granted money in Convocation to help to finance the Queen's aid to the Dutch rebels. Did not this discount any suggestion that the Homilies were designed to condition the people to submit without demur to 'a total subversion of the constitution'.[53] Then there was the moment when Lechmere, for all his radicalism, conceded that the Anglican doctrine by which 'the general duty of subjects to the higher powers is taught' was 'a godly and wholesome doctrine', and that for preaching it 'in the same general terms in which he found it delivered', Sacheverell would never have been prosecuted. But what the Doctor had done, said Lechmere, was to draw quite deliberate attention to the most obvious exception, and then reject it; thus implicitly denying the legality of the Revolution, in which the fact of Resistance was crystal clear to everyone. This was his crime; and this was why, in Lechmere's view, so much of the Defence had been 'altogether immaterial'.[54] In the reply to Article II, Sir Peter King with equal effect told the Lords that he was far from asking them to convict the accused on the basis of those 'strained innuendoes and forced constructions' of which he and his counsel had constantly complained; and he then proceeded to retail a string of verbatim quotations from the sermon on which he had based much of his original case, most of which the Defence had failed even to mention, let alone argue away.[55]

On the 10th, the second day of the reply, there was time before Parker's advent to savour again the wit of Thompson, as he made merry with Phipps's desperate plea that the only sense in which Sacheverell could have accused the administration of endangering the Church was in hinting at the failure of the 'inferior magistrates' to enforce the laws against vice, irreligion and blasphemy. Who, he enquired, had been the architects of Comprehension, Toleration and Moderation, those policies which the Doctor deemed so disastrous to the Church? 'I suppose . . . as men of characters and stations in the State were construed to be constables, excisemen and custom-house officers, so these persons who were to bring about Comprehension, and are now blowing up and undermining the Church in another manner, must be churchwardens, parish clerks and sextons'.[56] To this point Sir Thomas Parker returned during his monumental closing speech on the general charge of sedition, challenging specifically the Doctor's own pretence that 'his warmth of speech was only to stir up the magistrates to put the laws [*for the defence and security of the Church*][57] strictly in execution'. He asked the court to listen again to two pages of the sermon and to some of the words and phrases the defendant had chosen to use: 'what a vast scandal and offence must it give to all persons of piety and integrity to see men of characters and stations that shift and prevaricate with their principles'; 'what can unwary persons conclude . . . but that all religion is statecraft and imposture . . . and that the doctrines of the Church lie not so much in her Articles as her honours and revenues?'; 'in what moving and lively colours does the Holy Psalmist paint out the crafty insidiousness of such wily Volpones';* 'whatever these cunning, temporising politicians may think . . .'

> Is this the language of one that is only laying before magistrates the abuses of a few inferior persons . . . and desiring those magistrates to correct them?[58]

Yet all this, and much masterly logic besides, was to be forgotten once Parker turned in detail to Sacheverell's speech and began his final searing attack. What, in the first place, of the Doctor's pathetic, hand-on-heart protestations of innocence?

> My Lords, great regard is to be had to the word . . . much more to the oath of a clergyman, when he is free and unbiased. But when he stands in judgment, when the rod is over him . . . neither his word, nor his declaration, nor his oath is to be regarded. That method will acquit all that are accused; and the less conscience any such wretch has, the surer and easier will be his escape.[59]

What then of his plea that the charge had been patched up from disconnected sentences and inferences, and that if he had really been guilty, bare reading, without comment, would have convicted him?

> No, my Lords: even Doctor Sacheverell is not yet arrived at that pitch as to arraign the government as directly and openly

---

* The diarist noted: 'he only of all the Managers now mentioned that passage of wily Volpones, but barely, without insisting upon it'. Osborn MSS. 21/22: 10 March.

as to preach a general doctrine. This fallacy seems very gross. For is it reasonable to think that a man that intends to unhinge the government, to expose an administration, to fire the people, to raise sedition, should speak directly and plainly? . . . In such discourses . . . schemes of speech are to be contrived that have two meanings: the one more obvious and plain, to have its full effect upon the people, the other (that will occur to nobody else) a reserve, to be offered to a court of justice.[60]

As for the 'tenderest' charge nearest to his own profession, that of perverting the Scriptures, the Doctor had not deigned to answer it at all.[61] 'Will he thus give himself up for a falsifier of the Word of God, and yet have the confidence to hope for any reputation . . . in preaching it?'

> I am amazed [Parker went on] that a person in Holy Orders, in his distinguishing habit before this awful assembly, should dare to take the tremendous name of God into his lips and appeal to Him for the sincerity and integrity of his heart, at that very time when he stands charged with this black crime, and is neither able to repel it nor has the sincerity and honesty to repent.[62]

But there was one thing Doctor Sacheverell had said, Parker concluded, which the Managers would concede: namely, that his punishment was not all they aimed at.

> No, my Lords: what we expect from your Lordships' justice is the supporting our Establishment, the preventing all attempts to sap its foundation . . . and I hope the clergy will be instructed not to preach the doctrine of submission in such a way as to prepare the way for rebellion, but to follow the advice and example of my Lord Archbishop of York, rather than tread in the steps of Doctor Sacheverell. And we doubt not but that those to whom our proceedings have been so industriously misrepresented will see and own the favour shown to this man in the manner of the charge; and our care for the honour of the Church and clergy, in singling out for an example for these impious attempts against his country him that now plainly appears the shame of his own order.[63]

With these words Sir Thomas Parker brought to an end ten days of legal and political argument in the course of which forty-five major speeches had been delivered and well over 200,000 words uttered. The Commons, the lawyers and the prisoner had had their say. It was now for the Lords, as judge and jury combined, to consider their verdict.

IX THE VERDICT

From the time the Commons wound up their case on 10 March it took the peers ten days to come to their verdict and another day to pass sentence. It would be idle to suppose that even the verdict, let alone the sentence, was arrived at in an atmosphere of Olympian detachment and that it was governed solely by the arguments deployed by both sides in Westminster Hall. Some votes these arguments did sway. Lord Nottingham spoke exultingly immediately after Sacheverell's speech of 'many converts' among his brethren;[1] and no one imagined that Jekyll, King, Stanhope, above all Parker, had wasted their sweetness entirely on desert air. Yet there were scores of died-in-the-wool partisans on both sides whose votes were predetermined before a word had been spoken at the Lords' Bar. The duke of Buckingham, for one, was not disposed to humbug: throughout the trial he is said to have 'declared very plainly that he was more desirous to know which was the stronger party than which of them had the juster and better cause'. A large majority shared his attitude, if not his ingenuousness. It was their known commitment which led James Lowther to predict a bleak prospect for the Doctor as early as the second day, on the evidence of a mere procedural vote.[2]

All the same, the issue was by no means clear-cut by 10 March. A number of peers still waited to see which way the wind would blow when the party spokesmen in their own House began to debate the great questions which Managers and counsel had rehearsed. Others 'kept close their judicious sentiments, not knowing where to find them most acceptable'.[3] Still others watched the political barometer outside Parliament, conscious that the overheated state of public feeling about the Sacheverell case might, over the next few months, hold the key to the disposal of office and power. For all, an object of constant scrutiny was the Court, which was daily scanned for some irrefutable sign that the Queen's own mind on the impeachment had been finally made up: for since the Regiment crisis had sent Tory hopes prematurely soaring, the evidence on Anne's true feelings and intentions had been blurred, though seeming on balance to favour the Whigs.*

None was more keenly interested in the Queen's reaction than Robert Harley, eager to turn the fluid situation in the Upper House to Sacheverell's – and his own – advantage, and a group of six Whig noblemen whom of late he had made the special objects of his attention. These six notables, all disaffected for various reasons from the administration, were allotted a key part both in Harley's immediate parliamentary aims and in his long-term scheme for a decisive ministerial revolution. Even before the onset of the Sacheverell affair, Shrewsbury and Peterborough were already succumbing to his blandishments and Rivers was wavering. More recently the other three peers, the 'proud duke' of Somerset (Master of the Horse) and the Campbell brothers, Argyll and Islay, had been subjected to an adroit and assiduous political courtship. Harley fully realised that Sacheverell's case reached so far down to the roots of Whiggery that it was no ideal issue on which to rally malcontent members of the party against the administration; and he had employed the persuasive tongue of his former disciple, Henry St John, in the work of proselytisation. On 5 March the latter had reported how

> this moment I came from Lord R[ivers] to whom I opened in the best manner I could the duke of Shr[ewsbury]'s opinion in relation to the impeachment. I find that I can easily enough prevail with him, provided it were possible to draw the duke of Somerset into the same measure; but this he thinks impracticable, and urges a promise made by the duke of Ar[gyll] and himself to vote with Somerset in this affair. The latter, it seems, told the Queen, when she was commending Harcourt's argument . . . that indeed it was extremely fine, but that it had not convinced him.

* See pp. 115–16 above.

On the 9th followed a further bulletin, revealing equal uncertainty about Argyll's 'temper . . . with relation to the impeachment'.

> I believe it will be proper for you to endeavour to compound with him, rather than to insist much on convincing him. You will touch the true string if you insinuate that no one of those embarked in the same interest pretends to drive another, but that where a thing is judged to be right by some, it is natural for those to attempt persuading the rest, without any further consequence if they do not prevail.[4]

Most Tories, however, knew nothing of these clandestine efforts to pare down the ministry's majority in the Lords; so that few shared the unexpected euphoria of Nottingham, who began to think during the second week of the trial that there were some grounds for hoping for an acquittal. The general hope was still that the sentence on the Doctor might not be too severe and that his supporters in the Lords would make a brave showing, with enough desertions from the Court ranks to harass the ministry and further lower Whig morale. It was this erosion of his majority and the future embarrassments it presaged, rather than the prospect of any spectacular triumph for Sacheverell, which the Lord Treasurer feared most when he told Marlborough early in March of his uncertainty how the trial would end.

> . . . I certainly wish it had never begun; for it has . . . given opportunity to a great many people to be impertinent who always had the intention, but wanted the opportunity of showing it. Upon the whole, the great majority in the House of Lords which we had in the beginning of this session encourages people to commit follies . . .

For rank-and-file Whigs, however, it was enough to find few peers on the eve of the Lords' debates who doubted Dr Sacheverell would be convicted; and at Rose Castle the bishop of Carlisle, who had kept his horses ready for saddling at an hour's warning if the summons came from Lambeth, was relieved to hear from his friend, Wake, that 'the Doctor and his rabble' were likely to be suppressed without his assistance. In betting circles, which in London embraced much of polite society, it was noted with in-

P

terest that Tory ladies might pray for the Doctor's deliverance but would not put their money on it. Young Thomas L'Estrange, after taking tea with Lady Arran and Lady Harpur, found that the wagers were nearly all being laid against him, 'with some of them by a superiority [majority] of 10, some 15; but within 5, allowing for accidents too, they can be pretty positive'.[5]

There was perhaps more room for 'accidents' than the punters realised. They would have been very surprised, for instance, had they known of the enmeshed motives of the duke of Hamilton. As the leading figure among the Scottish Jacobites, his vote for Sacheverell must have seemed to most a foregone conclusion. But his closest friends on this occasion knew differently. He confessed to George Lockhart that

> he was much straitened in this affair, for his inclinations naturally led him to vote for the Doctor, but he was apprehensive it would be inconsistent with good policy, with respect either to private or public views; for he had then a lawsuit of great value depending, and if he voted for the Doctor the ministry would be displeased and certainly interpose to his prejudice; that he had endeavoured all along to gain and maintain an interest with the Scots Presbyterians . . . and should he vote for the Doctor, they would never forget it nor forgive him.

Lockhart was at great pains to hold him to the Tories but admitted that on the very eve of the verdict the duke had yet to reach a decision. The marquess of Kent, Anne's Lord Chamberlain and an anaemic Court Whig, was equally undecided, though for more orthodox reasons. In his perplexity he consulted his old friend, Colonel Cornwall, who 'told him, the surest way to know the Queen's mind was to ask her himself'.[6]

No sooner had the scene of the trial switched from Westminster Hall to the chamber of the Lords in the Old Palace, than Anne took a step which seemed to most people the clearest indication yet of where her sympathies lay. The eminent Lord Chief Justice of the Queen's Bench, Sir John Holt, had been ailing since Christmas. Early in February, though seriously ill, he had summoned up enough strength to make his one appearance of the term in court: thereafter he took to his bed in his elegant home in Bedford Buildings, and there on the afternoon of 5 March he died. The

names of but a handful of possible successors had only just begun
to be bandied around the coffee-houses when, with quite extraordinary despatch, on the following Saturday evening the Queen
made it known that her choice had fallen on Sir Thomas Parker.[7]
Two things struck almost everyone about this appointment. One
was its indecent haste: it was almost unheard-of for a new Lord
Chief Justice to be named before his predecessor had been laid in
his grave, and it could hardly be thought coincidental that it had
been done in this case immediately before a crucial transaction in
the House of Lords.[8] The other was the pointed award of the most
prestigious place on the judges' bench to the man who had out-
shone all the other Managers of Sacheverell's impeachment and
who, only the day before his appointment, had concluded the case
for the Prosecution. It was widely felt that by bestowing this
honour, on the advice of her Whig ministers,* the Queen had
done just 'enough to turn the scale [in the House of Lords], had it
been equal before'.[9] When it was also realised that two bishoprics
which had recently fallen vacant, Bristol and St David's, had just
been offered to a pair of moderate Low Church divines, Samuel
Bradford and Dr Barton, there was understandably some de-
pression in the Tory camp. 'A Chief Justice whom we are jealous
of', grumbled St John, 'and two bishops who will we are sure be
against us, must turn all our schemes and those who go on with
them into a jest'.[10]

By contrast, the news about Parker, released on the 11th, was
manna to the Whigs; for at Westminster they had just spent two
highly uncomfortable days, when for a while it had seemed that all
the labour and trouble of the past three months might be brought
to nothing on a judicial technicality. This came about as a result
of a wholly unexpected manoeuvre, cleverly conceived and executed
by the High Tory leader, Lord Nottingham, in conjunction with
his brother Heneage Finch, Lord Guernsey. The timing was im-
peccable. On the afternoon of Friday the 10th, after Parker had
indicated to the Lord Chancellor that the Commons' case was
finished, Nottingham rose to ask whether it was in order for him to

---

* The Whigs were naturally delighted with Parker's promotion, but there are two
versions of how it came about. One stems from John Oldmixon, who attributes it to
the influence of Godolphin and Sunderland on a rather reluctant Queen. The other,
the more probable, points to the dukes of Somerset and Devonshire (especially the
former) as Parker's patrons.

propose a question to the judges there in Westminster Hall. Devonshire, the Lord Steward, moved immediately that the Lords should adjourn to decide whether the question should be put there or in their own chamber. But they were soon back again, having decided – against some opposition from Wharton and others – that Nottingham had the right to pose his question in public. What the question was, no one yet knew. After the Serjeant-at-Arms had called for silence, all eyes turned on 'Dismal'.*

My Lords, the question I humbly propose to your Lordships that my noble lord on the woolsack may propose to the reverend judges is, whether by the law of England, and constant practice in all prosecutions by indictment or information for crimes and misdemeanours by writing or speaking, the particular words supposed to be criminal must not be *expressly specified* in such indictment or information.

Having sprung his mine he sat down, directing his saturnine stare at Cowper.† The latter, realising (as did every good Common lawyer in the House) the disturbing significance of the question he was being asked to put, was patently disconcerted. For a few moments he hesitated; and as he did so Secretary Sunderland seized the opportunity to try to retrieve a game which was suddenly threatening to slip away from the Whigs. He proposed and carried a second adjournment. And as their lordships trooped solemnly back again to their own chamber the crestfallen faces of the Commons began to clear, 'everybody supposing [as our diarist observed] Lord Wharton and Sunderland, etc., would not lose two points together'.[11]

In this, however, they were mistaken. The Junto's tactics were to argue either that the judges' opinions were unnecessary or that they should be heard *in camera*. Somers and Cowper, wrestling with the arguments put forward by Nottingham and Guernsey, took the line that because Common Law judges were appointed

---

* Wharton's unforgettable nickname for Nottingham – 'so they call him [Swift said] from his looks'.

† Brilliant though this was as a tactical move, Nottingham was an honest man; and we may believe him sincere when, soon after the trial, he wrote to his son, Daniel, that in the course of the impeachment 'some steps had been made which I thought not agreeable either to the law of the land or the usage of Parliament'. Finch MSS. Box VI, bundle 23.

to interpret the laws, they were constrained to act within the letter of those laws; but that since all contingencies could not possibly be provided for in express words, there was a need for other judges – lords of Parliament – to decide according to equity and not according to the law's strict letter. The supreme court, Parliament, was not 'tied up [Somers insisted] to the forms of the inferior courts or bound to proceed according to those laws which we prescribe to others'. But Nottingham still carried his point, with the sole proviso that the judges should be asked only for their opinion, not for their ruling. Westminster Hall was half empty, and all the Commons had departed, by the time the peers returned; but those Whigs who were left winced as they heard Baron Lovell, the junior judge, reply to the Lord Chancellor's questions:

> My Lords, I have always taken it to be so, and by constant experience we have practised it so, that all words and writings which are supposed to be criminal ought to be expressly mentioned in the information or indictment.

One by one, the other nine judges present delivered the identical opinion. As Sacheverell and his counsel had frequently reminded everyone, not a single article against him contained a direct quotation from his sermons. The pessimists feared, as they left the Hall that evening, that the whole prosecution was now in jeopardy, at least for this session; for there simply would not be time for the Commons to begin the whole process afresh before Parliament was prorogued.[12]

For three hours on Saturday, the 11th, the House of Lords debated the implication of the judges' answers of the previous day. Galleries crowded with members of the Commons, and the presence of the Queen incognito, bore witness that this was to be no formality. Peter Wentworth, a courtier less biased than most, judged the debate a triumph for the Whig leadership. Four prominent Tories spoke: Nottingham, Guernsey, Haversham, and Lord North and Grey.

> But Lord Somers and Lord Chancellor and Lord Halifax answered all the other lords' objections so clearly that Mr Lechmere and Sir Joseph Jekyll, that were next me, concluded the Doctor's business done, for they carried the matter so as to have

this question put: that in the judgment they would give of the
Doctor they would be guided . . . by the laws of England and
the laws and usages of Parliament. There was some struggle to
have the words 'laws and usages of Parliament' left out . . . but
the question was put with those words, and carried without any
division. Then Lord Treasurer moved that the clerks should
make out extracts of the books of Parliament of parallel cases
against Monday, and so to adjourn till that day.[13]

It was Tuesday before all the precedents had been gathered.
That afternoon, the hopes of the Tories rose once again as it
became clear that out of twenty-one cases unearthed, involving forty
impeached persons between 1620 and 1701, only one – the impeachment of Roger Mainwaring in June 1628 – appeared to justify
the method followed in framing the charges against Sacheverell,
and even here the parallel was not exact. Now it was ruthlessness,
not subtlety of argument, that was called for from the Junto. When
Nottingham demanded that the original Journals be produced to
demonstrate the precedents in full he was told by the duke of
Bolton, who had chaired the select committee, that they were not
all to be found; although 'when Lord Somers wanted that single
precedent of Dr Mainwaring [the cynics noted] it was found by
itself in an old box, wrote in parchment'. When, finally, Nottingham moved for an adjournment, telling their lordships that 'if
they would allow him time till next day, he would from his own
papers produce them precedents enough', his motion was nega-
tived – though only after a fierce debate and by a narrow majority
of five, with seven or eight Whig peers deserting the colours. 'No
bear garden was ever more noisy', wrote Ann Clavering; and the
chamber became noisier still when Nottingham embarked on a
palpable filibuster, announcing that 'since they would not adjourn,
though he was very much tired he must tell them his thoughts and
should speak an hour'. He had just managed half an hour, 'and
not one word [so the Whigs said] to the purpose', when the Queen
rose and left him in mid-sentence;[14] an event which not only de-
flated Nottingham but encouraged the Whigs to call out for a
final division on the critical main question, 'that by the law and
usage of Parliament in prosecutions by impeachments for high
crimes and misdemeanours . . . the particular words supposed to

be criminal are not necessary to be expressly specified'. At 8 p.m. the tellers finished counting the heads. There were 65 for the question, and only 47 against (several Tories having left the House in disgust). The Whigs could breathe again; and Nottingham was left to ponder, over supper at his brother Guernsey's, how a matter of such import could be determined 'upon one single precedent, not clear and plain but justly controverted, and which no man could or did affirm to be fact against 40 instances to the contrary'.[15]

It was now quite certain that the trial would be carried through to its end, whatever that might be. Nothing could be done on Wednesday, the 15th, a public fast-day. So far as Sacheverell's slim chances of escaping conviction were concerned, all now depended on the Lords' debate on the first article on 16 March. And as though to order, Clements, the publisher, was able to bring out the first edition of Sacheverell's speech to the court, most handsomely printed, on this same day. It was another masterstroke of timing and publicity, another nail firmly in the coffin of the public image of the Whigs. As one of their M.Ps sourly told his agent,

> the Doctor to show his entire submission and passive obedience to the supreme court of judicature has this day published his speech, that it may go all over England; and the people having no knowledge what reply was given to it may be disposed to arraign the justice of the Queen and Parliament.[16]

The government was furious, and that night, a post-night,* every letter going out of town was broken open by official order and copies of the speech removed.[17]

Thursday's debate was one of the longest any member of the House of Lords could remember. The peers normally kept temperate hours. But on 16 March 1710, having first despatched general business, they began their consideration of the Sacheverell case shortly after 11 a.m., when Wharton moved that the Commons be declared to have made good their first article, and they rose immediately after the division, twelve hours later.[18] In many

---

* The Post Office in Lombard Street despatched letters to all the English counties except Kent on only three evenings a week, Tuesday, Thursday and Saturday.

respects it was an extraordinary occasion. The Queen sat intent through the whole debate, except for the last hour or so. We know the names of at least thirty peers who spoke, a record for a single debate in Anne's reign. The great issues at stake, and the unforgettable experience of the events of 1688–9 which had left their mark on all but a handful of men in that chamber, brought to their feet peers who scarcely ever made speeches from one year's end to another, men such as Cholmondeley, Winchelsea, Carmarthen and Bishop Talbot. Some speakers – among them Haversham, Talbot and Burnet, the earls of Seafield and Anglesey, Lord North and Grey, and the old duke of Leeds – showed remarkable stamina. The first three alone, to judge from the printed versions of their speeches, published soon afterwards, consumed at least two and a half hours of the House's time: Nottingham, with predictable loquacity, spoke twice.

On the other hand, the quality of the debate was not always high. A few speakers, especially Talbot of Oxford, truly distinguished themselves; others held the House's attention in their characteristic ways, Wharton with his robust vigour, Argyll with his fiery uninhibited language, Burnet (for once) with his staggering erudition. But for some reason those party leaders from whom most might have been expected – Somers and Halifax on the Whig side, Rochester for the Tories – said relatively little. Of those who said more, not a few were barely audible;* some were downright tedious. There were too many personal apologias in the debate, most of them, naturally, from Tories such as Leeds and Bishop Compton who had taken up arms against James II and who felt bound to square their conduct then with their intention now to vote for Sacheverell. Above all there was far too much irrelevance, as Lord Cowper had cause to complain in the course of the evening. The strict question before the House – whether Sacheverell had indeed maintained and suggested what the Commons claimed he had, about Non-Resistance, the Glorious Revolution and William III – was too often lost sight of altogether, or remembered only to be the subject of a bare assertion of agreement or dissent.[19]

Except for their bishops, the Whigs throughout the debate had by far the more straightforward task, especially since they

---

* Anglesey, Seafield and, surprisingly, Secretary Sunderland seem to have been the worst offenders.

cautiously avoided any quarrel with the basic Anglican doctrine of Obedience.[20] For long afterwards, however, the spectators would remember Wharton dismissing with contempt, and with well-relished references to his own share in the events of 1688, the devious attempts of the Tories to wrap up that rebellion in clothes other than those of plain Resistance. They would remember his bluntly challenging words, 'if the Revolution is not lawful, many in this House and vast numbers without are guilty of blood, murder, rapine and injustice: and *the Queen herself is no lawful Queen*, since the best title she has to the crown is her parliamentary title, founded on the Revolution'. They would recall, too, the great skill with which the bishop of Oxford sought to reconcile the traditional doctrines of the Church with the practice and teachings of some of its leaders in 1688, and of many since: his demonstration that Scripture could be a general guide to conduct but not a provision for all contingencies, by considering the words 'honour thy father and thy mother':

> Suppose a parent in a frenzy . . . draws his sword and attempts to kill his innocent son, and the son has no way to escape from him; is he obliged by this duty of not resisting to stand still and let his father sheath his sword in his bowels? . . . May not the same law of self-preservation justify the political child, the body of the people, in defending their political life, i.e. their constitution, against plain and avowed attempts of the political parent utterly to destroy it?

Nor would the audience readily forget the inspired resurrection by the Whig prelates of Archbishop Laud's blessing on Charles I's expedition to help the rebels of La Rochelle; his call upon God to defend 'thy altars that are among us and in all the reformed churches'; and Talbot's wry comment: 'It seems the reformed churches were thought to have God's altars among them then, however they have been vilified since'.

Many peers took issue over the general question of political preaching. Burnet spoke of his alarm at the violence with which Non-Resistance doctrines had been proclaimed from the pulpit since the Jacobite attempt of 1708; Talbot enquired why High-flying parsons should give this one duty of Obedience priority over 'all the other duties of Christianity'; and both gave solemn warnings of the dire consequences that must follow 'unless an effectual stop is put to this distemper'. Argyll, in the most sharply anti-clerical speech from the Whig side, saw nothing very novel in these developments. To him it seemed plain that 'the clergy in all ages have delivered up the rights and liberties of the people and preached up the King's power in order to govern him; and therefore they ought not to be suffered to meddle with politics'. In reply, Anglesey defended the right of parsons to preach politics, at least on 30 January and similar occasions; Hooper, in contrast to the Low Church bishops, maintained that Passive Obedience preaching was positively necessary at a time when Resistance was being so openly justified; and North and Grey, who made the most uncompromising and closely-argued attack on Resistance theory, as contrary to natural law and 'the practice of Christ himself', argued that it was essential to counter the audacity of Hoadly, 'who had made the people the source of power and justice'.

Two things stand out from the dozen speeches from Tory peers of which we have some knowledge. One is their treatment of Sacheverell; the other is their uneasy preoccupation with the incongruities of the Tory party's philosophy, and their consequent attempts to exorcise the dangerous spirit of the Revolution without disavowing what they themselves had done more than twenty years before. The attitude to Sacheverell was remarkable. Haversham and Ferrers let him off lightly when they argued that his foolish, unguarded expressions were not enough to justify the charges in Article I. Anglesey admitted there was a good deal of nonsense in the St Paul's sermon, but added, 'I never knew nonsense to be a crime'.[21] Leeds declared 'he would vote the Doctor a fool or a madman, but wondered where the high crimes and misdemeanours were'; and Henry Compton went further still, 'said he was guilty of folly, madness and the greatest extravagance in the world', but ended, like all the rest, by professing himself unable to detect anything criminal in his references to the Revolution.

Their own references to the Revolution in this debate were, in all conscience, far more interesting and revealing. The earl of Anglesey seemed to argue that the case of the Revolution did not affect the validity of the Non-Resistance doctrine, since what had taken place in 1688 was a 'vacancy of throne'; and Haversham (an ex-Whig) followed a similar line with rather more sophistication.* The speech of Bishop Hooper encapsulated all the ingredients in the Tory dilemma: the different viewpoints of the individual and the Churchman, the tug of political realism against the roots of a traditional ideology. He 'thought himself at liberty to act as he did at the Revolution, though he owned himself to have preached up Passive Obedience as high as any'. He conceded the legality of Resistance in certain extraordinary cases, but differed from Talbot in believing that this right should be concealed from the people, 'who are naturally too apt to resist'. Therefore

> the Revolution was not to be boasted of and made a precedent; but we ought to throw a mantle over it, and rather call it a Vacancy or Abdication. . . . They who examined the Revolution too nicely were no friends to it; for at that rate the crown would roll like a ball and never be fixed.

The most extraordinary gyrations of all, however, were performed by the veteran Leeds, who argued even more strenuously than Hooper for the wisdom of an ostrich-like attitude.

> What is this I hear? King William an usurper! and the Revolution a rebellion! Indeed, if that enterprise had not succeeded to our wishes [i.e. if James had stayed and fought], both these assertions had been true; and the judges would have pronounced all of us who stood up in defence of our country, our religion and our laws, rebels. But since the Prince of Orange's cause has been avowed both by God and man . . . I wonder how there can be any debate among your Lordships about this matter. . . . My Lords, suffer not such matters as these to be made subjects of debate, nor any question to be started in Parliament about what was done at the time of the Revolution.[22]

As the debate went on hour after hour, however, it appeared that this warning was having little effect on Tories who felt both

---

* 'It is impossible, in my opinion, to prove that Resistance was made use of as a means to bring about the late happy Revolution. . . . "Means", my Lords, is a relative term and refers to some end: and the end and design of the Prince of Orange in coming hither, and of those that joined him when he was here, being to have the nation and rightful succession secured by a free parliament, it follows that whatever force was at that time made use of, could not be made use of as a means to bring about an end which was never intended . . .'

the fatal fascination of the subject and the urge to self-justification. Just after 9 p.m. one of the Whigs had proposed 'that the Commons had made good the first article of impeachment', but the debate still dragged on; and Ann Clavering was told that it was 'near ten', and at a time when 'Lord Guernsey was clearing himself of the Revolution' that the Queen suddenly wearied of it all, 'rose and left them, which so confounded him that he'd much ado to proceed'. The Master of the Horse, Somerset, offered to escort her back to St James's, but Anne told him 'no, not without he brought a lord of the other party [with him], for she would not have a vote lost on any score'.

But if Guernsey had tried the House's patience, his fellow-Tory, Carmarthen (Leeds's son), finally broke it. He embarked on a tedious recapitulation of the steps preceding the Revolution, and insisted (despite Richmond's protests that it was 'a long story') in spelling out his own part in them in minute detail. But when, over the rising tide of murmurs, he promised 'to keep them till the morning', the question was called for too insistently to be denied. Even then, the vote itself was postponed for almost another hour by a further procedural debate on whether the question 'be now put' (the issue being whether voting should take place in the chamber, as the Whigs demanded, or in Westminster Hall, as the Tories desired). And curiously it was on this 'previous question', and not on the article itself, that the only Lords' division took place on 16 or 17 March. The Whigs emerged clear victors by a majority of 17 (68 against 51), and 122 very weary peers drifted off to their coaches. All had stayed to the bitter end, except Bishop Manningham of Chichester, a nominal Whig, who 'stole away' before the vote.[23]

The next day's relatively tepid events gave many the impression, misleadingly as it turned out, that the Tory Peers regarded the crucial battle as having been fought and lost after Thursday night's vote. Our diarist, for instance, was so depressed by the collapse of opposition on the 17th that he reserved only five lines for the whole business of the day. 'The Lords proceeded to the 2nd, 3rd and 4th articles', he wrote, 'which one by one, with very little debate and no division, were given up'. His entry is more than a little inaccurate. Admittedly, discussion of the second article, the Toleration article, was more or less monopolised by Bishops Wake and Trimnell: the only opposition came from that notoriously eccentric Whig, Lord Scarborough, well known for his dislike of the dissenters, who failed to find a seconder among the Tories. All the same, the House spent at least two hours on this article, and its proceedings were decorated by a most elegant and lucid speech from the bishop of Lincoln, who was later to succeed Tenison as archbishop of Canterbury.[24] Unlike most of Thursday's speakers, Wake, after giving a revealing first-hand account of High Church participation in the Comprehension schemes of 1689, went on to subject the relevant words of the sermon itself to the most intensive and devastating scrutiny. Miss Clavering was delighted with the apostolic eloquence of both her bishops. 'Had we ever heard of two St Pauls I should have believed they had now been with us,' she wrote next day. Perhaps in her enthusiasm for Wake she was a little kind to Trimnell, 'who read his speech [remarked Ralph Bridges] and as dull a one, God knows, as any sermon he ever preached from St James's pulpit'.[25]

After Article II had been approved without a vote, the 'Church in Danger' article was disposed of to the accompaniment of only three short speeches, from Halifax, Nottingham and Ferrers.[26] The fourth article, however, sparked off a genuine debate, with at least twelve speakers, and the only real battle of the day. A warm defence of the present administration by Wharton was surpassed in vehemence by Burnet. He thought it appalling and amazing to hear the Queen's government traduced from the pulpit in this reign of all reigns, 'which was the wonder of the present age and would be so of posterity, and which therefore ought to be the object of our idolatry'. He accused Sacheverell of arraigning the Queen herself by his attack on those three great achievements to which Anne was personally committed, the Revolution, the Toleration and the Union. And there was uproar when, in full spate, the bishop went on to say that 'nothing could be more plain than his reflecting on her majesty's ministers; and that he had in particular so well marked out a noble peer there present by an ugly and scurrilous epithet (which he would not repeat) that it was not possible to mistake him'. Both sides rocked with laughter at this typically indiscreet mention of the unmentionable,* and a number of the younger and brasher peers called out in great glee to the bishop to

* cf. p. 82 above.

'name him! name him!' The Lord Chancellor had to intervene
to get Burnet off the hook, and to restore order. There were
further piquant moments to come. The House was intrigued to
hear Anne's uncle, Rochester, claim a special faculty for divining
insults to the Queen by virtue of his blood relationship to her, and
acquit Sacheverell apparently on the strength of these special
powers of detection. And later it was stirred by a barbed exchange
between the Jacobite duke of Hamilton and the Whig Lord Mohun,
given sharper point by the known enmity between them, a quarrel
which was to end in 1712 in their mutual destruction in the most
celebrated of all eighteenth-century duels. But in spite of the
renewed excitement, the Tories once again declined to expose
their numerical disadvantage by forcing a division on the fourth
article. They confined themselves to entering a Protest, signed by
thirty-seven lords, in the Books of the House.[27]

What they had in mind now was a procedural manoeuvre which,
had it succeeded, could hardly have failed to be to Sacheverell's
advantage. In the course of a very long debate on Saturday, the
18th,[28] they struggled hard to ensure that the final question to be
asked each peer in Westminster Hall, when the verdict was given,
should be put separately on each article. The ostensible grounds
for this were best expressed in the debate by Guernsey, who
claimed that a blanket verdict, 'guilty' or 'not guilty', would pre-
clude individuals from giving their judgment of the law as well as
of the fact (the argument being that while some might be satisfied
as to the *fact* that the Doctor was guilty of some, if not all, of the
charges, they might yet disagree that *in law* these offences, or
some of them, amounted to high crimes and misdemeanours).
The real object of the ploy, not surprisingly, was to fragment the
Whig-Court vote to the greatest degree possible; and it was only
after many hours of intricate argument that the move was defeated
by a majority of 12, and the message sent at last to the Commons
to acquaint them that the Lords would be in Westminster Hall on
Monday, 20 March, at 11 a.m. to deliver their verdict.[29]

Eleven o'clock on the fourth Monday of the trial arrived with the
Hall as full as ever, with the prisoner and his myrmidons standing
composed and confident at the Bar, but with no peers. Eventually
news filtered down that the Lords were being delayed by a debate

on whether the Doctor should be permitted (as the Tories desired) to remain at the Bar while the votes were being given. It was after two o'clock when one of Black Rod's assistants entered the Hall and was seen instructing Sacheverell to remove himself from the court. It was almost three o'clock by the time the last peer was in his place.[30] For the last time the Hall stilled as the Serjeant-at-Arms bellowed out, 'Our Sovereign Lady the Queen doth strictly charge and command all manner of persons to keep silence, upon pain of imprisonment.' Now the voice of Lord Cowper came across slowly and distinctly as he stood at the Woolsack.

Your Lordships having fully heard and considered of the evidence and arguments in this case have agreed upon a question, which is severally to be put to your Lordships in the usual order. The question is this: that Doctor Henry Sacheverell is guilty of high crimes and misdemeanours charged on him by the impeachment of the House of Commons.

Then, addressing himself in a louder voice to the most junior baron,

Lord Pelham, what is your Lordship's opinion: is Doctor Henry Sacheverell guilty of high crimes and misdemeanours charged upon him by the impeachment of the House of Commons?

The sixty-year-old Pelham, ennobled in 1706, stood up and removed his hat. He was widely known as a stout Whig,* so his reply surprised no one: it was *Guilty*. Next, Lord Hervey: *Guilty*. Then Lord Conway: *Not Guilty*. And so on, through the thirty-two barons, the twelve bishops (Chichester was again conspicuous by his absence), the two viscounts, the fifty earls, the two marquesses, the seventeen dukes and the chief officers of the government. With nine votes to cast, 61 had voted guilty and 51 not guilty. The last three dukes to vote were all of the blood royal – Charles Fitzroy, duke of Grafton (a grandson of Charles II by Barbara Villiers), and two of King Charles's bastards, the duke of Richmond and – weak-minded and henpecked by a Tory wife – the duke of Cleveland. The tussle for Cleveland's vote became one

---

* He was the father of Thomas Pelham-Holles, duke of Newcastle, the celebrated political manager of the Walpole and Pelham administrations.

of the favourite stories of the trial, a little embroidered no doubt in the telling.

The Duchess of Cleveland told her duke he was to vote for the Doctor, and speak as his brother Northumberland* did. To which end, of Monday she locked him up and bid the servants tell the Duke of Richmond he was gone out (fearing him). The Duke comes. The servants obey the Duchess's commands. His Grace, not satisfied, lights out of his coach, runs over the house, meets with one room locked, calls and was answered, 'I'm here, but can't get out. My wife's locked me up'. To which the Duke [of] Richmond says, 'I'll release you'. Away he runs, fetches a ladder, set it to the window, takes the Duke out and put him in his coach, and bids him say in the House as he did, for he'd speak loud.[31]

Richmond's enterprise and athleticism were repaid. Grafton's *Guilty* and his own were valiantly followed by Cleveland; and of the last six votes, beginning with that of the Lord Steward and ending with that of the Lord Chancellor, only Archbishop Sharp's was in favour of the prisoner.[32]

The Lord Chancellor now announced that he would need some time to make the count. He did so with great care, checking and rechecking. Eventually, satisfied (as he put it) that he had 'cast them up with as much exactness' as he could, he announced the verdict. 69 lords had voted the Doctor *guilty*, and 52 *not guilty*. Sacheverell was then called to the Bar. With great solemnity Cowper informed him of the judgment of the court. No person just convicted before the highest court in the land could have been less abashed than Henry Sacheverell. Speaking in what the diarist euphemistically called 'a very undisturbed accent', he announced that, having been removed from the Bar before judgment was given, he hoped he might now be allowed to put in a plea before sentence was passed. He had been advised by his counsel to offer, first, that 'no entire clause, sentence or expression contained in either of my sermons or dedications is particularly set forth in my impeachment', and second (a piece of characteristic

---

* George Fitzroy, duke of Northumberland, like Cleveland a son of Charles II and Barbara Villiers, and curiously enough the only Tory among the five descendants of the King in this Parliament.

cheek) that the impeachment was legally invalid since the articles had been exhibited 'in the name of the knights, citizens and burgesses', omitting the Scottish commissioners of shires! On Bolton's motion the House adjourned and, not surprisingly, after a very brief discussion, dismissed the Doctor's objections as frivolous and passed a resolution that they would proceed next day, in their own chamber, to consider what censure they should pass on him.[33]

After supper that night Lord Treasurer Godolphin, whose view of the proceedings had become increasingly jaundiced with every day of the trial (he had even spoken in support of the Tories in one or two of the recent procedural arguments in the Lords), sent a few lines by special messenger to the duke of Marlborough. His pen scarcely vibrated with elation. The best he could summon up was a partial but lugubrious sense of relief, as he wrote of the majority of 17 by which the Doctor had 'at last' been convicted. One member of the Cabinet had abstained:

> The duke of Somerset did not vote. Some of his friends said he was sick, but I fancy it was only his profound wisdom that kept him from the House. Tomorrow we are to go upon the consideration of the punishment, and if that be [not] made lighter than in itself is reasonable, I doubt some of our seventeen will desert from us. But this is plainly our case, and it is very well the session is so near an end. . . . Now, for aught I know, things may run on very disagreeably for six months longer.[34]

At the same time as he received Godolphin's note, Marlborough was sent a division-list of the great vote of 20 March.* His first reactions are a clear indication that even this vote had been closer than the government had bargained for. Seven of the lords who had voted *not guilty* caught his eye at once, four Court Tories and three Scottish Tories: 'I should have thought all these would have been on the other side'.† Yet in other respects there

---

* Probably a manuscript list. The printed version does not seem to have been published until the 21st.
† The names he picked out were those of the duke of Northumberland (see p. 115 above), the earl of Pembroke and Lords Lexington and Berkeley of Stratton; and among the Scots, Hamilton, Northesk and Wemyss. For the votes cast on 20 March, and for the further crucial defections and absences on 21 March, see below, Appendix B, 'The Judgment of the Lords'.

Q

had been few real surprises. Only two Whigs, Scarborough and Shrewsbury, had voted for the Doctor; both Scarborough's prejudices and Shrewsbury's long-standing unreliability being well known. The loss of the earl of Mar, an architect of the Union and a Court pensioner, had been disappointing, but not entirely surprising: he was, after all, on close terms with Harley (and it was he, it afterwards appeared, who had talked over Northesk and Wemyss).[35] But for the rest, things on the surface did not appear too desperate: five Court Tory or Court votes that might have gone the other way* had held firm; although Hamilton had deserted, his brother Orkney had not;[36] and the Whig front itself seemed to the outsider to be scarcely chipped, let alone cracked.

From the Hague it still seemed to Marlborough amazing that a man of Shrewsbury's experience should judge the Tories strong enough to break the mighty Whig–Court alliance. But to a very few men on the inside, the situation on the night of 20 March looked decidedly more disturbing – or from a Tory viewpoint, more promising. And one man especially, Robert Harley, was looking to the morrow as the most important day in British politics since he had been forced out of the government over two years before. His negotiations with the four disaffected Whigs, Rivers, Somerset, Argyll and Islay, had prospered since the early days of the month. Broad hints of the Queen's disillusionment with her present ministers; enticing promises of a completely reconstructed administration in which 'moderate' men of both parties, and not least the Whig magnates themselves, would call the tune; the assurance that a serious setback for the government over the impeachment would immensely facilitate its destruction: all helped on the work of conversion. Until a few days before the 20th Harley had continued to urge his conspirators to vote, along with Shrewsbury, for Sacheverell's acquittal. But although he had succeeded so far with Somerset that the duke had persuaded himself that it would be politic to take the waters at Epsom on the crucial day, with the rest he had had to be content with his second objective, the absolute necessity of a mild – nay a derisory – sentence. Rivers, Argyll and Islay had condemned Sacheverell too openly, either before or during the Lords' debates, to turn round at this stage

* Those of Byron, Hunsdon, Paget, De la War and Winchelsea.

and vote him *not guilty*. With Argyll there was another consideration, as Harley's emissary, Lord Orrery, explained.

He thinks too that an absolute acquittal would rather tend to promote a High Tory scheme than to ruin the interest of the Junto. Besides, he's afraid he should prejudice his interest in Scotland by it. . . . However, he thinks he may fairly oppose any excessive punishment that shall be proposed, and he believes the duke of Somerset may be brought to concur with him in that . . . for *the punishment designed to be proposed is an incapacity [from preaching], fine and imprisonment*.[37]

But how low were the Campbells prepared to go on the punishment? At first Argyll committed himself to oppose only the fine and a term of imprisonment; he thought that 'a man that has made so bad an use of a pulpit ought never to come into it again'. But after further pressure from Harley, he at last agreed that the punishment should be 'as mild as you please'.[38]

It was of great help to Harley that in the few days before the verdict the Queen's own predilections for a mild sentence were noised about; a number of peers who had applied to her for guidance had been given this clear impression.[39] Precisely how many Anne saw we cannot know. But she may well have influenced the abstention of the duke of Grafton on 21 March, and it is very likely that her views played a major part in what, apart from the behaviour of the Whig dissidents, was to prove the vital development of that day: the secession of the Scottish Secretary, Queensberry, and with him three more representative peers of Scotland, Loudoun, Rosebery and Orkney. Harley, too, had been working on these vulnerable Scots votes through the agency of Mar and Somerset; and the combined pressure on them was critical. Not without reason did Bonet report to Berlin that 'the Scottish peers have held the balance in this affair'; for we know that although Godolphin was almost half-prepared for the defection of the four Whig peers, he was astonished – and disgusted – by the behaviour of the Scots, and particularly that of Queensberry, from whom he had had specific assurances of support on the Sacheverell issue.[40]

Henry Sacheverell had not been brought before a parliamentary tribunal merely to ensure his conviction. The impeachment had been set on foot, and sustained in the face of great hostility, by the conviction that Parliament alone would inflict on the offender an 'exemplary punishment' – one that would effectively deter clergy-men of his kidney from using their pulpits in future to disseminate political 'poison'. For such a punishment the Commons' Managers had repeatedly called in Westminster Hall. At the start of the trial no self-respecting Whig would have settled for anything less than a life ban on the Doctor's preaching, a bar on further pre-ferment, a stiff term of imprisonment and a fine;* and the govern-ment had remained set on this well into the third week. But by the end of that week they were prepared to lower their sights quite considerably. The sentence which Lord Carlisle, a Junto lieutenant, proposed to the House of Lords on 21 March, and which Godolphin seconded, was even said to have been sanctioned by the Queen.[41] The Doctor was to be incapacitated from preaching not for life but for seven years. During that time he was to be debarred from receiving any ecclesiastical preferment other than that he already enjoyed. There was still to be a period of imprisonment, but it was to be only three months, and until such further time as he could 'find sureties for his good behaviour during the term of seven years before the two Chief Justices'. Finally his offending sermons were to be burnt by the Common Hangman at the Exchange. The House decided to take the four proposals into consideration one by one: and at once a storm broke over the heads of the hapless ministry so fierce that its supporters were soon clinging on desperately to prevent every part of the package from being swept away.

It was Argyll who started it all. 'Though he had voted in this matter against the Doctor to make impeachments easy', he an-nounced, 'and upon promise that no severe punishment should be insisted on, yet since he found they valued their word no more, he should leave them'. Then, to the stupefaction of the ministers, a period of one year's suspension only was proposed, either by the duke himself or by Islay (afterwards, no one seemed quite sure which, for as Sir John Cropley explained, 'the confusion [was] so

---

* Many would have gone further. There was much talk of unfrocking him (to which Sacheverell is reported to have responded, 'God be praised, he should make a very good layman'), of incapacitating him from holding any future office under the Crown, and even of inflicting a corporal punishment – 'nothing less [Lockhart wrote] than the pillory and being whipped at a cart from the Royal Exchange to Charing Cross'. Add. MSS. 47026, p. 11; Dyer, 23 March; D.Z.A. Rep. XI England 35D, f. 121: Bonet, 24 March; *Lockhart Papers*, i, 313.

great that . . . no two gave it that night alike'). The debate was so
acrimonious that for a while it seemed that this unthinkable disaster might have to be suffered, but in the end a compromise
proposal of three years was carried on a division by a mere six
votes: Wharton had sufficient sense of humour left to observe that
he was sure the Doctor would thank their lordships for it, 'for now
by law you have made him idle so long'. The Whigs had com-
promised on this, but surely they could not do so on the second
paragraph, incapacitating Sacheverell from further preferment
during his period of suspension? To do so would be to allow him
to be *rewarded* for committing high crimes and misdemeanours
(and indeed it was already being said – and with reason – that one
Tory patron had already offered him just such a reward). The
second proposal was therefore pressed to a vote. The result was
shattering. Somerset, now back in the House, and the other Whig
rebels voted against it; so did Queensberry and the renegade Scots
(Queensberry had intended to abstain and had actually left the
chamber, only to be brought back by Somerset and constrained
to vote with the opposition); there were three new Whig absentees
compared with the previous day (one of them, Somers, known to be
a genuine case of indisposition); and one extra Tory was present.
Thus the government's seventeen-vote margin of the 20th simply
melted away and the proposal was lost by 60 votes to 59.* After this,
it was almost a rout. The imprisonment proposal was abandoned
without so much as a debate. Only the burning of the sermons
was rescued, once it had become clear that the Tories were quite
happy to agree to it, provided (as Buckingham maliciously suggested) Garrard, the Lord Mayor, was ordered to attend the last
rites.[42]

For the government and all who supported it this had been a day
of complete mortification. Godolphin by the end of it all seemed
almost too sickened to care very deeply. 'So all this bustle and
fatigue ends in no more but a suspension of three years from the
pulpit, and burning his sermon at the Old Exchange'. The Whigs
were less restrained, and some of them, at least, were more conscious than the Treasurer that the votes of this day might well
prove a turning-point in the political history of the reign. Even
before the House rose Burnet had angrily told the peers that their

* See below, Appendix B, 'The Judgment of the Lords'.

sentence was equivalent to returning the Doctor thanks. Sir John Percival, watching from the gallery, was incredulous that all should have ended in this laughable sentence, and that 'after the Managers for the Commons had . . . painted him out not only black but scarlet; after the City had been at above ten thousand pound charge for raising the militia; the Queen one way or other at as much more* . . . our people put into a ferment and the stocks fallen'. That Sacheverell should still be capable of promotion in the Church, of actually being made a bishop by a friendly regime even while still under sentence, seemed utterly diabolical. 'We shall be soon overpowered,' Cropley feared, 'especially since from the pulpits we shall have all their thunder to depress us'. Miss Clavering shared his pessimism. 'Happy are those who wear a black robe when the doctrine they preach is to be disavowed, and yet not suffered to be punished. I should advise all housebreakers, etc., to wear that habit'. 'The ministry, thus insulted, is insupportable and to be overlooked', she warned her brother. ''Tis true the English never know when they are well. A Church ministry we now want and shall have, as soon as Johnny† can decently be thrown aside . . .'[43]

For the Commons, or for its Whig members at least, this was black Tuesday indeed. While the Lords were determining Sacheverell's future, the Lower House was debating a motion of thanks to the Managers 'for their faithful management in charge of the trust reposed in them'. The Tories turned the proceedings into a farce. One Tory said he could congratulate the Whigs only on a very well-read set of Managers, since almost all of them had read their speeches. Another was in favour of particular rather than general thanks, as for instance, to Sir David Dalrymple and Harry Mordaunt for their faithful management in never appearing. A third cruelly proposed that Jack Dolben should be thanked for giving up the rights of the Commons by explaining his words without leave of the House, and the criticism was so savage on that head that poor Dolben fled the chamber. Yet another Tory expressed surprise that the Whigs had ignored the only strong argument in favour of the motion – that if the House did not thank the Managers, no one else would. The motion was eventually carried

---

* One estimate, probably Harley's, put the cost to the government at £60,000. See H.M.C. *Portland MSS.* iv, 539; also p. 118 above.
† i.e. the duke of Marlborough.

by 175 votes to 116, but the news from the Lords soon put all that out of everyone's mind. Whig members were so incensed that during that evening the talk of the coffee-houses was that many would vote next day against the House demanding judgment of the Lords.[44] Indeed, Tory leaders in the Commons were so hopeful of large-scale desertions from the ministry that they prolonged the debate on 22 March, on the motion 'that this House will demand judgment', from 1 p.m. until 6 p.m. There was out-spoken criticism of the Lords from the Whig side: from the back benches their votes were called 'scandalous' and 'a reflection upon the proceeding'; even the Chancellor of the Exchequer, John Smith, expressly called it 'a ridiculous judgment'. But in the end, although there were a number of Whig abstentions, only four or five Whig members actually divided with the Tories against the motion, which was carried comfortably enough by 165 to 117.[45]

Nevertheless, what the Lords had done on 21 March left a raw wound which, so far as the Commons were concerned, remained unhealed for the rest of this session. How raw was shown on Thursday the 23rd, when the Speaker led a party of Whig members from St Stephen's Chapel through the Painted Chamber· and the intervening passages to demand judgment at the Lords' Bar (the stands in Westminster Hall were now being rapidly demolished, so that the courts of Justice could once again begin to function). Three times between the door of the chamber and the Bar, 'stiff Dick' Onslow, bristling with punctilios and loudly asserting his rights, clashed with Black Rod, and all Cowper's tact was required to prevent him carrying out his threat to take his whole flock back to the Chapel unless the Lords acquiesced in what was due to the dignity of the Commons.[46] Eventually Henry Sacheverell was brought, for the last time, to the Bar, and for the last time knelt there and was bidden to rise. There, in front of a House almost entirely Whig (for the opposition peers had deliber-ately stayed away, as a final mark of protest), the Speaker demanded, and the Lord Chancellor pronounced, the judgment of the Lords upon the prisoner: a judgment 'in which [as Cowper pointedly reminded him] you cannot but observe an extreme tenderness towards your character as a minister of the Church of England'.

As they listened to Cowper spelling out the sentence, in its pathetic baldness, no doubt the minds of some of the Whigs at the

Bar went back wrily to a quip of Harry Mordaunt's in their own House on the previous day, when he had 'begged leave to conclude with a misconstrued text of scripture, as the reverend divine had set the example. His words . . . were these: "Tis the Lords' doings, but not marvellous in our eyes".' But perhaps, too, there were some who were philosophical enough, and far-sighted enough, to see beyond immediate disillusionment; and to recognise, like the member for Shaftesbury when he wrote to the now-absent Stanhope, that at least "tis a judgment in favour of the best foundation of government this nation ever pretended to, for as much as we are dissatisfied with this judgment, we may remember that but very lately you would have been hanged for what the House of Commons have this day thanked you for'.[47]

Certain it was that they would need all their philosophy in the next few months. The Doctor's trial was over.

His triumph had barely begun.

X THE TRIUMPH

'His enemies . . . have had their turn. Now, his friends have theirs'. So wrote a midlands parson, a fortnight after the great deliverance.[1] During that fortnight there had indeed been abundant evidence from almost every part of England that the hour of the High Tories had come. They may not yet have been sure of the Queen. But they could no longer doubt that the current of popular feeling was flowing irresistibly for them, through all ranks of society. The reception of the news of Sacheverell's token punishment had varied from place to place only in the degree of enthusiasm, ecstasy, hysteria or violence evinced. To people in all walks of life, it seemed, this was a deliverance not just for one man but for a whole Church.[2]

London, naturally, had set the pattern. From Tuesday the 21st, the night of the sentence, to Thursday the 23rd, there was scarcely a major street in Westminster or in the western suburbs of London which did not have its bonfire, its illuminated windows or its crowd of people drinking the Doctor's health and blessing the Queen, to the clangorous accompaniment of church bells. At first the crowds were orderly. But by Thursday their growing unruliness had brought four companies of Trained Bands out again, 'with wind music before 'em'. Thereafter the demonstrations slowly subsided, although a group of hatters' apprentices stirred up a Sacheverell riot in Southwark, and things did not return to normal until after 30 March, when the Lord Mayor – at the Queen's personal command – made a formal order requiring magistrates, constables, and churchwardens 'at their peril' to exercise all possible care and vigilance in the restoration of order.[3]

But by then the whole country had caught fire. News had come in of mobbing in the streets of Oxford, 'the University resolved to defend Sacheverell with their blood', and Town vying with Gown in its enthusiasm. A tub containing Burgess's effigy and having Hoadly's treatise nailed to its sides had been ceremonially burnt, and a great procession had been held in the Doctor's honour appropriately headed by the bearer of a flag of defiance. If it had not been for the firm action of the Recorder in committing the ringleaders, 'the advantages of a liberal education' (thought the Vice-Principal of St Edmund Hall) would not have deterred the students from producing even more 'fine contrivances'.[4] By the 24th the post had brought the news of the sentence into Dorset and Wiltshire. Extravagances in Oxford were hardly remarkable in the circumstances. But who would have expected the sleepy town of Sherborne to go berserk? Certainly not one of its dissenting pastors, John England, who recalled

> scarce ever the like in this place, upon any occasion. In divers houses there were illuminations, many bonfires were made in several parts of the town; Dr Sacheverell's health was publicly drunk in our Town Hall, and that in *aqua mirabilis* too, and this upon their knees. . . . There being also some bottles of wine sent into the Church for another select company, the Doctor's health (as I am informed) was drunk by both sexes at the top of the tower, with lights in their hands to give notice of it. And as for us that are dissenters, we were . . . forced to keep our doors fast; and this was scarce sufficient to keep us from the rabble, who cursed the Presbyterians to the pit of Hell, beat a drum about the town, threatened to burn or pull down our meeting-houses, and having guns with them, they made a halt at several houses and fired at them, at my own in particular, to the affrightment of my family.

This had been only the start of a week of tumult and rejoicing, in which 'the better sort' of townsfolk had been prominent and which the vicar, Mr Lacy, had openly encouraged. Guns discharged from the church tower, the bells pulled by relays of ringers 'paid for the most part out of the Poor-Box', the continued baiting of dissenters, the public burning of one of Hoadly's books on the same day that

Sacheverell's sermons were consumed in London: little wonder that
what 'formerly has been esteemed a civilised town' seemed to the
Whigs and nonconformists there to have been transformed into
'the seat of Satan'.[5]

Salisbury was almost quiet by comparison. There was a bonfire
in High Street round which Sacheverell's health was drunk and
money distributed to the mob; but although St Thomas's church
bells were rung, the churchwardens of the other two parishes
managed to prevent the same happening there. There was high
excitement further west, however: ugly scenes in the streets of
Barnstaple and Frome, King William's effigy burnt at Cirencester,
and a man killed in a duel at Bristol. A huge fire blazed in Exeter
cathedral close on the 27th, to which all Hoadly's works were committed, and Sir Peter King arrived that night to find the populace
in so dangerous a mood that he slipped quietly out of town next
morning, rightly judging that the person of a leading Manager
was in some danger of injury.[6] Meanwhile the post which had
brought the glad tidings to Wiltshire on the 23rd had reached
Shropshire and the Welsh border counties on the 24th. Shrewsbury had erupted into a spontaneous outburst of joy and relief.
In Wrexham, as Sir Joseph Jekyll discovered some days later when
he arrived to preside over the Assizes, joy had soon degenerated
into riot: 'a great rabble of this town . . . went with a drum before
'em to several of the dissenters' houses and broke their windows,
and also those of the meeting-house', which only narrowly escaped
sacking. Wrexham's dissenters were luckier than those of Gainsborough whose meeting-house was broken into and severely
damaged; but Jekyll was still scandalised by the negligence of the
town's magistrates in failing to proceed against the offenders,
and after a second 'insurrection' on the 31st he charged even the
High Sheriff with culpable inertia.[7] Bonet, the Prussian minister,
reported sardonically to his government that in any other country
but England such scenes as these would have been interpreted as
the forerunners of civil war.[8]

Lawyers who, like Jekyll, had been prominently involved in the
Sacheverell trial found that their spring circuits brought political
feelings to the boil wherever they went. The Oxford circuit, in
which Harcourt and Lechmere were involved, and the Grand
Sessions in Cheshire, Flintshire and Denbighshire, over which

Jekyll and John Pocklington* presided, witnessed some remarkable scenes. Apart from his experiences in Wrexham, Jekyll had several affronts to complain of, especially at Ludlow, 'and suspected somebody put *aqua fortis* on his coach braces, for it fell in Bromfield'.[9] But his sufferings were nothing compared with those of Lechmere. The pleasure of receiving the freedom of Gloucester on 18 March was soon alloyed by a series of insults, at Hereford, Ludlow, Shrewsbury and Stafford: and they were the more difficult to stomach since his own treatment was in such pointed contrast with the royal receptions accorded everywhere to Sir Simon Harcourt. At Hereford bonfires, bells and the company of the county's leading gentry celebrated Harcourt's election as a freeman; at Shrewsbury a reception-committee of 400 mounted gentlemen escorted him over the last two miles into town, cheering him to his lodgings; while Stafford proved a replica of Shrewsbury, his entry not merely 'tumultuous' but (as other lawyers in the party testified to Sunderland) patently 'concerted, and with such circumstances as gives us a strong jealousy that there was something extraordinary in its design'. Lechmere's progress, on the other hand, was humiliating. His windows were smashed by the mob at Hereford on the 25th and he was treated with 'visible disrespect' by the city dignitaries and with little sympathy by the judge. To avert what he feared might be worse treatment still at Ludlow, he 'was forced to scamper over to Witley and steal into Mr Kettle's [his host's] by the back way', and then to leave at crack of dawn next morning. But his worst experience was outside Shrewsbury on 31 March, where the same party assembled to welcome Harcourt hissed and jeered him as he passed by on horseback with two fellow-barristers, and sped him on his way with shouts of 'No Manager, No Manager'.[10]

Although the first ferment of popular reaction to the Sacheverell verdict had begun to abate within a fortnight, there was not a chance that the emotions which produced it would be allowed to moderate. The clergy saw to that. The Whig member for Lincolnshire found, on his return home, that the local parsons were pressing their non-resistance doctrines even further 'than the Oxonian parsons at London'. From the other side of the land Jekyll told Sunderland: 'I have heard but one sermon since I came into the circuit which

* Whig M.P. for Huntingdonshire.

had not in its broad hints of the hardships the clergy lay under, or
. . . of the dangers of the Church'.[11] In just a few dioceses there
was relative restraint: the bishop of Carlisle, especially, congratulated himself that 'no sacrifices are here offered (nor fires
kindled) to Dr Sacheverell'.[12] But over the country at large the
fears which Sir John Cropley had confided to Stanhope on the
night of the punishment votes were realised with frightening
rapidity.

On 25 March a Sacheverellite parson named Cornwall, incumbent of a living near Ludlow, managed with the connivance
of the sheriff of Montgomeryshire virtually to hijack the pulpit
of Welshpool on the occasion of the Assize Sermon,* and from it
preached a sermon worthy of his mentor on the text: 'Who will
rise up for me against the evil-doers, or who will stand up for me
against the workers of iniquity'. His whole discourse was a thre-
nody on the lot of the clergy as a result of Sacheverell's impeachment, reduced to fettered servitude to 'some great men at Court'.
He proclaimed that 'the Church of England is wounded through the
sides of the clergy; that they ought to cry aloud and spare not'.
Both judges, appalled, agreed that the sermon was scurrilous and
seditious, reporting to the Secretary of State that while the preacher
had praised the Queen personally, 'yet he condemned her government by representing the subordinate magistrates as guilty of
maladministration'. It was like November the Fifth all over again;
yet the pressure which the judges exerted on the Grand Jury to
indict the offender for sedition proved fruitless, and Sunderland,
with Anne's co-operation, could only instruct the bishops of St
Asaph and Hereford to bring him to 'condign punishment' in their
consistory courts. Meanwhile, he had fearlessly preached the
identical sermon to an enthusiastic audience at Salop Assizes, while
the curate of Wrexham inflicted another on Judge Jekyll which
'came almost up to Mr Cornwall, though he took care to soften
or intricate his expressions so as to screen himself from a legal
prosecution'.[13] The measure of the government's disastrous failure
to achieve its prime object in the prosecution of Sacheverell, to
'padlock the mouths' of the Highflying divines, could be gauged

---

* Mr Mercer, vicar of Welshpool, had been nominated by Bishop Fleetwood of St
Asaph to deliver this address, but in the face of great pressure eventually stood down
under protest.

by everyone from the effrontery of these two Welshmen and the powerlessness of the Queen's judges to stir the local magistrates and Grand Jurors into lifting a finger against them.

Back at Westminster the Queen had prorogued Parliament on 5 April. She had done so, moreover, with a Speech from the Throne carefully calculated by the Cabinet to depress current Tory pretensions: one which explicitly gave the stamp of her approval to the Sacheverell prosecution – 'so necessary an occasion of taking up a great part of your time' – and condemned the 'pretence' that 'the Church is in any danger from my administration'.[14] Unless the Queen, with the advice of her Privy Council, decided to dissolve Parliament prematurely, the next General Election, under the provisions of the Triennial Act, could not possibly be held before the spring of 1711. At the moment, whatever some Whigs apprehended, there was not a hint in the Queen's conduct that she contemplated a change of ministry. Only in the full confidence that she had, as yet, no such intention would Godolphin have gone off to Newmarket races as soon as Parliament had risen,[15] to recruit his strength for weathering those 'very disagreeable' six months which he had forecast until the Tory gale blew itself out.

Those Tory peers and members of Parliament who took coach or horse for home in the early days of April had time to ponder on their journeys the one great problem facing their party. Even with the unstinting co-operation of the parish clergy, they and their friends could not hope to sustain indefinitely the massive impetus which the Sacheverell affair had given their cause. To capitalise on the prevailing national mood of loyalism and High Anglican zeal, they must somehow force a new Election before the winter. How could this be done? Only by persuading the Queen that an overwhelming majority of the electorate desired it, in her interest as well as theirs. Apart from using the press, there was in late Stuart England one very effective way of getting such a message across, as the Whigs had demonstrated in 1701: namely, *via* loyal addresses to the Crown from the county communities and from the borough oligarchies. Towards the end of March 1710, ominously for the ruling party, the first such addresses began to be hatched by the Tory gentry and clergy at Assizes in several parts of England. Gloucestershire led the way on 18 March, followed by Herefordshire on the 25th and Cornwall on the 29th. Hard on their heels came Devon, Northamptonshire, Warwickshire, and after a week's interval, Wiltshire on 15 April. Apart from the Cornish address, each one of them assured Anne of its county's determination to return loyal, Church-loving members whenever voters were given the chance, and some hinted even more broadly at their hopes of an early dissolution.

These addresses, as we shall see, proved to be only the beginning of an organised campaign of almost unprecedented dimensions, aimed first at precipitating an Election and then at ensuring victory in every constituency where public opinion counted for anything. It had been Sacheverell's achievement to make this campaign possible. But his involvement was far from ending here. In June and July 1710 he himself played a direct and essential part in it by undertaking what must surely be the most extraordinary Progress ever made by a private individual in Britain: when (as Steele later recalled) 'the anarchic fury ran so high that Harry Sacheverell swelling, and Jack Huggins laughing, marched through England in a triumph more than military'.[16]

In his last few years of teaching at Magdalen Sacheverell numbered among his wealthier pupils a Salopian of High Tory, crypto-Jacobite stock named Robert Lloyd. In March 1710, during the trial, Lloyd found that he had in his gift a handsome living, the rectory of Selattyn, worth £200 a year to its incumbent. The parish was in the diocese of St Asaph and lay close to Oswestry, just on the English side of the border with Wales. Since the living could be held along with a university fellowship it was an irreproachable gift from a grateful student to an old tutor; and as soon as the trial was over it was bestowed on Sacheverell.[17]

Bishop Fleetwood, understandably perturbed at the prospect of the Flag Officer in person invading his already troubled territories, took the full twenty-eight days allowed by law to decide whether to allow the Doctor institution. Sacheverell was not unduly concerned. He knew that the only possible objection to his accepting the cure was his inability to speak Welsh, and that since the same was true of many of his parishioners, this could hardly prove a permanent sticking-point.[18] When he did go up to Shropshire to take possession he proposed to do so in style. Meanwhile he was only too happy to stay in town for some weeks, basking in the adulation due to the saviour of the Church and the nation's martyr-hero, and restoring the blush of prosperity to his financial affairs. These were heady days. A 'Thanksgiving Supper' with his clerical devotees at the Queen's Arms, by St Paul's, 'with plenty of wine and a consort of music', was the prelude to a round of invitations and good dinners, among which the highlight was a visit to the prodigiously wealthy Sir Charles Duncombe at Richmond. The Doctor's lodgings were thronged with congratulators. He devised a characteristic way of conveying his own acknowledgments to those peers still in London who had voted for him. Cunningham described how, puffed up, 'he went from house to house to congratulate them all on his and their common safety, followed by a train of link-boys and blackguards'; at his every appearance on the streets 'he was huzza'd by the mob like a prize-fighter'. High on his list was that key defector, Argyll; but the duke had prior warning and sent a servant to forestall him, with the instructions, 'tell him what I did in Parliament was not at all done for his sake'. Meanwhile St Saviour's was crammed every Sunday for the afternoon service, at which the Doctor read prayers; and Dyer soon informed the world that no fewer than forty-six City ministers had undertaken to fill his pulpit by rota during the period of his suspension.[19]

Sacheverell fed greedily on his own notoriety: and there seemed no limit to its manifestations. He could afford the occasional rebuff – such as the news from Nottingham, a stronghold of Dissent, that he had been hanged in effigy from a signpost[20] – since already his very name was beginning to take on the character of a popular talisman. Ralph Bridges related towards the end of April how

> In Lincolnshire or Yorkshire (it matters not which) the gentlemen met in a large plain and distributed seventeen hundred and ten twelve-penny loaves to so many poor people, all marked thus, *Sacheverell 1710*. In the Town here every couple since Lent desires to be married by him; and 'tis common to christen children by his name. Dr Bradford* only I have yet heard refuse to name a child thus, and had liked to have turned away his curate for doing of it; and his reason was, that Sacheverell *was no Christian name*.[21]

* Rector of St Mary-le-Bow. See p. 211 above.

The provinces soon caught on to the London fashion, and at the beginning of May the son of a Tewkesbury attorney was baptised 'Sacheverell' before what was reputed to be the biggest congregation seen in the town church for a century. A number of Tory cockfighters renamed their birds 'Sacheverell', and there was heavy betting on a great contest at Cirencester between one of these birds and another called 'Burgess'.

A more personal consequence of his fame was that Henry Sacheverell became one of the most marriageable bachelors in London. Various eligible young females set their caps at him, and his acquaintance, Thomas Carte, heard in particular of one lady 'of 10,000*l* or more' who was resolved to disqualify him from his Fellowship. The Doctor, however, was already well on the way to being free from all financial worries, without resort to matrimony. His case was generally believed to have cost him about £800 since mid-December, including barristers' fees of at least £250. But it was being said on very good authority before the end of April that, through private donations alone, he had not merely cleared his debts but had built up already a surplus of 1,500 guineas. Such a combination of idolatry and sudden affluence would have tested the character of a man of far finer fibre than Sacheverell. But the same vanity which rendered him impervious to the growing disapproval of some of the more fastidious London clergy was to make him the ideal tool in the hands of the local Tory chiefs of the Midlands and the West Country, who were keenly aware that once Sacheverell could be lured away from London and persuaded that he could enjoy his triumph even more spectacularly in the provinces, they would have at their disposal the surest vote-catcher most of them would see in a lifetime.[22]

In mid-April, while Sacheverell was still junketing in London, the political world was given the first intimation – in the form of the duke of Shrewsbury's sudden appointment as Lord Chamberlain and admission to the Cabinet – that the hold of Godolphin and the Junto over the Queen might be relaxing. The Treasurer returned from Newmarket with indecorous haste, but after a few days of consternation calm was to all appearances restored in government circles. Those, however, who recognised, or thought they recognised, the hand of Harley behind this shrewd gambit waited expectantly for further developments; among them Francis

R

Atterbury, who early in May went down to Devon on his archidiaconal visitation and planned to make the maximum political capital out of the occasion by taking Henry Sacheverell with him.[23] But the Doctor did not linger in the West Country. On the 10th he was expected in Tavistock. By the 14th, at the latest, he must have been back in London; for the next day, a Monday, saw him bound for Oxford, which had not seen its champion since before the impeachment and was now preparing a sumptuous welcome for him.

The journey to Oxford, though accomplished in a single day, gave a slight foretaste of what lay ahead when Sacheverell at length went up to Shropshire for his induction. He left Town in a cavalcade of sixty-six horsemen, including his solicitor Jack Huggins, and a strong party of his Southwark parishioners who accompanied him as far as the Crown at Uxbridge. Leaving Uxbridge the 'convoy', according to one eyewitness, had grown to 300, and hundreds more tacked on in Beaconsfield, High Wycombe and West Wycombe. In Stokenchurch and Tetsworth there were more heavy reinforcements to take the place of those who had to turn back – plainly, the Doctor's itinerary had been well publicised beforehand – and those who could not follow came to cheer:

> The very lame forsook their crutches
> And tumbled over hedge and ditches.[24]

And so to Wheatley, six miles east of Oxford, where the Queen herself could not have been more splendidly received.

> Here [wrote one of the travellers] the Right Honourable the earl of Abingdon, with his brother Mr Charles Bertie . . . Mr Rowney, one of the members of Parliament for the city of Oxon, as also most of the noblemen, Heads of Houses, both the Proctors, most of the Fellows of Colleges, gentlemen, commoners, etc., welcomed the Doctor home to the University, which he had been such an ornament to, and ushered him into the town; where, having supped with the earl, he betook himself to his chambers in the college, which were crowded the next morning by visitors of the first rank and quality.[25]

At Magdalen Sacheverell remained for over a fortnight, enjoying the munificent hospitality of college after college, while the arrangements for his Progress were being finalised. Just as the celebrations were ending, news arrived from Epsom that Jack Dolben, the persecutor-in-chief, had died there suddenly after a short illness, wrongly diagnosed by his doctors;* 'by which', one Tory savagely observed, 'the hangman was saved a labour'.[26] Thus fortified both in body and mind, Sacheverell left Oxford on the Banbury road on the morning of Thursday, 1 June: with him went Huggins and a party of cronies, engaged to bear him company throughout the whole expedition, and over the first stage of his journey 'a vast retinue' of University men and townsfolk.[27] The choice of roads was itself a signal of intention. Travelling north-westwards, spending a night in Worcester and another at Shrewsbury, the rector-designate of Selattyn could have reached his parish very comfortably in three days. However, for one more concerned with feeding a fire than taking up a cure a more circuitous route was appropriate. In the event it took him over four weeks to reach Selattyn, and just under three weeks to get back to Oxford again. Precisely two days of this time (excepting the briefest of passing visits on 27 June) was spent among his new parishioners: on 1 July he was inducted; on the 2nd he took his one service (minus a sermon, naturally) in his new church; and he rarely, if ever, showed his face there again until he resigned the living in 1713. Seemingly the Church, whatever its other perils, was not in danger from pluralists and non-residents.[28]

Some of the statistics of the Progress can be left to tell their own story of its scale, its political significance and its triumphant success, enveloped as it was in an atmosphere of popular delirium which today would be the envy of any pop idol's public relations team. On his outward journey Sacheverell took in six counties on his way to the borders of Salop: Oxfordshire, Warwickshire, Staffordshire, Cheshire, Denbighshire and Flintshire. On his way back, he flaunted through Shropshire, Worcestershire, and briefly through Gloucestershire, before re-entering Oxfordshire. Although he visited Birmingham, Nantwich, Oswestry and several small market-towns, it was the parliamentary boroughs on or anywhere

---

* To quote *Squire Bickerstaffe's Elegy on the much-lamented Death of John Dolben, Esq.* (London, 1710):

> 'Death nick'd him, in a trice, like a false brother,
> Nor gave him time to say, Forgive me, Mother!'

244 of Doctor Sacheverell

near his route which saw most of him. He showed himself in no
fewer than twelve,* in some for no more than a few hours, but in
others, notably Lichfield, Shrewsbury and Worcester, for two or
three days. Little wonder Bromley wrote in July to an old friend at
University College that the Doctor 'was very welcome to us in
Warwickshire'.[29] A dozen other Tory members or prospective
candidates who were able to use the Progress most profitably for
their own publicity would have echoed these sentiments.

In the space of just over six weeks Henry Sacheverell was
honoured with ten civic receptions.† Three of these were informal
affairs, as when the members of the corporation of Ellesmere way-
laid him *en route* from Oswestry to Whitchurch, and treated him
'with a handsome cold breakfast'.‡ Mostly, however, they were full-
dress occasions of pompous, bibulous ceremony. At Banbury the
visitor 'was waited upon by [the] worshipful body, in scarlet gowns
and black gowns, and the Recorder made as good a speech as he
could to him, which introduced a more grateful present, a hamper
of the best wine in Banbury'.[30] A fortnight later, a mile out of
Lichfield, Sacheverell's party – including the High Sheriff of
Staffordshire and numerous gentry – was formally welcomed by
the two Bailiffs and the city Sheriff, by the aldermen and corporation in full rig, 'with their maces before them', and by the Town
Clerk flourishing his carefully-prepared speech. Oswestry surpassed all others in the lavishness of its civic banquet; but Worcester fell surprisingly short in this respect, since the Common
Council was far from unanimous§ and in the end could vote
only £20 of public money towards a 'cold treat' at the Bush
Inn.[31]

* Viz, Banbury, Warwick, Coventry, Lichfield, Stafford, Newcastle-under-Lyme,
  Shrewsbury, Bridgnorth, Ludlow (possibly), Wenlock, Worcester and Evesham.
† In Banbury, Warwick, Lichfield, Stafford, Newcastle, Nantwich, Ellesmere, Oswestry, Wenlock and Worcester. An eleventh, planned for Evesham, misfired.
‡ The Warwick Whigs insisted that only the Mayor, four aldermen and the Recorder
  visited the Doctor at his inn, the Woolpack, to pay their respects: that they 'at first
  ordered their gowns to be brought there', but 'had not the courage to put them on,
  and so moved without that grandeur to the Doctor's apartment' – to Sacheverell's
  disgust. Even so, they were much criticised by other burgesses for slighting the
  authority of Parliament. *The Flying-Post*, Nos 2243, 2246, 2248, 22 and 29 June,
  4 July.
§ For instance, in their anxiety to avoid undue disturbance, the burgesses ordered the
  constables to seize the drums heading Sacheverell's rather slender procession into
  the city, and also to remove the garlands with which the Cross had been festooned.

By the time he reached Worcester on 14 July, however, Sacheverell was so sated with hospitality that he was probably grateful for the relief. In the course of his progress, which followed hard on a fortnight of high living in Oxford, almost fifty vast dinners, not to mention many lavish suppers, were washed down by innumerable bottles of wine. Quite apart from public dinners and a score of meals given in his honour in the households in which he stayed, he sat down to dinner in at least twenty-two private houses. He dined with the earl of Denbigh at Newnham Paddox, with Lord Leigh at Stoneleigh, and with three other peers.* He graced the table of the great William Bromley at Baginton, and of Sir William Boughton at Lawford Park; of Sir Edward Cobb and Sir Edward Aston; of his first patron, Sir Charles Holt, at Aston. He pointedly accepted invitations from Tory candidates – like Richard Cresswell and Edward Cressett in Shropshire, for instance, and Sir Robert Jenkinson in Oxfordshire – whose expectation of a new Election was heightened by the news, in mid-June, that the Queen had replaced Sunderland as Secretary of State by a Tory, Lord Dartmouth.

At every stage of Sacheverell's journey prominent Tory landowners hastened to put their mansions at the disposal of his whole *entourage*. On only seven nights in seven weeks did their champion have to resort to an inn.† He stayed for ten extraordinary days at Combe Abbey with Lord Craven while he lorded it over Warwickshire, before moving on to Newhall, where George Sacheverell and his wife Mary welcomed the man who had brought fresh renown to the family name. In Staffordshire he was the guest for three days of Richard Dyott, Lichfield's long-serving member and noted 'Tacker', and he then encamped at Blithfield Hall, whose owner, Sir Edward Bagot, had been one of the county's knights of the shire from 1698 to 1708. Every great house he stayed in became a Mecca for the neighbouring gentry and clergy, flocking in to pay their respects.

In Cheshire his host was the bishop of Chester. In Denbighshire he divided his favours between Crossford, home of George

---

* Lord Willoughby de Broke, Viscount Kilmorey and Lord Folliot, the last two Nonjurors.

† Viz, in Banbury, Birmingham (for two nights), Newcastle-under-Lyme, Whitchurch, Shrewsbury and Stow-on-the-Wold.

Shackerley, the brother of the Tory member for Chester, and Chirk Castle, only two miles from Selattyn. There one of the wealthiest commoners in Britain, Sir Richard Myddelton, lived in resplendent style as the undisputed *grand seigneur* of the county and its representative at Westminster time out of mind. Vicarious pleasure and pride suffused the parsonages of England when Dyer's Letter brought them the news on 1 July that Sir Richard had invited the Doctor 'to make [Chirk] his home while his business kept him in the country', and had 'entertained him and his numerous retinue in a princely manner'. In Shropshire and Worcestershire came more munificent hospitality, from Roger Owen at Condover, from Whitmore Acton and Lord Kilmorey, and from Berkeley Green at Cotheridge; while at Sarsden in Oxfordshire, on the very last lap, Sir John Walter* was so excessively welcoming that rumour had it subsequently that Sacheverell had been 'Low-Church' there, 'that is laid flat under the table, which gave occasion for that sarcasm, "there lies the pillar of our Church" '.[32]

He did do other things from time to time besides feast and carouse. He laid the foundation stone of the desperately-needed new church of St Philip in Birmingham. At Newcastle-under-Lyme he christened a child 'Sacheverell'; and although it was a Thursday, the parish church was reported 'fuller than it has been in the memory of man'. He was kept very busy during his three-hour stay in Wrexham, where 'almost all the mad[a]ms went to get a kiss of him'.[33] He persuaded Lord Kilmorey to take the oaths to the government. But what ordinary people remembered most about the Progress were the perpetual noise, the colour and the crowds. Coventry greeted the hero of the hour with its town band, with beating drums and blaring trumpets. Lord Leigh conferred on him a singular honour, 'a triple discharge of his artillery, during which prosperity was drunk to the Church and health to the Queen, the 52 lords and the Dr by that noble lord . . .'[34] Church bells everywhere saluted him; although at Eccleshall, in Staffordshire, there was a delay while the Tory churchwardens wrested the keys from a recalcitrant 'Hoadleian' vicar, while at Worcester old Bishop Lloyd got tit-for-tat with his former antagonist by forbidding every parish minister to allow his bells to be rung, in 'very high affront to the highest court of judicature in

* Thomas Rowney's colleague as M.P. for Oxford.

this kingdom'. At St Nicholas's, some determined Sacheverellites did get in through the windows and up to the bell tower, only to find that the clappers had been removed.

There were astonishing scenes in Wales and in Shropshire. Not content with strewing their streets with flowers and decorating their houses with boughs, the citizens of Wrexham (to the mild alarm of Sacheverell's retinue) 'burned the effigies of Mr Hoadly, etc., in the bonfires which were lighted at our going through the town'. When the party approached Bridgnorth on 5 July they found 'the hedges two miles from the town . . . dressed with the finest of flowers and lined with people and the two steeples dressed out with fifty pounds' worth of flags and colours'.[35] In Shropshire too, the crowds reached new peaks. They had been high enough in Warwickshire: an estimated 5,000 had ushered Sacheverell into Coventry (or, as one of Walpole's clerks less elegantly put it, 'that impudent dog' had been 'attended with five thousand mob at his arse'); and at the approaches to Birmingham his reception committee was put at between 300 and 500 horse and between 3,000 and 4,000 foot.[36] But these scenes paled later beside the triumphant entry into Shrewsbury on 3 July, when a huge cavalcade of mounted gentry and yeomen, headed by the two prospective Tory candidates and numbered by most observers at 5,000, by some at 7,000, escorted him from Montford bridge to the town gate. Beyond there, 'the streets were crowded with such an infinite number of foot that he was an hour passing from the gate to the place where he was entertained at supper'. The church bells, which had begun ringing at five that morning, did not stop until eleven at night.

At Bridgnorth Sacheverell's arrival was another elaborately-staged electioneering exercise, engineered by Richard Cresswell, junior, a rakish but enterprising Jacobite who rightly saw this as the only way he and his partner could overthrow the established Whig interest of the Whitmores of Apley and Sir Humphrey Briggs among the borough's thousand voters. Cresswell sent circular letters to virtually every clergyman in Salop, and to many gentry also, inviting them to join the parade and to take dinner with him and 'the idol of the country' afterwards at the Cock and Castle. Shortly before the great day, we read in a letter of Gervase Scroop, there had been violent doings at Bridgnorth, both parties making bonfires where about one they drink Dr Sacheverell's health and the other his confusion. You have read the letter sent by some Shropshire gentlemen to the earl of Bradford concerning the fraudulent and sinister means they got the Shrewsbury address signed, by carrying it about to public houses at 10 and 11 at night. The Tory party at Bridgnorth put this letter into the bonfire with a pair of tongs as scorning to touch it with their hands . . . and read the gentlemen's names that subscribed to it, declaring them liars, which had not the bailiffs commanded the peace, would have caused bloodshed.[37]

5 July proved a triumph for Cresswell's organisation, though not for the forces of law and order. Sacheverell's escort into the borough was estimated by Tory sources (over-enthusiastically, perhaps) at 3,500 horsemen (including sixty-four clergymen) and almost 3,000 on foot: 'most of them had white knots edged with gold, and 3 leaves of gilt laurel in their hats'. On the other hand, a correspondent of the Whig *Flying-Post* reported anti-Sacheverell demonstrations as well, halters lowered down to Sacheverell out of upper windows, oranges on sticks thrust under his supporters' noses ('the best fruit that ever came to England'!), and at least one fatality in the fighting between the rival mobs.[38]

On 19 July Doctor Sacheverell returned to Oxford, amid scenes scarcely less enthusiastic than those which had marked his departure. For the rest of July and the whole of August, except for a brief excursion to his birthplace, Marlborough, he remained at Magdalen. His chief *direct* contribution to the Tory triumph of 1710 was by now made. At the Oxfordshire Assizes on 22 July Mr Justice Dormer, an unblushing Whig, was still prepared to announce categorically that there would be no dissolution and no new Election.[39] But few, even then, believed him; and there was barely a doubt left after 8 August, when Queen Anne took the decisive step of dismissing Godolphin, who had served with wisdom and assiduity since 1702, and replaced him with a Treasury Commission in which Harley was first in importance if not in name.

For three months past the stream of addresses which had begun to descend on the Court in the spring had become a cascade. Some few were relatively moderate. But the bulk of the ninety-seven Tory addresses which counties, boroughs, dioceses and arch-deaconries had sent up to the Queen by the time of Godolphin's dismissal, were charged with loyalist and pro-clerical fervour and redolent of all the most reactionary political thinking which the Sacheverell affair had stimulated. In this work, as in much else, the clergy were busy. The Stafford address was penned by 'parson Husband' and that of Herefordshire by 'rector Trahearne'.[40] Some addresses had been drafted or revised either precisely at the time of Sacheverell's visit, like the notorious concoction of the clergy of the Archdeaconry of Coventry, or very shortly beforehand, as with the offerings of Shrewsbury and Bridgnorth.* On 30 June the bishop of Worcester had reflected with acute apprehension on

> the great danger we are brought into by the turbulent preaching and practices of an impudent man . . . [who] is now riding in triumph over the middle of England, everywhere stirring up the people to address to her Majesty for a new Parliament. The danger is so great that I cannot but tremble to think of it, if her Majesty should dissolve the present Parliament and change her ministry, which is the thing driven at by the addresses.[41]

Even before the Progress the 'higher' addresses had been vehement enough. In May the corporation of St John's borough of Wootton Bassett, for instance, had professed themselves unwilling to

> continue silent at this time amidst the crowds of your Majesty's faithful subjects, who daily express their indignation against such doctrines as openly deny your Majesty's hereditary title, insolently invade your just prerogative, and hardly tolerate the Established Church. . . . The most effectual way by which we can evince the sincerity of these professions [they concluded] is

---

* For the Coventry address, originally drafted on 11 May but presented for Sacheverell's approval at Newnham Paddox on 5 June, see MS. Carte 230, f. 227; for Bridgnorth, whose address was drawn up late in June but presented at Kensington by Richard Cresswell a week after Sacheverell's tumultuous visit to the borough, see Monson MSS. 7/13/123 and *A Collection of the Addresses which have been presented to the Queen since the Impeachment of the Reverend Dr Henry Sacheverell* (London, 1711), Pt 2, p. 14. The Shrewsbury address was first drafted on 26 May; but it was later amended (see MS. note on British Museum copy of the *Collection*, Pt 2, p. 5) and not presented until 24 June.

to choose such persons to represent us, as are capable of paying allegiance only where it is due, as prefer the Crown to a faction, the Church to a conventicle, and our ancient, happy constitution to any New Model.

During the Progress and after it the tone became increasingly shrill, frequently hysterical. Harcourt's Cardiganshire Address, after rhapsodising on the Queen's divine right in words that were the pure milk of Toryism, went on to assure her

that as we have a just detestation and abhorrence of all schismatical and antimonarchical principles, which have, of late, been publicly professed, and industriously propagated, with an intent to lessen our duty to your Majesty, and veneration to our most holy Church; so we shall always be ready (by the example of the unshaken loyalty of our ancestors in the worst of times) with our lives and fortunes, to support and defend your Majesty's most sacred person, regal power and government. . . .

Denbighshire assured the Queen that 'while Republican and factious spirits, the implacable enemies of your Majesty's family and government are . . . reviving and maintaining those pernicious and fatal doctrines that paved the way to the execrable murder of your Majesty's royal grandfather, and laid these kingdoms in desolation and ruin', they did from the bottom of their hearts 'abhor and detest all those traitorous and damnable positions which assert the legality of deposing or resisting princes upon any pretence whatsoever'. The clergy of Coventry, having also been reminded by recent events of Charles I's 'barbarous murder', and declaring their unshakable belief in the Queen's 'undoubted hereditary right', looked forward to the time 'when your Majesty shall, to the great satisfaction of your loyal subjects (and of none more than the clergy), be pleased to call another Parliament, and give the Convocation leave to sit'.[42] And so it continued, in address after address: the words might vary, but the message was almost always the same.*

To Robert Harley, deeply engaged all summer in scheming the downfall of Godolphin and the Junto, the evidence which the first shoal of addresses had provided of 'the sense of the nation', and

* There were only fifteen Whig counter-addresses procured before the end of August.

even the popular demonstrations which had accompanied Sacheverell's Progress, had seemed like gifts from the gods. For his own
part, he had precious little sympathy with the sentiments paraded
in the former[43] and nothing but contempt for the latter; but he
needed them, and welcomed them, to prepare the ground for a
ministerial revolution which could never be easy or straightforward
so long as the army was dominated by Marlborough, the City
commanded by the Whigs, and the Lord Treasurer closely linked
with both.[44] Not least, he needed them to stiffen the wavering
resolution of the Queen, whose mind was undoubtedly set on an
early peace, but who hesitated many weeks before agreeing to part
with Godolphin, and whose doubts about the necessity of a dissolution took a long time to dispel.

Unfortunately for Harley the gods were too lavish in their gifts.
Contrary to his expectation, by the time the destruction of the old
ministry was completed in the fourth week of September – not
entirely in accord with his plans – and by the time the dissolution
of the old Parliament had become unavoidable (if a new one,
willing to support Tory ministers, was to meet before the winter),[45]
there was still no sign that the Sacheverell fever had burned itself
out. Harley and his chief collaborator, Shrewsbury, had no desire
to meet a new Parliament as violently High Tory as its predecessor
had been violently Whig. But they reckoned without the exceptional momentum and ferocity of the Tory election campaign,
and above all without the truly frightening commitment of the
clergy to the campaign. For, as Bishop Burnet recorded in November,

> besides a course, for some months, of inflaming sermons, they
> went about from house to house, pressing their people to show,
> on this great occasion, their zeal for the Church, and now or
> never to save it: they also told them in what ill hands the Queen
> had been kept, as in captivity, and that it was a charity as well as
> their duty to free her. . . .

Theirs, as Cunningham affirmed, was 'a furious zeal'; and helped
as they were by 'the [electorate's] hope of being eased by peace of
the great burthen of taxes', they proved irresistible. Most Whigs
accepted 'that the bent of the nation is against us'; but, like George
Whichcote, their defeated candidate in Lincolnshire, it was to

'this frenzy, heightened by the black-coats' that they mainly attributed the loss of so many seats.[46]

The most important single achievement of the Tory clergy and gentry in their Election campaign lay in ensuring that the platform on which their party eventually fought in October and November 1710, was essentially the same platform on which Henry Sacheverell had taken his stand seven months before. It was neatly epitomised in the infectious election-chant which carried the two Tory candidates for the county of Cornwall, John Trevanion and George Granville, to a resounding victory over the Whigs on 1 November:

> Trevanion and Granville, sound as a bell
> For the Queen, the Church, and Sacheverell.[47]

Contemporary reports from a variety of constituencies testify to the decisive success of the High Tories in keeping the Doctor's name in the forefront of the action:

> On Wednesday last [7 October] began at Norwich the election of knights of the shire for the county of Norfolk. The candidates for the Church party were Sir John Woodhouse and Sir Jacob Astley, Barts, and for the Whigs Ash Wyndham and Robert Walpole, Esqrs. The same was carried on with great heat. The two first had Dr Sacheverell's picture carried before them, and the cry was 'No Manager, No Scaffolder'. But that was not all, for they pelted Mr Walpole with dirt and stones and drove him out of his tent, spoiling his fine laced coat which they told him came out of the Treasury. With this heat and clamour it continued till about 9 at night when, the poll being cast up, Sir John Woodhouse had 3,217 voices and Sir Jacob Astley 3,200, Wyndham 2,781, Walpole 2,391.[48]

What was notable here was not merely that Walpole came at the bottom of the poll, but that he finished 400 votes below his Whig partner, a nonentity by comparison. Ash Wyndham's sin was less heinous, since he had only voted against Sacheverell in the House of Commons, whereas Walpole had prosecuted him before the supreme tribunal.

The Managers of the impeachment had a torrid time at this Election. Their opponents singled them out for particular attack.

At least five of them – Hawles, Boyle, Holland, Coningsby and Compton – preferred not to hazard their persons and reputations and declined to stand for re-election.[49] General Stanhope, who stood by proxy at Westminster and was crushingly defeated, had his reputation shamelessly traduced, being accused of sodomy and sacrilege as well as republicanism: he eventually squeezed in with some difficulty at Cockermouth. William Thompson, with little hope of re-election at Orford, tried his luck instead in the more popular borough of Ipswich, which had a large dissenting vote: he was defeated, though only by 23 votes. Spencer Cowper was dropped by his patron at Beeralston. In the end only ten Managers were re-elected (including Mordaunt and Dalrymple, who had played no part in the trial), and only four of them, significantly, had to survive a contest.* Speaker Onslow was tarred with the same brush. Handbills circulated in support of his successful Tory opponents in Surrey described them as 'true to the Queen and Church against all Managers of Oliver's party and principles, that once murdered their King and thousands of the nation to reign over us'.[50]

Even having voted against the Doctor, let alone having managed the impeachment, proved electoral death to many a Whig. Thousands of purported 'division lists' on the Sacheverell case were printed and circulated round the country, and they were used with great effect by Tory supporters in many regions for canvassing purposes.[51] Moreover, Serjeant John Pratt, who had not been in the last House of Commons but had declined to act as counsel for Sacheverell, was rejected by the electors of Marlborough, allegedly on that account.[52] The Doctor's influence seemed all-pervasive. His name was linked with the safety of the Church in the shouts of Tory election mobs and in the broadsheets of election publicists. His portrait rivalled the mitre as the favourite emblem on the rallying standards of the Tories. At Tewkesbury, William Bromley of Upton both used it in his campaign and had it carried before him in procession, with the church bells ringing, when he

---

* The ten re-elected were Montagu (after a hard and controversial struggle at Carlisle); Lechmere and Stanhope (in a sharp contest at Cockermouth); King, Jekyll, Smith and Powlet (in pocket boroughs normally controlled by the Whig nobility, though Powlet lost his seat at Winchester and survived a petition at Lymington); Mordaunt, on Wharton's interest at Richmond; Walpole, who took refuge at Castle Rising and King's Lynn; and Dalrymple at Haddington Burghs.

set out for London to take his seat. At Newcastle upon Tyne the supporters of Blackett and Wrightson, who defeated the old Whig member, William Carr, 'had red and blue favours in their hats with this motto in letters of gold, *For the Queen & Church B : W*; and Dr Sacheverell's picture was carried about the streets bedecked with laurels, etc., which the people followed huzzaing to it'. In Cambridgeshire, too, the familiar portrait proved a lucky talisman for the Tories. And in Yorkshire, where a hired mob of schoolboys carried the Sacheverell emblem aloft on placards round the seething hustings at York, Sir William Strickland, the former Whig member, was so incensed that 'he turned his backside on't when it was brought before the tribunal'[53] – a rare gesture of defiance and *lèse-majesté* which availed him nothing, for he was shatteringly defeated.

In fact it is permissible to describe the epic General Election of 1710 as a personal, as well as a great party, triumph. The anti-Whig reaction was nowhere more marked than in those counties and boroughs through which the Doctor had passed in the course of his Progress. In Staffordshire the Whigs were annihilated, losing the only four seats they had held in the Parliament of 1708–10.[54] In Warwickshire they lost Coventry, their only stronghold. In Salop, where the Whigs had previously been very strong, their rout was proportionately more spectacular. The Tories captured both the county seats (one of them for Sacheverell's patron, Lloyd), two at Bridgnorth (where Cresswell left so little to chance that he paid the expenses of twenty-seven voters to travel all the way from London[55]), two at Shrewsbury and one at Bishop's Castle.[56] The nearest thing to a personal setback for the Doctor happened in Southwark, where his patron, John Lade, stood against the powerful Whig brewing interest and was narrowly defeated.

When the last of the smoke had cleared in the second week of November, after at least 130 contests in England and Wales alone,* the Tories found they had carried 332 English members against 181 for the Whigs, while the Scottish results had still further widened the gap. The contrast with the previous Parliament,

* See W. A. Speck, *Tory and Whig: The Struggle in the Constituencies, 1701–15*, pp. 126–31. This was the highest number of contests in any eighteenth-century Election, except that of 1722, when there were 134 (*The History of Parliament: The House of Commons 1715–1754*, i, 116–24).

as Francis Annesley joyously wrote, was 'prodigious, and beyond the expectations of any man'.[57] The Election had settled one thing beyond doubt: that before very long peace would be restored at last to a distracted Europe.* But had it settled with equal certainty the future of the Church of England, for which its parish clergy and its country squires had fought with such passion? That question would depend no longer on Henry Sacheverell, whose *annus mirabilis* had now run its course, but partly on Queen Anne, and still more on Robert Harley. For Harley, that instinctive moderate, the election results of 1710 were almost, though not quite, as bitter as they were for the Whigs, who this autumn had reaped in anguish what a year earlier they had sown in anger and self-assurance.

* The Baltic countries apart, it should be added.

XI EPILOGUE

1. *After the Triumph: Sacheverell's Later Years, 1710–24*

When the General Election of 1710 was over Dr Sacheverell was still three months away from his thirty-seventh birthday. Given a continuance of his present robust health, he must have hoped that half a lifetime still lay ahead of him, more than enough time for the champion of the Church to enjoy to the full his due reward. He could not believe that the Tories would ever fail in gratitude to the man who (he himself, at least, never doubted) had brought them out of the wilderness. His ambitions had now moved on to a different plane from those of the aspiring young Magdalen Fellow of eight years before. The first bishopric that fell vacant once his suspension was over; in the meantime, a benefice at least double the value of Selattyn,[1] and a continuance of that political influence and social *cachet* in which he had revelled throughout the spring and summer: these, it seems, were the goals towards which pride and assurance now directed his expectations.

By the autumn of 1710 Sacheverell was already financially a man of substance. Besides the income from his fellowship and college offices and from his Southwark chaplaincy, he was now guaranteed £200 a year from Selattyn. He could well afford to sacrifice the £80 a year from the lectureship to which the parish of Newington Butts had elected him during his imprisonment: for his professional emoluments alone now placed him in the same income bracket as many gentry of the middle rank.* But in addition

---

* A useful yardstick of comparison may be found in the provisions of the Act of 1711 which fixed the property qualification for a M.P. representing a borough at £300 p.a. and that for knights of the shire (traditionally drawn from the social *élite* of the county communities) at £600 p.a.

his capital assets had accumulated remarkably since December 1709, mostly through the private and public bounty of scores of Tory sympathisers and corporate bodies. The financial contributions which had begun immediately he was taken into custody had already topped £2,000 by the end of April 1710, of which the expenses of the trial absorbed just over a third.* Throughout the summer the flow continued unstaunched. Hearne heard of 'great sums of money presented him in divers places' on his Progress; on his return to Oxford there were gifts of 60 guineas from Jesus College, 30 guineas from Queen's and many individual donations; a purse of 200 guineas, together with a generous private 'benefaction' from Lord Bruce, discharged Marlborough's debt of gratitude to its native son; and he was made a legatee in several wills, including – so rumour had it – that of 'a great lady newly deceased at Canterbury', who left him £1,000.[2] Add the money received from his printer for the right to publish his speech, and to reissue his old sermons and pamphlets (notably his two Oxford sermons of 1702), and here indeed was a martyr's crown that had proved to be worth its weight in gold.

When Sacheverell returned to London in the autumn of 1710 he advertised quite plainly his disinclination to devote himself during his suspension to the care of his Southwark parishioners. He took new lodgings in St Martin's Lane, Westminster – 'to be near his Parliament', as the Whigs would have it. In the first weeks of the new session, to be sure, not a day went by without the Doctor putting in an appearance in the Court of Requests or in the Commons' lobby. He was, after all, 'the sun' (he explained to his acquaintances), and the sun must show itself regularly and not hide behind clouds. His appearances in Southwark were confined to Sundays, when he exercised his mellifluous voice reading the prayers and lessons in St Saviour's, unaffectedly and with due reverence, and listening comfortably to his visiting preachers regaling 'the governors of boats and barges in their furbelowed galleries' with sermons after his own heart.[3]

His relations with his Tory satellites at Westminster were not all that he could have wished. Bromley, the new Speaker, looked elsewhere for his chaplain, and so did Harcourt, the new Lord Keeper of the Great Seal. Irrationally, Sacheverell had expected

* See p. 241 above.

S

otherwise. And he was even more peeved when numbers of High Tories in both Houses, wearying of his importunities and pretensions, began to shun his company. They were still a minority, however, and early in the New Year Sacheverell found himself in favour with the members of the October Club, a large and vociferous group of Tory backbenchers who were discontented with the restraint being shown by Harley and the new administration towards the defeated Whigs, and impatient with the seeming lack of official interest in a positive pro-Anglican programme. In March John Cass, an Octobrist and a London member of Parliament, gladly made use of the Doctor to stage a popular demonstration in the City in the Tory–Anglican cause. White Kennett noted with distaste that in his old parish church of St Botolph, Aldgate, there was

> a sermon by the Lord Bishop of Chester and prayers read by Dr Sacheverell, to make a mob and noise upon opening the schools of charity built up over the church porch by Colonel Case [Cass]. A procession to a public hall for dinner upon tickets at 7s 6d apiece. Some peers at the hall, though not at the church . . . and some commoners of the October Club, all under the wise direction of Capt. John Silk, who forced the use of the desk from Dr Bray for Dr Sacheverell and said there was order from above for it.

But although the Doctor still cut a figure in London in 1711 it was not always a popular or heroic one. In April, for instance, he badly overplayed his hand when he deluded himself into thinking he could influence the elections at the Bank of England. After buying £500 worth of stock to qualify himself to vote, and actively canvassing for the Tory list of candidates for the offices of Governor and Vice-Governor and for the twenty-four directorships, all he achieved in the end was his own mortification. His appearance at the General Court on election day, 13 April, was a disaster; for he was hissed by his fellow-shareholders, roundly told that 'this was no mob business' and forced to retreat in disorder with bystanders throwing dirt at his coach.[4]

Meanwhile his quest for fatter preferment was proving frustrating. A promise of the succession to the princely living of Hatfield, made twelve months before by the earl of Salisbury, showed no sign of materialising as the rector obstinately refused to die. An application to the bishop of Durham for the prebendary and livings of the late Theophilus Pickering in this lush diocese met with the suavest of snubs. Enough was enough for the wily Lord Crewe, who had been one of the six bishops to vote Sacheverell *not guilty* in the previous March, but who now replied 'that the Doctor's services and merits were public, and that his rewards ought to be so; that he would not be guilty of the presumption, as a private patron, to prevent the government from doing justice in preferring the man who had deserved so well of the Church and nation'. But the government showed no inclination to oblige while the suspension was in force. Even Harcourt was not to be moved, despite the receipt of a costly present, a double-gilded basin and ewer, from his erstwhile client: in fact, the gesture miscarried, for in the pretentious inscription with which the gift was engraved (as Canon Stratford perceived) 'the Doctor has so interwoven his own praises with my Lord Keeper's that his lordship is afraid he cannot make any public use of the plate'. In the summer of 1711, therefore, Sacheverell retired in some dudgeon to Oxford, where at least he had the satisfaction of hearing his friend, Tilly, rebuke the ministry from St Mary's pulpit for its ingratitude to its saviour, and then of caballing with Atterbury against the great university trimmer, William Lancaster, Provost of Queen's. Most of the Queen's ministers were glad to see the back of him; it was plain that in London they found him increasingly *de trop*.[5]

1712 was the year when the ministry of Robert Harley (now earl of Oxford) took the decisive steps towards peace; and at such a time Sacheverell's doings caused scarcely a ripple in the capital, though his self-esteem could still be repaired by occasional visits to the provinces.[6] However, as the time drew near when the Lords' sentence would expire Sacheverell's few close friends in the Commons, and his one true advocate in the Cabinet, Lord Harcourt, began to bestir themselves on his behalf. By the end of September 1712, in fact, Harcourt had already begged Lord Treasurer Oxford

to speak to the Queen that I may be ordered to present Dr Sacheverell to St Andrew's, Holborn. You will be subject to perpetual importunities if this opportunity be not taken. There cannot be so easy a way for the Queen to prefer him as this, for the presentation being in my gift,* as one of those under value, it may pass for my act whenever it is objected to.

But he had had to be content with a promise that this coveted rectory, described by Calamy as 'at that time one of the greatest parochial cures in the Christian world', would be held in storage for his client. Both Oxford and the Queen were adamant against preferring him before his sentence expired; and when, soon afterwards, Harcourt went further and pressed Sacheverell's claims to a bishopric, Anne would have none of it. She had always set her face against bringing controversial Highflyers on to the bench, and no party considerations which the Lord Keeper could urge would persuade her to make an exception in Sacheverell's, of all cases. Harcourt's pique at this rebuff was considerable; but it was nothing compared with the relief of William Lloyd of Worcester, that venerable eccentric, who at eighty-five had been wont of late to tell his friends that 'the thoughts of death are nothing near so terrible as of the possibility of the Doctor's succeeding me'.[7]

Henry Sacheverell's suspension ended on 23 March 1713. London greeted the event with a nonchalance which would have been unthinkable three years earlier. There was, it is true, a certain amount of activity by paid bellringers and a discharge of cannon in Southwark organised by a group of the Doctor's parishioners; but there was surprisingly little evidence of spontaneous enthusiasm, in contrast to the demonstrations in such towns as Worcester, Norwich, Wells and Frome, whence news soon came in of flag-

---

* The Crown's rights of patronage over this benefice, *via* the Lord Keeper or Lord Chancellor of the day, seem to have been curiously ambiguous, for all the confidence with which Harcourt here asserted them. Hatton, surveying the London parishes in his *New View of London* (1708), described St Andrew's, Holborn, as 'a rectory, the present incumbent is the reverend Dr Manningham, in the gift of the most noble duke of Montagu' (ibid. i, 118). In 1721 a committee of the Lords, called on to arbitrate in a dispute which had arisen in St Andrew's parish over the appoint- ment of preachers to officiate in a subsidiary chapel then under construction there, referred in their report explicitly to 'the duke of Montagu, the patron of the living, and Dr Sacheverell, the present incumbent' ([Joseph Trapp,] *The Case of the Patron and Rector of St Andrew's Holborn* (1722), p. 11). Likewise after Sacheverell's death, both Hearne and the editor of the *British Journal* speculated on whom Montagu would prefer to this valuable living (*Remarks and Collections*, viii, 224; *British Journal*, xci, 13 June 1724).

bedecked steeples, streamers hung at windows, bonfires, and people singing in the streets. In the metropolis, thought the Hanoverian resident, 'the mob seemed already to have forgotten him'.[8]

Not quite. When on the afternoon of the 29th, Palm Sunday, Sacheverell climbed the pulpit steps of St Saviour's for the first time since December 1710, the multitude of people who flocked either to hear him inside the church or to see him outside it was variously described as 'great', 'prodigious', 'inconceivable to those who did not see it, and inexpressible to those who did'. Those who did get in were given full value. He spent two hours all told over prayers and sermon together, preaching on the text from Luke 23, verse 34, *Father, forgive them, for they know not what they do*, and contriving to draw a barely-disguised parallel between his own sufferings in the past three years and those of Jesus Christ.[9] He had more than one good reason to feel satisfied with the Palm Sunday sermon; for he already had in his pocket £100 which his publisher had paid him for the right to print it. Jonathan Swift, on hearing from Sacheverell that Clements intended to print 30,000 copies, expressed the belief that 'he will be confoundedly bit, and will hardly sell above half'. Swift proved an uncannily accurate judge of a shrinking market.

> For people expected politics and more noise of the Church [wrote Kennett, soon afterwards], but excepting the title* and the text, there was but little mischief in it; and so the hawkers suffered much, and the bookseller received no money for one half of the impression.[10]

It may well be, as Kennett was assured by members of the congregation, that there had been 'some bolder strokes in the preaching which were struck out by a wiser hand'. Certainly Sacheverell had no desire to jeopardise at this stage the prize that was all but his. On 12 April he preached at Camberwell before Chief Justice Trevor, a political ally both of Oxford and of Henry St John, Viscount Bolingbroke. Next day his presentation to St Andrew's, Holborn, was announced.

Sacheverell was once reported to have said, very characteristically, while dining with his benefactor, Harcourt, that 'no prefer-

---

* *The Christian Triumph : or The Duty of Praying for our Enemies.*

ment in the Church could ever make him amends for the trouble and fatigues he had undergone in visiting and receiving visits after the glory of his trial'.[11] But neither on that account, nor on account of the frustration of his hopes of a bishopric, would he or any clergyman in his senses have dreamt of turning down the rectory of St Andrew's. It was financially more valuable than at least half a dozen of the poorer bishoprics.[12] The tithe income of the living was £400, but its net value from all sources was generally put at around £700 a year, perhaps rather more. Although its acceptance meant resigning both his Magdalen fellowship and his Shropshire rectory (though not the chaplaincy of St Saviour's, which he kept until his death),[13] it also meant that Sacheverell became one of the richest clergymen in the Church of England, private incomes aside. Together with Southwark, it was said, St Andrew's 'contains more souls which he has the care of than the whole diocese [Rochester] of his tutor and speech-maker, and yields almost double the income'.[14] Here at the top of Holborn hill, in the heart of one of London's most populous parishes and in the largest of all Wren's parish churches,* he found both a charge and a physical setting commensurate with his reputation. Aloft in his splendid hexagonal pulpit, his aesthetic senses could rejoice in one of the noblest church interiors of its type in the country: the rich wainscoting, the spacious galleries, the six graceful Corinthian columns supporting a magnificent fretted and camerated ceiling, the high altar of porphyry and gilded wrought iron;[15] and he could reflect with some complacency that from this church in recent memory two rectors, Stillingfleet and Manningham, had moved on to episcopal palaces and lawn sleeves. If the Tories were to consolidate their present supremacy in Church and State, might not he yet follow in their footsteps?

But though few could have guessed it in the summer of 1713, that supremacy had only one more year to run. The declining fortunes of a ministry riven by personal feuds, and of a party distracted by divisions over both basic principles and practical policies, are in a sense mirrored in two incidents which are a yardstick to Sacheverell's own falling stock. On 29 May 1713, after preaching a full-blooded party sermon to the House of Commons

* Wren had rebuilt the church in 1687 and had refaced, and added a further story to, the tower in 1704.

on the anniversary of Charles II's Restoration,* and dining with the Speaker, he was given a triumphal reception at the convivial tables of the October Club in King Street. In the following December, when he went to preach at St Paul's before the Corporation for the Sons of the Clergy, his procession was hissed by the crowd gathered to watch it at the Royal Exchange. And while the whole party's morale was shaken by Queen Anne's desperate illness that Christmas, Sacheverell himself was sickened still more by the grisly death in March 1714 of his friend Sir George Newland, father of the 'charioteer' of the trial, who was impaled on his own railings after a fall from the window of his second-floor bedroom.

The dismissal of Lord Oxford in late July, followed swiftly and inexorably by the death of Anne, the succession of the Elector George of Hanover, the disintegration of the Tory administration and – after a short interval – the dissolution of the old Parliament, did not in themselves deprive the High Church party of all hope. On the contrary, marshalled by Atterbury, the clergy at least threw themselves into the 1714–15 Election campaign with almost as much fervour as they had displayed in 1710. Along with such slogans as 'No Hanover' and 'Down with the Roundheads' the cry of 'High Church and Sacheverell' was heard for the last time at the hustings.[16] Sacheverell himself had been widely suspected in the autumn of 1714 of doing all in his power to generate it. In August, three weeks after the Queen's death, he had thrust himself back in the limelight by a violent attack on the duke of Marlborough's public entry into London, on his return from self-imposed exile, describing it as 'an unparalleled insolence and a vile trampling upon royal ashes'. He still had enough impudence to appear at Court in September, when the London clergy presented their loyal address to the new King, but was put to flight by the jibes of the Whigs, and 'getting to the outward door, the footmen hissed him on a long lane on both sides till he got into a coach'.[17] When he left London and appeared first in Oxford, then

* Henry Clements soon afterwards published this sermon, at 3*d* per octavo copy, under the title *False Notions of Liberty in Religion and Government destructive of both*. It was straight Non-Resistance fare and ended with an uninhibited blast against his Whig persecutors as 'traitorous, heady and high-minded men' (p. 22). The invitation to Sacheverell to preach had been moved by Sir John Pakington, and seconded by William Newland and Sir William Whitlocke.

the Party. And if by these Means they have Exasperated the Nation, and rais'd any Ferment or Sedition in it, that may give any Trouble or Disquiet, I am sure no Man can be more Sorry for it than My Self, or would more heartily Labour to Prevent it.

My Lord, if My Return to Town can any ways contribute to it, or give any Farther Satisfaction, or tend to Confute these unjust Calumnys cast upon Me, I will with all the Speed my affairs will permitt, Obey Your Lordships Commands, & beg leave in the mean time to Assure Your Lordship of My Duty, wch I shall be ever Ambitious inviolably to Pay, as becomes,

My Lord,

Your Lordship's most
Obedient Son, & most
faithfull Servant

H. Sacheverell

Oxon
Octr 31. 1714

Sacheverell's autograph

in Wiltshire, and then in Warwickshire, where he preached a highly provocative sermon at Sutton Coldfield on the Sunday before George I's coronation, the Whigs clamoured that another Progress was afoot. One can understand their alarm, for even in distant Carlisle at coronation time the Doctor's health was publicly drunk immediately after the King's and Sacheverell mobs disfigured the celebrations at Bristol, Taunton, Birmingham and Nuneaton. He himself protested that his motives were no more sinister than to see his mother in Salisbury for the first time in three years – and then only because her 'age and great infirmities disqualify her to come to me' – and to visit his octogenarian kinsman at Newhall, in whose will he hoped to be generously remembered! But these ingenuous pleas did not satisfy John Robinson, that notably moderate church-man who had been Lord Privy Seal in Oxford's cabinet and who had succeeded Henry Compton as bishop of London. Determined that there should be no repetition of the events of June–July 1710, which in his view had degraded the cloth, he wrote urgently to the absent rector, positively ordering him back to his London charge and warning him sternly against meddling in politics; and with this injunction Sacheverell reluctantly complied, confining his electioneering thereafter mainly to sounding the trumpet from his pulpit in Holborn.[18]

The heavy defeat which the Tories suffered at the polls in Jan-uary 1715 pushed many High Churchmen who for some years had teetered on the brink of Jacobitism into a position of more overt sympathy with the Pretender's cause. There is evidence that Henry Sacheverell was one of them. But after the failure of the Fifteen rebellion (when a Jacobite mob, sacking Cross Street chapel in Manchester, chanted his name), there was little likelihood that he would take very seriously suggestions emanating from the Pre-tender's court that he should go and settle there.[19] He had too much to lose at home. In the summer of 1715 George Sacheverell, the former High Sheriff of Derbyshire, died, abundantly gratifying his distant kinsman's expectations by leaving him the manor of Callow in Derbyshire. By marrying George's widow Mary in June 1716 (she was ten years his senior), Henry Sacheverell com-pleted his metamorphosis into a north-country squire of £400 a year, although it was not until 1717 that he went north to take possession of his estate. Formerly he had been a very well-to-do clergyman. Now, by almost any standards he was a rich man. In addition to his Derbyshire manor he acquired another landed estate at Wilden in Bedfordshire. In 1720 he bought an elegant house, 'with a garden and appurtenances', in South Grove, Highgate – an increasingly fashionable resort of London commuters, favoured particularly by the wealthy community of Sephardi Jews in the City. Lost causes, or even doubtful causes, were not now for him.[20]

Once marriage and prosperity quenched much of the fire in Sacheverell's belly, surprisingly little was heard of him as a public figure. In Oxford his name could still from time to time stir up old passions (in May 1717 a mob took possession of the streets for two hours to prevent the Whig Constitution Club burning the Doctor – together with the Pope – in effigy). But in London by the early 1720s it had become a fading memory: a name heard occasionally in connection with squabbles with his parishioners, or the unseemly attempt to eject from his church, at evening service in January 1719, the notorious Unitarian, William Whiston;[21] but scarcely ever heard in connection with politics. Perhaps he realised himself, in the end, the essential anachronism of a crusading pulpit politician in the pudding-time of George I. At any rate, Sacheverell devoted much of these last years to the further beautification of St Andrew's, adorning the sanctuary and commissioning a glorious east window* from Joshua Price. He lived high – well beyond his income, to judge from his will, which consisted largely of detailed arrangements for the sale of lands to pay off his debts.† And a constitution heavily punished over the years by alcohol was gradually undermined.

On an icy day in January 1723, not long before his forty-ninth birthday, the rector of St Andrew's slipped on the stone doorstep of his Highgate house, fell heavily and broke two of his ribs. A few days later, though still badly shaken, he was well enough to

* Destroyed in an air raid in 1941.
† Apart from creating a trust for his wife, to whom he also left his Highgate house, and making some provision for his sister, Susanna Banner, he left only two legacies: £200 to Magdalen College, and a further £200 along with the bulk of his library (and careful instructions to destroy most of his papers) to his friend the Rev. Joseph Trapp. The story that he left £500 in his will to the exiled Francis Atterbury as a debt of gratitude, which seems to have originated in 1729 and found its way in more recent times into Beeching's *Atterbury* and into the *D.N.B.* article on Sacheverell, has no foundation.

send a short message to Bishop Atterbury, who was imprisoned in the Tower for his complicity in a Jacobite plot: he was 'in hopes [he told the bishop] of doing well'.[22] But in fact he was never the same man again. In January 1724 he revised his will, and in the following May added a codicil excusing himself for having made no provision whatever, even by the smallest of legacies, for his servants. 'A complication of disorders', as Hearne termed them in his diary, steadily overcame him, and he died at Highgate on the evening of Friday, 5 June. The following Thursday his body was privately interred at St Andrew's in a vault previously prepared under the communion table, the place being marked on the chancel floor with a plain marble tablet, bearing the simplest of inscriptions which he himself had composed and written into his will:

Infra jacet Henricus Sacheverell, S.T.P., hujusque ecclesiae Rector.
Obiit 5to die Junii, Anno Dni 1724.

For one who had conducted much of his life amid a plethora of words, he made his end with a surprising verbal economy.

Unfortunately his shade was not allowed to rest in peace. In 1747 the sexton of St Andrew's was imprisoned for stealing his lead coffin, and the opening of the vault revealed that by the strangest of ironies the coffin of the most notorious high-class prostitute of the day, Sally Salisbury, had been placed immediately next to that of her former rector. The Whig wits were enraptured, and produced two revised epitaphs more suitable, as they thought, to their respective reputations. The first ran thus:

> Lo! to one grave consigned, of rival fame,
> A reverend Doctor and a wanton dame.
> Well for the world both did to rest retire,
> For each, while living, set mankind on fire.

The second was even pithier:

> A fit companion for a high-church priest;
> He non-resistance taught, and she profest.

2. *The Failure of High Church Toryism, 1711–c. 1725*

Before he died, Henry Sacheverell must have known that whatever he had achieved in 1709–10, by his St Paul's sermon and by his trial, in the long run he had failed – he and those High Church clergy who shared his philosophy if not his audacity. They had failed to see the Church of their pipe-dreams, reformed and re-purified, made a reality. They had failed to reforge the old links between Church and Crown, which had in truth been damaged beyond repair between 1685 and 1689. They had failed to win a decisive victory over either heresy or unbelief, and they had not materially increased the effectiveness of Anglican discipline over the laity. Most galling of all, although they had impeded the progress of nonconformity they had failed to halt it. The hope of destroying Dissent at its roots, by stamping out its academies and schools, had proved illusory. Even the hated practice of Occasional Conformity had not been effectively eradicated. Finally, at the purely secular level the Election of 1715 had demonstrated, and that of 1722 had confirmed, that shorn of the influence and patronage of the Crown, parson and squire alone could not guarantee a permanent Tory supremacy in the House of Commons, that supremacy on which both churchmen and laymen had pinned so many hopes. Thus, while the short-term effects of the Sacheverell trial had been spectacular, its long-term benefits to the Tory–Anglican alliance proved grievously disappointing.

These disappointments by no means stemmed only from the change of dynasty and the consequent change of ministry in 1714. Even the years of Tory supremacy from 1710 to 1714, which Doctor Sacheverell's impeachment had done so much to make possible, yielded the High Churchmen only meagre rewards.

Hopes were genuinely high in the last three months of 1710 that the political transformation achieved in the summer and autumn would usher in a golden age of Toryism and a parson's paradise. 'Your son shall be welcome to me', White Kennett wrote at that time to the rector of Waterstock, 'and I will endeavour to try to get some suitable employment for him, though it is very hard to do so at this time when such crowds of young divines are flocking hither in hopes from the new ministry'.[23] And relatively few doubted at this stage that the new ministry was well disposed.

Uneasiness about Harley's influence there may have been. But who could say that this influence would remain pre-eminent? Although Nottingham had not been given office, was not Lord Rochester back in favour as Lord President of the Council? Were not Buckingham and Ormonde, High Tories of the old model, now in the Cabinet? St John, the newly-appointed Secretary of State, had admittedly consorted for some years with Harley; but it was not forgotten that earlier in his career he had seconded Bromley in sponsoring the first two Occasional Conformity bills.

If the ministry would lead, men argued, the Queen would surely follow. Happy omens were detected in the Queen's Speech on 27 November. The promise to maintain the *Indulgence* granted by the law to *consciences truly scrupulous*, as opposed to the guarantee in previous Speeches to uphold the Toleration of tender consciences, seemed a deliberate change to Sacheverell's language. Nowhere did hope run higher than in Convocation, when it met again after an intermission of over three years at the beginning of December 1710.* Surely, it was felt, the new House of Commons, elected on a 'Church in Danger' platform in the post-Sacheverell delirium, would co-operate as never before with the elected representatives of the clergy to achieve the security and reform of the Church? The fact that the new Prolocutor of the Lower House, Atterbury, and the new Speaker of the Commons, Bromley, were both true sons of Christ Church and Oxford seemed somehow to epitomise all the fervent hopes of resolving the Anglican dilemma through sustained legislative action.

But these hopes proved unrealistic. Eager though the High Tory members were to bring about the new Jerusalem, their parliamentary energies were inevitably much absorbed by other matters: by the financial problems consequent on a long and exhausting war, by political vendettas against their defeated opponents, by the making of peace with France, and in the next Parliament by the gnawing anxieties attendant on an ailing Queen and an uncertain succession. Furthermore, they were never quite able to tear the reins of parliamentary management from Harley's tenacious hold. Some mark they did leave on the statute-book and on the religious life of the nation, though it hardly matched the loud noises in support of the Church of England which regularly issued forth

* A Convocation had been elected in 1708, but it had not been allowed to sit.

from the benches of St Stephen's Chapel and the conclaves of the October Club. In the course of four years, an Act to finance the building of fifty new churches in the suburbs of London and Westminster (1711),* a somewhat emasculated Occasional Conformity Act (the product of an unprincipled compact in December 1711 between the Tory earl of Nottingham and the Whig Junto), and an Act to ensure some measure of Toleration for the episcopalians in Scotland (1712) were the only substantial achievements. The Excommunication bill of 1713 was dropped. The Schism bill, the one really vicious blow against the dissenters, which would have deprived them of the capacity both to educate their youth and train ⁺heir prospective clergy in their own institutions, came far too late in the day. Bitterly resisted by the parliamentary Whigs, who fully atoned for their conduct in 1711,[24] and ingeniously obstructed by the Harleyites (some of them the products of dissenting academies themselves), it did pass into law in June 1714. But Queen Anne died on the very day it was due to take effect, and the new regime never enforced it.

The dissenters were not unscathed by the years of Tory reaction. Nottingham had boasted that the Occasional Conformity Act of 1711 would not be without teeth:† and his point was underlined both by the rapid re-establishment of Anglican monopoly thereafter in such important municipal corporations as Bristol and Coventry, and by the many civic dignitaries and J.Ps, among them Aldermen Abney and Fryer of London, who abandoned their meeting-houses and condemned themselves to seven years of private family worship rather than resign their posts.[25] The mob violence of 1710 also left its scars: Dr Burgess's congregation, for one, was far from having recovered its former numbers and prosperity by the time of the Queen's death.[26] On the other hand, the refusal of the Presbyterian leaders in London to accept a penny

* Although only twelve were eventually built – far too few to relieve the chronic shortage of churches in the expanding suburbs – they remain the most impressive memorial to the Anglican zeal of the early eighteenth-century Tories.
† He claimed at the time of its passing that it was 'exactly the same with the last [that of 1704], save only the last two clauses which we left out as unreasonable favours to dissenters, and two clauses added, which were just and fair condescensions to 'em'. Hatton-Finch MSS. 281: to Lady Nottingham, [20] Dec. 1711. See also Philip Yorke's comment on the harshness of some of the Act's clauses, Add. MSS. 35584, f. 144.

from Harley's government for the losses suffered in the Sacheverell riots is indicative of the continued confidence of Dissent in its future: only in the face of the Schism bill did this confidence temporarily waver.[27] By a curious irony, the Presbyterians were to be weakened far more by their own doctrinal disputes after 1720, when any threat to their existence had long since passed, than by anything Tory parliaments could do before 1715.

But Parliament was not only, nor even mainly, responsible for the frustrations experienced by High Church divines during the four years which followed the Sacheverell affair. Another factor was that very revival of Passive Obedience and Non-Resistance teaching and of Divine Right theory which had done much to precipitate the affair in the first place, and which had proved the most important single issue in the trial. It was soon to prove a dangerously double-edged weapon in the hands of the clergy; and this was particularly so after the Convocation sitting in 1710–11, under pressure from some members of the ministry, had declined to take any resolution expressly sanctioning these doctrines – despite the fact that such a resolution was believed in some quarters to have been 'the main design' of the Atterbury party.[28] Thereafter such doctrines became increasingly involved in the great revival of Nonjuring propaganda which characterised the years immediately after 1710, and partly for this reason they became more and more associated with the alarming spread of outright Jacobitism through the ranks of the lower clergy.[29]

Thus divisions were sown among the High Churchmen, many of whom – like Bishop Dawes of Chester, later archbishop of York – remained unbendingly firm to Hanover; and while Jacobitism undoubtedly gained a lot of ground in the Tory party between 1710 and 1714, it never gained enough ground to put the Harley administration under irresistible pressure to overturn the legal succession.[30] At the same time, the fact that it produced its own antidote from within, with the emergence of a distinct Hanoverian Tory group among the clergy as well as among the politicians, only served to highlight afresh the illogicality and inconsistency of the position taken up by Sacheverell's counsel and by many of his supporters in the House of Lords in 1710: the paradox (as George Lockhart said of the Hanover Tories) of men who 'pretended to reconcile the doctrine of Non-Resistance and Passive Obedience with the principles on which the Revolution was founded and by which the deposing of Kings was justified'.[31]

To most Highflyers, however, it seemed that the root cause of their troubles between October 1710 and July 1714, in or out of Parliament, was the attitude of the ministry and, to their intense chagrin, of the Queen herself. 'Sir Peter King told me yesterday', Kennett wrote to a friend in November 1710, 'that the words which her Majesty said to him upon enquiry into some of the City affairs were these, which he has thought himself obliged by the Queen to communicate to the people: *I would have my people satisfied that though I have changed my ministers I have not altered my measures; I am still for Moderation and will govern by it*'.[32] This pledge she kept for the rest of her life, except perhaps in her last months when her relations with Robert Harley had disintegrated. Harley's commitment to moderate courses in Church affairs, and to moderate men to control those affairs, remained as strong after 1710 as it had been in the days of his opposition to the Occasional Conformity bills and to the 'Tackers'. Indeed there is good cause to believe that his resolution was stiffened in 1710, first by the intolerable pressures to which some High Tories and High Churchmen subjected him during the delicate series of operations by which he brought down the Godolphin ministry, then by the unbridled extremism of the clerical Election campaign, which contributed much to his subsequent difficulties with the House of Commons. From that period, certainly, dates his disillusionment with Atterbury: 'I must say,' he told Canon Stratford with uncharacteristic bitterness, 'the follies and worse of our friends have done more hurt than all our enemies' efforts'.[33]

The lack of wholehearted support from Harley and the Queen for the more ambitious objectives of the High Church party was crucial.* For one thing, it crippled the effective use of Convocation as the vehicle of a full-scale Church reform programme.[34] For another, it meant that the commanding heights of the Church of England, its bishoprics and some of its most influential deaneries, continued to be denied to the true Highflyers under a Tory ministry, scarcely less than they had been under a Whig one. For advice on appointments Anne leant almost exclusively on her

* Rochester died in May 1711. In any event, in this closing period of his life he showed himself surprisingly hostile to extremism in both Church and State.

prime minister and on the statesmanlike Archbishop Sharp of York.[35] The eventual disposal of the two bishoprics which had fallen vacant during the Sacheverell affair, Bristol and St David's, was a token of what the 'hot men' were to expect in the field of preferments. Bristol went to John Robinson, a career diplomat and a self-confessed anti-Sacheverellite acceptable to the Whigs; St David's was given to Philip Bisse, a reconciler rather than a crusader, who as bishop of Hereford in 1714 scandalised the city Tories by appearing at King George I's proclamation 'at the head of the clergy, with a joyful and entirely pleased countenance'.[36] When York fell vacant in 1714 it went to Dawes, 'a man of a moderate and cool spirit', his predecessor's choice. Of those who had stood at Sacheverell's shoulder in Westminster Hall or who had supported him most vociferously from their pulpits in 1710, only Atterbury and Smalridge in the end received bishoprics from Queen Anne. Smalridge was a moderate and (in 1714, at least) a pro-Hanoverian, thoroughly acceptable to Harley; while of Atterbury's promotion to the see of Rochester in 1713, at a time when Sharp was mortally ill, Secretary Dartmouth wrote: 'I never knew the Queen do anything with so much reluctancy as the signing of his *congé d'élire*. . . . She said, Lord Harcourt had answered for his behaviour, and she had lately disobliged him by refusing the like request for Dr Sacheverell, and found if she did not grant this, she must break with him quite'. All the same, she seriously contemplated withholding from Atterbury the deanery of Westminster, which traditionally supplemented Rochester's beggarly revenue.[37]

If, however, the years of Tory supremacy down to 1714 proved bitterly disappointing to High Churchmen, the decade after 1714 – the first decade of the long Whig oligarchy of Hanoverian England – brought the full consciousness of irrevocable failure. The blows fell one by one, not perhaps as quickly as they had feared, nor as heavily, but unmistakable in their import. The very accession of a Lutheran prince, an occasional conformist who could not even read the Prayer Book in its native language, crushed any lingering hopes of a resuscitated alliance of Church and monarchy. High Churchmen may have confessed disappointment in Anne and her Tory ministry. But whenever they had looked ahead and contemplated Hanover, few can have failed to echo the words of Bishop

T

Hooper in his Thanksgiving sermon to Parliament in July 1713: 'many, many years we shall pray for; many, that she may perform her whole work, and many, that she may enjoy it'.[38] Understandably, but tactlessly, there were Tory preachers in London during August 1714 who 'so bemoaned the Queen as if Monarchy and the Church had died with her', and Kennett was not surprised to find that bold spirits such as Richard Welton at Whitechapel* had 'preached ever since the demise with a *double entendre* and with an eye directly on another king'.[39] The Election results of January 1715 were a bitter setback to the bulk of the parish priests, especially after many had campaigned 'like madmen' on behalf of known Jacobite candidates.[40] And the Jacobite rebellion brought lasting discredit on the already tarnished cause of Non-Resistance and Passive Obedience. When hundreds of country clergymen were known to have sympathised with, if not actively supported, the action of the rebels; when resistance to the legally-constituted authority in the country was condoned, and that in favour of a Catholic Pretender; when even three Tory bishops refused to subscribe to the declaration of loyalty to the throne and abhorrence of the rebellion agreed to by the rest of their brethren – where then was that 'great doctrine' which Bishop Lake had said on his deathbed 'he looked upon . . . as the distinguishing character of the Church of England'?[41]

But the disastrous effects of the Fifteen did not end there. From it dates the ruthless determination of the triumphant party that Church preferments, no less than all other offices in the kingdom, must be brought wholly under the control of the Whig patronage machine. In the early months of George I's reign there had been some disposition to compromise in Church appointments. But the rebellion left no room for compromise, a fact signalised beyond all doubt in December 1715 when the arch-enemy of traditional churchmanship, Benjamin Hoadly, was preferred to the see of Bangor and took his seat, crutches and all, in the House of Lords. From then on it became increasingly clear that in the future convinced, unrepentant High Churchmanship would condemn any aspiring young divine to second-class citizenship in the Angli-

---

* Welton had earned some notoriety by preaching a sermon during the high noonday of Whig power before 1710 on the text *O put not your Trust in Princes*. See *Modern Fanatick*, Pt iii, p. 16; also pp. 45, 105 above.

can ministry. The last doors were bolted and barred in 1723, when Edmund Gibson became bishop of London and Walpole's 'pope': a man of great ability and energy to whom Tories were far greater threats to the establishment than dissenters, and for whom the only firm foundation for Anglicanism was 'a clear Church–Whig bottom'.[42] No less than nine sees fell vacant in this one year, 1723; and men of Gibson's choice and Gibson's principles filled every one of them.

By that time the remaining buttresses of the High Church revival of Queen Anne's reign had also gone. In 1717 Convocation, for so long the chief sounding-board for the discontents of the lower clergy, was rudely muffled by the government with episcopal connivance. Hoadly, by his notorious sermon before the King on the text 'My Kingdom is not of this world', and the Lower House of the Canterbury assembly, by reacting to its ultra-Erastianism like a pack of ravening wolves, were the immediate causes of its prorogation. But it was the whole sorry history of this faction-ridden body, stretching back to 1689, which condemned it after November 1717 to a silence which was not to be broken until the middle of the nineteenth century. In January 1719 further affliction had followed when Parliament repealed both the Occasional Conformity and Schism Acts. The Whigs thus repaid their debt to the dissenters, and indeed added a small bonus in the shape of an Act for Quieting and Establishing Corporations.

And yet, amid the desolation of all the hopes and plans which the Sacheverell affair had nurtured, High Church parsons and their Tory patrons were left with a few scraps of consolation. Bills to reform or 'regulate' the universities of Oxford and Cambridge by the crudest instruments of government control were allowed to drop in 1717 and 1719. More significant still, Stanhope's bold attempt in the winter of 1718–19 to bring the dissenters close to complete civil equality with churchmen, not by repealing the Test Act outright but by devices which would render it redundant, was beaten off; and Whigs such as Cowper and Walpole, in the debates on Stanhope's bill,* upheld the sanctity of the Anglican Test as

---

* Stanhope aimed to combine these devices, along with the repeal of the Occasional Conformity and Schism Acts, in a comprehensive bill 'for strengthening the Protestant interest', introduced into the Lords in Dec. 1718. See N. Sykes, *William Wake*, ii, 122–7; B. Williams, *Stanhope*, pp. 391–5.

vigorously as any Tory. These lessons, at least, most Whigs had learned from the *annus mirabilis* of Doctor Sacheverell: the Church of England must not be tried too far; it was politic for any ministry to try wherever possible to work *with* its clergy, rather than against them; and whatever anti-clerical prejudices Whig backbenchers might privately indulge, they must never again be encouraged or allowed to 'roast a parson', and so allow High Church fanaticism its only remaining recourse – to stir up the embers of popular emotional support.[43] With this last lesson in mind Walpole's ministry dealt with Atterbury in 1723, after the revelation of his Jacobite plot, not by spectacular public prosecution but by a safe and expeditious bill of Pains and Penalties. With all these lessons in mind Walpole and his successors were able to preserve religious tranquillity, within the framework of an Erastian polity, throughout most of the eighteenth century. That they also stultified Church reform, and encouraged spiritual inertia, did not greatly disturb them.

APPENDICES
BIBLIOGRAPHY
NOTES
INDEX

Appendix A:
THE ARTICLES
OF IMPEACHMENT

ARTICLES exhibited by the knights, citizens and burgesses in Parliament assembled, in the name of themselves and of all the Commons of Great Britain, against Henry Sacheverell, Doctor in Divinity, in maintenance of their impeachment against him for high crimes and misdemeanours.

Whereas his late Majesty King William the Third, then Prince of Orange, did with an armed force undertake a glorious enterprise, for delivering this kingdom from Popery and arbitrary power; and divers subjects of this realm, well affected to their country, joined with and assisted his late Majesty in the said enterprise; and it having pleased Almighty God to crown the same with success, the late happy Revolution did take effect and was established.

And whereas the said glorious enterprise is approved by several Acts of Parliament, and amongst others, by an Act made in the first year of the reign of King William and Queen Mary, entitled *An Act declaring the Rights and Liberties of the Subject, and settling the Succession of the Crown*; and also by one other Act made in the same year, entitled *An Act for preventing Vexatious Suits against such as acted in order to the bringing in their Majesties or for their Service*; and also by one other Act made in the same year, entitled *An Act for appropriating certain Duties for paying the States General of the United Provinces their Charges for his Majesty's Expedition into this Kingdom and for other Uses*: and the actings of the said well-affected subjects in aid and pursuance of the said enterprise are also declared to have been necessary and that the same ought to be justified.

And whereas the happy and blessed consequences of the said Revolution are: the enjoyment of the light of God's true religion established among us, and of the laws and liberties of the kingdom; the uniting her Majesty's Protestant subjects in interest and affection by a legal Indulgence or Toleration granted to dissenters; the preservation of her Majesty's sacred person; the many and continual benefits arising from her Majesty's wise and glorious administration; and the prospect of happiness for future ages by the settlement of the succession of the Crown in the Protestant line, and the Union of the two kingdoms [of England and Scotland].

And whereas the Lords Spiritual and Temporal, and Commons in Parliament assembled, did by their Address of the seventeenth of December, in the year of our Lord one thousand seven hundred and five, lay before her Majesty the following vote or resolution, viz, 'That the Church of England, as by law established, which was rescued from the extremest danger by King William the Third of glorious memory, is now, by God's blessing, under the happy reign of her Majesty in a most safe and flourishing condition; and that whoever goes about to suggest and insinuate that the Church is in danger under her Majesty's administration is an enemy to the Queen, the Church and the kingdom'; and by their said Address did humbly beseech her Majesty to take effectual measures for making the said vote or resolution public, and also for punishing the authors and spreaders of such seditious and scandalous reports; and on the twentieth day of the same December, her Majesty was pleased to issue her royal proclamation accordingly.

Yet nevertheless the said Henry Sacheverell preached a sermon at the Assizes held at Derby, August the fifteenth, in the year of our Lord one thousand seven hundred and nine, and afterwards published the same in print with a Dedication thereof. And the said Henry Sacheverell also preached a sermon at the cathedral church of St Paul, before the Lord Mayor, aldermen and citizens of London, on the fifth day of November last, being the Anniversary Thanksgiving to Almighty God for the deliverance from the Gunpowder Treason, and for beginning the late happy Revolution by giving his late Majesty a safe arrival here, and for completing the same by making all opposition fall before him till he became our King and Governor; which said sermon he, the said Henry Sacheverell, afterwards likewise published in print, with a Dedication thereof to Sir Samuel Garrard, baronet, Lord Mayor of the city of London; and with a wicked, malicious and seditious intention to undermine and subvert her Majesty's government and the Protestant succession as by law established, to defame her Majesty's administration, to asperse the memory of his late Majesty, to traduce and condemn the late happy Revolution, to contradict and arraign the resolutions of both Houses of Parliament, to create jealousies and divisions amongst her Majesty's subjects, and to incite them to sedition and rebellion.

ARTICLE I

He, the said Henry Sacheverell, in his said sermon preached at St Paul's, doth suggest and maintain that the necessary means used to bring about the said happy Revolution were odious and unjustifiable; that his late Majesty, in his Declaration disclaimed the least imputation of Resistance; and that to impute Resistance to the said Revolution is to cast black and odious colours upon his late Majesty and the said Revolution.

ARTICLE II

He, the said Henry Sacheverell, in his said sermon preached at St Paul's, doth suggest and maintain that the aforesaid Toleration, granted by law, is unreasonable, and the allowance of it unwarrantable. And asserts that he is a

False Brother with relation to God, religion or the Church who defends Toleration and liberty of conscience; that Queen Elizabeth was deluded by Archbishop Grindal, whom he scurrilously calls a False Son of the Church and a perfidious prelate, to the toleration of the Genevian discipline; and that it is the duty of superior pastors to thunder out their ecclesiastical anathemas against persons entitled to the benefit of the said Toleration, and insolently dares or defies any power on earth to reverse such sentences.

ARTICLE III

He, the said Henry Sacheverell, in his said sermon preached at St Paul's, doth falsely and seditiously suggest and assert that the Church of England is in a condition of great peril and adversity under her Majesty's administration; and in order to arraign and blacken the said vote or resolution of both Houses of Parliament, approved by her Majesty as aforesaid, he in opposition thereto doth suggest the Church to be in danger, and as a parallel, mentions a vote that the person of King Charles the First was voted to be out of danger at the same time that his murderers were conspiring his death; thereby wickedly and maliciously insinuating that the members of both Houses who passed the said vote were then conspiring the ruin of the Church.

ARTICLE IV

He, the said Henry Sacheverell, in his said sermons and books, doth falsely and maliciously suggest that her Majesty's administration, both in ecclesiastical and civil affairs, tends to the destruction of the constitution; and that there are men of characters and stations in Church and State who are False Brethren, and do themselves weaken, undermine and betray, and do encourage and put it in the power of others who are professed enemies to overturn and destroy the constitution and Establishment; and chargeth her Majesty, and those in authority under her both in Church and State, with a general maladministration. And as a public incendiary, he persuades her Majesty's subjects to keep up a distinction of factions and parties, instils groundless jealousies, foments destructive divisions among them, and excites and stirs them up to arms and violence. And that his said malicious and seditious suggestions may make the stronger impression upon the minds of her Majesty's subjects, he the said Henry Sacheverell doth wickedly wrest and pervert divers texts and passages of Holy Scripture.

All which crimes and misdemeanours the Commons are ready to prove, not only by the general scope of the same sermons or books, but likewise by several clauses, sentences and expressions in the said sermons or books contained; and that he, the said Henry Sacheverell, by preaching the sermons and publishing the books aforesaid, did abuse his holy function, and hath most grievously offended against the peace of her Majesty, her crown and dignity, the rights and liberties of the subject, the laws and statutes of this kingdom, and the prosperity and good government of the same. And the said Commons, by protestation, saving to themselves the liberty of exhibiting at any time hereafter any other article or [*sic*] impeachment against the said Henry Sacheverell, and also of replying to his answers, or any of them, and of offering proofs of all the premises, or any of them, and of any other article or impeachment that shall be exhibited by them, as the case according to course of Parliament shall require, do pray that he, the said Henry Sacheverell, may be put to answer to all and every the premises; and that such proceeding, examination, trial, judgment and exemplary punishment may be thereupon had and executed, as is agreeable to law and justice.

Appendix B:
THE JUDGMENT
OF THE LORDS

The two pairs of lists which follow illustrate the collapse of the anti-Sacheverell majority in the House of Lords between 20 and 21 March 1710.

The first, a list of the sixty-nine peers who voted Sacheverell *Guilty*, and of the fifty-two who voted him *Not Guilty*, on Monday, 20 March, is the official version published after the trial. The second, listing the fifty-nine peers who voted for, and the sixty peers who voted against the government proposal made next day to incapacitate Sacheverell from receiving further preferment during his suspension, has been reconstructed from the contemporary evidence cited in notes 37–42, pp. 323–4 below, collated with the *Lords' Journals*.

As regards their party affiliations, the peers have been classified in four categories: Whig (W), Court (C), Court Tory (CT), Tory (T) (see my *British Politics in the Age of Anne*, pp. 425–35). This is exactly as contemporaries would have classified the English peers in the session of 1709–10; and although the classification does not fit every one of the Scottish representative peers entirely satisfactorily, for the sake of simplicity it has been applied to the very few anomalous cases. In 1709–10 all the peers in the first two categories were expected to support the ministry on every issue, while the Court Tories were regarded as safe supporters in normal circumstances. The lists for the 'No Preferment' vote on 21 March demonstrate the absences, and still more the crucial defections to the Tories, which applied the *coup de grâce* to the impeachment of Dr Sacheverell (see pp. 225–9 above).

I. THE 'GUILTY' VOTE OF 20 MARCH 1710

Peers voting 'Guilty'	*Peers voting 'Not Guilty'*
1. Lord Pelham (W)	1. Lord Conway (T)
2. Lord Hervey (W)	2. Lord Guernsey (T)
3. Lord Halifax (W)	3. Lord Haversham (T)
4. Lord Herbert (W)	4. Lord Weston (T)
5. Lord Ossulston (W)	5. Lord Leominster (T)
6. Lord Cornwallis (W)	6. Lord Guilford (T)
7. Lord Rockingham (W)	7. Lord Stawell (T)
8. Lord Colepeper (W)	8. Lord Dartmouth (CT)

Peers voting 'Guilty'	*Peers voting 'Not Guilty'*
9. Lord Byron (CT)	9. Lord Osborne (T)
10. Lord Mohun (W)	10. Lord Craven (T)
11. Lord Hunsdon (C)	11. Lord Berkeley of Stratton (CT)
12. Lord Paget (C)	12. Lord Lexington (CT)
13. Lord Fitzwalter (W)	13. Lord Leigh (T)
14. Lord De la War (C)	14. Lord Howard of Escrick (T)
15. Bp Fleetwood of St Asaph (W)	15. Lord Chandos (T)
16. Bp Trimnell of Norwich (W)	16. Lord North and Grey (T)
17. Bp Wake of Lincoln (W)	17. Lord Willoughby de Broke (T)
18. Bp Talbot of Oxford (W)	18. Lord Ferrers (T)
19. Bp Cumberland of Peterborough (W)	19. Bp Dawes of Chester (T)
20. Bp Moore of Ely (W)	20. Bp Hooper of Bath & Wells (T)
21. Bp Burnet of Salisbury (W)	21. Bp Sprat of Rochester (T)
22. Earl of Islay (W)	22. Bp Crewe of Durham (T)
23. Earl of Glasgow (C)	23. Bp Compton of London (T)
24. Earl of Rosebery (CT)	24. Viscount Weymouth (T)
25. Earl of Seafield (C)	25. Viscount Saye and Sele (T)
26. Earl of Orkney (CT)	26. Earl of Northesk (CT)
27. Earl of Leven (C)	27. Earl of Wemys (CT)
28. Earl of Loudoun (CT)	28. Earl of Mar (CT)
29. Earl of Crawford (W)	29. Earl Poulet (T)
30. Earl of Cholmondeley (W)	30. Earl of Jersey (T)
31. Earl of Wharton (W)	31. Earl of Scarborough (W)
32. Earl of Greenwich and Duke of Argyll (W)	32. Earl of Plymouth (T)
33. Earl of Grantham (W)	33. Earl of Abingdon (T)
34. Earl of Orford (W)	34. Earl of Rochester (T)
35. Earl of Bradford (W)	35. Earl of Nottingham (T)
36. Earl of Warrington (W)	36. Earl of Yarmouth (T)
37. Earl of Portland (W)	37. Earl of Sussex (T)
38. Earl of Holderness (W)	38. Earl of Anglesey (T)
39. Earl of Berkeley (W)	39. Earl of Scarsdale (T)
40. Earl of Radnor (W)	40. Earl of Thanet (T)
41. Earl of Carlisle (W)	41. Earl of Berkshire (T)
42. Earl of Sunderland (W)	42. Earl of Denbigh (T)
43. Earl of Winchelsea (CT)	43. Earl of Northampton (T)
44. Earl of Stamford (W)	44. Earl of Pembroke (CT)
45. Earl Rivers (W)	45. Duke of Hamilton (CT)
46. Earl of Manchester (W)	46. Duke of Buckingham (T)
47. Earl of Westmorland (W)	47. Duke of Leeds (T)
48. Earl of Leicester (W)	48. Duke of Shrewsbury (W)
49. Earl of Bridgewater (W)	49. Duke of Northumberland (CT)
50. Earl of Dorset (W)	50. Duke of Beaufort (T)
51. Earl of Lincoln (W)	51. Duke of Ormonde (T)
52. Earl of Derby (W)	52. Archbp Sharp of York (T)

Peers voting 'Guilty'	*Peers voting 'Not Guilty'*
53. Marquess of Dorchester (W)	
54. Marquess of Kent (W)	*Absent* Lord Ashburnham (T)
55. Duke of Queensberry (C)	
56. Duke of Roxburgh (W)	
57. Duke of Montrose (W)	
58. Duke of Bedford (W)	
59. Duke of Schomberg (W)	
60. Duke of Bolton (W)	
61. Duke of St Albans (W)	
62. Duke of Grafton (W)	
63. Duke of Richmond (W)	
64. Duke of Cleveland (W)	
65. Duke of Devonshire (W)	
66. Duke of Newcastle, L.P.S. (W)	
67. Lord President Somers (W)	
68. Lord Treasurer Godolphin (C)	
69. Lord Chancellor Cowper (W)	

Absent:
Earl of Suffolk (W)
Absented:
Duke of Somerset (W)
Bp Manningham of Chichester (W)
Bp Hough of Lichfield (W)

2. THE 'NO PREFERMENT' VOTE OF 21 MARCH

Peers voting against Sacheverell	*Peers voting for Sacheverell*
1. Lord Pelham (W)	1. Lord Conway (T)
2. Lord Hervey (W)	2. Lord Guernsey (T)
3. Lord Halifax (W)	3. Lord Haversham (T)
4. Lord Herbert (W)*	4. Lord Weston (T)
5. Lord Ossulston (W)	5. Lord Leominster (T)
6. Lord Cornwallis (W)	6. Lord Guilford (T)
7. Lord Rockingham (W)	7. Lord Stawell (T)
8. Lord Colepeper (W)	8. Lord Dartmouth (CT)
9. Lord Byron (CT)	9. Lord Osborne (T)
10. Lord Mohun (W)	10. Lord Craven (T)
11. Lord Hunsdon (C)	11. Lord Berkeley of Stratton (CT)
12. Lord Paget (C)	12. Lord Lexington (CT)
13. Lord Fitzwalter (W)	13. Lord Leigh (T)
14. Lord De la War (C)	14. Lord Howard of Escrick (T)
15. Bp Trimnell of Norwich (W)	15. Lord Chandos (T)

* Herbert was not noted by the Clerk of the House as being among those present on the 21st. But this was probably an error. He was elected to a committee on a private bill the same day.

Peers voting against Sacheverell	*Peers voting for Sacheverell*
16. Bp Wake of Lincoln (W)	16. Lord North and Grey (T)
17. Bp Talbot of Oxford (W)	17. Lord Willoughby de Broke (T)
18. Bp Cumberland of Peterborough (W)	18. Lord Ferrers (T)
19. Bp Moore of Ely (W)	19. Lord Ashburnham (T)
20. Bp Burnet of Salisbury (W)	20. Bp Dawes of Chester (T)
21. Earl of Glasgow (C)	21. Bp Hooper of Bath and Wells (T)
22. Earl of Seafield (C)	22. Bp Sprat of Rochester (T)
23. Earl of Leven (C)	23. Bp Crewe of Durham (T)
24. Earl of Crawford (W)	24. Bp Compton of London (T)
25. Earl of Cholmondeley (W)	25. Viscount Weymouth (T)
26. Earl of Wharton (W)	26. Viscount Saye and Sele (T)
27. Earl of Grantham (W)	27. Earl of Northesk (CT)
28. Earl of Orford (W)	28. Earl of Wemys (CT)
29. Earl of Bradford (W)	29. Earl of Mar (CT)
30. Earl of Warrington (W)	30. Earl of Rosebery (CT)
31. Earl of Portland (W)	31. Earl of Orkney (CT)
32. Earl of Holderness (W)	32. Earl of Loudoun (CT)
33. Earl of Berkeley (W)	33. Earl of Islay (W)
34. Earl of Radnor (W)	34. Earl of Greenwich and Duke of Argyll (W)
35. Earl of Carlisle (W)	35. Earl Poulet (T)
36. Earl of Sunderland (W)	36. Earl of Jersey (T)
37. Earl of Winchelsea (CT)	37. Earl of Scarborough (W)
38. Earl of Stamford (W)	38. Earl of Plymouth (T)
39. Earl of Manchester (W)	39. Earl of Abingdon (T)
40. Earl of Westmorland (W)	40. Earl of Rochester (T)
41. Earl of Leicester (W)	41. Earl of Nottingham (T)
42. Earl of Bridgewater (W)	42. Earl of Yarmouth (T)
43. Earl of Dorset (W)	43. Earl of Sussex (T)
44. Earl of Lincoln (W)	44. Earl of Anglesey (T)
45. Earl of Derby (W)	45. Earl of Scarsdale (T)
46. Earl of Suffolk (W)	46. Earl of Thanet (T)
47. Marquess of Dorchester (W)	47. Earl of Berkshire (T)
48. Marquess of Kent (W)	48. Earl of Denbigh (T)
49. Duke of Roxburgh (W)	49. Earl of Northampton (T)
50. Duke of Montrose (W)	50. Earl of Pembroke (CT)
51. Duke of Bedford (W)	51. Earl Rivers (W)
52. Duke of Schomberg (W)	52. Duke of Queensberry (C)
53. Duke of Bolton (W)	53. Duke of Hamilton (CT)
54. Duke of St Albans (W)	54. Duke of Buckingham (T)
55. Duke of Richmond (W)	55. Duke of Leeds (T)
56. Duke of Cleveland (W)	56. Duke of Shrewsbury (W)
57. Duke of Devonshire (W)	57. Duke of Northumberland (CT)
58. Duke of Newcastle (W)	58. Duke of Beaufort (T)
59. Lord Treasurer Godolphin (C)	59. Duke of Ormonde (T)

60. Lord Chancellor Cowper (W)

[59 voters + 1 teller]

Absent or Absented :
Bp Manningham of Chichester (W)
Bp Hough of Lichfield (W)
Bp Fleetwood of St Asaph (W)
Duke of Grafton (W)
Lord President Somers (W)

60. Duke of Somerset (W)
61. Archbp Sharp of York (T)

[60 voters + 1 teller]

Absent :
NIL

Note. Two absentees of 20 March returned, Suffolk voting against Sacheverell and Somerset for him.

BIBLIOGRAPHY
The words in **bold** *type denote abbreviated titles*

I. PRIMARY SOURCES

1. Manuscript Collections

Add[itional] MSS. 6116, 6696, 17677DDD, 33273, 35584, 42176, 47025-6 (British Museum)

MS. Ballard 3-7 incl., 9, 31, 34, 38, 45, 49 (Bodleian Library, Oxford)

Blenheim MSS. A.1-20, B.2-3, B.2-4, B.2-8, C.1-16, D.1-32, D.2-2, E.26; Box VII, bundle 18 (duke of Marlborough, Blenheim Palace)

B.M. Loan 29 (British Museum, duke of Portland's loan: Harley and Newcastle [Holles] papers)

F. Bonet's despatches to Prussia: Rep. XI England 34B, 35D (Deutches Zentralarchiv, Merseburg, E. Germany)

Brogyntyn MSS. (National Library of Wales, Aberystwyth)

MS. Carte 129, 230 (Bodleian Library, Oxford)

Chevening MSS. (the late Earl Stanhope)

Cholmondeley (Houghton) MSS. 67 (Cambridge University Library)

Drake/King MSS. (Devon Record Office)

Finch MSS. (Leicestershire and Rutland Record Office)

Forester MSS. (Salop Record Office)

Fox-Strangeways MSS. (Dorset Record Office)

Gibson Papers (Lambeth MSS. 929-30, 941) (Lambeth Palace Library: microfilm in Bodleian Library, Oxford)

Hatton-Finch MSS. (Northamptonshire Record Office)

King MSS. (T. C. D. Lyons) (Library of Trinity College, Dublin)

Kreienberg's despatches to Hanover: Cal. Br. 24 England (Staatsarchiv Hannover)

Lansdowne MSS. 773, 825, 885, 987, 1013-14, 1024 (British Museum)

Lichfield Cathedral Archives

Lonsdale MSS. (Cumberland and Westmorland Record Office)

F. F. Madan Transcripts (by kind permission of Mr C. W. Brocklebank)

Magdalen College MS. 310 (Library of Magdalen College, Oxford)

Monson MSS. (Lincolnshire Record Office)

Nicolson, William, bishop of Carlisle, MS. diaries (Tullie House, Carlisle: part originals, part transcripts)

MS. North a.3 (Bodleian Library, Oxford)

Ogilvie of Inverquhurity MSS. (Scottish Record Office, Register House, G.D. 205, Portfolio 4)

Osborn MSS. Box 21, No. 22 ('Account of the Trial of Dr Sacheverell') (Yale University Library)

Panshanger MSS. Sir David Hamilton's diary (Hertfordshire Record Office)

Penrice and Margram MSS. (University Library of Wales, Aberystwyth)

P.C. [Privy Council Registers] 2/82 (Public Record Office)

Polwarth MSS. (Scottish Record Office, Register House, G.D. 158, HMC. 2123)

Portland (Holles) MSS. (Nottingham University Library)

MS. Rawlinson B.376, C.151 (Bodleian Library, Oxford)

Shaftesbury MSS. (Public Record Office)

S.P. [State Papers] 34/12, 34/24, 44/108–9 (Public Record Office)

Stowe MSS. 57, II, III, IV; 58, IV, V, VI, VII (Huntington Library, California)

Stowe MSS. 750 (British Museum)

Trumbull MSS. LIII, LIV; Add. MSS. 133 (Berkshire Record Office)

Wake MSS. (Christ Church Library, Oxford)

Walton MSS. (Sir Richard Hamilton)

2. *Printed Primary Sources*
a. *Full-length Contemporary Accounts of the Sacheverell Affair and Trial*

Compleat History *A Compleat History of the Whole Proceedings of the Parliament of Great Britain against Dr Henry Sacheverell* (232 + 249 + 16 pp., for J. Baker, London, 1710)

High Church Display'd *High Church Display'd: Being a Compleat History of the Affair of Dr Sacheverell . . . In several Letters to an English Gentleman at the Court of Hanover* (387 pp., publisher unnamed, London, 1711) (a rare and valuable work, on the title page of which are the words: 'Fit to be kept in all Families, as a Storehouse of Arguments in defence of the Constitution')

Tryal *The Tryal of Dr Henry Sacheverell before the House of Peers for High Crimes and Misdemeanours* (456 pp., for Jacob Tonson, London, 1710) (the official transcript of the trial, 8vo edn., published by order of the House of Lords)

b. *Pamphlets, Broadsheets and Sermons*

(*Note:* The pamphlet and sermon literature bearing either directly on the Sacheverell affair or on the issues it dramatised is of mammoth proportions. I have confined this list to items referred to in the text or notes of this book. Much fuller bibliographies can be found in the works of F. Madan and A. T. Scudi, cited below under Secondary Authorities.

All items, unless otherwise stated, were published in London in 1710.)

U

An Answer to a Letter from a Citizen of New Sarum
The Answer *of Henry Sacheverell, D.D., to the Articles of Impeachment exhibited against him by the Honourable House of Commons* (8vo edn)
The Ballance of the Sanctuary: or Sacheverell weighed and found Light
The Banb—y Apes, or the Monkeys chattering to the Magpie: in a Letter to a Friend in London (London, n.d. [1710])
The Bishop of Lincoln's and Bishop of Norwich's Speeches in the House of Lords
The Bull-Baiting: *or Sach—ll dress'd up in Fireworks: Being Remarks on a Scandalous Sermon bellow'd out by Dr Sach—ll* by JOHN DUNTON (London, 1709)
The Case of the Patron and Rector of St Andrew's Holborn [by JOSEPH TRAPP] (London, 1722)
The **Character** *of a Low-Church-Man: Drawn in Answer to the True Character of a Churchman, shewing the False Pretences to that Name* [by HENRY SACHEVERELL] (1st edn, n.pl., 1702)
Charnock's Remains: *or S—l his Coronation* [by THOMAS BRERETON?] (London, 1713)
The Cherubim with a Flaming Sword that appeared on the Fifth of November last . . . : Being a Letter to my Lord M[ayor], with Remarks upon Dr Sa—ll's Sermon (London, 1709)
Chuse which you Please: *or Dr Sacheverell and Mr Hoadly drawn to the Life, being a Brief Representation of the Respective Opinions of each Party, in relation to Passive Obedience and Non-Resistance*
A Collection of *the* **Addresses** *which have been presented to the Queen since the Impeachment of the Reverend Dr Henry Sacheverell* (2 parts, London, 1711)
The Danger of Priestcraft to Religion and Government, with some Politick Reasons for Toleration: occasioned by a Discourse of Mr Sacheverel's intitul'd The Political Union [by JOHN DENNIS] (London, 1702)
Daniel Danery's (The Queen's Waterman) Letter to the Lord Treasurer: Concerning a Discovery of the Ring-Leaders of the Late Tumult
A Defense of the Lord Bishop of London in answer to Mr Whiston's Letter of Thanks to his Lordship . . . To which is added, A Vindication of the Reverend Dr Sacheverell's late Endeavour to turn Mr Whiston out of his Church (London, 1719)
Derby Sermon (1709) See SACHEVERELL, H., *The Communication of Sin*
A Description of the High Court of Judicature for the Tryal of Dr Henry Sacheverell
Doctor Burgess's Character of the London Mob
Mr D—en's Letter to His Brother M—rs, dated from Elizium the 4th of June (broadsheet)
Fast-Day Sermon (1702) See SACHEVERELL, H., *A Defence of Her Majesty's Title* (etc.)
Four Letters *to a Friend in North-Britain, upon the Publishing the Tryal of Dr Sacheverell* [by ARTHUR MAINWARING]
The Free Debates *betwixt the H—— L—— and the H—— C—— on Doctor Sacheverell*

High-Church Politicks: *or The Abuse of the 30th of January considered. With Remarks on Mr Luke Milbourne's Railing Sermons and on the Observation of that Day*

An **Impartial Account** *of What Passed most Remarkable in the last Session of Parliament, relative to the Case of Dr Henry Sacheverell*

Leicester Assize Sermon (1706) See SACHEVERELL, H., *The Nature, Obligation and Measures of Conscience*

A Letter from a Member of Parliament to Mr H[enry] S[acheverell] concerning the Tacking the Occasional Bill (1705)

A Letter to a Convocation Man, *concerning the Rights, Powers and Privileges of that Body* [by FRANCIS ATTERBURY AND OTHERS] (London, 1697)

A Letter to a Noble Lord, *occasioned by the present Proceedings against Dr Henry Sacheverell:* By a hearty lover of the Church and present happy Constitution

A Letter to Dr Henry Sacheverell, in which are some Remarks on his Vindication . . . : by a GENTLEMAN OF OXFORD

The Life, Character and Memorable Actions of Dr Sacheverell

The Life, Character and Pious Deportment *of the Reverend Dr Henry Sacheverell, From his Cradle thro' the Whole Course of his Life: Together with an Account of every Day's Procession and Proceedings . . .* (anon. broadsheet)

The Managers Pro and Con: *or the Account of what is said at Child's and Tom's Coffee-Houses for and against Dr Sacheverell*

The Measures of Resistance to the Higher Powers by LUKE MILBOURNE

The Modern Fanatick: *With a True Account of the Life, Actions, Endowments, etc., of the famous Dr S—l* by WILLIAM BISSET

The **Modern Fanatick,** *Pt ii: Containing what is necessary to clear all the Matters of Fact in the First Part; and to confute what has been printed in the pretended Vindication of Dr Sacheverell* by WILLIAM BISSET (London, 1711)

The **Modern Fanatick,** *Pt iii: Being a further Account of the Famous Doctor and his Brother of like Renown* by WILLIAM BISSET (London, 1714)

A **Modest Reply** *to the Unanswerable Answer to Mr Hoadly, with some Considerations on Dr Sacheverell's Sermon* (London, 1709)

The Officers' Address to the Ladies

An Ordinary Journey no Progress: *or a Man doing his own Business, no Mover of Sedition* [by JOSEPH TRAPP]

Oxford Assize Sermon (1704) See SACHEVERELL, H., *The Nature and Mischief of Prejudice* (etc.)

The Peril *of being Zealously Affected, but not Well: or Reflections on Dr Sacheverell's Sermon* [by GEORGE RIDPATH] (London, 1709)

The **Pious Life** *and Sufferings of the Reverend Dr Henry Sacheverell from his Birth to his Sentence, received at Westminster Hall, March 23, 1710*

The **Political Union:** *A Discourse shewing the Dependance of Government on Religion in General: and of the English Monarchy on the Church of England in Particular* by HENRY SACHEVERELL (Oxford, 1702)

Pray for the Peace of Jerusalem: A Sermon preached at Sherborne . . . on the Public Fast, March 15th, 1709-10 [Postscript dated 29 March] by JOHN ENGLAND

A **Prelude** to the **Tryal of Skill** *between Sacheverellism and the Constitution of the Monarchy of Great Britain*

The **Priest** turn'd **Poet,** *or the Best Way of Answering Dr Sacheverel's Sermon . . . being a Discourse paraphrased in Burlesque Rhime* [by P.J.]

[**Progress**] *Dr Sacheverel's* **Progress** *from London to his Rectory of Salatin*

Public Peace Ascertained : with some Cursory Reflections upon Dr Sacheverell's two Late Sermons. In a Sermon preached on Tuesday, Nov. 22, 1709 by RICHARD CHAPMAN, Vicar of Cheshunt (London, 1709)

Remarks *on Dr Sach——'s Sermon at the Cathedral of St Paul: Being Design'd as a Seasonable Antidote against the Spreading Malignity of that Pestilent Discourse* by WILLIAM BISSET (London, 1709)

Remarks upon a Sermon preached by Dr Henry Sacheverell at the Assizes held at Derby, Aug. 15, 1709 . . . containing a just and modest Defence of the Societies for Reformation of Manners against the Aspersions cast upon them in that Sermon [by JOHN DISNEY] (London, 1711)

Resistance and Non Resistance: *Or an Account of the Debates in the H—of L—s on the First Article of Impeachment*

SACHEVERELL, H., [see **Political Union** (1702)]

——, [see *The* **Character** *of a Low-Church-Man* (1702)]

——, *A Defence of her Majesty's Title to the Crown and a Justification of her Entering into a War with France and Spain: as it was delivered in a Sermon* [on 2 Chron. vi, 34] *preached before the University of Oxford on 10th day of June 1702, being the Fast appointed for imploring a Blessing on her Majesty and Allies engaged in the Present War* (Oxford, 1702 [without the full title]; London, 1710)

[——], *The New Association of those called Moderate-Church-Men with the Modern Whigs and Fanaticks, to undermine and blow up the Present Church and Government* (4th edn, London, 1705; first publ. 1702–3)

——, *The Nature and Mischief of Prejudice and Partiality: stated in a Sermon preached at St Mary's in Oxford, at the Assizes held there March 9th 1703–4* [on 1 Timothy, v, 21] (Oxford, 1704; edn cited, 2nd edn, London, 1708)

——, and PERKS, JOHN, *The Rights of the Church of England Asserted and Proved* (London, 1705)

——, *The Nature, Obligation and Measures of Conscience: delivered in a Sermon preached at Leicester, at the Assizes held there, July 25th, 1706* [on Acts, xxiii, 1] (Oxford, 1706)

——, *The Nature, Guilt and Danger of Presumptuous Sins: set forth in a Sermon preached before the University of Oxford, at St Mary's, Septemb. 14th, 1707* [on Numbers, xv, 30, 31] (Oxford, 1708)

——, *The Communication of Sin: A Sermon preached at the Assizes held at Derby, August 15th, 1709* [on 1 Timothy, v, 22] (London, 1709)

——, *The Perils of False Brethren, both in Church and State: set forth in a Sermon preached before the Right Honourable the Lord Mayor, Aldermen and Citizens of London at the Cathedral Church of St Paul, on the 5th of November, 1709* [on 2 Cor., xi, 26] (London, 1709)

——, *The Christian Triumph: or The Duty of Praying for our Enemies, illustrated and enforced from our Blessed Saviour's Example on the Cross: in a*

Sermon preached at St Saviour's in Southwark on Palm-Sunday, 1713 [on Luke, xxiii, 34] (London, 1713)

——, *False Notions of Liberty in Religion and Government destructive of both: a Sermon preached before the Honourable House of Commons, at St Margaret's, Westminster, on Friday, May 29, 1713* [on 1 Peter, ii, 16] (London, 1713)

——, Preface to *Fifteen Discourses of William Adams* (London, 1716)

Sacheverell against Sacheverell: *or The Detector of False Brethren prov'd Unnatural and Base to his own Grandfather and other Relations. In a Letter to Dr Henry Sacheverell from his Uncle* by BENJAMIN SACHEVERELL (London, 1711)

Mr Sacheverell's Assize-Sermon . . . without Prejudice and Partiality examined . . . By a Moderate and True Son of the Church of England (London, 1704)

Dr Sacheverell's Answer to the Articles of Impeachment exhibited against Him (London and Edinburgh, 1710)

Dr Sacheverel's Letter to her Majesty (broadsheet)

A Search after Principles: In a Free Conference between Timothy & Philatheus concerning the Present Times

Secret Memoirs *of the Life of Dr Henry Sacheverell*

The Sins and Vices of Men's Lives, *the chief cause of their ignorance and corrupt opinions in religion. A Sermon preached before the University of Oxford, at St Mary's, on December the 11th, 1709* by WILLIAM TILLY, Fellow of Christ Church

Some Account of the Family *of Sacheverell, from its Original to this Time*

Some Considerations humbly offered to the Right Reverend the Lord Bishop of Exeter by BENJAMIN HOADLY (London, 1709)

Submission to Governours Considered: *in a Letter to a Friend and Admirer of Dr Sacheverell* [by ABRAHAM JEACOCKE]

The Thirteenth Chapter to the Romans Vindicated *from the Abusive Senses put upon it. Written by a Curate of Salop* [W. FLEETWOOD] *and directed to the Clergy of that County . . .*

Mr Toland's Reflections on Dr Sacheverell's sermon preached at St Paul's Nov. 5, 1709. In a Letter from an Englishman to an Hollander by JOHN TOLAND

A **True Answer:** *or Remarks upon Dr Sacheverell's Speech, Mar. 7, 1710: Being a Modest and Reasonable Comparison betwixt his Sermon at St Paul's and that at Westminster*

A True Answer to Dr Sacheverell's Sermon before the Lord Mayor . . . in a Letter to one of the Aldermen [by WHITE KENNETT] (London, 1709)

A True List of the Names of those Persons committed to the several Goals [sic] *in and about Westminster . . . on account of the Tumult, March the 1st* (broadsheet)

University Sermon (1707) See SACHEVERELL, H., *The Nature, Guilt and Danger of Presumptuous Sins*

A Vindication of the Last Parliament: in Four Dialogues between Sir Simon and Sir Peter (London, 1711)

A **Vindication** *of the Reverend Dr Henry Sacheverell from the . . . Aspersions cast upon him in a late infamous Pamphlet, entitled The Modern Fanatick* [by CHARLES LAMBE] (London, 1711, 2 edns)

A Visit to St Saviour's, *Southwark, with Advice to Dr Sacheverell's Preachers there* by a Divine of the Church of England [WHITE KENNETT]
Vulgus Brittanicus: or The British Hudibras (London, 1711)
The Welshman's Tales concerning the Times: viz, the Parson's Progress
Mr Whiston's Account of Dr Sacheverell's Proceedings in order to exclude him from St Andrew's Church in Holborn by WILLIAM WHISTON (London, 1719)
The Wisdom *of Looking Backward to Judge the Better of One Side or t'Other: By the Speeches, Writings, Actions and other Matters of Fact of Both Sides, for the Four Years Last Past* by WHITE KENNETT (London, 1715)
The Worcester Triumph: *or a True Account of Dr Sacheverell's Entrance and Reception in that City, July 14th, 1710* (broadsheet)

c. Contemporary Histories, Journals, Memoirs, Diaries

Boyer, Annals ABEL BOYER, *The History of the Reign of Queen Anne digested into Annals,* vol. viii (1710), vol. ix (1711)
Boyer, Political State ABEL BOYER, *The Political State of Great Britain, 1711–1714* (originally publ. monthly; 2nd edn, 4 vols, 1718)
Boyer, Queen Anne ABEL BOYER, *The History of the Life and Reign of Queen Anne* (1722)
Burnet GILBERT BURNET, *A History of my own Time* (6 vols, Oxford, 1833)
Calamy EDMUND CALAMY, *An Historical Account of my own Life, 1671–1731* (2 vols, 1830)
Chamberlen PAUL CHAMBERLEN, *An Impartial History of the Life and Reign of Queen Anne* (1738)
C.J. *Journals of the House of Commons*
Cunningham ALEXANDER CUNNINGHAM, *The History of Great Britain from the Revolution in 1688 to the Accession of George I* (2 vols, contemp., but published 1787)
Defoe, Tour DANIEL DEFOE, *A Tour through the Whole Island of Great Britain* (Everyman edn, 2 vols, 1927)
Evelyn's Diary *The Diary of John Evelyn* (ed. E. S. de Beer, abridged edn, Oxford, 1959)
Journal to Stella JONATHAN SWIFT, *Journal to Stella* (ed. T. Roscoe, in *The Works of Jonathan Swift,* vol. i, 1888)
Life of Sharp (1825) *The Life of John Sharp D.D., Lord Archbishop of York: collected from his Diary, Letters and other Authentic Testimonies by his son, Thomas Sharp* (2 vols, 1825)
L.J. *Journals of the House of Lords*
Lockhart Papers *The Lockhart Papers* (ed. A. Aufrere, 2 vols, 1817). Vol. i includes the *Commentarys* (1707–14) of George Lockhart of Carnwath, M.P.
Luttrell NARCISSUS LUTTRELL, *A Brief Historical Relation of State Affairs from September 1678 to April 1714* (6 vols, Oxford, 1859)
Oldmixon JOHN OLDMIXON, *The History of England during the Reigns of King William and Queen Mary, Queen Anne, King George I* (1735)
Remarks and Collections *Remarks and Collections of Thomas Hearne* (various editors, Oxford Historical Soc., 1885–1907), vols i [1705–7], ii [1707 to May 1710], iii [May 1710 to 1712], viii [1722–5]

d. Printed Correspondence

Atterbury Epist. Corr. *The Epistolary Correspondence . . . of . . . Francis Atterbury, D.D.* (ed. J. Nichols, 4 vols, 1783–7)

Clavering Corr. *The Correspondence of Sir James Clavering* (ed. H. T. Dickinson, Surtees Society, 1967)

Coxe, Marlborough W. COXE, *Memoirs of the Duke of Marlborough* (Bohn edn, 3 vols, 1847–8)

H.M.C. Ailesbury MSS. Historical Manuscripts Commission, Report on the marquess of Ailesbury's manuscripts

H.M.C. Ancaster MSS. Historical Manuscripts Commission, Report on the manuscripts of the earl of Ancaster

H.M.C. Bath MSS. Historical Manuscripts Commission, Report on the marquess of Bath's manuscripts, vols i, iii

H.M.C. Dartmouth MSS. Historical Manuscripts Commission, Report on the earl of Dartmouth's manuscripts, vol. i

H.M.C. Egmont MSS. Historical Manuscripts Commission, Report on the earl of Egmont's manuscripts, vol. ii

H.M.C. Portland MSS. Historical Manuscripts Commission, Report on the duke of Portland's manuscripts, vols ii, iv, v, vii

H.M.C. Stuart MSS. Historical Manuscripts Commission, Report on the Stuart Papers at Windsor Castle, vols i, ii

H.M.C. Townshend MSS. Historical Manuscripts Commission, Report on the manuscripts of Marquess Townshend

H.M.C. 11th Rep. Appx. Pt. vii Historical Manuscripts Commission, 11th Report, Appendix, Part vii (Report on the Le Strange papers)

Letters of Humphrey Prideaux *Letters of Humphrey Prideaux, sometime dean of Norwich, to John Ellis . . . 1674–1722* (ed. E. M. Thompson, Camden Soc., 1875)

Priv. Corr. *The Private Correspondence of Sarah, Duchess of Marlborough* (2 vols, 1838)

Wentworth Papers *The Wentworth Papers* (ed. J. J. Cartwright, 1883)

e. Other Correspondence

SIR GEORGE SITWELL *Letters of the Sitwells and Sacheverells* (2 vols, Scarborough, 1901)

f. Newspapers, Newsletters and Periodicals

The British Journal
The Daily Courant [ed. Samuel Buckley]
Dyer John Dyer's MS. Newsletters (complete sets for 1709 and 1710 in B.M. Loan 29/320–1)
The Evening Post
The Examiner [ed. Jonathan Swift, 2 Nov. 1710 to 14 June 1711]
The Flying-Post [ed. George Ridpath]
The Observator
The Post-Boy [ed. Abel Roper]

A Review of the State of the British Nation [ed. Daniel Defoe]
The Supplement
The Worcester Post-Man

g. *Other Contemporary or Near-Contemporary Works*

CALAMY, EDMUND, *The Nonconformist's Memorial* (revised by S. Palmer, 2nd edn, 1803)

ECTON, JOHN, *A State of the Proceedings of the Corporation of the Governors of the Bounty of Queen Anne* (2nd edn, continued to 1720; Dublin, 1725)

HATTON, EDWARD, *A New View of London: or An Ample Account of that City* (2 vols, 1708)

KIDDER, RICHARD, *The Life of Richard Kidder, D.D., Bishop of Bath and Wells, written by Himself* (Somerset Record Society, xxxvii, 1924)

NELSON, ROBERT, *The Life of George Bull, Late Bishop of St David's* (1714)

NEWTON, WILLIAM, *The Life of the Right Reverend Dr White Kennett, Late Lord Bishop of Peterborough* (1730)

NICHOLLS, W., *A Defence of the Doctrine and Discipline of the Church of England* (2nd edn, 1715)

SWIFT, JONATHAN, *The History of the Four Last Years of Queen Anne's Reign* (*Prose Works*, ed. H. Davis, vol. vii)

TOLAND, JOHN, *A State Anatomy of Great Britain* (1717)

h. *Compilations incorporating Contemporary Material*

Camden Misc. xxiii   *Camden Miscellany*, vol. xxiii (Royal Historical Society, 1969), printing 'An Anonymous Parliamentary Diary, 1705–6' and 'Sir John Pakington's speech on "The Church in danger" [8 Dec. 1705]', ed. W. A. Speck

Foxcroft   H. C. FOXCROFT, *A Supplement to Burnet's History of My Own Time* (1902)

House of Lords MSS.   *The Manuscripts of the House of Lords: New Series, in continuation of the volumes issued under the authority of the Historical Manuscripts Commission*, vol. viii [1708–10] (reprint, 1966)

Parl. Hist. vi   *Cobbett's Parliamentary History of England*, vol. vi (1810)

State Trials, xv   T. B. HOWELL, *A Complete Collection of State Trials and Proceedings for High Treason and Other Crimes and Misdemeanours*, vol. xv [1710–19] (London, 1816)

The Divided Society   G. HOLMES and W. A. SPECK (eds), *The Divided Society: Party Conflict in England, 1694–1716* (1967)

II. SECONDARY AUTHORITIES

(*Note:* Books or articles cited only once in the Notes, in a specific context, have not been included here unless their general importance seemed to warrant it.)

ABBEY, C. J., and OVERTON, J. H., *The English Church in the Eighteenth Century* (2 vols, 1878)

BEBB, E. D., *Nonconformity and Social and Economic Life, 1660–1800* (1935)

BEDDARD, R. A., 'The Guildhall Declaration of 11 December 1688 and the Counter-Revolution of the Loyalists', *Historical Journal*, xi (1968)

BENNETT, G. V., *White Kennett, 1660–1728, Bishop of Peterborough* (1957)
——, 'King William III and the Episcopate', in *Essays in Modern English Church History*, eds. G. V. Bennett and J. D. Walsh (1966)
——, 'Robert Harley, the Godolphin Ministry and the Bishoprics Crisis of 1707', *English Historical Review*, lxxxii (1967)
——, 'Conflict in the Church', in *Britain after the Glorious Revolution, 1689–1714*, ed. G. Holmes (1969)
BLOXAM, J. R., *A Register of the Presidents, Fellows, Demies . . . and other members of Saint Mary Magdalen College in the University of Oxford* (8 vols, Oxford, 1853–5)
BROCKETT, A., *Nonconformity in Exeter, 1650–1875* (Manchester, 1962)
CARPENTER, E., *The Protestant Bishop: The Life of Henry Compton, 1632–1713* (1956)
CRAGG, G. R., *Reason and Authority in the Eighteenth Century* (Cambridge, 1964)
EVERY, G., *The High Church Party, 1688–1718* (1956)
FEILING, K., *A History of the Tory Party, 1640–1714* (1924)
HART, A. T., *The Life and Times of John Sharp, Archbishop of York* (1949)
——, *William Lloyd, 1627–1717* (1952)
HOLMES, G., *British Politics in the Age of Anne* (1967)
HUTCHINS, J., *The History and Antiquities of the County of Dorset*, vol. i (3rd edn, 1861)
JAMES, F. G., *North country Bishop* [Nicolson of Carlisle] (New Haven, 1957)
MCLACHLAN, H., *English Education under the Test Acts* (Manchester, 1931)
MCLACHLAN, H. J., *Socinianism in Seventeenth Century England* (Oxford, 1951)
MACRAY, W. D., *A Register of the Members of St Mary Magdalen College, Oxford* (New Series, vol. iv [Fellows, 1648–1712], 1904)
MADAN, F., *A Bibliography of Dr Henry Sacheverell* (Oxford, 1884)
MICHAEL, W., *England under George I*, vol. i (transl. L. B. Namier, 1936)
NIGHTINGALE, J., *The History and Antiquities of the Parochial Church of St Saviour's, Southwark* (2 vols, 1818)
PLOMER, H. R., *A Dictionary of the Printers and Booksellers in England, Scotland and Ireland . . . 1668–1725* (1922)
SCUDI, A. T., *The Sacheverell Affair* (New York, 1939)
SEDGWICK, R. (ed.), *The History of Parliament: The House of Commons, 1715–1754* (2 vols, 1970)
SMITHERS, P., *The Life of Joseph Addison* (Oxford, 1954)
SPECK, W. A., *Tory and Whig: The Struggle in the Constituencies, 1701–1715* (1970)
STRAKA, G. M., *Anglican Reaction to the Revolution of 1688* (Madison, Wisconsin, 1962)
SYKES, N., *Edmund Gibson, Bishop of London* (Oxford, 1926)
——, *Church and State in England in the Eighteenth Century* (Cambridge, 1934)
——, 'Queen Anne and the Episcopate', *English Historical Review*, l (1935)
——, *William Wake, Archbishop of Canterbury* (2 vols, Cambridge, 1957)
——, *From Sheldon to Secker: Aspects of English Church History, 1660–1768* Cambridge, 1959)

298   *Bibliography*

THOMAS, R., 'Comprehension and Indulgence', in *From Uniformity to Unity, 1662-1962*, eds. G. F. Nuttall and O. Chadwick (1962)

TREVELYAN, G. M., *England under Queen Anne* (3 vols, 1930-4)

WHITING, C. E., *Nathaniel, Lord Crewe, Bishop of Durham* (1940)

——, *Studies in English Puritanism from the Restoration to the Revolution* (1931; reprint, 1968)

WILSON, W., *The History and Antiquities of Dissenting Meeting-Houses in London* (4 vols, 1808-14)

NOTES

PROLOGUE

1. On the great party battles of the early eighteenth century and their effects on society, see, in general, J. H. Plumb, *The Growth of Political Stability in England, 1675–1725* (1967); Geoffrey Holmes, *British Politics in the Age of Anne* (1967); W. A. Speck, *Tory and Whig: The Struggle in the Constituencies, 1701–15* (1970); Holmes and Speck, *The Divided Society* (1967). Recent studies of individual politicians (e.g. H. Horwitz, *Revolution Politicks* [1968] and H. T. Dickinson, *Bolingbroke* [1970]) also vividly illustrate the divisiveness of party.

2. D[eutches] Z[entral] A[rchiv], Rep XI England 35D, f. 93: Bonet to Frederick I, 21 March 1710; Ogilvie of Inverquhurity MSS. G.D. 205/4; John Pringle to Sir William Bennett, 21 March 1710.

3. Only recently have students of the eighteenth century grasped the full extent of this dilemma. The work of the late Norman Sykes and of G. V. Bennett, in particular (see Bibliography, p. 297), has pointed the way.

CHAPTER I

1. H.M.C. *Portland MSS.* iv, 295: W. Stratford to [? Francis Gastrell], 22 April 1706.

2. *The Pious Life and Sufferings of the Reverend Dr Henry Sacheverell* (1710), p. 4; *V.C.H. Warwicks*, iv, 239–40, 244; H.M.C. *Portland MSS.* iv, 59; Sir G. Sitwell, *Letters of the Sitwells and Sacheverells*, i, 269–70, 276 n.; ii, 49, 51 n., 54.

3. See *Some Account of the Family of Sacheverell* (1710), p. 5. The dedication of the 1710 edn of Henry Sacheverell's *The Political Union* (1st edn, 1702) to George Sacheverell of Newhall begins: 'The many favours I have received from you in the course of a long friendship, and the relation I have the honour to bear to your family . . .'

4. John Hutchins, *History and Antiquities of the County of Dorset* (3rd

edn, 1861), i, 413–14. See also A. T. Scudi, *The Sacheverell Affair* (1939), pp. 12–13; *High-Church Politicks*, pp. 4–5, for Milbourne, who was the son of a nonconformist minister.

5. *Sacheverell against Sacheverell*, p. 13. I have based this paragraph largely on the postscript to this pamphlet by Benjamin Sacheverell (pp. 13–16) and on the informative, partly independent account in J. Oldmixon, *History of England* (1735), p. 429. Apparently they were not consulted by William Hunt when he compiled his *D.N.B.* article on Henry Sacheverell, although this article contains some useful additional data on the subject's forbears. See also Hutchins, *Dorset*, i, 423; John Nichols, *History and Antiquities of the County of Leicester*, iii, 510.

6. All three brothers had Oxford educations (at New Inn Hall, Trinity and Merton respectively), though only John and Timothy took degrees (1636 and 1641). See *Alumni Oxonienses 1500–1714*, iv, 1297–8.

7. E. Calamy, *A Continuation of the Account of the Ministers . . . Ejected* (1727), i, 424–6.

8. E. Calamy, *The Nonconformist's Memorial* (revised by S. Palmer, 2nd edn, 1803), iii, 223–4.

9. J. and J. A. Venn, *Alumni Cantabrigienses*, Pt I, iv, 1; *Sacheverell against Sacheverell*, pp. 4, 6–7.

10. They were Timothy, b. November 1675 and Timothie, b. July 1679 (family piety again). These details, preserved in the F. F. Madan MSS. and extracted from the parish registers of St Peter's, correct a number of garbled accounts current in 1710–11, e.g.

Some Account of the Family, p. 3.

11. *Pious Life*, p. 4; Oldmixon, p. 429; *Some Account of the Family*, pp. 3–4; *Sacheverell against Sacheverell*, p. 2; Katherine Hearst to Robert Coxe, 1 Jan. 1711, printed in *A Vindication of . . . Sacheverell* (2nd edn, 1711), p. 15.

12. Walter Wilson, *The History and Antiquities of Dissenting Meeting Houses in London*, iii, 495–6; cf. *D.N.B.* entry on Burgess.

13. Boyer, p. 406; Oldmixon, p. 429; Katherine Hearst to Robert Coxe, 1 Jan. 1711, loc. cit.

14. *Pious Life*, pp. 4–5; *Secret Memoirs*, p. 18; J. R. Bloxam, *Register of . . . Magdalen College*, vi, 98; P. Smithers, *Life of Joseph Addison*, p. 13.

15. It is part of Addison folk-lore that the poet had a fondness for Sacheverell's sister, Susanna.

16. Smithers, *Addison*, pp. 13, 16, 24–5; *Some Account of the Family*, p. 4; Katherine Hearst to Robert Coxe, loc. cit.; W. Bisset, *The Modern Fanatick*, p. 4; *Vindication*, pp. 14, 17, 30; MS. Rawlinson B. 376, ff. 59–60; Sacheverell to John Robinson, bp of London, 31 Oct. 1714 (see also p. 265 above).

17. The shoulder of mutton episode was later admitted by one of Sacheverell's eulogists, appropriately named Charles Lambe, who merely denied Bisset's accusation that Sacheverell's quarrel had been with a fellow-member of the College. *Vindication*, p. 47; *Modern Fanatick*, p. 21. For the 1693 incident, see Bloxam, op. cit. p. 98.

18. W. D. Macray, *A Register of the Members of St Mary Magdalen*

19. *Modern Fanatick*, pp. 19–20; *Vindication*, pp. 33–4. Cf. Scudi, *The Sacheverell Affair*, pp. 21–2, and Hutchins, *Dorset* (3rd edn), i, 425, on Sacheverell as a Latin scholar.
20. William Whiston to Henry Clements (the bookseller), London, 17 Jan. 1711, 'to be communicated to Dr Henry Sacheverell' (later published, after Sacheverell had failed to reply, in *Modern Fanatick*, Pt ii [1711], pp. 25, 26). Cf. Nicolson MS. diary, 23 Jan. 1711, confirming that the letter was sent to Sacheverell and summarising its contents; *Modern Fanatick* (1710), p. 26; an unconvincing alternative version suggesting that Holt admired Sacheverell too much 'to bury so promising a young gentleman in such a place', in *Vindication*, pp. 37–8.
21. See *Vindication*, p. 34. Sacheverell was ordained at Eccleshall church, 19 September 1697, to the title of Cannock 'ad inserviendum curae animarium'. He had subscribed to the Articles and oaths the previous day. Lichfield Cathedral Archives, B/A/1/18, f. 30 v, B/A/4/22. I owe these references, and other information about Cannock, to Miss Jane Isaac of Lichfield Joint Record Office.
22. *Modern Fanatick*, p. 27. Bisset's evidence was both retrospective (compiled in 1710, much of it on the basis of recollected conversations) and hostile; but it has the ring of truth, and only one of his accusations about Sacheverell at Cannock was later contradicted –

and that only in part – by the author of the *Vindication*, Charles Lambe.
23. *Vindication*, pp. 39–40. Cf. Bisset's more scathing account, and the accusations that Sacheverell's behaviour had been disreputable (op. cit. pp. 27–8; also *Modern Fanatick*, Pt ii [1711], p. 27).
24. *Modern Fanatick*, p. 27. Uncontradicted by Lambe. Abraham Jeacocke of Birmingham claimed ten years later that he 'never could entertain any esteem for the Doctor's performances', which gave off 'more heat than light'.
25. Quoted in Smithers, *Addison*, p. 43.
26. Paul Chamberlen, *An Impartial History of the Life and Reign of Queen Anne* (1738), p. 331.
27. *The Private Correspondence of Sarah, Duchess of Marlborough* (1838), ii, 142, 143; *Modern Fanatick* (1710), p. 16, Pt iii (1714), pp. 14–15; Chamberlen, loc. cit.; Oldmixon, p. 429; Boyer, *Queen Anne*, p. 406; [Thomas Brereton?], *Charnock's Remains: or S—l his Coronation* (London, 1713); T. Hearne, *Remarks and Collections*, ii, 229; Cunningham, ii, 293.
28. See, e.g., Bloxam, *Register*, vi, 99. Cf. William Hunt in *D.N.B.*
29. 18 Jan. 1710: printed in Bloxam, vi, 100.
30. MS. Ballard 34, ff. 77–8: Sacheverell to Wm. Lancaster, [?4] Feb. 1710, endorsed 5 Feb.; cf. *The Managers Pro and Con* (3rd edn, London, 1710), p. 22.
31. 'Vir . . . vinolentus, loquax, audax'. See *Remarks and Collections*, ii, 229. The inset passage is roughly translated from

Hearne's tortuous Latin. Cf. ibid. iii, 65, expressing Hearne's astonishment, in 1710, that anyone could be taken in 'by so conceited and ignorant and impudent a man as that Doctor, who, whatever good he may accidentally produce, is certainly a rascal and knave himself'.

32. *A Letter to Dr Henry Sacheverell . . . by a Gentleman of Oxford* (1710), pp. 11–12.

33. *High Church Display'd* (1711), p. 2.

34. *Modern Fanatick*, p. 40; *Remarks and Collections*, iii, 98–9.

35. Ibid.

36. Magdalen College MS. 310.

37. Though see *Modern Fanatick*, p. 23.

38. For the brief account of Sacheverell's Magdalen career I have drawn partly on Bloxam, op. cit. 98, and Macray, op. cit. iv, 172, and partly on additional information kindly supplied from the Vice President's Register by Dr G. L. Harriss.

39. He served as Pro-Proctor in 1703 and was later appointed a Delegate of Appeals, the capacity in which he took his revenge on poor Ryley.

40. *Modern Fanatick*, p. 15; Macray, op. cit. iv, 172 n.

41. The sermon was later published at Oxford on 1 July under the title *A Defence of her Majesty's Title to the Crown and a Justifica-tion of her Entering into a War with France and Spain*.

42. F. F. Madan MSS. The imprimatur bore the date 2 June 1702, but the sermon (on Proberbs, viii, 15) was undoubtedly delivered during May.

43. *The Select Works of Mr John Dennis* (1718), i, 357–80. Playwright and pamphleteer, Dennis was a deeply committed Whig.

44. Much of this paragraph is heavily indebted to the bibliographical researches of Dr W. A. Speck.

45. Viz, *The True Character of a Church Man*, published probably in December 1701 and written by Richard West.

46. W. A. Speck, *Tory and Whig : The Struggle in the Constituencies* (1970), Appx D.

47. B.M. Loan 29/190, ff. 212–13: Sir J. Pakington to Thos. Foley, n.d., and Foley to Harley, Witley, 1 Sept. 1702; H.M.C. *Portland MSS.* iv, 73. At the end of the Parliament Stratford was promoted to a canonry of Christ Church. H.M.C. *Bath MSS.* i, 71.

48. *The Nature, Guilt and Danger of Presumptuous Sins* (Oxford, 1708); *The Nature and Mischief of Prejudice and Partiality* (2 edns, Oxford, 1704; 3rd edn, Oxford, 1705; 4th edn, London, 1708).

49. *More Short Ways with the Dissenters*, [April] 1704.

50. *Remarks and Collections*, i, 138–9.

CHAPTER II

1. See R. A. Beddard, 'The Guildhall Declaration of 11 December 1688 and the Counter-Revolution of the Loyalists', *Hist. Journal*, xi, 1968, p. 411 and *passim*.

2. Evelyn's Diary, 15 Jan. (de Beer, abridged edn, p. 897); *L.J.* xiv, 110; G. Every, *The High Church Party*, p. 27; A. T. Hart, *William Lloyd*, pp. 118–19. See also G. M.

Straka, *Anglican Reaction to the Revolution of 1688* (Madison, Wisconsin, 1962), p. 31, and in general chs 3, 4.

3. MS. Ballard 45, f. 67a: R. Sare to A. Charlett, 30 April 1691; Evelyn's Diary, 7 May (op. cit. pp. 937–8) and *The Life of Richard Kidder . . . by Himself*, pp. 62–3, for the experiences of William Beveridge and Kidder; Burnet, iv, 135–6; *Letters of Lady Rachel Russell* (1826 edn), pp. 198–216 *passim* (Tillotson's letters of 19, 24 Sept. 1689, 9, 25 Oct. 1690); *Life of Sharp* (1825), pp. 108–9 for John Sharp. In general, Every, op. cit. pp. 61–6.

4. 'Such a cross stumbling block in my way [the ex-bishop of Norwich called the oath] that I have no hopes to get over it.' H.M.C. *11th Rep.*, Appx Pt vii, p. 113: William Lloyd to Sir Christopher Calthorpe, 29 June 1702. Cf. Lansdowne MSS. 987, f. 202.

5. The most serious efforts were made in 1660–1 and during the Exclusion crisis of 1679–81. See R. Bosher, *The Making of the Restoration Settlement*; R. Thomas, 'Comprehension and Indulgence', in G. F. Nuttall and O. Chadwick (eds), *From Uniformity to Unity*; N. Sykes, *From Sheldon to Secker*, ch. 3; H. Horwitz, 'Protestant Reconciliation in the Exclusion Crisis', *Journal of Eccl. Hist.* xv, 1964.

6. Burnet, iv, 56–7; Intro. to [W.] Nicholls, [*A*] *Defence [of the Doctrine and Discipline of the Church of England]* (2nd edn, 1715), pp. 117–19.

7. Hartlebury MSS: Lloyd's Visitation Papers, 1702, cited in Hart, *Lloyd*, p. 194. See also *Letters of*

Humphrey Prideaux (Camden Soc. 1875), p. 154: 18 July 1692; *Life of Sharp* (1825), i, 341, for Sharp's motion in the Lords, 1705, on evasion of church attendance.

8. G. R. Cragg, *Reason and Authority in the 18th Century*, chs 1–2.

9. Francis Atterbury *et al*, *A Letter to a Convocation Man* (1697), p. 2; Wm. Tilly, *The Sins and Vices of Men's Lives* (Oxford, 1710, but preached 11 Dec. 1709), p. 14.

10. Author of the notorious book *Christianity not Mysterious* (1696). See J. G. Simms, 'John Toland, Donegal Heretic', *Irish Historical Studies*, xvi, 63, 1969.

11. Stowe MSS. 58, IV, p. 80: Rev. W. Wotton to Jas. Brydges, 8 Jan. 1710.

12. Evelyn's Diary, op. cit. p. 913; Burnet, iv, 387; H. J. McLachlan, *Socinianism in Seventeenth Century England* (1951), pp. 294–321 *passim*. The issues involved were immensely complex, and divines who engaged themselves against the Socinians ran the risk of incurring charges of diversionism themselves. See, e.g., MS. Ballard 3, ff. 51–2.

13. Burnet, vi, 185–6; W. Tilly, University Sermon, Oxford, 11 Dec. 1709; Evelyn's Diary, op. cit. p. 924 and entries for 1690–3 *passim*; C. Trimnell, Fast Day Sermon, 14 Jan. 1707; W. Fleetwood, Thanksgiving Day Sermon, 19 Aug. 1708.

14. E.g. *A Letter to a Convocation-Man*, p. 2; *High-Church Politicks*, p. 57; Burnet, iv, 387; *Camden Misc.* xxiii, 1969, p. 48; Wake MSS. Arch. W. Epist. 17 misc. i. 243: W. Wotton to Wake, 21 March 1710. Cf. MS. Ballard 3,

f. 90: Wake to Charlett, 2 Sept. 1708.

15. Lansdowne MSS. 773, f. 17; MS. Ballard 3, ff. 30, 34; H.M.C. *Portland MSS.* v, 321; Lansdowne MSS. 1014, f. 110.

16. John Ecton, *A State of the . . . Bounty of Queen Anne* (2nd edn, 1725), p. 103. In addition there were almost 2,000 small benefices, chiefly curacies and chapelries, which in the past had been considered too poor to be charged. Ibid. pp. 98–101.

17. G. Miège, *The New State of England* (1699 edn), Pt ii, p. 163. The Tudor inheritance is brilliantly analysed in C. Hill, *Economic Problems of the Church from Archbishop Whitgift to the Long Parliament* (Oxford, 1956).

18. MS. Ballard 9, f. 30: Tenison to Queen Anne (copy), 31 Jan. 1712.

19. The figures for Gloucester are derived from a contemporary census utilised by Gregory King. For Lincoln, see Defoe, *A Tour through the Whole Island of Great Britain* (Everyman edn), ii, 91.

20. *The Examiner*, No. 42, 24 May 1711.

21. Every, pp. 10, 13–15; Lansdowne MSS. 1024, f. 372; E. Carpenter, *The Protestant Bishop*, p. 218; MS. Ballard 3, f. 28.

22. *A Letter out of Suffolk to a Friend in London* (London, 1694), quoted in J. Birch, *The Life of the Most Reverend John Tillotson* (1753), pp. 290–1; Burnet, iv, 211–12; H. C. Foxcroft, *A Supplement to Burnet's History*, p. 314; G. V. Bennett, 'King William III and the Episcopate', in Bennett and J. D. Walsh, eds, *Essays in Modern English Church History*, pp. 118–22.

23. Burnet, iv, 248.

24. Intro. to Nicholls, *Defence*, p. 126; cf. MS. Ballard 5, f. 127: Edmund Gibson to Charlett, 28 May 1698.

25. Intro. to Nicholls, *Defence*, pp. 126–30; N. Sykes, *William Wake*, ii, 81–116; MS. Ballard 4, f. 12: Nicolson to Charlett, 6 May; MS. Ballard 6, f. 13; Atterbury's Visitation charges to the Clergy of Totnes, 1702 and 1703 (see J. Nichols [ed.], *The Epistolatory Correspondence . . . of . . . Francis Atterbury, D.D.* [hereafter *Atterbury Epist. Corr.*], ii, 211–30, esp. p. 227.

26. Atterbury's Visitation Charge, 1703, *Epist. Corr.* ii, 229; see also p. 227; Bishop Hooper's speech in the House of Lords, 6 Dec. 1705 (*Parl. Hist.* vi, 498); B.M. Loan 29/145/4: Thos. to Robert Harley, 27 June [1707]; H.M.C. *Bath MSS.* i, 52–4; H.M.C. *Ancaster MSS.*, p. 441.

27. G. V. Bennett's forthcoming life of Atterbury will illuminate these struggles; meanwhile his *White Kennett*, pp. 44–68, contains the clearest, most succinct recent account.

28. 6 Dec. 1705, *Parl. Hist.* vi, 496–7. In the same debate Simon Patrick of Ely 'complained of the undutifulness of the clergy to their bishops and the difficulty they had to govern them regularly'.

29. *Remarks and Collections of Thomas Hearne*, iii, 20.

30. *A Vindication of . . . Dr Henry Sacheverell* (2nd edn, 1711), p. 22.

31. Burnet, iv, 393.

32. *Atterbury Epist. Corr.* ii, 227–8.

33. G. V. Bennett, 'Conflict in the Church', in G. Holmes (ed.),

Britain after the Glorious Revolution, p. 165.
34. H. T. Dickinson (ed.), *Correspondence of Sir James Clavering*,
p. 76; Burnet, vi, 193-4 (cf. iv,
459-60); Every, *High Church
Party*, p. 131; [Ridpath], *The
Peril*, pp. 16-17; MS. Ballard 3,
f. 47.
35. Mainwaring, *Four Letters to a
Friend in North Britain* (1710), p.
4. For the identification of the
authorship of this famous pamphlet, see H. L. Snyder's arguments
in *Huntington Lib. Quarterly*,
xxxiii, 1970, pp. 138-44; H.M.C.
Portland MSS. iv, 507; Lansdowne MSS. 825, f. 8.
36. See Atterbury's Latin sermon of
17 May 1709, *Concio ad Clerum
Londinensem*, in *Sermons and Discourses* (1820), i, 396 ff.; Bennett,
'Conflict in the Church', loc. cit.
p. 169; Benjamin Hoadly, *Some
Considerations humbly offered to
the Right Reverend the Lord Bishop
of Exeter* (1709); *Chuse which you
Please* (1710). See also p. 31 n. *
above.
37. E.g. White Kennett at Aldgate
and Thomas Bennett at Colchester. See G. V. Bennett, *White
Kennett*, pp. 187-90; Thos. Bennett, *Charity Schools Recom-
mended* (London, 1710).
38. For High Church indifference to
the work of the S.P.C.K. (established 1698), see Burnet's scathing criticism in the House of
Lords in 1705, *Parl. Hist.* vi, 491.
Only the S.P.G. (1702) had something like broad-based support.
39. Fowler to Sharp, 6 April 1699
and T. Caryl to Sharp, Feb. 1697,
quoted in A. T. Hart, *Sharp*, pp.
181-2; *Life of Sharp* (1825), i,
X

170-89; *Atterbury Epist. Corr.* ii,
251; Calamy, i, 410.
40. Intro. to Nicholls, *Defence*, pp.
133-4, 145-6.
41. My italics.
42. Burnet, v, 161; *Parl. Hist.* vi, 78,
80, 83; *The Bishop of Lincoln's and
Bishop of Norwich's Speeches in
the House of Lords, March 17*
(London, 1710), pp. 28-9.
43. *The Examiner*, No. 42.
44. For Sheffield, and sixteen other
congregations in England with
more than 1,000 hearers in 1715,
see the information gathered by
the contemporary minister, John
Evans, printed in E. D. Bebb,
*Nonconformity and Social and
Economic Life*, p. 38 n. For Halifax, Defoe, *Tour*, ii, 197-8. For
Manchester, R. Halley, *Lanca-
shire, its Puritanism and Nonconformity*, ii, 294.
45. Defoe, *Tour*, ii, 38 (see also i, 32
for Colchester). Cf. figures in
Bebb, op. cit., pp. 51-2, with
those for the Bristol 'census' of
1695 in D. V. Glass, 'Gregory
King's Estimate of the Population of England and Wales, 1695',
Population Studies, iii, 1950, p.
347 n.
46. For these and many other conformist counties, see Bebb, op.
cit. Appx 2.
47. Figures for 1690 are based on the
evidence of the first year's licences; those for 1716 on the highest
figure for each county arrived at
by Evans and by the compiler of
another contemporary survey,
Daniel Neal. It is reasonable to
take the higher figure in each
case, since Evans clearly had the
more reliable sources of information in some counties, and
Neal in others.

48. For a detailed review of the immigrant Protestant congregations in England by 1688, see the invaluable work of C. E. Whiting, *Studies in English Puritanism from the Restoration to the Revolution* (1931), pp. 360-4.
49. *Camden Misc.* xxiii, 83.
50. Particularly of H. McLachlan, *English Education under the Test Acts* (Manchester, 1931), to which this section is mainly indebted. McLachlan's identification, and dating, of academies was generally more complete than that of Irene Parker, *Dissenting Academies in England* (Cambridge, 1914), pp. 137-42.
51. Thomas Secker and Joseph Butler.
52. Trumbull MSS. LIII: Ralph Bridges to Sir W. Trumbull, 12 Jan. 1709; *Camden Misc.* xxiii, 48; *Modern Fanatick*, p. 11.
53. See Calamy, i, 400: 'the allowance of the law is of necessity a sufficient establishment'. Cf. Pakington in 1705: 'This [acquiescence in Occasional Conformity] emboldens the dissenters to call their Toleration an Establishment'.
54. Intro. to Nicholls, *Defence*, p. 135; Calamy, loc. cit.; *Calendar of State Papers Domestic, 1697*, p. 467.
55. E.g. at Stafford and Pembroke in 1710. Sir J. C. Wedgwood, *Parliamentary History of Staffordshire*, ii (1920), 295; *The Post-Boy*, Nos 2404, 2411, 10 and 26 Oct. 1710.
56. Walton MSS. ii, 83: Rev. Humphrey Whyle to Sir J. Mordaunt, 27 Nov. 1703; *Life of Sharp* (1825), i, 367-8; Representation from the Lower to the Upper

House of Convocation, Dec. 1704; Every, *High Church Party*, pp. 116-17; [Ridpath], *The Peril*, p. 17.
57. Dec. 1702 to Jan. 1703.
58. Burnet, v, 51-4; Walton MSS. ii, 85: Whyle to Mordaunt, 20 Dec. 1703; Nicolson's MS. diary, 3, 4, 7 Dec. 1702, 16 Jan. 1703, 28 Nov. 1704. Sharp, too, was opposed to 'the Tack', though remaining convinced that the Occasional bill itself 'must pass some time or other'. *Life of Sharp* (1825), i, 305-6.
59. *Atterbury Epist. Corr.* iii, 51: Atterbury to Trelawney, 6 Sept. 1701. See also H.M.C. *Bath MSS.* i, 52-4: Harley to Tenison, 11 Aug. [1702], and in general, G. V. Bennett, 'King William III and the Episcopate', loc. cit. esp. p. 129. But cf. Lambeth MSS. 930 (Gibson Papers), f. 13: Somers to Tenison [1699].
60. See, e.g., *The Life of Dr Henry Compton* (1713), p. 67.
61. Burnet, iv, 519; Bennett, 'King William III and the Episcopate', p. 129; MS. Ballard 38, ff. 187, 190: T. Rowney to A. Charlett, 24 Oct., 26 Nov. 1702.
62. For contemporary notes on the 'Church in Danger' debate in the Commons, in which at least sixteen Tories made speeches in support of Bromley and Seymour, see *Camden Misc.* xxiii, pp. 44-9.
63. D.Z.A., Rep XI England 35D, f. 51: F. Bonet to Frederick I of Prussia, 26 April 1710; Dyer, 29 May 1705; Blenheim MSS. A.1-20: St John to Marlborough, 25 May. Ninety Tackers were eventually re-elected.
64. In the former category came 2

Anne, c. 11 (Queen Anne's Bounty Act), 3 and 4 Anne, c. 18 (Recovery of Small Tithes) and 6 Anne, c. 27. The 1707 Act discharged roughly 3,900 livings of £50 p.a. or under from the payment of First-Fruits and Tenths. J. Ecton, *State of the . . . Bounty*, p. 4.

65. Chatsworth MSS. C. 361: Aaron Kinton to John Whildon, 8 Aug. 1702.

66. James Clavering to Lady Cowper, 11 May 1708, printed in Holmes and Speck, *The Divided Society*, p. 57.

67. Cunningham, ii, 274-5.

68. H.M.C. *Portland MSS.* iv, 177; H.M.C. *Bath MSS.* i, 76.

69. Trumbull Add. MSS. 133, Letter 32: St John to Trumbull, 30 May 1704.

70. *Life of Sharp* (1825), i, 341.

71. Blenheim MSS. D.2-2: Gelli-

brand to Sunderland, 24 May 1711.

72. H.M.C. *Portland MSS.* iv, 533.

73. *Letter Books of John Hervey, First Earl of Bristol* (1894), i, 72.

74. *Camden Misc.* xxiii, 48.

75. King MSS. T. C. D. Lyons 1080: Francis Annesley to Archbishop King, 6 May 1704.

76. Finch MSS. Box VI, bundle 23: Bromley to Nottingham, 31 Dec. 1708; Trumbull MSS. LIII: Ralph Bridges to Trumbull, 7 Dec. 1708, 12 Jan. 1709; Dyer, 11, 13, 25 Jan.; Add. MSS. 47025: Sir J. Percival to E. Southwell, 7 May; MS. Ballard 49, f. 166: Sir W. Whitlocke to Charlett, 24 Feb.; MS. Ballard 7, f. 31: Smalridge to same, 26 Feb.; B.M. Loan 29/171: Harley to Wm. Stratford, 19 Dec. 1709.

77. *Modern Fanatick*, pp. 9, 12.

78. Ibid. p. 9.

CHAPTER III

1. See, e.g., Cunningham, ii, 82, for an allusion to his activities, *c.* 1706.

2. J. Dunton, *The Bull-Baiting*, p. 4; H. Sacheverell, *The Nature, Obligation and Measures of Conscience* (London, 1706); H.M.C. *Portland MSS.* iv, 321; J. Bennett to T. Hearne, *c.* 5 Jan. 1709, *Remarks and Collections*, ii, 162.

3. MS. Carte 230, f. 225: Thos. Carte to John Carte, 7 April 1710.

4. Oxford Assize Sermon (1704), p. 5.

5. Leicester Assize Sermon (1706), p. 20.

6. Ibid. p. 32.

7. University Sermon of Sept. 1707, p. 9.

X2

8. Burnet, v, 434.

9. [Ridpath], *Peril*, p. 6; *The Bull-Baiting*, p. 3; *Modern Fanatick*, p. 17.

10. *Remarks and Collections*, viii, 224: 14 June 1724.

11. Cunningham, ii, 275-6; [W. Kennett], *A Visit to St Saviour's, Southwark* (1710), p. 16.

12. Sacheverell wrote Part I of the pamphlet *The New Association of those called Moderate-Church-Men with the Modern Whigs and Fanaticks* in 1702 and Part II in 1703. See F. Madan, *A Bibliography of Dr Henry Sacheverell* (Oxford, 1884), p. 11.

13. *Political Union*, pp. 5, 6.

14. Oxford Assize Sermon, Preface, p. 2.

15. *Political Union*, p. 20; Oxford Assize Sermon, p. 24.
16. Oxford Assize Sermon, p. 14. The innuendo was naked enough: 'Her Majesty succeeding so *opportunely* to the throne . . .'; 'blessed be God, there is *now* a person on the throne who so justly weighs the interest of Church and State . . .'; 'If his Majesty's person or authority was brought under any disregard or contempt it was owing to their false counsels and ensnaring practices who . . . betrayed him into a jealousy of his best friends'. *Character of a Low-Church-Man*, pp. 2, 13–14; *Political Union*, p. 24. Cf. *Four Letters*, p. 10; *Modern Fanatick*, pp. 21–2; ibid. Pt ii (1711), p. 24; *The Review*, No. 144; *Vindication*, pp. 36–7.
17. p. 13.
18. Oxford Assize Sermon, 9 March 1704.
19. *Political Union*, p. 24; Leicester Assize Sermon, p. 21.
20. *Political Union*, p. 20. See also the striking paragraph on the supporters of Comprehension in *Character*, p. 8.
21. *Political Union*, p. 24; Oxford Assize Sermon, p. 16; Leicester Assize Sermon, p. 5.
22. Oxford Assize Sermon, pp. 23–4.
23. Leicester Assize Sermon, p. 21; Oxford Assize Sermon, p. 14; University Sermon, Sept. 1707, p. 7.
24. *Character*, p. 24.
25. *Political Union*, p. 20; Oxford Assize Sermon, p. 2; *Character*, p. 14; Derby Sermon, epistle dedicatory.
26. Oxford Assize Sermon, pp. 11–12; Derby sermon, epistle dedi-

catory and pp. 8–9, 10, 13; *Character*, pp. 11–12.
27. Leicester Assize Sermon, pp. 19–20; cf. pp. 30–3; Derby Sermon, pp. 15–16.
28. Burnet, v, 434.
29. Ibid.; J. Nightingale, *History and Antiquities of the Parochial Church of St Saviour's, Southwark* (1818), i, 90, 93. Cf. Trumbull MSS. LIII: Ralph Bridges to Sir W. Trumbull, 25 May.
30. Trumbull MSS. LIII: Bridges to Trumbull, 12 April, 6 May.
31. My account of the Southwark election of 1709 is mainly constructed from the letters of Ralph Bridges and others to Sir William Trumbull in Trumbull MSS. LIII (Berks R.O.), 28 March to 25 May, with Trumbull's endorsements. There are extracts printed in H.M.C. *Downshire MSS.* I, Pt ii, 872–6.
32. Trumbull MSS. LIII: Bridges, 12 April.
33. Ibid.: Bridges, 6 May, 25 May. The competition was too keen, those appointed being the bishop of Chester (Sir William Dawes), Dean Atterbury and Dr Birch.
34. Ibid.: Withers, 6 April; Bridges, 12 April. Withers was an East India and Africa merchant who had been Prime Warden in 1701–2.
35. Ibid.: Bridges, 28 March.
36. *Modern Fanatick*, p. 17. For Gouge, see also Bridges to Trumbull, 12 April, loc. cit. Sacheverell was particularly annoyed with him – and Annesley – for having split the High Church interest in the election.
37. *Modern Fanatick*, pp. 17–18, an account somewhat toned down in

Vindication, pp. 31–2; *Modern Fanatick*, Pt ii (1711), pp. 6–7.

38. Trumbull MSS. LIII: Trumbull to Sacheverell (draft), 30 May; Trumbull to Bridges (draft: written on Bridges's letter of 25 May).

39. Wake MSS. Arch. W. Epist. 23, f. 200: Rev. Maurice Wheeler to Wake, 21 Dec. 1709; Oldmixon, p. 429; Burnet, vi, 434.

40. G. Pole to T. Hearne, 28 Aug., *Remarks and Collections*, ii, 242.

41. Derby Sermon, p. i.

42. H. R. Plomer, *A Dictionary of the Printers and Booksellers . . . 1668–1725* (1922), p. 280.

43. 'Clements' examination before the Commons' [14 Dec. 1709], paper in Cholmondeley (Houghton) MSS. 67; *The Daily Courant*, 27 Oct.

44. No. 1811, 29 Oct. to 1 Nov.

45. He served as Master of the Company, 1701–2. *List of the Wardens of the Grocers' Company* (London, 1907), p. 36; Oldmixon, p. 427.

46. See pp. 40–1 above; for Garrard's extreme politics, see also *Toland's Reflections*, p. 10; Add. MSS. 17677DDD, f. 364.

47. Lansdowne MSS. 1024, f. 199: Garrard's statement to the House of Commons, 14 Dec.

48. A point made by the author of *High Church Display'd* (1711), p. 3.

49. *The Bull-Baiting*, p. 6.

50. *Four Letters*, p. 9: my italics. Cf. *The Priest turn'd Poet* (1709), p. 2: '. . . those of sense among 'em [the Tories] curse him and such as employed him'; Ogilvie of Inverquhurity MSS. (G.D. 205/4): Robert Pringle to Sir William Bennett, 2 March 1710 – 'a miscreant and tool of ane certain party'; Oldmixon, pp. 429–30,

esp. his reference to 'Those who were in the secret of Sacheverell's mission' for 'fomenting faction and stirring up rebellion'; *Lockhart Papers*, i, 310–11, for the extraordinary implication that Robert Harley was one of his instigators (George Lockhart's account of much of the Sacheverell affair, save what pertains to the Scots, is, for him, unusually inaccurate).

51. See the terms of his will, dated 10 February 1723 (and codicil 28 May 1724), P.R.O. Prob. 11/604, ff. 180–1.

52. *Modern Fanatick*, pp. 11, 23.

53. *London in 1710* (transl. by W. H. Quarrell and M. Mare), pp. 34–5.

54. The Reverends J. Bennett and D. Evans (in MS. Rawlinson, printed in *Remarks and Collections*, ii, 304–5, 317), and W. Bisset (*Remarks on Dr. Sach—'s Sermon*, pp. 2–7, and *Modern Fanatick*, pp. 1–2).

55. *The Cherubim with a Flaming Sword*, p. 8.

56. Bisset, *Remarks*, p. 3; *Modern Fanatick*, pp. 1–2; cf. *Remarks and Collections*, ii, 229.

57. So John Bennett timed the sermon (see n. 54 above). The timing is confirmed by Bisset, *Remarks*, p. 3. Bisset, whose pamphlet appeared over a week after the sermon, wrily remarked that Sacheverell's prolixity 'was a piece of fanaticism I should never have thought he would have been guilty of'.

58. For Jones, see *D.N.B.* and Hearne, loc. cit.

59. Dedication to *The Priest turn'd Poet*, by J— P— (1709), p. 1.

60. All the quotations and page references which follow are from

the standard 2nd octavo edn of the sermon, published by Henry Clements, by far the most widely read edition.

61. *The Perils of False Brethren*, p. 5; cf. p. 53 above.
62. Ibid. pp. 7–8.
63. Ibid. pp. 9–10.
64. Ibid. p. 10.
65. Ibid. pp. 11–14.
66. Ibid. p. 15.
67. Ibid. pp. 16–17.
68. Ibid. p. 19: my italics.
69. Ibid. pp. 18–20.
70. It had been applied to Godolphin in a pamphlet of 1707, *Vulpone, or Remarks on some Proceedings in Scotland*, and more recently in Mary Manley's scurrilous book *New Atalantis*. For evidence that the nickname, or its English equivalent, were in common use in political circles, see H.M.C. *Dartmouth MSS.* i, 296; H.M.C. *Portland MSS.* iv, 522 (cf. ibid. p. 520); Penrice and Margam MSS. L.683: Sir Edward Stradling to Sir Thomas Mansel, 19 June 1710: 'whatever Sir Fox and the Lady [Marlborough] may do, I fancy the Junto will stay to be turned out'.
71. *The Perils of False Brethren*, pp. 20–2.
72. Ibid. pp. 22–3.
73. *Remarks and Collections*, ii, 304–5: Rev. D. Evans to T. Hearne, 10 Nov. 1709.
74. That lowest of Low Churchmen, William Bisset, wrote a few days later: 'I must needs say it grieved me not a little to see him ride in triumph through the City, as being conqueror'. *Remarks*, p. 7.
75. Lansdowne MSS. 1024, f. 199; Boyer, *Annals*, viii, 205. My italics.

76. *Modern Fanatick*, p. 24.
77. *Remarks*, p. 7.
78. '*Pour peu que le sermon soit approuvé*', as l'Hermitage put it in a report to the Dutch States-General. Add. MSS. 17677DDD, ff. 364–5.
79. See, e.g., W. A. Speck, 'Conflict in Society', in G. Holmes (ed.), *Britain after the Glorious Revolution*, p. 150.
80. Cunningham, ii, 276; Add. MSS. 17677DDD, ff. 364–5: l'Hermitage, 16 Dec.; Luttrell, v, 509, 510; *Toland's Reflections*, pp. 10–11; Dyer, 10 Nov.; *Modern Fanatick*, p. 18; Boyer, *Annals*, viii, 205; *Daily Courant*, No. 2510, 9 Nov.
81. *Modern Fanatick*, p. 18; *Remarks*, p. 7.
82. Without an exceptionally slow delivery the sermon as printed could not have taken a full 90 minutes to deliver. The main section jettisoned was apparently a further denunciation of the Societies for Reformation of Manners. Bisset noted a number of lesser changes, e.g. in print Sacheverell called not on 'the bishops' but on the 'superior pastors' of the Church to 'thunder out their ecclesiastical anathemas'. *The Bull-Baiting*, p. i; Bisset, *Remarks*, pp. 3–4; *Modern Fanatick*, p. 19. John Bennett told Hearne on 1 December that the printed version was 'verbatim as 'twas preached' – the only witness I have found categorically to say so.
83. *Wentworth Papers*, p. 99: Peter Wentworth to Lord Raby, 16 Dec. 1709.
84. Cholmondeley (Houghton) MSS. 67: 'Clements' Examination'.

85. *Clavering Corr.* p. 53: 26 Nov.
86. Cholmondeley (Houghton) MSS. loc. cit.
87. I owe most of my bibliographical information to the kindness of Dr W. A. Speck.

88. *Tryal*, pp. 103, 143; Burnet, v, 435.
89. This is Dr Speck's estimate, and I see no reason to challenge it.
90. Wake MSS: Nicolson to Wake, 5 Jan. 1710.

CHAPTER IV

1. [*A*] *Review* [*of the State of the British Nation*], vi, 106: 8 Dec. 1709.
2. *The Thirteenth Chapter to the Romans Vindicated*, by a Curate of Salop (1710), p. 1.
3. *Remarks and Collections*, ii, 317: J. Bennett to T. Hearne, 1 Dec.; Trumbull MSS. LIII: Ralph Bridges, 7 Dec.
4. *Review*, vi, 107.
5. *A True Answer to Dr Sacheverell's Sermon before the Lord Mayor*, pp. 3–4, 11, 21. See also *The Life of the Right Reverend Dr White Kennett* (1730), p. 103.
6. Bisset, *Remarks*, p. 7.
7. The Whigs were not alone in thinking so. This was the view of well-informed neutrals too, e.g. Friedrich Bonet, the long-serving Prussian minister in London. D[eutches] Z[entral] A[rchiv], Rep XI England, 34B, f. 303: 16 Dec.
8. *The Observator*, 30 Nov.; Dyer, 3 Dec. He went to Lothbury at the invitation of Samuel Hilliard.
9. Richard Chapman, *Public Peace Ascertained* (Dec. 1710), preface; *A Modest Reply to the Unanswerable Answer to Mr Hoadly, with some Considerations on Dr Sacheverell's Sermon* (written 2 Dec., publ. 10 Dec.), p. 23.
10. Burnet, v, 435; *An Impartial Account of what pass'd most Re-*markable in the Last Session of Parliament (1710), p. 2.
11. Cunningham, ii, 276.
12. The Manager concerned was Sir Thomas Parker. See p. 204 above. For the reference in the Lords: *Parl. Hist.* vi, 879; also pp. 221–2 above, and Burnet, v, 435.
13. H. C. Foxcroft, *A Supplement to Burnet's History of My Own Time* [hereafter Foxcroft], p. 427.
14. See *High Church Display'd*, pp. 6–7.
15. Add. MSS. 6116, f. 18.
16. Burnet, v, 435. Burnet's information is dependable on this point. He must have had it directly from Eyre, who as M.P. for Salisbury knew the bishop well.
17. The Prussian minister in London, Bonet, had explained to his court in Berlin on 16 December that one of the main reasons for not referring the case to the ordinary courts or the Church courts was that '*cela n'aurait pas fait d'éclat*'. D.Z.A. Rep XI England 34B, f. 304. See also the Attorney-General's speech, 27 Feb. 1710, in *The Tryal of Dr Henry Sacheverell* (printed for Jacob Tonson, London, 1710), p. 25.
18. See, e.g., *Tryal*, pp. 88, 146.
19. Mainly Edward Harley's Memoir, H.M.C. *Portland MSS.* v, 649; Lansdowne MSS. 885, ff. 81–2, Lord Coningsby's History of

312 *Notes to Pages 84–91*

Parties presented to George I; ibid. 1024, f. 98: White Kennett's diary; Stowe MSS. 57 (correspondence of James Brydges, Paymaster of the Forces); Trumbull MSS. LIII: Ralph Bridges, 7 Dec.; Coxe, *Marlborough*, iii, 30; Hardwicke's and Dartmouth's notes to Burnet, v, 435, 443; Cunningham, ii, 276–8 (the most circumstantial evidence); Trumbull MSS. LIII: Ralph Bridges to Trumbull, 20 Dec.; B.M. Loan 29/238, f. 310: [Robert Monckton] to Newcastle, 10 Dec.; Swift, *The History of the Four Last Years of Queen Anne's Reign* (*Prose Works*, ed. H. Davis, vol. vii), p. 6, and *Memoirs relating to that Change . . . in the Queen's Ministry*.

20. See the revealing article by H. L. Snyder, 'The Duke of Marlborough's Request of his Captain-Generalcy for Life: a Re-examination', *Journal of the Society of Army Historical Research*, vol. xlv, 1967, pp. 70–82; also pp. 114–16 above for the Court crisis over the Essex regiment in January 1710, when Somers failed to give Marlborough adequate backing.

21. See the speech of Wharton's client, Nicholas Lechmere, in *Tryal*, p. 36; cf. Mainwaring, *Four Letters*, p. 3.

22. Coxe, *Marlborough*, iii, 30: letter headed 'Wednesday, six o'clock' [30 Nov. or 7 Dec.].

23. H.M.C. *Portland MSS*. v, 649.

24. Lansdowne MSS. 1024 (Kennett's diary), f. 198; Stowe MSS. 57, III: Brydges to Thos. Stanwix, 30 Dec.; cf. the dissenting voice of one Whig M.P. quoted in Calamy, ii, 224.

25. Blenheim MSS. E.26: Mainwaring to duchess of Marlborough, 'Thursday evening' [15 Dec.]; Dyer, 17, 22, 29 Nov., 3, 8, 10 Dec.; Penrice and Margam MSS. L.1446: C. Williams to Mansel, 29 Nov.; B.M. Loan 29/171: Harley to Stratford, 27 Aug., 4 Nov., 6 Nov.; B.M. Loan 29/147/7: Rochester to Harley, 18 Nov.; *L.J.* xix, 17–19; Luttrell, vi, 520.

26. Blenheim MSS. C.1–16. I am grateful to Professor H. L. Snyder for confirmation of this point.

27. B.M. Loan 29/238, f. 310: [Robert Monckton] to Newcastle, 10 Dec. 1709 (cf. H.M.C. *Portland MSS*. ii, 209); Trumbull MSS. LIII: Ralph Bridges to Trumbull, 20 Dec., wrongly cited in H.M.C. *Downshire MSS*. I, ii, 885–6.

28. Most recently, early in 1708, when according to Cunningham, ii, 144, Somers was supported by Cowper and Townshend.

29. Cunningham, ii, 276–8.

30. Edward Nicholas, M.P. for Shaftesbury, and Thomas Harley, M.P. for Radnorshire.

31. John Dolben was the son of John Dolben, archbishop of York (1683–6) and the younger brother of the High Tory M.P. and lawyer, Sir Gilbert Dolben.

32. Trumbull MSS. LIII: to Sir W. Trumbull, 14 Dec. 1709.

33. Trumbull MSS. loc. cit.; H.M.C. *Egmont MSS*. ii, 243–4; Lansdowne MSS. 1024, f. 198; *C.J.* xvi, 241; *Compleat History*, pp. 3–5; Dyer, 13 Dec.; *High Church Display'd*, pp. 4–5.

34. Boyer, *Annals*, viii, 222; B.M. Loan 29/171: R. Harley to W. Stratford, 19 Dec. 1709.

35. *Compleat History*, p. 6; Dyer, 15 Dec.
36. Lansdowne MSS. 1024, ff. 198–9.
37. Kennett's diary, loc. cit.; *Compleat History*, p. 6; *Wentworth Papers*, p. 100.
38. As n. 37; also H.M.C. *Egmont MSS.* ii, 244; Burnet, v, 438; Oldmixon, pp. 427, 430; Boyer, *Annals*, viii, 223; Add. MSS. 17677DDD, f. 364; *High Church Display'd*, pp. 5–6. On Garrard's loss of caste, see also *A Search after Principles: In a Free Conference between Timothy & Philatheus concerning the Present Times* (London, 1710), p. 11.
39. *Compleat History*, p. 5. There are alternative versions with slight verbal differences, e.g. in Kennett's diary, loc. cit., and in Dyer, 15 Dec.
40. *Compleat History*, p. 6; *Wentworth Papers*, pp. 99–100; *Impartial Account*, p. 1; *High Church Display'd*, p. 6; *A Letter to a Noble Lord*, p. 16; Luttrell, vi, 524; *The Supplement* No. 300, 16 Dec. Sir Stephen Lennard was M.P. for Kent, 1708–9.
41. *C.J.* xvi, 241.
42. See *C.J.* xvi, 242.
43. H.M.C. *Egmont MSS.* ii, 244: Percival to Archdeacon William Percival, [15] Dec.; *Impartial Account*, p. 3; *Compleat History*, p. 7; Blenheim MSS. E.26: Arthur Mainwaring to duchess of Marlborough, 'Thursday evening' [15 Dec.]; Register House, G.D. 158. HMC 2123: Geo. Baillie to Marchmont, 24 Dec.; *C.J.* xvi, 246.
44. Dyer, 24 Dec.; Add. MSS. 17677DDD, f. 369: l'Hermitage, 20 Dec.; Trumbull MSS. LIII: Ralph Bridges to Trumbull, 20

Dec.; Lansdowne MSS. 1024, f. 200; H.M.C. *Portland MSS.* iv, 530; *C.J.* xvi, 245, 256; *Impartial Account*, p. 4; *High Church Display'd*, pp. 8–9. For the arguments deployed in the debate 'of several hours' on 22 December, see *Compleat History*, pp. 8–9.
45. Dyer, 24 Dec.; Lansdowne MSS. 1024, f. 200. But cf. *Life of Sharp* (1825), ii, 328.
46. H.M.C. *Portland MSS.* iv, 530: Stratford to Harley, 21 Dec.; Wake MSS. Arch. W. Epist. 23, f. 200: M. Wheeler to Wake, Gloucester, 21 Dec.; Burnet, v, 439; Trumbull MSS. LIV: Ralph Bridges, 9 Jan. 1710.
47. Lansdowne MSS. 1024, f. 201.
48. *Dr Sacheverel's Letter to her Majesty* (broadsheet, printed for T. Harris, 1710): dated 4 Jan. 1710.
49. *Peter Went Out and Wept Bitterly. A Sermon prepared to be preached before the Lord M— at his parish church, on the 22nd of January* (London, 1710). The sermon was put into the press well before it was preached – if it ever was preached.
50. To Trumbull, 9 Jan., loc. cit.
51. Ibid.
52. By a resolution of the Commons on 4 February 1710 the Committee which had drawn up the articles was ordered to do service as Managers for the House during the trial; but on 10 February four additional Managers were nominated, one of them being Walpole.
53. Stowe MSS. 57, III: Brydges to John Drummond, 15 July 1710.
54. Hardwicke's n. to Burnet, v, 435. As a young man in his teens in the 1730s Philip Yorke, later 2nd earl

of Hardwicke, would have known Jekyll, then the veteran Master of the Rolls. Alternatively he may have learnt of his opinions from the Somers papers, to which he had access.

55. Lansdowne MSS. 885, ff. 81–2.
56. Dyer, 29 Dec.; *Parl. Hist.* vi, 809.
57. These errors were to be devastatingly exposed during the trial by Sir Thomas Parker (see p. 154 n. above) and in print by the learned author of the pamphlet *The Ballance of the Sanctuary: or Sach-*

everell Weighed and found Light (written in May 1710), who described Sacheverell as 'a notorious Scripture plunderer' (pp. 11–13).

58. For proceedings on the 11th and 12th in the Commons, see Trumbull MSS. LIV: Bridges to Trumbull, 13 Jan.; Add. MSS. 17677DDD, f. 385; Cunningham, ii, 285–6; *Compleat History*, p. 11; Boyer, *Annals*, viii, 225–6; Dyer, 12 Jan.; *Impartial Account*, p. 7; *C.J.* xvi, 261–2.

CHAPTER V

1. *House of Lords MSS.* viii, 340.
2. *L.J.* xix, 33; *C.J.* xvi, 262–3; Boyer, *Annals*, viii, 226. For the fees, which Bromley and another Tory M.P., Gilfred Lawson, had promised to pay on his behalf but now refused, see *Clavering Corr.* p. 65.
3. There were sixty-five peers present on 12 January. See *L.J.* xix, 32.
4. *L.J.* xix, 33; Dyer, 14 Jan.; Trumbull MSS. LIV: Ralph Bridges, 13 Jan.
5. *House of Lords MSS.* viii, 345; Dyer, 14 Jan., 25 Feb.; Trumbull MSS. LIV: Ralph Bridges, 13 Jan.; *Remarks and Collections*, iii, 28; Nicolson's MS. diary, 26 Jan. 1711.
6. *L.J.* xix, 37.
7. Lansdowne MSS. 1024, f. 202. Sacheverell had just been elected to a Lectureship at Newington Butts.
8. Burnet, v, 441 n.
9. Dyer, 24 Dec.
10. The petition was offered on 16 January and granted on the 17th. See the original in House of Lords

MSS. 2640 (cf. *House of Lords MSS*, viii, 351); *L.J.* xix, 39; Burnet, v, 439–40.
11. *Life of Sharp* (1825), i, 383; cf. Luttrell, vi, 540.
12. *The Answer of Henry Sacheverell, D.D. to the Articles of Impeachment* (8vo edn, London, 1710), pp. 7, 12–13, 21. The reference in *A Prelude to the Tryal of Skill*, p. 23, to Atterbury as 'the reputed chief penman of Dr Sacheverell's Answer' can probably be discounted in view of the wholly different tenor of Sacheverell's speech at the trial for which Atterbury *was* largely responsible. (Cf. also Oldmixon, pp. 431–2.)
13. Luttrell, loc. cit.; Dyer, 24 Jan.; Cunningham, ii, 286; *L.J.* xix, 64.
14. pp. 11–12 (cf. the reference to the Answer in Dyer, 24 Jan., which could not have been made without some advance knowledge). See also Burnet, v, 440; *The Answer*, p. 27; *Tryal*, pp. 166–7: speech of Sir T. Parker.
15. *The Free Debates betwixt the H— L— and the H— C— on Doctor*

Sacheverell (copy in Magdalen College Library, in vol. N.2.20). Cf. *Dr Sacheverell's Answer to the Articles of Impeachment Exhibited against Him* (London and Edinburgh, 1710), p. 1, intro.

16. House of Lords MSS. Parchment Collection, Box 30.
17. *The Free Debates*; Dyer, 26 Jan., estimating the cheering crowd at Westminster Gate at 200 or 300; Luttrell, vi, 538–9; *L.J.* xix, 48–9.
18. *L.J.* xix, 43; *C.J.* xvi, 277 (my italics).
19. *C.J.* xvi, 277–8, 283; Luttrell, vi, 539; Dyer, 26 Jan.
20. Dyer, 28 Jan.; *L.J.* xix, 52.
21. *C.J.* xvi, 291–3; *Compleat History*, p. 25.
22. *L.J.* xix, 56 (my italics).
23. Ibid.; Trumbull MSS. LIV: Ralph Bridges, 13 Jan.
24. For these informal 'whips', see G. Holmes, *British Politics in the Age of Anne*, pp. 300–7 *passim*.
25. See G. S. Holmes, 'The Attack on "the Influence of the Crown", 1694–1716', *Bull. Inst. Hist. R.*, xxxix, 1966.
26. *C.J.* xvi, 293; Burnet, v, 440; Foxcroft, p. 427; Add. MSS. 17677DDD, f. 400: l'Hermitage, 7 Feb.; *Compleat History*, pp. 27–8; Boyer, *Queen Anne*, p. 412; Lonsdale MSS: James Lowther to W. Gilpin, 7 Feb.
27. Edward Harley's Memoir, H.M.C. *Portland MSS.* v, 649.
28. Elizabeth Hamilton, *The Backstairs Dragon*, pp. 128–31.
29. Probably at the Queen's request. See Swift, *Memoirs relating to that Change . . . in the Queen's Ministry* (*Prose Works*, ed. Davis and Ehrenpreis, viii, 116).
30. Marlborough had planned to dispose of it to General Meredith.

Hill's colonelcy dated only from 1705 (see W. Coxe, *Memoirs of Sir Robert Walpole* (1798), ii, 14–15).
31. Add. MSS. 42176, f. 291.
32. The longest account is still that of Coxe, *Marlborough*, iii, 6–20, and it can be usefully supplemented and corrected by H. L. Snyder, 'The Duke of Marlborough's request of his Captain-Generalcy for Life', loc. cit. A good contemporary account is in George Baillie's letter to Lord Marchmont, 19 Feb. 1710, in Register House, G.D.158. HMC 2123.
33. Lansdowne MSS. 885, f. 82; Cunningham, ii, 278–9, 286–7; cf. Coxe, *Marlborough*, iii, 31; *Wentworth Papers*, p. 110; Stowe MSS. 58, V, pp. 124–6: Walpole and Thomas Coke to James Brydges, 15 Feb. 1710; D.Z.A. Rep. XI England 35D, f. 160: Bonet, 17 Feb.; Register House, G.D. 158. HMC 2123: Baillie to Marchmont, 19 Feb.
34. Finch MSS. Box VI, Bundle 23: unsigned letter of 28 Jan.; Blenheim MSS. E-26: 'The account of what passed when Mrs Masham made the Queen put in her brother over so many people's heads'; *An Account of the Conduct of the Dowager Duchess of Marlborough* (1742), p. 235; see also Cunningham, ii, 279.
35. Add. MSS. 17677DDD, f. 419; *The Daily Courant*, Nos 2610–11, 6–7 March; Dyer, 9 March.
36. *L.J.* xix, 60; Dyer, 9, 11 Feb.; Add. MSS. 17677DDD, f. 403; *C.J.* xvi, 385 for the shopkeepers' petition of 25 March.
37. Finch MSS. Box VI, bundle 23: Nottingham to Lord Finch, 14 Feb.; *Wentworth Papers*, pp. 110–11; Dyer, 18 Feb.; *L.J.* xix, 66.

38. *C.J.* xvi, 325, 336, 337; Dyer, 21 Feb.
39. D.Z.A. Rep. XI England 35D, f. 96: Bonet, 21 March. This sum would include the cost of erecting the royal box.
40. See G. Holmes and W. A. Speck (eds), *The Divided Society*, p. 65. Dodd's chief claim to distinction was in having negotiated the merger of the Old and New East India Companies.
41. Dyer, 31 Jan., 28 Feb.; *Remarks and Collections*, ii, 351; W. Kennett, *The Wisdom of Looking Backward* (1715), pp. 7–8; L. Milbourne, *The Measures of Resistance to the Higher Powers* (London, 1710, publ. 18 Feb.); Boyer, *Queen Anne*, p. 416; *The Life of the Right Reverend Dr White Kennett* (1730), p. 102.
42. Boyer, loc. cit.; *The Evening Post*, No. 85, 25–28 Feb.
43. For example, *A Letter to the Right Reverend the Lord Archbishop of York, occasioned by the Prosecution of Dr Henry Sacheverell: By a True Son of the Church of England; The Judgment of King James the First and King Charles the First Against Non-Resistance, Discovered by their own Letters*; Tindal's *The Jacobitism, Perjury and Popery of High Church Priests*; Milbourne's *The Measures of Resistance to the Higher Powers*; *St Paul and Her Majesty Vindicated* (attempting to show that Non-Resistance was not, as so often claimed, a Pauline doctrine); and *Monarchy Sacrificed: or A Melancholy Memorial to stop the Mouths of a Present Faction.*
44. H.M.C. *Ancaster MSS.* p. 49; *Wentworth Papers*, p. 112; *L.J.* xix, 77, 81.
45. *Wentworth Papers*, p. 113: Lady Wentworth to Lord Raby, 6 March; *Clavering Corr.* p. 70; Cunningham, ii, 290; *L.J.* xix, 81; Wake MSS. Arch. W. Epist. 23, f. 202; Add. MSS. 47026, p. 10.

CHAPTER VI

1. M.P. for Ripon.
2. This account is based mainly on *C.J.* xvi, 338–40; Dyer, 28 Feb.; and the anonymous broadsheet *The Life, Character and Memorable Actions of Dr Sacheverell* (1710).
3. *Tour*, i, 362.
4. The Lords gave careful thought to the avoidance of morning traffic jams. See their order of 25 Feb. in *L.J.* xix, 81.
5. Add. MSS. 47026, pp. 10, 12.
6. Cunningham, ii, 290; Add. MSS. 47026, pp. 16–17; *Clavering Corr.* pp. 70, 77; *The Officers' Address to the Ladies* (1710), p. 2.
7. Blenheim MSS. B.II-3: 30 March. William was the eldest son of Francis Godolphin, Viscount Rialton, and Lady Henrietta Godolphin, *née* Churchill. He was later marquess of Blandford.
8. There can be no doubt that money was thrown to the mob with some prodigality. House of Lords MSS. 2665: MS. minutes of evidence before the House, 2–3 March, by Henry Bendish and Matthew Raper; Blenheim MSS. Box VII, 18: MS. depositions before the London J.Ps, March 1710, vol. II, especially Dr

Fauquier's evidence. For the progress to Westminster see also *The Life, Character and Pious Deportment of . . . Dr Henry Sacheverell* (broadsheet, 1710); Boyer, *Queen Anne*, p. 416; Oldmixon, p. 434; Dyer, 28 Feb.; Trumbull MSS. LIV: Ralph Bridges's postscript of 27 Feb. to letter of 25 Feb.; *Four Letters*, p. 6; House of Lords MSS. 2665: Ward Gray Ashenhurst's evidence. For the size of the accompanying mob I am indebted to a note in the F. F. Madan MSS.

9. *L.J.* xix, 81–3; Dyer, 25 Feb.; *The Tryal of Dr Henry Sacheverell before the House of Peers* (published by Jacob Tonson, by order of the House of Lords, London, 1710), 8vo edn, p. 5 [the official transcript of proceedings – hereafter referred to as *Tryal*]; Yale University, Osborn MSS. Box 21, No. 22: 'Account of the Trial of Dr Sacheverell', unfoliated [hereafter cited as Osborn MSS. 21/22, followed by date of entry]. The official version times the entry of the peers at 'about eleven', the author of the Osborn diary (normally very observant) at 'between 10 and 11'.

10. Wren had left space for 200 of them. Luttrell, vi, 549–50.

11. *Tryal*, p. 6; Dyer, 2 March; Cunningham, ii, 290; Osborn MSS. 21/22: 27 Feb.; *C.J.* xvi, 341–52 *passim.*

12. *Tryal*, pp. 25–8, *passim.*

13. Osborn MSS. 21/22: 27 Feb.

14. Ibid.

15. *Tryal*, p. 32.

16. Ibid. p. 34.

17. Osborn MSS. 21/22: 27 Feb.

18. *Tryal*, p. 36.

19. Ibid, pp. 36–40 *passim.*

20. Boyer, *Queen Anne*, p. 416; H.M.C. *Ancaster MSS.* p. 439; *The Evening Post*, No. 85, 25–28 Feb.; Panshanger MSS: Sir David Hamilton's diary, 27 Feb.

21. The procession is described in *Life, Character and Pious Deportment.*

22. *Tryal*, p. 77.

23. Burnet, v, 440; Osborn MSS. 21/22: 28 Feb.

24. There are some 30 pages of notes, representing various drafts, in Cholmondeley (Houghton) MSS. P.67, though the speech as delivered covers only 4 pages of the printed *Tryal*, pp. 90–4.

25. Osborn MSS. loc. cit.

26. See, e.g., H.M.C. *Portland MSS.* iv, 533.

27. *Tryal*, pp. 93–4.

28. Boyer, *Annals*, viii, 263.

29. Boyer, *Annals*, viii, 263–4; *Tryal*, pp. 106–7, 109; H.M.C. *Portland MSS.* iv, 533; Add. MSS. 47026, p. 9: Sir John to Philip Percival, 2 March; Osborn MSS. 21/22: 28 Feb.

30. *Tryal*, p. 88.

31. This, he said, was 'plain and obvious to everyone's observation'. Ibid. p. 86.

32. Ibid. pp. 73, 93, 105, 109.

33. Ibid. p. 73.

34. Ibid. pp. 74, 86.

35. Ibid. pp. 88–9: my italics.

36. Ibid. pp. 91, 92.

37. Ibid. pp. 74, 106.

38. Ibid. p. 97.

39. Ibid. p. 87.

40. Ibid. pp. 105, 89–90.

41. Ibid. pp. 77, 94, 88.

42. Ibid. pp. 81, 88, 77–8, 100.

43. Ibid. pp. 91–2, 110.

44. Luttrell, vi, 551; Boyer, *Queen Anne*, pp. 415–16; Osborn MSS. loc. cit.; *Tryal*, pp. 113–14.

Buckingham's motion was opposed principally by Somers.
45. This word is significantly not in the printed version. The section was probably omitted with the co-operation of Jacob Tonson, the official printer. See *Mr D—en's Letter to His Brother M—rs, dated from Elizium the 4th of June* (broadsheet, London, 1710).
46. Osborn MSS. loc. cit.; *Tryal*, pp. 131–2; Burnet, v, 440; cf. H.M.C. *Portland MSS.* iv, 533 on Powlet.
47. *Tryal*, p. 113; cf. pp. 131–3 for Powlet's claim that as a result of the Act the number of dissenters was 'daily' decreasing.
48. Ibid. p. 115; cf. p. 132.
49. Ibid. pp. 132, 134.
50. Ibid. pp. 115–16, 134.
51. Ibid. pp. 119–20. See pp. 117–18 for a still more ingenious proof adduced by King.
52. Ibid. p. 17.
53. Ibid. pp. 130–1. Cf. Cowper on this point, p. 135.
54. Osborn MSS. 21/22: 1 March.

55. Ibid.; *Tryal*, p. 145.
56. *Tryal*, p. 146.
57. Ibid. pp. 142, 148.
58. Ibid. pp. 143–4.
59. Ibid. p. 150.
60. Osborn MSS. 21/22: 1 March; cf. D.Z.A. Rep. XI England 35D, f. 114: Bonet, 3 March.
61. Cf. *Tryal*, p. 150: 'My Lords, those words had relation only to the prisoner at the Bar'.
62. For this whole incident, see Osborn MSS. loc. cit.; *Tryal*, p. 150; Add. MSS. 17677DDD, f. 421: l'Hermitage, 3 March; Boyer, *Queen Anne*, p. 416; Oldmixon, p. 434 (Boyer and Oldmixon have some inaccuracies); *L.J.* xix, 87.
63. *Tryal*, pp. 153–4.
64. Ibid. p. 157.
65. Ibid. p. 158.
66. Ibid. pp. 159–61.
67. Ibid. p. 162.
68. Ibid. pp. 167–8.
69. Osborn MSS. 21/22: 1 March.
70. Add. MSS. 17677DDD, f. 421.

CHAPTER VII

1. Boyer, *Queen Anne*, p. 416; Cunningham, ii, 293; Burnet, v, 444; Dyer, 28 Feb.; F. F. Madan MSS. (for the gentlemen's coaches); *High Church Display'd*, p. 95; *Priv. Corr.* ii, 427–9: Shute to Sunderland, Sunday afternoon [5 March].
2. *House of Lords MSS.* viii, 367, and Lords' Committee Book (1704–10), 1 March: evidence of Cowper's coachman, Sarles Goatley.
3. *L.J.* xix, 86, 88; Luttrell, vi, 551.
4. Blenheim MSS. Box VII, bundle 18: depositions of George Gosdin, Thomas Talboys and Thomas

Gray; T. B. Howell (ed.), [*A Complete Collection of*] *State Trials*, xv (1816), 552–3 (Talboys's evidence), 553 (Captain Edward Orrell's evidence), 565 (Mr Darnell's speech); S.P. 34/12/14: Talboys to Hy. Boyle, 7 March; Dyer, 2 March; Shute to Sunderland, 5 March, loc. cit.; H.M.C. *Portland MSS.* iv, 533–4. For Burgess's meeting-house, built *c.* 1705, see Walter Wilson, *The History and Antiquities of Dissenting Meeting Houses in London* (1808–14), iii, 492–4.
5. Dyer, 2 March; *State Trials*, xv, 553, 668–9; Ogilvie of Inver-

quhurity MSS. G.D. 205/4: John Pringle to Sir W. Bennett, 2 March; *Lockhart Papers*, i, 311; Add. MSS. 17677DDD, ff. 421–2: l'Hermitage, 3 March; *High Church Display'd*, p. 96; Blenheim MSS. Box VII, 18: John Smith's deposition; H.M.C. *Portland MSS.* iv, 532–3.

6. Blenheim MSS. Box VII, 18: depositions of Joseph Burgess and Sarah Sawery. The reconstruction of the rioting which follows is so involved, and is based on the analysis and collation of so many sources, that it would scarcely be practicable here to document every statement. I have therefore confined myself in the main to supplying the references for a few important quotations. The principal sources used were some seventy of the depositions made after the riots before the J.Ps of London, Westminster and Middlesex, preserved in the Sunderland papers at Blenheim Palace (Blenheim MSS. Box VII, bundle 18, 2 MS. vols); the testimony of over fifty witnesses at the treason trials of Daniel Dammaree, Francis Willis and George Purchase; the evidence taken by the Lords, 2–4 March (House of Lords MSS. 2665); the letters of Abigail Harley in H.M.C. *Portland MSS.* iv, 532–4; reports in *The Evening Post* and *The Flying-Post*; Dyer's Newsletters of 2 and 4 March: and the accounts of Burnet, Boyer, Dyer, Cunningham, Calamy, Oldmixon and of the well-informed author of the pamphlet *High Church Display'd* (1711).

7. Blenheim MSS. VII, 18: Anne Newth's deposition.

8. Ibid.: deposition of Martin Kneebone, woollen-draper, who accompanied Jackson on his reconnaissance.

9. *State Trials*, xv, 557–9. Cf. *Daniel Danery's* (*The Queen's Waterman*) *Letter to the Lord Treasurer: concerning a Discovery of the Ring-Leaders of the Late Tumult* [1710].

10. Blenheim MSS. VII, 18: Sarah Sawery's deposition. The broadsheet *Doctor Burgess's Character of the London Mob* (1710) accused some of the mob of defiling the pulpit with excrement.

11. Henry Hunter, *The History of London and its Environs*, i (1811), 589; Oldmixon, p. 434.

12. *Vulgus Brittanicus: or The British Hudibras* (1711), pp. 56–7.

13. Sarah Sawery's deposition, loc. cit.

14. *State Trials*, xv, 656.

15. House of Lords MSS. 2665: Bendish's evidence, 2 March; W. Wilson, op. cit. iv, 389, 390.

16. *State Trials*, xv, 622: Hugh Victor's evidence; Dyer, 4 March; Blenheim MSS. Box VII, 18: deposition of Culbridge, clerk to Samuel Blaikerby, J.P.; Bendish's evidence to the Lords, loc. cit.

17. *High Church Display'd*, p. 96.

18. *State Trials*, xv, 554.

19. Ibid. pp. 554–5.

20. Blenheim MSS. Box VII, 18: Sarah Sawery's deposition.

21. As well as the evidence given in the trial of George Purchase, see Ogilvie of Inverquhurity MSS. G.D. 205/4: Pringle to Bennett, 2 March.

22. See Trevelyan, *England under Queen Anne*, iii, 56; also Boyer, *Queen Anne*, p. 416; Cunningham, ii, 294.

23. *House of Lords MSS.* viii, 367:

Sunderland's evidence to the Select Committee; S.P. 44/108: Sunderland to Brigadier Tatton, Whitehall, 1 March.

24. S.P. 44/108: Whitehall, 1 March.
25. Boyer, *Queen Anne*, pp. 416-17; *Annals*, ix, 266-7; Cunningham, ii, 294; Calamy, ii, 228.
26. S.P. 44/108, ff. 199, 223: Sunderland to Bedford, 1 March (copy); Sunderland to Argyll, 2 March (copy, endorsed 'the like letter sent with some alterations to Genl. Churchill and to Majr. Genl. Withers').
27. This was the estimate of the Dutch agent in London, l'Hermitage, Add. MSS. 17677DDD, f. 432.
28. See L.C.J. Parker's summing-up at the trial of Purchase, *State Trials*, xv, 668.
29. Ibid. xv, 556.
30. Ibid. xv, 626.
31. Burnet, v, 444; Foxcroft, p. 427; *Impartial Account*, p. 11; House of Lords Papers 2665 (evidence of Thos. Wilson and Matthew Bunce); *House of Lords MSS.* viii, 368 (Burnet's evidence to the Select Committee); Lansdowne MSS. 1024, f. 206; Blenheim MSS. VII, 18; depositions of Joseph Bennett, Elizabeth Andrews, William Sutherland, John Smith *et al.*
32. They were patrolling the streets by 5 a.m. Pringle to Bennett, 2 March, loc. cit.
33. Add. MSS. 47026, pp. 17-18.

34. *Wentworth Papers*, p. 113: to Lord Raby, 6 March.
35. Abigail to Edward Harley, 2 March, in H.M.C. *Portland MSS.* iv, 532.
36. Boyer, *Queen Anne*, p. 418; Oldmixon, p. 435; Dyer, 2, 9 March; *An Ordinary Journey no Progress* (1710), p. 4; *Life, Character and Pious Deportment* (1710).
37. Usually of ten or twenty nobles. See Luttrell, vi, 554; Dyer, 9 March; 13 April, 27 May. *A True List of the Names of those Persons committed to the several Goals [sic] in and about Westminster ... on account of the Tumult, March the 1st* (London, 1710) contained 105 names.
38. The proclamation was published on the 3rd. For its wording, see *London Gazette*, No. 4660. The *True List* included only two persons described as 'gent.', and even they could not be indicted.
39. H.M.C. *Portland MSS.* iv, 527; Monson MSS. 7/12/137: Charles Bertie to Sir J. Newton, 4 Sept.; Lansdowne MSS. 1014, f. 105; MS. Ballard 4, f. 99: T. Tanner to A. Charlett, 14 Dec.; Cunningham, ii, 217.
40. On the whole question of the Palatines and their reception, see the valuable article of H. T. Dickinson, 'The Poor Palatines and the Parties', *E.H.R.* lxxxii, 1967. See also Cunningham, ii, 216-17.

CHAPTER VIII

1. The Scottish M.P. Robert Pringle, writing the same night, put the start of proceedings an hour later. Ogilvie of Inverquhurity MSS. G.D. 205/4: to Sir W. Bennett, 2 March.

2. *Tryal*, pp. 177–8; H.M.C. *Portland MSS.* iv, 533; Osborn MSS. 21/22: 2 March.
3. H.M.C. *Portland MSS.* iv, 533.
4. Osborn MSS. 21/22: 3 March.
5. H.M.C. *Portland MSS.* iv, 533: Abigail Harley, 4 March; MS. Ballard 7, f. 35: Smalridge to Charlett [4 March].
6. *Tryal*, pp. 178–96.
7. Cunningham, ii, 342; cf. Arthur Onslow, n. 6 to Burnet, v, 441.
8. Osborn MSS. 21/22: 3 March; MS. Ballard 7, f. 36, for Smalridge.
9. *Tryal*, p. 179.
10. Ibid. p. 180.
11. Ibid. pp. 180, 181.
12. Sir Keith Feiling, *History of the Tory Party*, p. 417; Trevelyan, *Queen Anne*, iii, 53.
13. *Tryal*, p. 182: my italics.
14. Ibid. p. 184.
15. Burnet, v, 441–2.
16. *Tryal*, pp. 186–8.
17. Ibid. pp. 188–9.
18. Ibid. pp. 191–3.
19. *Life, Character and Pious Deportment* (1710).
20. Osborn MSS. 21/22: 3 March.
21. *Tryal*, p. 211; cf. Dodd in ibid. p. 203.
22. Ibid. pp. 201, 204, 212, 217.
23. Ibid. pp. 223–4.
24. Ibid. p. 209.
25. Ibid. p. 214.
26. Ibid. pp. 243–4.
27. Osborn MSS. 21/22: 4 March; *Tryal*, pp. 247–8.
28. MS. Ballard 7, f. 35: to Charlett, [4 March].
29. *Tryal*, pp. 263–4.
30. Ibid. pp. 268–9.
31. Ibid. p. 267.
32. Ibid. pp. 264, 271, 273; cf. King's speech, 9 March, p. 406.
33. Ibid. pp. 278–9.

34. *England under Queen Anne*, iii, 55.
35. Osborn MSS. 21/22: 6 March; *Tryal*, p. 303; H.M.C. *Portland MSS.* iv, 534–5.
36. *Tryal*, pp. 312–16.
37. Ibid. p. 333.
38. Burnet, v, 444 and n. (c); MS. Ballard 31, f. 82; Oldmixon, p. 435; MS. Carte 230, f. 225; *Modern Fanatick*, p. 23; *Four Letters*, p. 9.
39. *Tryal*, p. 334.
40. Ibid. pp. 334–5.
41. Ibid. p. 336.
42. Ibid. pp. 337–8.
43. Ibid. pp. 339–40.
44. Ibid. pp. 341–2.
45. Ibid. p. 345.
46. Ibid. pp. 347–8.
47. Ibid. pp. 348–9.
48. Ibid. p. 350.
49. Osborn MSS. 21/22: 7 March; Dyer, 7 March.
50. MS. Ballard 31, f. 82; 34, f. 79; H.M.C. *Portland MSS.* iv, 535; *Clavering Corr.*, p. 70; *Four Letters*, p. 9; Hatton–Finch MSS. 281: Nottingham to Lady Nottingham, 7 March; Osborn MSS. 21/22: 7 March; H.M.C. *11th Rep.*, Appx, Pt vii (*Le Strange MSS.*), p. 117; *Modern Fanatick*, p. 23; Burnet, v, 444; Cunningham, ii, 292–3.
51. Osborn MSS. loc. cit.
52. Oldmixon, p. 437; Osborn MSS. 21/22: 9 March.
53. *Tryal*, pp. 360–1, 364.
54. Ibid. pp. 388–91 *passim*.
55. Ibid. pp. 394, 396–7.
56. Ibid. p. 419.
57. Cf. Sacheverell's speech, ibid. p. 340.
58. Ibid. pp. 433–6.
59. Ibid. p. 439.
60. Ibid. p. 441.

61. 'If I am guilty of it', he had said on 7 March, 'there is another tribunal, another Bar, at which I am to appear, and whereby . . . I shall be judged and condemned'. Ibid. p. 344.
62. Ibid. p. 446.
63. Ibid. p. 447.

CHAPTER IX

1. Hatton–Finch MSS. 281: to Lady Nottingham [7 March].
2. Cunningham, ii, 296 (see also ibid. p. 299); Lonsdale MSS.: Lowther to Gilpin, 28 Feb.; cf. pp. 142-3 above for this vote.
3. Ogilvie of Inverquhurity MSS. G.D. 205/4: Pringle to Bennett, 21 March.
4. H.M.C. *Portland MSS.* iv, 666, 536.
5. Nottingham to Lady Nottingham, [7 March], loc. cit.; *Lockhart Papers*, i, 313; Coxe, *Marlborough*, iii, 25: Godolphin to Marlborough, 5 March; Lonsdale MSS.: James Lowther to Gilpin, 11 March; Wake MSS.: Nicolson to Wake, 23 March; H.M.C. *11th Report*, Appx, Pt vii (*Le Strange MSS.*), p. 117: 16 March.
6. *Lockhart Papers*, i, 313-14; *Wentworth Papers*, p. 146.
7. Dyer, 11 Feb., 7 March; Luttrell, vi, 547, 556; *The Post-Boy*, No. 2311, 7 March.
8. H.M.C. *Ancaster MSS.*, p. 440; Osborn MSS. 21/22: 12 March.
9. Thomas to Sir Nicholas L'Estrange, 16 March, loc. cit.; cf. Osborn MSS. 21/22: 12 March. 'This evening the Queen declared herself in this affair, and 'tis thought gave a decisive turn to it . . . by appointing in Council Sir Thomas Parker to succeed Lord Chief Justice Holt, at this nick of time on purpose 'tis believed to show her approbation of his speeches & the whole proceeding'.
10. H.M.C. *Portland MSS.* iv, 536. Hall of Bristol had died on 6 February, Bull of St David's about a fortnight later. By 14 March it was known that Barton had 'absolutely refused' the poor see of Bristol, thereby disappointing Hoadly, who had hopes of succeeding to his Prebendary, and Bradford, the rector of St Mary-le-Bow, later turned down St David's. For the great contemporary interest in these vacancies, see Luttrell, vi, 555; Dyer, 14 March, 7 April; Coxe, *Marlborough*, iii, 30; Lansdowne MSS. 1014, f. 110; H.M.C. *Portland MSS.* iv, 532; Lonsdale MSS: Lowther to Gilpin, 14 March.
11. Osborn MSS. 21/22: 10 March; *Compleat History*, Pt ii, p. 178; *Tryal*, p. 448; *House of Lords MSS.* viii, 342; cf. Boyer, *Queen Anne*, p. 427.
12. Cunningham, ii, 296, 298; *Compleat History*, Pt ii, p. 179; Osborn MSS. loc. cit.; Boyer, loc. cit.; *House of Lords MSS.* viii, 342-3.
13. *Wentworth Papers*, pp. 114-15; cf. Boyer, *Queen Anne*, p. 427; Dyer, 11 March.
14. Osborn MSS. 21/22: 14 March; *Clavering Corr.*, pp. 70-1: Ann to James Clavering, 18 March.
15. Hatton–Finch MSS. 281: Nottingham to Lady Nottingham, 14 March. For proceedings on 14

March in general, see ibid.; *Clavering Corr.*, loc. cit.; *House of Lords MSS.* viii, 343; Dyer, 16 March; *L.J.* xix, 105–6.

16. Lonsdale MSS.: Lowther to Gilpin, 16 March.

17. Trumbull MSS. LIV, f. 25.

18. *House of Lords MSS.* viii, 343; Osborn MSS. 21/22: 16 March; Dyer, 18 March; Trumbull MSS. LIV, f. 11; Ralph Bridges to Trumbull, 19 March.

19. Apart from the sources cited above, there are excellent accounts of this debate in Boyer, *Queen Anne*, pp. 429–39 and in the Shaftesbury Papers in the P.R.O. (30/24/21/182) – a long, extremely interesting, but unsigned report, to which Professor Henry Snyder kindly drew my attention. In addition I have drawn on the pamphlet *Resistance and Non Resistance: Or an Account of the Debates in the H— of L—s on the First Article of Impeachment*; on the printed speeches of Burnet, Talbot and Haversham; on the MS. notes of Lord North and Grey (Bodl. MS. North a.3, ff. 135–44); on Burnet, v, 447–9; on Ann Clavering's letter of 18 March, loc. cit.; and on Trumbull MSS. LIV, f. 25: Ralph Bridges, 28 March.

20. *Resistance and Non Resistance*, pp. 3–5.

21. Ibid. p. 6; Boyer, p. 433; Osborn MSS. 37/76/4: 'Proceedings in Parliament against Dr Henry Sacheverell'.

22. Cunningham, ii, 298. See also *Lockhart Papers*, i, 312: 'the duke of Leeds on this occasion added also success, as an essential point for rendering it [the Revolution] legal'.

23. Osborn MSS. 21/22: 16 March; D.Z.A. Rep. XI England 35D, ff. 99–100.

24. This speech was printed in full soon afterwards, and is reproduced in *Parl. Hist.* vi, 861–73. See the remarkable tribute of a Nonjuror in *Remarks and Collections*, iii, 35.

25. *Clavering Corr.* p. 72; Trumbull MSS. LIV, f. 11.

26. Boyer, *Queen Anne*, pp. 440–1. Cf. *Clavering Corr.* Trumbull MSS., loc. cit. for the implication that there was no debate at all on the 3rd article.

27. *L.J.* xix, 111; Boyer, *Queen Anne*, p. 441; *Clavering Corr.* p. 72; *Parl. Hist.* vi, 879; Trumbull MSS. LIV, f. 11: Ralph Bridges, 19 March.

28. This debate is very fully reported in Boyer, *Queen Anne*, pp. 441–3 and there is an 8-page first-hand account in Osborn MSS. 21/22: 18 March. See also *Clavering Corr.* pp. 72–3; Luttrell, vi, 558–9.

29. *C.J.* xvi, 376.

30. Osborn MSS. 21/22: 20 March; Dyer, 21 March; Boyer, *Queen Anne*, p. 444.

31. *Clavering Corr.* p. 75: Ann to James Clavering, 23 March.

32. *Tryal*, pp. 450–2; D.Z.A. Rep. XI England, 35D, ff. 94–5: Bonet, 21 March.

33. *Tryal*, pp. 452–3; Luttrell, vi, 559; Boyer, *Queen Anne*, p. 444; Osborn MSS. 21/22: 20 March.

34. Coxe, *Marlborough*, iii, 25.

35. Ibid. p. 27; *Lockhart Papers*, i, 314–15.

36. *Priv. Corr.* ii, 416.

37. H.M.C. *Portland MSS.* iv, 537: 14 March (my italics).

38. Ibid.; H.M.C. *Portland MSS.* iv,

538: Orrery to Harley, 15 March.

39. Burnet, v, 449; *Wentworth Papers*, p. 146; *Lockhart Papers*, i, 313.
40. Cunningham, ii, 79–80, 300; Blenheim MSS. B.2–8: Godolphin to Marlborough, 17 March; *Priv. Corr.* ii, 416; *Wentworth Papers*, p. 115; Bonet, 24 March, loc. cit. (transl.); MS. Carte 129, f. 445, for the Scottish votes on 21 March.
41. Chevening MSS.: Sir John Cropley to Stanhope [March 1710]; Osborn MSS. 21/22: 21 March; Bonet, 21 March, loc. cit.
42. This account has been reconstructed from *L.J.* xix, 118; Boyer, *Annals*, viii, 331; Osborn MSS. 21/22: 21 March; *Clavering Corr.* p. 74; Add. MSS. 47026, pp. 17–18: Sir John Percival to Archdeacon Percival, 24 March; Trumbull MSS. LIV, f. 25; Chevening MSS. loc. cit. and

Cropley to Stanhope, 21 March; Coxe, *Marlborough*, iii, 25–6: Godolphin to Marlborough, 21 March.
43. Coxe, *Marlborough*, iii, 25–6; *Clavering Corr.* p. 74; Add. MSS. 47026, p. 17; Chevening MSS.: 21 March.
44. See p. 134 above.
45. For Commons' proceedings on 21–22 March: *C.J.* xvi, 378, 380; Osborn MSS. 21/22: 21–22 March; Bonet, 24 March, loc. cit. f. 99; *Impartial Account*, pp. 13–15; Chevening MSS. loc. cit.; Ogilvie of Inverquhurity MSS. G.D. 205/4: Pringle to Bennett, 21 March; Cunningham, ii, 300–1; Boyer, *Queen Anne*, p. 445; Add. MSS. 47026, p. 12.
46. *C.J.* xvi, 382: a memorandum by the Clerk of the House of Commons, which describes the fracas in detail.
47. *Clavering Corr.* pp. 75–6; Chevening MSS. loc. cit.

CHAPTER X

1. MS. Carte 230, f. 225: Thos. to John Carte, Coleshill, 7 April.
2. Finch MSS. Box VI, bundle 23: Nottingham to Lord Finch, 24 March.
3. Dyer, 23, 25, 30 March; Luttrell, vi, 562; *The Daily Courant*, No. 2635, 4 April; Boyer, *Annals*, viii, 331–2; ix, 194–7.
4. Lansdowne MSS. 1024, f. 210: Robert Pearce to Kennett, 6 April; H.M.C. *Portland MSS.* iv, 539.
5. John England, *Pray for the Peace of Jerusalem* (1710), Postscript, 29 March 1710.
6. *An Answer to a Letter from a Citizen of New Sarum* (1710), p.

1; Dyer, 1 April; D.Z.A. Rep. XI England 35D, f. 26; Bonet, 11 April; *A Vindication of the Last Parliament : in Four Dialogues between Sir Simon and Sir Peter* (1711), pp. 298–9.
7. S.P. 34/12/14: Jekyll to Sunderland, Wrexham, 4 April; cf. Whichcote to Newcastle, Gainsborough, 27 March, B.M. Loan 29/238, f. 320.
8. Despatch of 11 April, loc. cit.
9. Ibid.; H.M.C. *Portland MSS.* iv, 539: R. Knight to Harley, 4 April.
10. Knight to Harley, loc. cit.; P.C. 2/82, pp. 550–1, for the circuit dates; Brit. Mus. Stowe MSS.

750, f. 22: William Brydges to Sir T. Parker, 2 April; Huntington Lib. Stowe MSS. 58, V, p. 205: F. Woodhouse to J. Brydges, 15 April; S.P. 34/24, f. 34; G. Parker, A. Grosvenor *et al.* to Sunderland, April 1710; S.P. 34/12: deposition of John Stainer, gent., of Aston, Shropshire, 5 April 1710; *The Post-Boy*, No. 2324, 6 April; Dyer, 28, 30 March, 1 April.

11. B.M. Loan 29/238, f. 320; S.P. 34/12/41: 4 April.

12. Wake MSS: Nicolson to Wake, 11 May.

13. Ibid.; S.P. 34/12/1: Jekyll to Sunderland, Welshpool, 25 March; S.P. 44/108: Sunderland to bp of St Asaph, 2 April; to Jekyll, 2 April; to bp of Hereford, 3 April; Lansdowne MSS. 1013, f. 132; 1024, f. 210; *The Post-Man*, 4 April; Dyer, 7 April; H.M.C. *Portland MSS*. iv, 92.

14. Bonet took the speech as an outright declaration against Sacheverell and his adherents. D.Z.A. Rep. XI England 35D, f. 19.

15. Ibid. f. 41.

16. Francis Hicks (pseud.), *A Letter to Sir Miles Warton concerning Occasional Peers* (London, 1713/15).

17. Trumbull MSS. LIV, f. 25; MS. Carte 230, f. 226; Kennett, *Wisdom*, pp. 54–5; Dyer, 28 March.

18. *Vindication*, pp. 43, 47; Dyer, 27 April.

19. *Modern Fanatick*, p. 52; Dyer, 28 March, 7 April; Cunningham, ii, 300 and Bonet, 24 March, for Sacheverell's round of visits to the peers.

20. Wake MSS: Nicolson to Wake, 25 May.

Y

21. Trumbull MSS. LIV, f. 16.

22. Ibid.; D.Z.A. Rep. XI England 35D, f. 96: Bonet, 21 March; Dyer, 28 March, 18 May; *The Flying-Post*, No. 2225, 13 May; MS. Carte 230, f. 226; Cunningham, ii, 300–1.

23. Drake/King MSS. 346 M/F 59: Sir Francis Drake to Sir Peter King, 5 May.

24. *The Welshman's Tales concerning the Times* (May, 1710); see also *Dr Sacheverel's Progress from London to his Rectory of Salatin*, an account by one of his Southwark parishioners (hereafter cited as *Progress*), pp. 3–5; Boyer, *Annals*, ix, 202.

25. *Progress*, p. 5.

26. *Remarks and Collections*, iii, 12; Stowe MSS. 57, IV, 19.

27. *Progress*, p. 6.

28. The main sources I have drawn on for the journey, apart from the *Progress* (which is only spasmodically useful), are the Newsletters of Dyer, who gave it a coverage quite invaluable to the historian and whose factual information and dates, as opposed to his partisan gloss, are remarkably reliable; Boyer's *Annals*, ix, 202 ff.; a series of bulletins in the Tory *Post-Boy* and (of more dubious value) in the Whig *Flying-Post*; a number of pamphlets, e.g. *The Banbury Apes* and *The Worcester Triumph*; and a variety of contemporary correspondence, to which specific references will be given where appropriate.

29. MS. Ballard 38, f. 147: to Charlett, 1 July.

30. Oldmixon, p. 448.

31. *The Worcester Triumph* (1710); *Flying-Post* No. 2254, 20 July

(letter from Worcester, dated 17 July).

32. Dyer (3 Aug.) calls it rather a 'noble' entertainment. But cf. *Modern Fanatick*, p. 29; ibid. Pt ii, p. 28; and the purported letter from Walter to Sacheverell printed in *Vindication*, p. 42.

33. Dyer, 29 June; Brogyntyn MSS. 1003: Mrs E. Lloyd to —?—, Bodderiot (Wrexham), 23 July.

34. Dyer, 13 June. Lord Leigh expended more ammunition to celebrate the final collapse of the Whig ministry in September (*Atterbury Epist. Corr.* i, 28).

35. *Progress*, p. 13; *The Post-Boy*, 11 July.

36. *Progress*, p. 12; *The Post-Boy*, 13 June; Add. MSS. 33273, f. 31; MS. Carte 230, ff. 227–8; Dyer, 22 June.

37. Monson MSS. 7/3/124: 1 July.

38. Dyer, 27 July; *The Post-Boy*, 11 July; *The Flying-Post*, 6, 18, 22 July (a Whig correspondent of this paper insisted that the escort numbered only 1,400 horse and foot, including sixty parsons); *Progress*, p. 16.

39. See H.M.C. *Portland MSS.* vii, 6: William Stratford to Harley, 22 July.

40. Stowe MSS. 58, V, 205; 58, VI, 36.

41. King MSS. T. C. D. Lyons 1373: Bishop Lloyd to Archbishop King.

42. *A Collection of Addresses*, Pt 1, p. 36; Pt 2, pp. 6, 8, 1.

43. Significantly, the address he himself presented on behalf of the county of Radnor on 27 April was most restrained; it made no exaggerated claims for the royal prerogative, no assertions of divine, hereditary right, and

ended with the typically moderate aspiration 'that all schisms, divisions and factions being laid aside, we may have no contention among us but who shall be the most conformable to the present Establishment'. Ibid. Pt 1, p. 9.

44. In this connection see his memorandum for the Queen, 4 July 1714, recalling the situation in 1710, in B.M. Loan 29/10/6.

45. See H.M.C. *Bath MSS*. iii, 437: Sir T. Hanmer to M. Prior, 15 June 1710.

46. Burnet, vi, 16 (drafted on 16 Nov.); Cunningham, ii, 340; Portland (Holles) MSS. Pw2/291: Whichcote to Newcastle, 17 Oct. 1710.

47. Quoted in E. Handasyde, *Granville the Polite*, p. 109.

48. Dyer, 14 Oct.

49. Stowe MSS. 57, IV, 161; Fox–Strangeways MSS.: W. Hillman to Charles Fox, 30 Sept. 1710.

50. *The Post-Boy*, No. 2407, 17 Oct.

51. Stowe MSS. 58, VII, 125: W. Wotton to Brydges, 13 June; H.M.C. *Dartmouth MSS.* i, 297: W. Blathwayt to Dartmouth, 14 Aug.

52. Dyer, 14 Oct.; *Wentworth Papers*, p. 141.

53. Dyer, 7, 23 Nov.; W. A. Speck, *Tory and Whig*, p. 42, quoting *The Letters and Papers of the Banks Family*, p. 13.

54. In addition, a moderate Court Tory and pro-Hanoverian, Walter Chetwynd, who had supported the impeachment, lost his seat at Stafford on petition.

55. Forester MSS. 1224/21/41: Sir W. Forester to G. Weld, 31 Aug. 1710.

56. In Shropshire the Whigs survived only at Wenlock, a tiny borough

where they had long been un-
challenged; and even here they
were pressed to a contest.

CHAPTER XI

1. Swift, *Journal to Stella*, 24 Aug.
1711.
2. *Remarks and Collections*, iii, 12;
Modern Fanatick, p. 4; Kennett,
Wisdom, p. 70, citing letter from
Oxford, 25 Aug.; H.M.C. *Ailes-
bury MSS*. p. 202: Sacheverell to
Bruce, 10 Aug.; Dyer, 20
May.
3. *Clavering Corr.* p. 103; *Modern
Fanatick*, p. 30; *A Visit to St.
Saviour's*, pp. 6, 9, 16.
4. *Clavering Corr.* pp. 103, 111;
Lansdowne MSS. 1024, f. 278;
Boyer, *Political State*, April 1711;
Trevelyan, *England under Queen
Anne*, iii, 104, quoting Somers
MSS.
5. Trumbull MSS. LIV, f. 16:
Ralph Bridges to Trumbull, 26
April 1710; Kennett, *Wisdom*, pp.
123, 136–7, quoting letters from
Durham and Oxford, 6 April, 11
July; H.M.C. *Portland MSS*. vii
(Stratford to Edward Harley letters), 23, 39, 72–3, 76 (for the inscription on the basin, see Lambeth MSS. 941 [Gibson Papers],
f. 25); *Journal to Stella*, 24 Aug.
1711.
6. For a celebrated visit to Lichfield
in 1712, see J. Boswell, *The Life
of Samuel Johnson* (Everyman
edn), i, 14–15.
7. H.M.C. *Portland MSS*. v, 228:
Harcourt to Oxford, 29 Sept.
1712; Calamy, ii, 228; Burnet, vi,
176, Dartmouth's n.; *Modern
Fanatick*, Pt iii, p. 4.
8. Cal. Br. 24 England 113a, f. 44:
Kreienberg to Hanover, 24

March; *Worcester Post-Man*, Nos
196, 197 (27 March, 3 April).
9. *Parl. Hist.* vi, 1208; Kennett,
Wisdom, pp. 277–8; *Worcester
Post-Man*, No. 197 (3 April).
10. *Journal to Stella*, 2 April; *Wisdom*, pp. 278–9. The Dutch agent,
l'Hermitage, had heard before the
sermon was preached that Sacheverell had been offered £200 for
it. Add. MSS. 17677GGG, f. 113.
11. *Wisdom*, pp. 279–80.
12. Add. MSS. 17677GGG, f. 130;
Modern Fanatick, Pt iii, p. 2.
13. W. Thompson, *History and Antiquities of St Saviour's*, p. 90.
14. *Modern Fanatick*, Pt iii (1714), p.
2. For Atterbury's promotion to
Rochester, see p. 273 above.
15. See especially T. B. Bumpus,
Ancient London Churches, pp.
278–80; Hatton, *New View of
London* (1708), i, 115–16; *The
Parishes of St Andrew, Holborn,
and St Giles in the Field* (1861),
pp. 3–4.
16. C. J. Abbey and J. H. Overton,
*The English Church in the Eigh-
teenth Century*, i, 88; *An Account
of the Riots, Tumults and other
Treasonable Practices since His
Majesty's Accession to the Throne*
(London, 1715), p. 16.
17. Lansdowne MSS. 1024, f. 463:
Kennett to Nicolson (copy), 25
Sept.
18. Lansdowne MSS. 1013, f. 200;
Wake MSS: Nicolson to Wake, 1
Nov. (cf. H.M.C. *Ailesbury MSS*.
p. 216); *Account of the Riots*
(1715), pp. 4–5, 9–11, 14; *A Full*

57. King MSS. T. C. D. Lyons 1382:
to Archbishop King, 28 Nov.

and Impartial Account of the Late Disorders in Bristol (London, 1714), pp. 7–8 (cf. pp. 18–19); MS. Rawlinson B. 376, ff. 59–60: Sacheverell to Bishop Robinson, Oxford, 31 Oct. 1714; W. Michael, *England under George I*, i, 115; John Nichols, *The History and Antiquities of the County of Leicester*, iii, 512; [H. Sacheverell], *A Sermon preached January 31, 1714/15* [on Matthew, xxiii, 34–6], *as it was taken in Short-Hand by one of his Parishioners: to which is added a postscript, containing notes of another sermon, on the twentieth of the same month* (London, 1715).

19. H.M.C. *Stuart MSS.* i, 533; ii, 70; also *Modern Fanatick*, Pt iii, p. 8 on a Jacobite sermon preached by Sacheverell at St Martin's in March 1714. For the Manchester riot, and other Sacheverell riots during the Fifteen, see Sir T. Baker, *Memorials of a Dissenting Chapel: its Foundation and Worthies*, pp. 21–2 (I owe this reference to Mr Oliver Westall), and Scudi, *The Sacheverell Affair*, p. 138. For Sacheverell's own activity in the midlands during the Rebellion, H.M.C. *Townshend MSS.* p. 160: William Eden to Lord Townshend, 25 Aug. 1715.

20. F. F. Madan MSS., citing the will of Geo. Sacheverell of Newhall, dated 5 May 1715; ibid. and *D.N.B.* article on Sacheverell, for the marriage; H.M.C. *Portland MSS.* vii, 223; P.R.O. Prob. 11/604, f. 180: copy of the will of Henry Sacheverell D.D., 10 Feb. 1723[-4]; Defoe, *Tour*, ii, 3; London County Council, *Survey of London*, xvii (1936), 65–6. I am greatly indebted to Mr Clyve

Jones of the Institute of Historical Research for resolving some thorny problems concerning Sacheverell's association with Highgate.

21. *Mr Whiston's Account of Dr Sacheverell's Proceedings* (1719); *A Defence of the Lord Bishop of London . . . To which is added, A Vindication of the Reverend Dr Sacheverell's late Endeavour to turn Mr Whiston out of his Church* (1719). See also p. 10 above for Whiston.

22. MS. Rawlinson C.151, ff. 44–5: newsletters to Monsr Dorval, 7, 10, 14 Jan. 1723. The house was No. 19, South Grove; not 'in the Grove, Highgate', as stated by F. Prickett, *History and Antiquities of Highgate* (1824), p. 111.

23. Lansdowne MSS. 1014, f. 120; cf. H.M.C. *Dartmouth MSS.* i, 296: Sir Michael Warton to Lord Dartmouth, 10 Aug. 1710.

24. Calamy, ii, 284–8.

25. Ibid. ii, 245–6.

26. W. Wilson, *Dissenting Meeting-Houses in London*, iii, 493. Burgess himself died in 1713.

27. Kennett, *Wisdom*, pp. 121–2; G. Holmes and W. A. Speck (eds), *The Divided Society*, pp. 121–2.

28. Kennett, *Wisdom*, pp. 113–14.

29. G. V. Bennett, *White Kennett*, pp. 114, 125–6.

30. See G. Holmes, *British Politics in the Age of Anne*, pp. 279–80, 337.

31. *Lockhart Papers*, i, 475–6.

32. Lansdowne MSS. 825, f. 75.

33. H.M.C. *Portland MSS.* v, 650–1; B.M. Loan 29/171: Harley to Stratford, 16 Sept. 1710.

34. On this, see Atterbury's disillusioned letter to Trelawney, 10 Feb. 1713, in *Atterbury Epist. Corr.* iii, 313–14. In general,

G. V. Bennett, 'Conflict in the Church', in G. Holmes (ed.), *Britain after the Glorious Revolution, 1689–1714*, pp. 171–2; also the fuller account in N. Sykes, *William Wake*, i, 124 ff.

35. *Life of Sharp* (1825), i, 332–3, 336. Cf. ibid. ii, 4–5.

36. On Robinson, the leading English expert on Baltic politics, see *Clavering Corr.* p. 75; Lansdowne MSS. 1013, f. 130; also p. 265 above. On Bisse, see Sykes, *Wake*, i, 124–30 *passim*, and (for the Hereford incident) Hereford R.O., Brydges MSS. A.81. I owe this last reference to W. A. Speck.

37. *Life of Sharp* (1825), i, 332–3, for Dawes; Wake MSS: Nicolson to

Wake, 17 Sept. 1711, for Smalridge; Burnet, vi, 176 n.; Lansdowne MSS. 987, f. 242, on Atterbury's promotion.

38. George [Hooper], bishop of Bath and Wells, *A Sermon Preached before Both Houses of Parliament ... on Tuesday, July 7, 1713*, p. 21.

39. Lansdowne MSS. 1013, f. 200: to Samuel Blackwell, 21 Aug.

40. King MSS. T. C. D. Lyons 1603: Wake to Archbishop King [Dec. 1714].

41. Quoted by Abbey and Overton, op. cit. i, 138.

42. N. Sykes, *Wake*, ii, 119; *Edmund Gibson*, pp. 408–9.

43. Cf. *Impartial Account*, p. 16.

INDEX

Managers, of Sacheverell's impeachment,
see under House of Commons
Manchester, 28, 265
Manningham, Thomas, bishop of
Chichester, 220, 223, 260n., 262
Mar, earl of, 226, 227
Marlborough, duchess of, 12, 113, 114,
124, 129, 135n.
Marlborough, duke of, 1, 45n., 79, 84,
85, 87, 88, 89, 97, 98, 104, 106, 114–15,
178, 209, 225–6, 230, 251, 263
Marlborough, Wilts, 4 and n., 6–7, 248,
253, 257
Mary II, Queen, 21, 29, 43
Masham, Mrs Abigail, 113, 114, 115
Milbourne, Rev. Luke, 5, 45, 119
Militia regiments, 157, 170, 171–2
Mohun, Lord, 157, 222
Montagu, George, 89
Montagu, Sir James, 79–80, 89, 97n.,
130–1, 133, 253n.
Moore, John, bishop of Norwich and
Ely, 30–1
Morality, private, decline of, 26, 55
Mordaunt, Lieut.-General Harry, 118,
230, 232, 253
Moss, Dr Robert, 129, 137n.†, 180, 196
Myddelton, Sir Richard, 246

Nesbitt, John, Independent
meeting-house of, 174
Newcastle, duke of, 79n., 87n., 103, 170
Newcastle-under-Lyme, 244n.†, 245n.†,
246
Newington Butts, parish of, 104, 256
Newland, Sir George, 128, 263
Newland, William, 128 and n., 263n.
Nicolson, William, bishop of Carlisle,
16n., 30, 31, 31n., 40–1, 75, 209, 237
Nonjurors, 18, 22–3, 24, 33, 142, 246,
271
Non-Resistance and Passive Obedience,
doctrines of, 22, 23, 31n., 33–4, 52,
65–6, 80, 84–5, 90, 98 and n.†, 106–7,
119, 120, 130–1, 138–42, 152–3, 181,
182, 184–6, 190–2, 197, 197–8, 203,
205, 217–19, 263n., 271, 274;
Harcourt's version of, 182–4, 187
North and Grey, Lord, 213, 216, 218
Northesk, earl of, 225n.†
Northumberland, duke of, 115, 224
Nottingham, earl of, 23, 29, 200, 207,
209, 211–13, 213, 214–15, 216, 221,
269, 270 and n.†
Nye, Rev. Stephen, 26

Occasional Conformity, 17, 35, 39–40,
43, 53, 54, 66, 67, 80, 145, 270; Bills

against (1702–4), 40–1, 44, 46, 54;
Act against (1711), 270, 275
October Club, 258, 263, 270
Onslow, Sir Richard (Speaker, 1708–10),
91–3, 123, 124, 231, 253
Onslow, Thomas, 118
Orford, earl of, 42n., 79 and n., 87
Orkney, earl of, 226, 227
Ormonde, duke of, 115, 269
Orrell, Edward, 163, 165–6, 167, 168–9,
172, 173
Orrery, earl of, 227
Oswestry, 27n., 239, 244 and n.†
Oxford University, 3, 11, 12–13, 14n.,
16n., 16–17, 18, 38, 50, 54, 57, 90,
104, 106–7, 191, 234, 242–3, 248, 257,
259, 266, 269, 275
Oxfordshire, 245, 246, 248

Pakington, Sir John, 18–19, 38, 263n.
Parker, Sir Thomas, Lord Chief Justice
(March 1710), 72n.†, 80, 97n., 137,
149–55, 166n., 181n., 183, 195, 201,
202, 203–6, 211 and n.
Parliament, 28, 36n.*, 43, 54, 72, 80, 86,
89, 93, 101, 140, 182–3, 214, 238, 251,
269–70, 275; *see also* Commons,
House of; Lords, House of;
Impeachment
Passive Obedience, doctrine of, *see*
Non-Resistance
Patrick, Simon, bishop of Ely, 30–1
Pelham, Lord, 223
Pembroke, earl of, 225n.†
Percival, Sir John, 90, 94, 95, 126, 230
Peterborough, earl of, 208
Phipps, [Sir] Constantine, 105, 187–8,
189–90, 191, 193, 193–4, 195–6, 203
Pocklington, John, 236
Poulet [John], Lord, 45–6
Powlet, Lord William, 94 and n., 97n.,
143, 144, 253n.
Pratt, John, 105, 106, 107–8, 118, 253
Presbyterians, 23–4, 35, 37, 38, 52, 57,
134, 210, 234, 271; ministers of, 5–6,
7, 23–4, 69, 160, 166, 234, 270–1;
meeting-houses of, 37, 160, 161–3,
164, 166–7, 169, 234
Pretender, *see* Stuart, Prince James
Edward
Purchase, George, 160n., 173, 175

Quakers, 24, 37
Queensberry, duke of, 79, 227, 229

Raymond, [Sir] Robert, 105, 106, 107–8,
118